AREA HANDBOOK
for the
DEMOCRATIC REPUBLIC OF SUDAN

Co-Authors

Harold D. Nelson

Margarita Dobert
Gordon C. McDonald
James Mc Laughlin
Barbara J. Marvin
Philip W. Moeller

Research and writing were completed April 1972

(This handbook supersedes DA Pam 550-27, August 1960)

Published 1973

DA Pam 550-27

Library of Congress Catalog Card Number: 72–600260

FOREWORD

This volume is one of a series of handbooks prepared by Foreign Area Studies (FAS) of The American University, designed to be useful to military and other personnel who need a convenient compilation of basic facts about the social, economic, political, and military institutions and practices of various countries. The emphasis is on objective description of the nation's present society and the kinds of possible or probable changes that might be expected in the future. The handbook seeks to present as full and as balanced an integrated exposition as limitations on space and research time permit. It was compiled from the information available in openly published material. An extensive bibliography is provided to permit recourse to other published sources for more detailed information. There has been no attempt to express any specific point of view or to make policy recommendations. The contents of the handbook represent the work of the authors and FAS and do not represent the official view of the United States government.

An effort has been made to make the handbook as comprehensive as possible. It can be expected, however, that the material, interpretations, and conclusions are subject to modification in the light of new information and developments. Such corrections, additions, and suggestions for factual, interpretive, or other change as readers may have will be welcomed for use in future revisions. Comments may be addressed to:

The Director
Foreign Area Studies
5010 Wisconsin Avenue, N.W.
The American University
Washington, D.C. 20016

PREFACE

Many political, economic, and social changes and developments have occurred in Sudan since publication of the 1960 edition of the *Area Handbook for the Republic of Sudan.* Consequently, a thoroughly revised new edition is now presented to bring up to date the material about a country and society that hope to serve as a link between Arab North Africa and Africa south of the Sahara.

The first edition of the handbook was published four years after the country achieved its independence from British and Egyptian administration. An underdeveloped country lacking national unity and political stability throughout its short span of sovereignty, Sudan embarked on a socialistic course after a military coup d'etat in early 1969. In early 1972 it had concluded a seventeen-year civil war generated by regional ethnic, political, and religious differences.

After research and writing of the new revised handbook were completed, relations between Sudan and the United States continued to improve. In a move initiated by the Sudanese government of President Jaafar al Numayri, diplomatic relations between the two countries were resumed on July 25, 1972. Official ties had been severed by the Sudanese in June 1967 following the Six-Day Arab-Israeli War.

The revised handbook, in a shorter and somewhat different form from that of the first edition, seeks to provide a compact and objective exposition of the dominant social, political, and economic aspects of Sudanese society. It is designed to give the reader an understanding of the forces operating in the society. There remain, however, a number of gaps in information to which attention has been called.

The spelling of place names, proper names, and other Arabic words follows the usage of the Board on Geographic Names of the United States Department of the Interior. An exception is made in the case of words of Arabic origin that appear in *Webster's Seventh New Collegiate Dictionary.* Such words appearing in this handbook retain their anglicized spelling.

The original *Area Handbook for the Republic of Sudan* published in 1960 was prepared by a research team composed of Howard J. John, Archibald G. MacArthur, Jean McEwen, Wyatt MacGaffey, and Mildred C. Vreeland under the chairmanship of John A. Cookson.

COUNTRY SUMMARY

1. COUNTRY: Democratic Republic of Sudan; formerly the Anglo-Egyptian Condominium of Sudan; date of independence, January 1, 1956; capital, Khartoum.

2. SIZE: 967,500 square miles.

3. TOPOGRAPHY: Primarily a broad plain rising gradually to mountains in northeast near Red Sea coast and plateaus and low mountains near southern and western borders. Blue Nile and White Nile rivers join in northeast to form the Nile River, which flows northward into Arab Republic of Egypt. Extensive swamps in Southern Region, especially along sluggish White Nile.

4. CLIMATE: Ranges from desert region of the northern border, where rainfall is very rare, to semiarid climate in central plains and humid equatorial rain belt, with rainfall up to sixty inches per year, along southern border. Maximum daily temperatures range from 85°F to 115°F in most areas throughout year. Dry season ranges from twelve months in north to less than three months along southern border.

5. POPULATION: Estimated at 16.2 million in 1972; growth rate at least 2.5 percent. Rural densities generally low except in irrigated farm areas along Nile River. Various ethnic groups in six northern provinces, including about 12 million people, are Arabs or arabized. About 4 million people, mostly in the three southern provinces, trace genetic and cultural origins to black Africa.

6. LANGUAGES: Roughly 115 different languages, including twenty-six major ones. Arabic, the official language, spoken widely in north but by few people in south, where English is recognized as working language.

7. RELIGIONS: According to unofficial 1968 estimates, 66 percent of population, including majority in six northern provinces, were Muslims; 4 percent, mostly in southern areas, were Christians; the rest adhered to indigenous beliefs and practices.

8. EDUCATION: In 1969 about 18 percent of eligible school-age children enrolled in free state-operated primary and secondary schools; others were in limited number of private institutions in north. Public system included 4,630 schools. Educational advancement limited by teacher shortage and insufficient facilities. In north Arabic is language of instruction in elementary schools;

English, at secondary level. After March 1972 English being considered for use in Southern Region schools. Literacy rate in 1970 estimated at 10 percent for entire population; lower in south.

9. HEALTH: High incidence of diseases reflects difficult ecological conditions, inadequate diets, insufficient medical care, and mobility of large part of population. Malaria, tuberculosis, and bilharziasis considered major health problems. Government health services capable of coping with major epidemics collaborated with international agencies in various disease eradication programs.

10. GOVERNMENT: Single-party state under President Jaafar al Numayri, who came to power through coup d'etat by socialist and modernist military officers in May 1969. Eventual establishment of elected legislature is planned. Agreement on permanent constitution delayed by seventeen-year armed conflict between Arab-dominated north and black African south and political conflicts between religious, regional, and ethnic divisions in north. Administration highly centralized until March 1972; agreement ending civil war granted new degree of regional autonomy to newly designated Southern Region, consisting of Bahr al Ghazal, Upper Nile, and Equatoria provinces; north consists of six provinces.

11. JUSTICE: Court system and legal code developed during former British colonial rule. Penal Code drawn from similar criminal law of British colonial India; Commercial Code based in part on Egyptian model. Common law and judicial precedent play major role in legal system. Personal and family law matters governed by customary law of various ethnic groups and by Islamic law administered by separate court system. Civil and criminal cases heard by three levels of courts; chief justice was top legal authority and served also as administrative head of Islamic system of law. Strong tradition of independent judiciary.

12. ECONOMY: Money economy, prosperity depend on export of long-staple cotton fiber grown by small-scale tenants on large-scale government-owned and -managed Nile irrigation projects. Government completely dominates commercial agriculture and in late 1960s began to take over important industrial and commercial firms. Apart from limited government mechanization projects, most nonirrigated farming and food grain production is by small-scale subsistence farmers employing laborious traditional methods. About 25 percent of population are nomadic herders; another 25 percent move seasonally with their herds; livestock also raised by most sedentary cultivators, but national herd is largely unproductive. Industry still very limited; service sectors largely undeveloped.

13. PRINCIPAL EXPORTS: Seventy percent cotton fiber, cottonseed, and byproducts; others are gum arabic, sesame, groundnuts.

14. PRINCIPAL IMPORTS: Machinery and transport equipment, textiles.

15. CURRENCY: 1 Sudanese pound (£S) equals US$2.87; £S is divided into 100 piasters.

16. COMMUNICATIONS: Postal and telecommunications services provided by central government. Modern telephone system linked Khartoum, Khartoum North, Omdurman, Wad Madani, Atbarah, Singi, Dunqulah, Al Qadarif, Port Sudan. Radio links between Khartoum and southern provincial capitals. External services to neighboring countries, Middle East, Moscow, East Berlin; planned marine cable to provide improved service with Saudi Arabia. Government-owned domestic radio broadcasting to major population concentrations; television service in capital city complex and Al Jazirah area and planned for Atbarah and Port Sudan. All newspapers nationalized in 1970; two daily newspapers circulated in early 1972.

17. RAILROADS: Government-run Sudan Railways carries 80 percent of freight traffic and 60 percent of all passenger traffic. Started in 1897, mostly completed by 1930, but several recent extensions have been made. Important sections of country not served by rail transport.

18. INLAND WATERWAYS: Sections of Nile River navigable north from Khartoum to Egypt. White Nile and Bahr al Ghazal navigable south from Khartoum to Equatoria Province, but steamer voyage is time consuming and expensive for freight, and service is poor. Purchase of new equipment planned. A few other rivers navigable in high-water season summer and fall.

19. PORTS: Port Sudan handles all overseas surface shipments, has been major bottleneck at peak export season; administration of port has consequently been detached from Sudan Railways and placed under independent port authority.

20. ROADS: Inadequate road network inhibits development of cash farming. Motor vehicle traffic concentrated largely around Khartoum; remainder of country depends heavily on railroad. More than three-fourths of roads were unsurfaced tracks impassable in rainy season.

21. CIVIL AVIATION: Air transport service provided by government-owned Sudan Airways and by Sudan International, owned jointly by Sudanese and Kuwaiti interests. International airport at Khartoum; sixteen other airfields play important part in domestic transport; thirty-six smaller landing strips scattered throughout country.

22. INTERNATIONAL MEMBERSHIPS AND AGREE-MENTS: Member of United Nations and its specialized agencies and Organization of African Unity. Bilateral trade and aid agreements with Soviet Union, People's Republic of China, Democratic People's Republic of Korea (North Korea), Yugoslavia, United Kingdom, Kuwait, Libya.

23. ARMED FORCES: Total personnel strength approximately 52,000 officers and men. Army increased from 18,000 in 1966 to nearly 50,000 in 1972, mainly infantry; most equipment for enlarged forces supplied by Soviet Union since 1969; air force of 1,500 men, very few fully trained; aircraft included small numbers of Soviet-built jet fighters and helicopters; 600-man navy equipped with modest fleet of Yugoslav vessels.

SUDAN

TABLE OF CONTENTS

LIST OF ILLUSTRATIONS

LIST OF TABLES

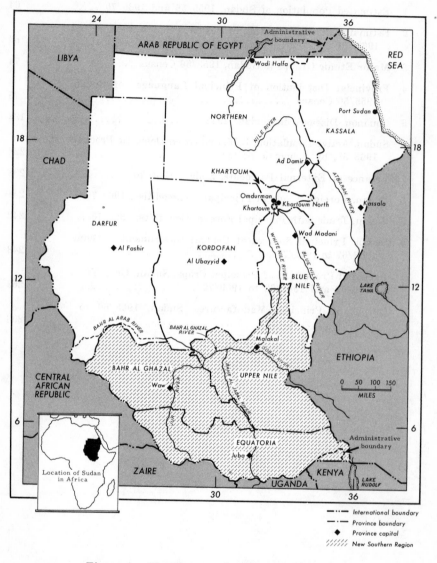

Figure 1. The Democratic Republic of Sudan

SECTION I. SOCIAL

CHAPTER 1

GENERAL CHARACTER OF THE SOCIETY

The Democratic Republic of Sudan—an independent state since January 1, 1956—is the largest country on the African continent. A little less than 1 million square miles in area, it straddles the Nile River from southern boundaries with Kenya, Uganda, and Zaire—until late 1971 Congo (Kinshasa)—to the northern frontier with the Arab Republic of Egypt (see fig. 1). It is bounded on the west by Libya, Chad, and the Central African Republic and on the east by Ethiopia and the Red Sea.

Spanning nearly 18 degrees of latitude, the country provides sharp contrasts in terrain and climate (see ch. 3). From south to north the topography ranges from tropical forests and savanna through vast swamplands, open semitropical savanna, and scrublands to the sandy and arid hills that lie between the Red Sea and the vast stretches of the Libyan and Sahara deserts. Because of the scant amount of precipitation that falls over much of the country, the Nile and its White Nile and Blue Nile tributaries are a vital lifeline to all populous areas except the well-watered Southern Region.

Sudan is the home of more than 16 million people, a land of over 100 languages, diverse ethnic groups, and persistent regional loyalties and cultures (see ch. 4). It has tried to become a link between the Middle Eastern and African worlds, and both are strongly represented within its boundaries. There is, however, no single Sudanese society with characteristic attitudes and institutions, its citizens consciously sharing a national identity. Instead, Sudan is a conglomerate of many tribal and regional social systems that have in common only a nominal unity within a formal national government structure (see ch. 5).

In the more productive regions, such as Kordofan and Blue Nile provinces in the country's midsection, and along the main lines of communication live settled village farmers—most of them Muslim in religion and Arab in ways of life. These peoples, and also those who have become residents of the urban centers, recognize a centralized administration within the concept of a nation-state.

1

In the deserts and the arid grasslands of the north, the nominally Muslim nomads have a social organization in which lineage (see Glossary) and kin responsibilities are still unquestioningly accepted as supreme.

The Nilotic cattle-raising people of the upper Nile—East African in culture and religion—are engrossed in their herds and are generally indifferent to outsiders. They as well as the southern subsistence farmers living in scattered homesteads have long resisted arabization, and northerners have consequently regarded them throughout history as inferior infidels. Since independence these southern groups have remained generally out of reach of direct administration.

Cities and towns are few, and of the ten with populations of more than 20,000 only the triple city of Khartoum, Khartoum North, and Omdurman bears any resemblance to a modern cosmopolitan urban center. The other towns, with the exception perhaps of industrialized Atbarah and Port Sudan, differ from the villages only in size. Their inhabitants cherish essentially village values. Although they are aware of and generally subservient to central authority, their strongest attachment is still to family, tribe, or region.

Evolution in the direction of modern social and political institutions is apparent only in Khartoum. Even there the array of government buildings offers a facade, behind which labor insufficient numbers of trained administrators and technical specialists who must cope with plans for national development. European clothing styles and other evidences of modernization frequently serve to cloak traditional conservatism and grudging concession to change. The genuine intellectual acceptance of changing realities is characteristic only of a dynamic few, most of whom have been educated either at the University of Khartoum or at institutions abroad.

Diversity also characterizes the religious affiliations and practices of the people who inhabit Sudan; moreover, religious diversity has unmistakable political implications (see ch. 9). About two out of three Sudanese—mainly Arabs and arabized peoples of the northern provinces—profess Islam. The strictly orthodox Muslims are a minority, and many of the nominal Muslims persist in former practices, values, and traditional African beliefs.

The roughly 4 million people of the three southern provinces adhere mainly to indigenous beliefs, and most of them have maintained a marked lack of interest in the call of Islam. About 4 percent of the entire population are Christians, mainly southerners educated in foreign-operated mission schools before the mid-1960s.

Living standards in Sudan vary considerably from area to area and between rural and urban environments (see ch. 7). Only in the larger urban centers are there people with enough money to aspire to higher education and consumer durables, neither of which is cheaply acquired. Except in the progressive area of modern agricultural activity, rural Sudanese lead frugal lives as subsistence farmers or pastoralists; many of them still engage in commercial exchanges by barter.

A high incidence of disease is attributable to difficult ecological conditions, diets low in nutritional value, insufficient medical care, and the continuous mobility of nomadic and semisedentary peoples. Life expectancy is short by the standards of more developed countries, and most of the modern medical facilities are confined to the cities. Large numbers of rural inhabitants continue to rely on traditional diagnosis and treatment in times of illness.

All Sudanese governments have faced a major problem in dealing with the chronic ethnic fragmentation that deterred national development and divided the population into two distinct cultures: the Muslim north and the black African south. The overt conflict began in 1955 with the mutiny of southern troops of the Sudanese army; it expanded into armed rebellion and progressed rapidly to a state of civil war (see ch. 9; ch. 14). The basic cause of the seventeen-year conflict was southern resentment of northern domination in social, political, and economic affairs. It grew out of inherited differences in culture and lifestyle and was nurtured by animosities dating from the nineteenth century, when northern Arabs made slave raids into the south (see ch. 2).

Before a cease-fire was concluded between opposing forces in March 1972 and agreement was worked out granting considerable autonomy to the three provinces of the new Southern Region, the cost in human suffering and national progress had reached ominous proportions. An estimated 500,000 persons had died from war-related causes, and some 750,000 more had fled their homes, many as refugees to neighboring countries. Hundreds of village settlements had been burned to the ground, and all schools in the south had been closed for a number of years.

Much of the political instability that has characterized the country since independence has been generated by conflicts in longstanding ethnic, religious, and regional loyalties (see ch. 2). Many of these internal divisions dated from Sudan's entry into modern political history in the early nineteenth century, when its conquest by the Egyptians brought the entire country under the nominal control of the Ottoman Empire. Foreign rule, brutal and oppressive, eventually provoked organized revolt, and large numbers of Sudanese flocked to the banner of the Mahdi, a self-proclaimed messianic deliverer who promised to wipe out the foreigners and establish an Islamic state that would follow the true precepts of the Prophet Muhammad. The foreigners were expelled, and during the fourteen years of Mahdist control opposing factions within the country were mercilessly persecuted.

The depredations of the Mahdists, which brought the country to the verge of ruin, ended with their military defeat by joint British and Egyptian forces. Between the end of the Mahdist interlude and the achievement of independence half a century later, Sudan was ruled by a joint but British-dominated Anglo-Egyptian administration—the condominium—which introduced twentieth-century Western concepts of the state, education, law, and health. At the same time in Khartoum a political consciousness developed among the few Sudanese who were being exposed to westernized education, and it was from this educated elite that the challenge to foreign rule was to come.

In the 1930s political parties arose roughly on the lines of the sectarian divisions. The followers of the Mahdi's precepts acquiesced in the gradualist British rule and wished eventually to see Sudan as an independent nation. Their rivals favored union with Egypt.

The question of Sudan's future had been the source of much recrimination between Great Britain and Egypt, which had long advocated Sudanese-Egyptian political unity, and it was not until the Egyptian revolution in 1953 that Egypt agreed on the right of the Sudanese to self-determination. Between 1953 and 1955 the British administrators left the country after relinquishing their appointments to qualified Sudanese.

The British policy of devolution of powers to local leaders, carried out over several decades before their departure, had tended to preserve regional exclusiveness—a problem not so agreeably resolved. The new sovereign government was faced with the need to foster among the many and diverse peoples the concept of national identity. The idea of unity had been cautiously cultivated by the British, but at independence few Sudanese outside the centers of political activity were more than vaguely aware of what was taking place.

Throughout the 1960s many of the social problems remained unresolved. The horizons of the vast majority of people were local; the wider community was unreal, and responsibilities within it as citizens of an independent polity could be conveyed to them only slowly. Illiteracy was widespread, even in the cities. Superstition and traditional practices regulated the political and socioeconomic structures of the rural peoples. Tribal and

4

family feuds were common, and many groups preferred to settle such disputes through customary procedures rather than submit to the arbitration of westernized courts.

From the outset of independence the arabized peoples of the northern and central provinces, who had had access to higher education and who predominated among professional men and legislators, dominated the affairs of the nation. The Nilotes and other southerners—illiterate, isolated, and long resentful over ill treatment and exploitation by northerners—viewed the central government with hostility and suspicion.

Although Sudan had a provisional constitution and a parliament during its first two years of sovereignty, political rivalries and a long period of economic difficulties soon paralyzed public administration. A military coup d'etat in November 1958 brought General Ibrahim Abboud to power and an end to parliamentary government. Abboud failed to carry out promises to return Sudan to civilian rule, however, and popular resentment against military rule led to a wave of riots and strikes that forced him to relinquish control in October 1964. The Abboud regime was followed by a provisional civilian government and a series of political coalitions between 1966 and 1969. None were able to agree on a permanent constitution or to cope with major problems of factionalism, economic stagnation, and ethnic dissidence.

A second coup in May 1969 brought the central administration under the control of the second Sudanese military government within a decade. Although the ruling Revolutionary Command Council (RCC) led by General Jaafar al Numayri banned all formal political parties, the religious, ethnic, and ideological forces they represented remained as latent divisive elements in 1972. The stated aim of the new regime was the building of a politically united Sudan with social and economic development guided by socialist precepts that would free the country from underdevelopment and dependence on Western influences.

In carrying out its announced goals the revolutionary military government moved for a time to closer political and economic ties with the Soviet Union (see ch. 9; ch. 10; ch. 12). Although formal political parties had been disbanded, the Sudan Communist Party (SCP)—the largest in Africa—increased its influence under the RCC. After an abortive coup in mid-1971, allegedly generated by Communists of the SCP and those within the government, Numayri's drastic action to crush the remnants of the party reduced it as a threat to Sudanese socialist aims. In October 1971 Numayri was confirmed by referendum as the country's first president. His domestic policies since then have reflected a strong desire to bring an end to ethnic conflicts. In foreign affairs he has sought to maintain amicable relations with the neighboring state of Egypt while at the same time protecting Sudanese independence. With the government's political security reinforced by the agreement to end the southern rebellion, primary attention could be given to the tasks of economic development, which presented a number of problems that had yet to be resolved.

The economic profile of Sudan is marked by the predominant development of agriculture and slowly expanding industrialization (see ch. 12). Land is abundant, and more than 85 percent of the population derives a livelihood from agricultural and pastoral activities. In most of the northern sector, the availability of water is a critical factor governing the production of food and export crops. The scant annual rainfall often provides little drinking water for humans and livestock, and the periodic shortage of vegetation for grazing animals fosters extensive patterns of nomadic migration. The population density is low in comparison to the available arable land. The country is generally self-sufficient in essential foods, although the level of nutrition in the diets of many people is low by modern standards of health (see ch. 7).

The agriculturally based economy has both modern and traditional sectors. The modern sector, which is largely government developed and sponsored, concentrates on the production of a single crop, cotton (see ch. 13). Using the waters of the Nile and its tributaries, the central government has invested large sums of capital in irrigation projects to increase agricultural output. Although improved since the mid-1960s, industrial development has been limited generally to the processing of agricultural products and to the provision of import substitutes. The traditional sector consists of livestock herding by various nomadic and semisedentary tribesmen and cultivation of drought resistant food crops that are dependent on the summer rains or irrigation by traditional methods.

The development of an integrated economy is slowed down by the continued existence of the large traditional sector and by the major dependence on cotton as an export commodity. The need to diversify in order to offset the dangers of crop failure or low cotton prices is recognized by the government, and throughout the 1960s efforts at diversification received the attention of agricultural technicians and budget planners.

The inadequate transportation system is a major hindrance to Sudan's economic development (see ch. 3; ch. 12). In early 1972 the system consisted of a single railroad with several feeder lines, supplemented by river steamers, a government-owned airline, and

6

about 1,300 miles of roads capable of all-weather use. Pending electrification using the various dams constructed by the government in its quest for irrigation water, the economic infrastructure also suffers from a shortage of cheap power.

With the exception of copper, which was yet to be exploited, surveys of the early 1970s had revealed few minerals in significant quantities. Oil exploration rights along the Red Sea coast have been granted to several foreign companies, but as of early 1972 oil had not been discovered.

The government's role in the country's economic activity has increased steadily since independence, beginning with the control of cotton production and marketing. Since its commitment to socialism in mid-1969, public sector involvement has increased rapidly. Under its nationalization policy since mid-1970, the central government has taken over all medium-sized and large commercial firms in the modern sector, including all commercial banks.

Sudan's precarious economic position, demonstrated by its lack of appreciable growth from 1965 through 1971, has been the product of its expenditures to cope with the long civil war, which had generated rising inflation since 1960. The country also suffers from a chronic trade deficit, and borrowing from international sources had increased to meet the costs of national development projects. In 1970 the Sudanese government adopted a new five-year development plan, prepared with the help of Soviet advisers. The second in a series of long-term development plans since independence, it calls for substantial improvements in many areas, particularly in agricultural and industrial output and in education. Achievement of its goals is based on projections of private sector contributions and external assistance. The country faces immense problems in its quest for national economic development, and success of the plan will depend heavily on the government's ability to secure reasonable foreign assistance. A separate plan growing out of the peace agreement of early 1972 had been devised to cope with the special needs of the south.

In early 1972 under the progressive leadership of President Numayri, Sudan was moving to meet its internal problems with solutions that appeared to be more pragmatic than those adopted by preceding Sudanese governments. This approach already had achieved an initial resolution of the country's protracted civil war. Having diminished its earlier ideological attachment to the to the Soviet Union, the government was attempting to achieve a practical balance in its relations with countries that could and would assist in the attainment of Sudanese goals (see ch. 10). Although diplomatic and economic overtures had been made to nations of the East and the West as well as to those of the Muslim world, Sudan was concentrating its primary attention on the establishment of good relations with all neighboring African states.

CHAPTER 2

HISTORICAL SETTING

To the individual Sudanese, history often means the tales of his community or tribe, its origins, wanderings, heroes, and wars. The existence of diverse ethnic and language groups that often regarded one another as alien has been the usual pattern in the country's history. There was seldom need or incentive for the development of large political entities.

The principal ways of life, until modified by modern technical innovations, were subsistence agriculture, pastoralism, and trade conducted largely by barter. The more important markets, towns, and political centers arose within the more densely settled agricultural areas and often at the junctions of trade routes—the Nile River and its tributaries, the caravan route across Africa and its branches (see fig. 2). There a local potentate might exact tolls and possibly gain hegemony over a sizable area. Conflict among small groups, particularly between agricultural and pastoral people for control of land and trade, was ever present.

Above the purely local level the history of the country may be treated as three regional histories. The region south of the Sudd marshland—more closely related to equatorial Africa than to northern Sudan—was known to outsiders until the nineteenth century mainly in myth; it remains one of the least known areas of Africa. The more densely settled central and western area of Darfur Province, separated from eastern Sudan by desert, usually remained independent of outside control and maintained closer relations with adjacent territories to the west than with the Nile River valley. It is only along the Nile, where successive kingdoms had some contact with the major civilizations of the Mediterranean and the Arab world, that a more or less continuous history may be discerned.

The Nile River valley north of the modern towns of Kosti and Sannar has been throughout history the most densely populated area of the country and the center of the most important kingdoms. Here, as in the rest of the country, major periods of history were defined by migrations of new people, who sought out the best lands, drove many of the previous inhabitants into less hospitable regions, and absorbed or were absorbed by the rest.

A long period of Egyptian-influenced civilization in the kingdom
of Meroe was ended in the first centuries A.D. by a Nilotic (see
Glossary) migration from the south. After a period of which
little is known, the kingdoms of Muqurra and Alwa arose and
enjoyed centuries of relative stability until they were brought

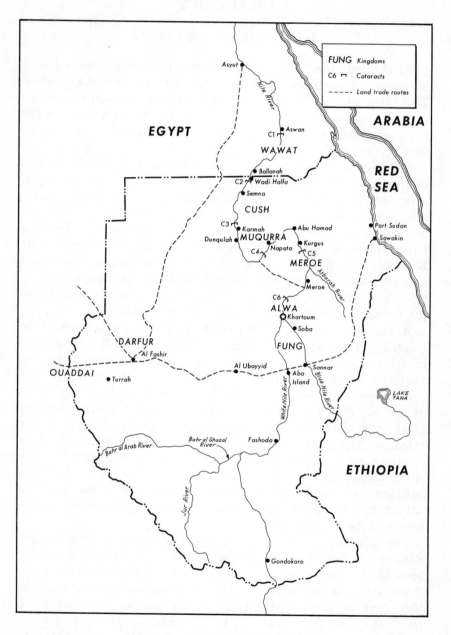

Figure 2. Historical Sites of Sudan

down by the major migration of the modern period: the arrival of the Arabs from Egypt and the Mediterranean coast from the thirteenth to the fifteenth centuries.

Although these river kingdoms seldom exerted real control far beyond the Nile River valley, they were the centers of power in the Sudan area. They traded with Darfur and the south. They raided for slaves in the south or battled with the ruler of Darfur for control of the intervening area of Kordofan. The major efforts at military conquest and subjection came from the north, however, where the usually stronger rulers in Egypt looked toward the upper reaches of the Nile as a prime direction for expansion.

At all times the contact with Egypt was the primary means by which the people of northern Sudan came into contact with the main currents of civilization. To be educated in the Egyptian capital was a mark of prestige both in the twelfth century B.C. and in the twentieth century A.D. At times Egypt was also a conquering power, interested in the past in controlling the river in order to dominate trade and obtain gold and Negro soldiers and slaves and interested in more recent times in having control of the river and its potential for irrigation and power. Egypt, however, never extended control far beyond the river valley. Even when the Egyptian goverment was strong, Sudan was secondary to its Mediterranean interests; when Egypt was weak, control over Sudan was quickly lost.

The Egyptian conquest in the nineteenth century, after which the northern valley was administered and some of the rest of the country was controlled by Egypt, gave rise to a legal claim to sovereignty that was not disavowed until 1953, when it was agreed that the Sudanese should determine their future status. In 1955 the matter was put to a vote of the Sudanese Parliament; representing the south and Darfur as well as the dominant people of the valley—themselves divided in opinion—Parliament voted for independence, which was achieved on January 1, 1956.

As the Anglo-Egyptian Sudan, the country in 1899 entered a period of more than fifty years of colonial status, during which time British and European concepts of the nation, government, law, education, and medicine were introduced. As government became more established, the goals of the rulers shifted from pacification and the construction of the transport and communications necessary for control to the development of a uniform adminstrative system and the provision of some means of economic development and social services.

A challenge to the right of foreigners to rule came from the small but influential Sudanese elite, composed of secondary school and university graduates, leaders of the labor unions, and holders

11

of posts in government service. Under this pressure the benevolent paternalism of the early years gave way to a debate on the speed of progress toward self-government and independence. Although the process was complicated by the Egyptian claim to sovereignty, the achievement of independence was without violence and with relatively little bitterness. The transfer of power was, in effect, from an alien to a national elite. At independence the first task facing the government was to foster among diverse peoples an awareness of national identity and work toward a time when national allegiance would take precedence over parochial loyalties.

Among the problems requiring solution were two of long standing. Sudanese-Egyptian relations, an issue for nearly 4,000 years, remained a subject around which factions immediately developed; failure to find a modus vivendi with Egypt threatened internal as well as external security. The second issue—the task of dealing with the population of the three southern provinces—was to remain a chronic problem as Sudan struggled to become a viable nation-state. Independence brought new problems without solving the old—the kind of foreign policy that should be adopted; what to do about the country's dependence on the single crop of cotton; priorities of economic development, education, and local government; and the deterioration of relations between the Muslim north and the Nilotic south.

As the new problems were superimposed on the old ones, modern political groups formed, but even their adherents retained ties with roots in ethnic and religious organizations.

After independence was achieved, no one group was able to retain majority support in a web of conflicting loyalties and issues. The result was a series of weak coalitions in which each faction sought power for itself. Parliamentary government failed thirty-four months after Sudanese sovereignty when political parties and factions could neither compose their differences within a coalition government nor accept the role of loyal opposition outside the government. On November 17, 1958, motivated by the economic difficulties and political maneuvering that paralyzed public administration, General Ibrahim Abboud overthrew the parliamentary regime in a bloodless coup d'etat and formed a military government. General Abboud did not carry out his early promises to return Sudan to civilian rule, however, and popular resentment against military rule led to a wave of riots and strikes that, on October 26, 1964, forced him to relinquish power.

Between 1965 and 1969 Sudan had a second series of civilian coalition governments that were again unable to agree on a permanent constitution or to cope with major problems of factionalism, economic stagnation, and ethnic dissidence. Dissatisfaction culminated in a second military coup on May 25, 1969, led by Colonel Jaafar al Numayri. The new military government set about to effect a strongly nationalist and socialist program for the country. Within the three southern provinces, where southern Sudanese political groups had agitated for autonomy or secession since independence, the chronic state of insurgency against the central government continued as Numayri came to power (see ch. 9).

EARLY HISTORY

Ancient Egypt and Cush

For 2,000 years after Egypt became a united kingdom around 3,000 B.C., the known history of the Sudan area is limited to the story of Egyptian interest and influence in the extreme north. In the three long periods of ancient Egyptian power, there was increasing contact with Sudan; during the intermediate periods of Egyptian weakness, no control was maintained in the south. The first contacts arose from trade, when, toward the end of the Old Kingdom (3500–2700 B.C.), Egyptian caravans obtained ivory, incense, and ebony from the south, and a few military forays returned with slaves.

During much of the Middle Kingdom period (2400–1580 B.C.) the Egyptians controlled the Nile as far as Semna from a series of forts along the river, in order to gain control of the important gold supply in the district called Wawat. The Semna frontier seems to have been also the ethnic boundary between predominantly Mediterranean and negroid peoples at that time. The first records of a Sudanic culture began after 1900 B.C. in an area centered on Karmah. The Egyptians called the district Cush, a term later applied to an undefined wider area.

Not until the period of the New Kingdom (1580–1100 B.C.) and the disappearance of the Karmah culture was Egyptian administrative control firmly established. Although the Egyptian records sometimes listed a great number of tributary districts extending eastward to the Red Sea and southward to the junction of the Blue Nile and the White Nile, Cush, the territory actually administered by Egypt, ended at the fourth cataract.

As Cush came under regular Egyptian administration, Egyptian government and religious officials and artisans moved into the area. Local chiefs, their loyalty ensured by the drafting of their children to serve as pages in the capital, continued to be responsible for the delivery of tribute. The Egyptian language, art forms, and religion were adopted; the temple at Jabal Barkal, built about 1450 B.C., remained the religious center of the region for 1,000 years.

Egyptian power waned in the eleventh century B.C., and little is known of Cush during the next 300 years. In the eighth century B.C. Cush was an independent state able to take advantage of Egyptian weakness; it became a world power after its rulers moved north and established the twenty-fifth dynasty in Egypt. It fell to the Cushite rulers to defend their new realm against the Assyrians, who already had conquered much of the Middle East; by 675 B.C. the last Cushite ruler of Egypt, Taharqa, had been defeated and driven back to the capital of Cush at Napata.

Meroe

During the next several centuries Cush developed independently of Egypt. From the capital at Napata the rulers of Cush conquered areas to the south and east, and at some time in the sixth or fifth century B.C. the capital was moved to a more central location at Meroe. In the north the desert seems to have taken over. The raids by Blemmyes—nomads from the area between the Nile and the Red Sea thought to be the ancestors of the modern Beja—took place more frequently. The kingdom gradually became less Egyptian in culture. By 200 B.C. the use of Egyptian hieroglyphs had given way to the use of Meroitic writing, apparently an adaptation of Egyptian writing to the local language; in 1972 it still had not been deciphered.

Extending from the third cataract in the north to the Soba area in the south, the kingdom reached its height in the third and second centuries B.C. Ruins of palaces, pyramid tombs, and temples attest to a highly centralized political structure whose rulers were able to command the skills of artisans and large labor reserves. Irrigation made possible the support of a large population. Fragments of architecture showing Roman, Greek, and Indian influence indicate that the kingdom was not completely isolated. Contact with the Greeks and later the Romans in Egypt was not always peaceful. After attacks from Meroe, a Roman army razed Napata in 23 B.C., and the northern part of the kingdom declined rapidly in importance, although southern Meroe lingered into the fourth century A.D.

The gradual migration of Nilotic people from the south brought the Meroitic kingdom to an end. By the second and third centuries A.D. a new people, called Noba or Nobatae in contemporary descriptions, were living on the west bank of the river. As Meroe grew weaker, they moved into the fertile areas from which the more civilized Meroitic people had long excluded them.

No more is known of the region, except that until the fifth century A.D. both Blemmyes and Nobatae were subsidized by the Romans to keep the peace. By then a mixed Nilotic-Meroitic kingdom had grown up with a capital at Ballanah.

In the south the dwindling Meroitic power was subjected to the pressure of the Nilotic migrants from the west and south and from the expansion of a more powerful state in the east. By A.D. 350, when an army from the Axumite kingdom in Ethiopia invaded the area, the Meroe central power had ceased to exist.

The Christian Kingdoms of Nubia

By the sixth century A.D. three new related kingdoms—Nobatia, Muqurra, and Alwa—had emerged in the area of the Nile River valley that was formerly Meroitic. In all three the Nilotic conquerors were the ruling people, and at least in the two northern kingdoms Nubian was the official language. By the time historical records began, however, the distinctions between the immigrants and earlier inhabitants were no longer clear. To the writers of the Mediterranean world the region had come to be called Nubia. Like the term *Cush, Nubia* indicated specifically a small area along the Nile in the northermost part of the country but was also used generally for the whole area south of Egypt.

The earliest written references to the Nubian kingdoms occur in accounts by Christian authors of the conversion of the Nubian kings in the late sixth century. Conversion probably began earlier, however, for Christianity had been prevalent in Egypt from the third century and was adopted by the Ethiopian king Ezana of Axum at some time before his raid on the Nile Valley in A.D. 350.

In accepting Christianity, the rulers of the Sudan area accepted the Monophysite form that prevailed throughout Egypt. The churches of the Nile River valley and Ethiopia recognized the authority of the Coptic patriarch of Alexandria. Their bishops were appointed in Egypt, and after a time the use of Greek in liturgy gave way to the use of the local language written in Coptic script.

Although the Nubian kingdoms lasted for many centuries, their existence was challenged almost immediately by the conquest of Egypt in 640 by Muslim Arab invaders. Arab raids reached Dunqulah in 642 and again in 652, but they were stopped; the mainstream of the invasion moved west across North Africa. It was probably in response to Arab pressure that Nobatia was incorporated into Muqurra at some time before 700. After the initial raids, however, a treaty between the Arabs and Muqurra was concluded and remained in effect for centuries. Arab domination in Egypt cut Sudan off from the rest of the Christian world and, as Islam engulfed Egypt, the position of the patriarch of Alexandria was threatened. It became difficult for the Nubians to obtain either literature or Egyptian-trained clergy.

An Arab traveler who visted Muqurra and Alwa in the late tenth century was particularly impressed by the fertility of the Dunqulah area, the wealth and cavalry of the king of Soba, and the numbers of churches and monasteries of both kingdoms. He reported also that a number of Muslims were settled in the north, that some of the local people had adopted Islam, and that there was a Muslim quarter even in Soba.

After 1252 the Mameluke sultans of Egypt ended the earlier policy of coexistence with the Christian kingdoms and sent a number of successful expeditions against Muqurra, but the fall of the kingdom is attributable less to battles than to the steady immigration from the thirteenth to the fifteenth centuries of a new wave of Arabs.

The fourteenth and fifteenth centuries were times of political anarchy. Arab tribes took over northern Sudan. In many areas territorial government was largely replaced by tribal organization; and settled agriculture, by pastoralism. Some groups of displaced persons left the valley; others were absorbed into Arab life or managed to live under Arab patronage. By the sixteenth century the people of the north had been converted to Islam and the modern population patterns largely formed. A similar process was repeated in Darfur in the west and in Alwa, the southernmost of the Nile kingdoms.

Darfur and Sannar

Darfur first appears in Sudanese history as the area around the Jabal Marrah range of western Darfur Province, where the caravan route across Africa branches into roads leading northwest to the coast and northeast to the Nile River. It is the area populated by the Fur (see ch. 4). During the fifteenth and sixteenth centuries the people of most of the surrounding territory were converted to Islam.

After a period of disorder in the late sixteenth century when Darfur was conquered briefly by its western neighbor, the Sultanate of Bornu, a new power emerged among the Fur, who established a sultanate that was to last for three centuries. The Fur rulers made Islam the official religion and drove their former rulers, the Daju and Tungur, into fringe areas. The conversion of the people was achieved primarily during the reign of Ahmed Bakr (1682–1722), who brought in teachers, built mosques and schools, and both encouraged and compelled his subjects to adopt Islam.

During the late eighteenth century the Fur, expanding over eastern Darfur and conquering much of central Kordofan, moved their capital eastward to Al Fashir. The Fur sultanate remained intact within its central area until 1916, when its independence was ended by British occupation and inclusion in the Anglo-Egyptian Sudan.

A new Islamic kingdom emerged in eastern Sudan shortly after 1500 when a people called the Fung, in alliance with an Arab tribe, defeated the remnants of Alwa. The origin of the Fung is much debated; they probably came to Sannar from the upper Blue Nile River or the area immediately to the east; they were Muslim and claimed descent from the Umayyads, some of whom had fled southward from Egypt after their defeat in the struggle for the caliphate in the eighth century. By 1533 the Fung governed directly the area centered in Al Jazirah and around the trade route junction at Sennar, and the tribes and districts north to the third cataract recognized Fung suzerainty.

As with the earlier collapse of Muqurra, the fall of Alwa opened the way for large-scale Arab immigration, causing some indigenous groups to flee and others to become Muslim and intermarry with the newcomers. Several of the larger present-day religious orders trace their foundations to the sixteenth and seventeenth centuries (see ch. 6).

The Fung kingdom reached the height of its political power in the mid-seventeenth century after it repulsed the advance of the Shilluk down the White Nile River, bringing some of that tribe under its government. By the end of the century many of the northern Arab tribes were virtually independent. In the mid-eighteenth century there was a second brief period of expansion when the Fung defeated an Abyssinian invasion and reassumed control over central Kordofan. After 1760 the kingdom gradually declined. The more distant areas of the kingdom ceased to recognize Sannar. Fung records attribute the decline to the dynasty's loss of real power to the hereditary viziers, chiefs of the subject people of the Sennar area. One of them, Muhammad Abu al Kaylak, had led the Fung army successfully against and Abyssinians and Kordofan; in 1760 he deposed the reigning sultan, after which he and his descendants became more powerful than the nominal sultans. Continued internal dissension and fragmentation of the kingdom marked the last years of the dynasty.

MODERN HISTORY

Turko-Egyptian Rule, 1821–81

The political vacuum created in the Sudan area as Fung control disintegrated made easy an Egyptian conquest when a strong government was installed in Cairo. Egypt since 1503 had been a part of the Ottoman Empire, but during much of that time power had rested with the Mameluke emirs who served as Egypt's governors. By the end of the eighteenth century Ottoman control was only nominal, and Egypt was prostrated by the rapacity and irresponsibility of the rival Mameluke emirs. In 1798 the situation was abruptly altered by Napoleon Bonaparte's conquest; involvement in the diplomacy of the Napoleonic wars awakened Egypt to external political realties, and forces loosed by Egypt's adaptation to nineteenth-century Europe led to the creation of modern Sudan.

After the withdrawal of French troops, the Ottoman sultan in 1805 appointed one of his officers, Muhammad Ali, to be the pasha (governor) of Egypt. Muhammad Ali's first task was to rid his army of the Mamelukes. To build a new army he wanted Negro slave recruits. He also needed money for his vast projects, and gold was rumored to be abundant in Sudan; he therefore undertook to conquer the northern region.

The Egyptian army by the end of 1821 had conquered the area as far south as Sannar. All of Sudan except Darfur, the Beja country, and the almost unknown south recognized Muhammad Ali's sovereignty. The first results of the conquest were disastrous; the invading army lived off the land, the commanders imposed heavy taxes on peoples scarcely governed during the previous forty years, and slave raids in the south caused whole tribes to retreat into the hills. In 1822 there were uprisings all along the Nile, but the reinforced Egyptian army moved in from Kordofan to reconquer the valley. During the early 1820s tribes that offered any opposition to the Egyptians were decimated, and fertile Al Jazirah, the stronghold of the Fung, was depopulated. In 1822 and 1823 an estimated 30,000 Negroes from the upper Nile were captured for the army.

The invasion caused many shifts in fortunes of tribes and clans; the Ababda, for example, gained a monopoly of the desert caravan trade in part of the north, and the Shaiqia—in part because they had offered such fierce initial resistance—were employed as irregular soldiers in the enforcement of tax collection.

Although the new rulers were called Turks, Muhammad Ali's government in Egypt and Sudan was his own creation, and the main influence on the Sudanese was Egyptian.

By the early 1830s political control was effective over the north, and government had become less harsh. By granting tax exemptions when it seemed necessary, the support of some tribal and religious leaders was gained, and people were attracted back into the devastated agricultural land of Al Jazirah. Higher levels of government were organized as elsewhere in the Ottoman Empire. After a brief experiment with more direct rule, smaller population groups were left under traditional tribal or district sheikhs. In 1835 government was further centralized by the appointment of a *hakimdar* (governor general). Khartoum, already chosen as a military headquarters, then became the administrative center of the country.

Changes in economic and social life under Turko-Egyptian rule occurred primarily among the townspeople, who increased in number as administrative centers developed. Money came into more common use. State monopolies were formed for the export of such local products as gum arabic and ivory. Among the economic innovations were some, such as the attempt to build an iron foundry in the Kordofan Hills, that failed immediately; but others, including the more widespread planting of indigo, sugar, and cotton for commercial exploitation, were profitable.

Some of the Sudanese townsmen went to Cairo for their education; others were employed in the administration, spoke Turkish, and were addressed as *"effendi,"* the Turkish title of respect. More frequent contact with the centers of Islamic training encouraged greater orthodoxy in religion. The nineteenth-century reform movements gained adherents; although local religious brotherhoods earlier had been the centers of religious life, under Turkish rule a few of the *turuq* (religious orders) organized throughout the Islamic world became powerful in Sudan. One of these, the Khatmiyyah, was particularly favored as it maintained close ties to Cairo and brought support to the government. Religious courts, staffed by Egyptian and Sudanese Islamic judges or cadis trained at Al-Azhar University in Cairo, were organized by the administration to function as the courts of law.

Sudan nevertheless remained an area over which the Egyptians had less than firm control; outside the towns the role of the Turkish official was mainly to collect taxes by force. In many cases the ruler of Egypt would decree reforms for Sudan to find later that nothing had been done, either because of the inertia or corruption of subordinates or because they chose to obey the more compelling orders for revenue or slaves.

The immediate successors of Muhammad Ali, Abbas I (1849–53) and Muhammad Said (1854–63), paid only sporadic notice to Sudan, but the reign of the Khedive Ismail (1863–79) proved a crucial period. Although the administration of the north had become well established and less foreign—Arabic was replacing Turkish as the language of administration; more Sudanese were appointed to responsible positions; and some modernization of communication, law, and education had been introduced—the expansion of Egyptian hegemony and the uneven efforts to govern and modernize Sudan were achieved at the expense of growing unrest. There were mutinies in the army and widespread resentment over the quartering of troops and the use of forced labor on government projects. Finally, the issue of the slave trade became all-important.

Ismail, like Muhammad Ali before him, tried to force Egypt to become a modern state in order to ward off the increasingly evident danger of European intervention, particularly after the opening of the Suez Canal in 1869. He tried to rebuild his army like a European army, recruiting Egyptian peasants rather than Sudanese slaves. Because he no longer wanted slave recruits and both his own European training and European diplomatic pressures encouraged it, he sought to suppress the slave trade.

Slavery had been an institution of Sudanese life throughout history, and the northern Sudanese Negroes were impressed into the Egyptian army under the pharaohs as well as under Muhammad Ali. In the nineteenth century, however, the raids reached massive proportions. Thousands of men were taken as the annual raids extended further into the south, destroying tribal stability and economy. Accounts of the horrors of the slave trade related by European travelers were the first cause of European interest in the area. Most raiding was done by private traders—usually northern Sudanese, other Arabs, or renegade Europeans, who were given government monopolies over certain areas.

The suppression of slavery in Sudan required an extension of territorial control: Ismail hired many Europeans in his effort to modernize Egypt and assigned a number to Sudan. He commissioned Sir Samuel Baker to establish Egyptian rule in the Gondokoro region of Sudan and to suppress the slave trade there. Baker set up a few military outposts, and his successor, Charles George Gordon, who was appointed governor of Equatoria Province in 1873, weakened the trade considerably.

In 1877 Egypt signed the Slave Trade Convention, under which all trade in slaves should end immediately and all private sale of slaves should end by 1889. It seems to have been this commitment, made two years before he was deposed for the financial failure of his government, that led Ismail to appoint Gordon governor general of Sudan with specific orders to improve communications and to suppress slavery.

The Mahdiyyah, 1881–98

After the deposition of Ismail in 1879 and the resignation of General Gordon in 1880, the Sudan governors general, either because of their own indecision or because of the weakness of the Cairo government, could neither continue Gordon's active policies nor change them. The slave trade revived to some extent, but there was no longer a large market, and the former traders remained dissatisfied. The army could not be adequately maintained, and the disbanding of some units created an unemployed soldiery. The burden of taxation increased, often at the will of an extortionate local taxgatherer. Resentment against the "Turks" tended to be locally centered—there was no concept of a Sudanese national entity—but widespread. In this situation the weakened government failed to recognize the threat posed by the appearance of a man—Muhammad Ahmad—who, combining the force of personal magnetism with the zeal of religious fanaticism, dedicated himself to the mission of expelling the Turks.

Ahmad, the son of a boatbuilder from Dunqulah, had attended Koranic schools in the Khartoum area. He became a disciple of the head of the Sammaniyyah order, Muhammad al Sharif, and later, as a sheikh of the Sammaniyyah, spent several years in semiseclusion on Aba Island in the White Nile. There he gained some prominence as an ascetic and mystic and attracted a group of students. In 1879, according to his own version of what happened, when on one of his regular visits to his former teacher, he found Sharif impiously celebrating the circumcision of his son with feasting and dancing. Ahmad remonstrated to Sharif, who expelled him from the order. After the conflict Ahmad became a follower of a rival Sammaniyyah leader, to whose position he succeeded in 1880. During the next year one of the men who came to join his order was Abdullahi ibn Muhammad, a Taaishi from southern Darfur who was considered a seer in his tribe. The meeting of the two men rapidly became surrounded by legend, but within a year Ahmad declared himself the Mahdi— in Islam the guide or messiah who would inaugurate the era of true religion—and set forth with Abdullahi as his most trusted aide.

The expectation of the Mahdi had been widespread during the preceding years of unrest. Ahmad's fundamentalist movement demanded a return to the simplicity of early Islam, abstention from alcohol and tobacco, the proper seclusion of women, and a reduction in the lavish celebrations of marriage and circumcision. He criticized particularly the rivalry among religious groups, the sterile legalisms of the theologians, and the depravity of the Turkish oppressors, whom he called infidels. The inauguration of such a religious society required the expulsion of the alien rulers. Many orthodox religious leaders opposed him, as did most of the townspeople, who did not share his religious fanaticism or his hatred of the Turks.

By 1882 the Mahdi had found political support in Al Ubayyid

and more widespread support for his religious appeals and his denunciation of the tax collectors. The government sent a group of the *ulema* (see Glossary) to talk with him, but he ignored their rejection of his claims; soldiers were sent to arrest him, and they were ambushed. His followers, the Ansar, numbered in the thousands. In 1882 he gained control of Kordofan by surrounding Al Ubayyid with a force of 30,000, many of them former soldiers in the Turkish army, and starving the population into submission. A large Egyptian army under the command of British General William Hicks was overwhelmed, and Hicks was killed. During the next months the Mahdi took Darfur, and Rudolph Slatin, the Austrian governor of the province, became his prisoner for the next decade.

As the Mahdi gained control of most of the country, the British-commanded Egyptian garrisons alone prevented his assumption of power. The government of William Gladstone in England, committed to a nonimperialist policy, decided that the only means of avoiding a full-scale British invasion of Sudan was to convince the Egyptians to withdraw. Gordon, reappointed governor general, reached Khartoum early in 1884, shortly before the Mahdi's troops laid seige to the town. In August 1884 British popular opinion forced the Gladstone government to decide that a British relief force should be sent to rescue Gordon. The advance unit reached Khartoum on January 25, 1885, to find that Khartoum had fallen and General Gordon had been killed three days earlier.

By the end of 1885 the Mahdist forces controlled all of Sudan, but the regime had to be maintained by constant fighting. The Mahdi introduced a highly autocratic government, imposed harsh religious law, and sought to revive regular administration and trade. He died of typhus six months after the battle of Khartoum, however, and the major work of pacification and government devolved on his deputies—three caliphs chosen by the Mahdi in emulation of the Prophet Muhammad. Rivalry among the three, each supported by the people of his native region, continued until 1891, when Abdullahi, with the support primarily of the Baggara Arabs, overcame the opposition of his main rival.

The British government's decision to occupy Sudan resulted from international developments in the decade after 1885. It had become apparent that the British occupation of Egypt was to last longer than had been the original intention. The northern frontier and the Red Sea coast had been almost constant battlegrounds; control over the Nile waters had become of major importance as plans were made for a vast irrigation dam at Aswan. The European powers had moved in from their coastal holdings in Africa, and by 1895 most of the interior of the continent had been occupied. In the early 1890s it appeared that France, Belgium, and Great Britain might converge around the Nile headwaters. In 1894 the approximate spheres of Great Britain in Sudan and Belgium in the Congo were agreed on but a French mission began to move east into the Bahr al Ghazal.

In 1895 Rudolph Slatin escaped from his ten years' imprisonment, and his book *Fire and Sword in the Sudan* did much to stir British public opinion in favor of a campaign against the Mahdists. The decision to occupy northern Sudan was made in March 1896, and an army under General Herbert Kitchener took Dunqulah in September. The second stage of conquest took almost two years, which were spent chiefly in the construction of a railway across the desert from Wadi Halfa to Abu Hamad and along the river to Berber. Little resistance was met until the invading force reached the Atbara-Nile junction in February 1898, where the army of the caliph (Abdullahi) was defeated; it withdrew to Omdurman. The Nile Expeditionary Force reached Omdurman on September 1. The following day the caliph launched an attack with his army of nearly 60,000, equipped with little more than fanaticism. About 11,000 of the Mahdist troops and only forty-eight of the expeditionary force were killed in this battle at Omdurman. The caliph himself escaped to Kordofan, where he was killed in battle in November 1898.

With the death of the caliph organized resistance ended, and in many areas the fall of his regime was welcomed. It had taken several years for the Mahdist regime to consolidate its control. From 1892 until 1896 the caliph had been strong enough to institute a more or less regular administration. An appointed governor, a member of the caliph's tribe, ruled in each province—Dunqulah, Berber, Northeast, Southeast, Darfur, Kordofan, and Equatoria. But the economy of the country was in chaos, and the population had declined possibly by as much as one-half from death by famine, disease, and war. None of the area's traditional institutions or loyalties remained intact, tribes were divided in their attitudes toward the Mahdi, the religious brotherhoods were weakened, and the orthodox religious leaders were gone.

As an aftermath of the conquest came the revelation that British suspicions of French designs on the upper Nile were fully justified. A few days after the Battle of Omdurman, it was reported that white men were in Fashoda. Kitchener arrived at the village two weeks later to find a small French company in occupation. The so-called Fashoda incident proved the climax of a long period of British-French rivalry and hostility. In December 1898 the diplomatic struggle ended in favor of the British; the French mission withdrew from Fashoda on orders from Paris.

The Anglo-Egyptian Condominium, 1899–1952

Since the British and Egyptian occupation of Sudan had been legally undertaken on behalf of the khedive, the Egyptian ruler, and his government against which the revolt of 1885 had been directed, some means had to be devised by which both governments could share in governing the area. The solution was found in the Condominium Agreement of January 19, 1899. Sudan was defined as all territory south of the twenty-second parallel that had previously been administered by the khedive's government or that might subsequently be reconquered by the two governments. Article III specified that "the Supreme military and civil command in the Sudan shall be vested in one officer, termed the Governor-General of Sudan. He shall be appointed by Khedival Decree on the recommendation of Her Britannic Majesty's Government and shall be removed only by Khedival Decree with the consent of Her Britannic Majesty's Government."

During the first five years of the condominium, from 1899 until about 1916, the emphasis was on the establishment of order and administrative regularity. At first nearly all of the growing personnel were military officers from the army in Egypt. The autocratic powers of the governor general were first exercised by Lord Kitchener; he was succeeded in 1899 by Sir Reginald Wingate. Second in authority, and the governor general's main adviser on native affairs, was Rudolph Slatin, the inspector general.

In 1910 the governor general's authority was limited slightly by a law requiring the approval of the governor general in council for all legislation and the budget. The council was composed of the governor general, the inspector general, the civil, legal, and financial secretaries, and two to four others appointed for three-year terms by the governor general; it retained full legislative authority until after World War II. The first young civilians recruited directly from British universities for service in Sudan arrived in 1901; later they became the nucleus of the Sudan Political Service.

The basic policy to be followed in governing the people was outlined in 1899 in Kitchener's directive to territorial officers. Administration was based on the system introduced by the Turkish-Egyptian government in the nineteenth century. In each province—Berber, Dunqulah, Kassala, Sannar, Fashoda, Khartoum, and Kordofan—a British governor (*mudir*) was aided by two inspectors, also British, and a number of district officers (*mamur*), who usually were Egyptian.

During the first years of the administration, sweeping changes were made as the basic institutions of a modern government were organized. By the early 1900s a criminal code and a code of criminal procedure were adapted from the codes in India (see ch. 14). Commissions were appointed to establish rules of land tenure and to adjust claims and counterclaims in dispute because of grants made by successive governments. The taxation system was revised; the basic taxes remained those on land, the amount depending on the type of irrigation, on the number of date trees, and on the size of herds, as under previous administrations, but rates were fixed for the first time. The governors had wide latitude to govern personally in their provinces and applied reforms gradually as they were able. Government in the south, where it existed, remained limited to the keeping of peace.

There was little resistance to British rule. There was some religious resentment, usually stirred up by a local teacher. Tribal resistance in the south lasted longer, particularly along the Ethiopian border, which divided a number of tribes, but most disturbances of the peace after 1920 were tribal raids rather than direct opposition to government.

Another major concern of the early governors was to determine exactly the area for which they had assumed responsibility. A treaty with Ethiopia in 1902 defined the long border to the southeast, and the status of the Lado area in the extreme south was determined by treaty with Belgium in 1909. The western boundary proved the most difficult problem. Darfur was the only major area not under condominum government. Sultan Ali Dinar had assumed power as the Mahdist state disintegrated but, although he recognized Ottoman sovereignty, the condominium government stopped at his borders. As France moved into Ouaddai in the early 1900s the status of the small areas between Ouaddai and Darfur, historically claimed by both, came into dispute.

When World War I broke out, Ali Dinar announced his loyalty to the Ottoman Empire, and the British, who had already declared a protectorate over Egypt, promptly ousted him and incorporated Darfur into Sudan, bringing to an end the ancient Fur sultanate. The boundary between Sudan and French Equatorial Africa was delimited after Franco-British negotiations at the Versailles Peace Conference in 1919.

By the end of World War I the boundaries of Sudan were established; regular government had been instituted; transport and communication had been greatly expanded; and initial steps had been made in education, health facilities, and the training of Sudanese for technical work in government departments. After twenty years, however, the dispartity between the north, where most of the modernization had occurred, and the south had increased; so too had the disparity in the north between the educated few of the towns and their uneducated countrymen. British consideration of administrative problems led to a basic policy conclusion that of the two means available for associating the Sudanese with the government—either employing them in the central bureacracy or transferring authority to Sudanese institutions—the second was less disruptive and more conducive to the even development of the country. The first, however, was put into effect first, primarily because of unrest that developed as a result of Egyptian claims.

Egyptian army personnel and subordinate officials in the civil government formed a substantial group in Sudan. When after 1919 a series of crises occurred in British-Egyptian negotiations on the future of Egypt, there was support for union with Egypt and independence among a vocal minority in the larger Sudanese towns. In 1924 Governor General Sir Lee Stack was murdered in Cairo, and Great Britain demanded, among other things, the withdrawal of all Egyptian officers and military units from Sudan. After some discussion it was decided not to terminate the condominium arrangement, but the Sudan Defense Force was formed to replace the Egyptian army units, and Sudanese rapidly replaced Egyptians at the lower administrative levels.

The major administrative trend of the 1920s was toward devolution, the transfer of some government functions to local persons with recognized authority. The traditional authorities were the sheikhs—of villages, tribes, and districts—in the north and tribal chiefs in the south. The number of people recognizing them, the nature of their authority, and the degree of authority they still held after a century of Turkish, Mahdist, and British rule varied considerably. In many areas devolution required the creation of an authority or the amalgamation of small groups into one. The first powers delegated were judicial, since the role of the sheikh in settling disputes among his people had long been one of his major functions. In some cases the fusion of local groups under sheikhly authority, at first only in legal matters, was successful enough for the unit later to assume some additional powers of local government.

The policy of devolution was devised to prevent complete bureaucratic centralization of government, but it also contributed to a continuation of three types of political and social life in the country. Devolution was little more suited to the south than was bureaucracy.

Devolution was most successful among some groups in the north whose systems of tribal authority had not been completely destroyed by the Mahdi or by early direct British rule and whose economy was still compatible with traditional organization; among the Kababish of Kordofan, for example, the experiment seemed fully successful. The mainstream of political development, however, was in the towns and among the educated, to whom devolution seemed a return of archaic methods of government. In their view British policy in the south—aimed at preserving less advanced tribal society from Arab influence—was expressive of a "zoo mentality," a term coined, however, by British self-critics.

Economic and social changes transformed the settled areas of the Nile valley much more quickly than the west or south. Some communications existed in the north in 1898. During the next two decades the telegraph, the railway, bridges over the rivers, automobiles, and the first airplanes linked northern Sudan but only occasionally reached more distant areas, where the district officers made their rounds by camel. Port Sudan opened in 1909. Khartoum became a city of department headquarters, commercial buildings, law courts, mosques, and schools. The Gordon Memorial College, for which Kitchener had raised money in Great Britain in 1899, opened in Khartoum in 1903 with a primary curriculum. By 1913 a secondary course was offered, and by the late 1920s students could obtain primary and secondary education in the major towns and additional training as teachers, mechanics, veterinarians, or medical technicians.

Most important for future economic development were the plans made for Nile irrigation (see ch. 13). Although cotton had long been a crop of Al Jazirah, commercial growing was not organized until early in the twentieth century. After the construction of the Sannar Dam in 1926 made possible the irrigation of a much larger area, the Jazirah area became the densely populated center of the country and cotton the country's major export.

Birth of Sudanese Nationalism

The removal of Egyptian personnel from Sudan had—as intended—reduced the degree of political ferment. The change had given the Sudanese a greater opportunity to gain experience in government and to consider their future apart from that of Egypt. Specifically Sudanese nationalism that began to develop in the 1930s immediately ran into the complexities of the Condominium Agreement. The educated Sudanese wanted more rapid economic development, social progress, and liberalization of firm control of the central government by the governor general and council. Nationalism was spurred somewhat because, at the very time when Sudanese spokesmen were beginning to voice demands for more schools and hospitals, the worldwide economic depression hit the Sudanese cotton market; a sharp decline in government revenue slowed the process of development and postponed the day when social services could be extended.

Any change in government required a change in the Condominium Agreement. Neither Great Britain, which in practice had full authority in Sudan by virtue of the clause vesting authority in the governor general, nor Egypt, which had regained its formal independence as a kingdom in 1922, could agree to modification. Moreover, the British regarded their role as in part the protection of the Sudanese from Egyptian domination. Thus much of the earliest expression of Sudanese nationalism was a reaction against the fact that little could be done in Sudan until Great Britain and Egypt reached some agreement. The Sudanese feared that the eventual result of British-Egyptian friction might be the attachment of northern Sudan to Egypt and southern Sudan to the neighboring British colonies of Uganda and Kenya.

Most educated Sudanese were in government employment and were aware of the legal and political intricacies involved. In 1929, when Great Britain and Egypt settled the major issue of control of Nile waters, there was hope that further progress would follow, even though the agreement seemed favorable to Egypt and was denounced later by Sudan. When Egypt and Great Britain settled most of their outstanding differences in the Treaty of Alliance of 1936, which provided for an end to British military occupation, the basic question of Sudan's future status was left in abeyance, however; this resulted when Great Britain would not agree to recognize Egyptian suzerainty. It was agreed that Egyptians could again be employed in the Sudanese government if qualified Sudanese could not be found, but the Condominium Agreement was untouched.

The signing of the treaty occasioned the first organized expression of Sudanese nationalism. The Graduates' General Conference, formed in 1936 among Sudanese having some secondary education, was organized primarily to prove the existence of an educated group that was unwilling to accept determination of the country's future without reference to Sudanese wishes. Their demands were moderate, but after the beginning of World War II they pressed for recognition of the right of self-determination, quoting the principles of the Atlantic Charter in support of their stand. Reminded by the British that they represented only a very small fraction of the Sudanese public, the graduates went outside their limited number to make their appeal through religious groups, which were the only organizations commanding widespread popular loyalties.

The secular nationalists were divided first of all on the issue of complete independence or union with Egypt; so too were religious leaders. Although at first British policy had been to suppress all vestiges of Mahdism, in part by giving support to the powerful Khatmiyyah brotherhood, led by the Mirghani family, which had been the Mahdi's major opponent, policy had changed during the struggle against pro-Egyptian nationalism in the 1920s. Limited recognition had been given to Abd al Rahman al Mahdi, the posthumous son of the Mahdi, during World War I as a means of influencing public opinion against the Ottoman cause. Abd al Rahman, as leader of the Mahdi sect, the Ansars, gradually emerged as a spokesman for proindependence sentiment as opposed to the Mirghani followers, who favored union with Egypt. Two coalitions having some secular membership and the religious support of either Abd al Rahman or Ali al Mirghani formed the wings of the nationalist movement and, after 1942, the first political parties. The more radical nationalists, in alliance with the Khatmiyyah, tended to look to union with Egypt and formed the Ashigga party, later renamed the National Unionist Party (NUP). The more moderate favored Sudanese independence in cooperation with Great Britain and formed the Ummah party.

At the end of World War II Sudanese, Egyptian, and British leaders alike agreed that new plans were essential for a new era. Economic depression followed by war had caused postponement of many projects; but plans were made, and Sudanese demands increased rapidly. Early in the war the Sudan Defense Force had defended the borders against the Italians in Eritrea and Ethiopia; later, Sudanese had served outside the country. The first political parties had formed. Among the significant changes made by the government between 1945 and 1950 were the establishment of the first government schools in the south, the legalization of trade unions, the reorganization of Gordon Memorial College as a university, the inauguration of Sudan Airways, nationalization of the management of the Jazirah Scheme, and the inauguration of a comprehensive project of economic development among the Azande.

Political innovation came with greater difficulty. In the midst of new tensions caused by new Anglo-Egyptian discussions concerning Sudan, the first changes in Sudan government since 1910 were instituted. Provincial councils had been formed in 1944, and an advisory council for northern Sudan was constituted in 1946 to advise the Governor-General's Council. Two years later, in changes made unilaterally by Great Britain since Egypt would not agree to them, Sudan obtained an executive council to replace the Governor-General's Council and a partially elected legislative assembly. Since the pro-Egyptian party boycotted all preparatory work and the elections, the legislature was dominated by moderates and the proindependence party. The British and Sudanese proceeded to draw up the Self-Determination Agreement, enacted in 1952. The Egyptians—still demanding that their sovereignty over Sudan be recognized—unilaterally terminated the Condominium Agreement and declared Farouk I king of both Egypt and Sudan.

Independence

The thirty-year deadlock on the matter of Sudanese sovereignty was broken only by the revolution in Egypt in late 1953, which brought the monarchy to an end and Muhammad Naguib to power. Naguib, whose mother was Sudanese, was trusted in Sudan and was prepared to recognize the right of the Sudanese to self-determination. By early January 1953 all of Sudan's organized parties had accepted the Egyptian proposals. Under this joint pressure, on February 12, 1953, Great Britain agreed that the Condominium Administration would give way to Sudanese self-government over a three-year transitional period, after which the Sudanese themselves would decide their status by plebiscite. During this period the governor general's powers were very limited. An elected bicameral Parliament held legislative power, and Sudanese rapidly replaced British government personnel.

The progress toward self-government suggested by Great Britain and Egypt was followed at first but was later ignored as the Sudanese Parliament gained full initiative. Although the unionist party, somewhat surprisingly to the British, won firm majorities in the 1953 elections to the Senate and the House of Representatives, the party reversed its policy in 1954 and 1955. Prime Minister Ismail al Azhari and most of his followers, for many years the major spokesman for the unity of the Nile River valley, chose Sudanese independence. The strength of popular opinion against union with Egypt had become apparent, both among the opposition and in the south, particularly after Gamal Abdul Nasser replaced General Naguib in 1954; and the men in government, their support for Egypt always having been based in part on the usefulness of Egyptian support against the British, realized that independence was at hand and that their own positions as leaders of an independent country were at stake. Although the future of the country was to have been determined originally by an elected constituent assembly and a plebiscite, independence was achieved by a simple declaration adopted unanimously by the Sudanese Parliament on December 19, 1955. On January 1, 1956, Sudan became an independent republic.

The country obtained independence, however, without solving the problems necessary to agree upon a permanent constitution. Instead, the Constituent Assembly had adopted the Transitional Constitution; its most noteworthy feature was the replacement of the governor general as head of state by the five-member Supreme Commission, elected by Parliament. The Parliament was to consist of an indirectly elected Senate and a popularly elected House of Representatives. Most executive power was placed in the hands of the prime minister, elected by the House and confirmed in office by the Supreme Commission. The Supreme Commission also oversaw the operation of the judiciary. The multi-headed executive and the lack of a permanent constitution were to prove major problems in the future.

Although independence was achieved with a minimum of conflict and bitterness, the government inherited several major problems and conflicts. Sudanization of the administration was achieved with remarkable speed and good will; the Sudan government provided compensation and pensions for the British officers of the Sudan Political Service who left the country and retained those who could not be replaced. Replacement of British administrators in the south by northern Sudanese, however, increased or revived the southern tribes' fears of domination by Arab northerners.

Development of North-South Differences

The Sudan of precolonial times stopped at a line that wavered between the tenth and twelfth parallels or from the northern edge of the Nuba Mountains to the upper Nile swamps. The area to the south had never been a part of any of the earlier states. By the sixteenth century all of the various peoples of the north had adopted Islam and some degree of political and cultural arabization.

There are no clear lines of racial or religious distinction between the southern peoples and the northerners; instead the distinctions are cultural. The southerners were protected by geographic barriers from the advance of Islam and retained the traditional cultural, religious, and political forms of adjacent black Africa (see ch. 5). Only the Nile provided any potential link between the northern and southern areas.

During the nineteenth century the slave trade opened for the first time a relationship between the Sudanese Arabs and Africans, but this contact resulted only in adding deep and lasting hatred to the existing cultural cleavages. As Sudan had direct access to slave markets of the Middle East, slave raiding by northerners intensified in the second half of the century and continued long after it had been generally suppressed in the rest of Africa. Because of the disruptions caused by the Mahdiyyah period, the trade was not even formally suppressed until the beginning of the twentieth century.

The raids of the slave era had two lasting results. First, the Arabs and other arabized northerners came to look upon the southerners as their natural inferiors, an attitude that northerners still openly displayed in the 1960s. Second, the southerners developed a permanent fear of the Arabs that did not diminish with the ending of the slave trade. They continued to regard the peaceful northern traders in their midst as exploiters and to associate them with the cruelty of their forebears.

The establishment of the condominium formally brought the south under British colonial rule, but this remote and poor area was almost entirely ignored by the government until after World War I, except for efforts to suppress intertribal warfare. Nevertheless, social welfare efforts were begun by Christian missionaries, who had been active in limited numbers before the Mahdiyyah period and who had returned during the condominium period. A number of mission schools were opened, and converts were made. This also had the effect of separating the north and south, as Christianity and English rather than Islam and Arabic became the symbols of the elite. Northern influence may actually have been growing because the lower ranks of the colonial administration and most of the region's limited trade remained in Arab hands. From the first, however, the British treated the three southern provinces as a separate region to which access by northerners was restricted.

As the colonial administration of the south took on more substance in the late 1920s, the British reinforced their decision to treat the south separately. Some officials considered eventually making the region a part of British East Africa, with which its people were more culturally aligned. The separation policy was officially clarified by a 1930 government directive barring virtually all northern Sudanese from entering or working in the south. Thus, only two decades after the ending of slave raiding, all contact betwen southerners and northerners ceased; however, a permanent memory of the earlier era remained. The announced reason for the British policy was a desire to protect the less advanced southern culture from submersion by the north. The actual objective was the creation of self-contained racial or tribal units based on indigenous customs and traditional usage and beliefs. English was made the official lingua franca in place of

Arabic in the army and police, and the spread of Arab customs was curtailed. As the level of education increased, the few southerners receiving higher training were sent to schools in East Africa rather than Khartoum.

Although potentially a rich agricultural zone, the south's economic and social development was limited by its climate and its distance from markets. During the 1930s and 1940s the colonial government could not afford the expenditures required for major development projects. Thus, the region was not brought up to an economic level where it could compete with the north, and the rail and road lines that would have been required to tie the south to East Africa were not built. The southern economy remained stagnant, and government service provided the only job market for the increasing number of graduates of the small school system.

After World War II as the British—no longer interested in the imperial burden of colonies—prepared to withdraw from Sudan, a decision was made to reverse the forty-year-old policy of separate, if limited, development in the south. Deciding that the vague plans for amalgamating the region with East Africa were economically impractical, the British in 1946 decided to accede to the demands of Sudanese Arab nationalists and firmly link the two halves of the country. Although the decision had little impact until 1953, northern traders, officials, and teachers returned to the south, gradually at first, but then—as the British withdrew—in large numbers.

Although the south had no political parties or elected officers, the indigenous educated leaders had all protested the British plans in 1947. During the independence negotiations the question of the south had been pushed aside; the northerners gained British agreement that the southern provinces were to be administered exactly as were the northern provinces. After having been included in the plans for self-government but having had no effective means of exerting any influence, southern representatives were sent to the legislature in 1948 and in 1953. They shared a general fear of northern domination but were unable to formulate demands except to propose internal autonomy or federal government, systems that were effectively blocked by northern attitudes, the economic dependence of the south on the north, and the absence of experienced southern administrators.

By 1953 the southerners began to feel they were about to be overcome economically, culturally, and religiously. They particularly resented the threat of Arabic replacing English as the only language of government, a move that effectively deprived the few educated southerners of all job opportunities. They also felt threatened by the replacement of trusted British district commissioners with unsympathetic northerners. This loss was to be countered by offering new jobs to all Sudanese as the colonial officials left. When the several hundred new appointments were announced, however, only four junior administrative posts were given to southerners. This event left the southern elite feeling betrayed. The majority saw the arrival of northern officials as the first step in the replacement of the limited, benevolent British colonial rule by a new, active, and hostile Arab colonialism. The less advanced tribesmen were willing to believe assertions that the era of slave trade was about to begin again.

Southern political leaders pressed for a federal relationship of the three southern provinces to the central government, but the widespread hostility of southerners toward control by the Arab majority in the north led to the revolt of southern units of the army in August 1955. Several hundred northern traders and officials were killed. The revolt was quickly suppressed and seventy southerners were executed. The situation in the south improved temporarily after 1956, but northern domination and the government policy of arabizing the country through unified administration and the teaching of the Arabic language continued to arouse the southerners (see ch. 9).

Although the government made rapid progress in some areas, as in plans for economic development and for more rapid expansion of the educational system, the political coalition of independence was subjected to frequent reshuffling. Political loyalties were pulled in several directions—between north and south, between religious and secular emphasis, and between socialism, communism, and conservatism, complicated by the rivalry between the Khatmiyyah and the Ansar.

Political Alignments

Independence removed the major issue on which party policies had been formed, and Azhari not only forfeited Egyptian support but also became the prime target of Egyptian propaganda. The new alignment was implicit in the statements issued in December 1955 by Abd al Rahman and Mirghani who, meeting for the first time in several years, urged Azhari to form a coalition government. He yielded to his critics and formed a coalition cabinet in February 1956, but he had by this time alienated the Khatmiyyah by making clear his lack of enthusiasm for it and proclaiming his preference for a secular party. The coalition included some opposition elements, but Azhari himself took the key posts of prime minister and minister of interior, and his strongest supporter, Mubarak Zarruq, was given the portfolios of foreign affairs and justice.

34

In June, when the People's Democratic Party (PDP), formed under Mirghani's leadership by Khatmiyyah members of the NUP, announced its existence, twenty-one representatives and fourteen senators declared their allegiance to it. The PDP and Ummah representatives then voted against Azhari, and on July 5 Abdullah Khalil was elected prime minister. The new coalition of the Ummah and PDP, backed by the Ansar and Khatmiyyah, seemed a temporary compromise between the two religious leaders in the face of the growing secular threat of the NUP.

By forming the alliance the Ummah obtained power in government after three years of being the opposition party. The Khatmiyyah, by creating a new party, also bettered its political position. The coalition was a realignment of conservative factions but ones that were traditionally hostile. Nevertheless, they held together for the remaining year of the Parliament's tenure and after adjournment in July 1957 cooperated in preparation for elections to be held in February 1958.

The 1958 Elections

For the 1958 elections the membership of the House of Representatives was increased to 173, each member to be elected directly by adult males. The constituencies were drawn on the basis of the 1956 census, each deputy representing from 40,000 to 60,000 persons.

The people in some rural areas considered political matters the concern of the chief or the elders or simply failed to attach any significance to the choice being made. Among urban voters, however, a high percentage cast their votes.

The election gave a plurality in the House of Representatives and in the Senate to the Ummah and a majority to the Ummah-PDP coalition. The results gave the Ummah sixty-three seats; the NUP, forty-five; the PDP, twenty-seven; and the Southern Liberals, twenty. Negotiation appeared to have played a greater part in election preparation than regular campaigning.

Two results were particularly important. The NUP, without major religious support, won one-fourth of the seats, largely from the urban centers or the Jazirah Scheme agricultural workers. The Ummah increased its share of seats from about one-fourth to one-third. It undoubtedly benefited from being in power at the time of the election; it also profited from independence, which relieved it of the charge of partnership with the British, and from increased anti-Egyptian sentiment.

Two weeks before the Sudanese elections, Nasser held a plebiscite in Egypt and Syria on the formation of the United Arab Republic (UAR). He also opened a boundary dispute with Sudan by insisting that persons living between the twenty-second parallel—the boundary defined in the Condominium Agreement—and the border of the territory actually administered from Khartoum since 1902 were Eygptian and should vote in the plebiscite. Although he withdrew his demands, the crisis worked to the disadvantage of the PDP and probably also of the NUP.

In the south the vote represented a rejection of the men who had cooperated with the government—all three of the southerners in the preelection cabinet were defeated—and a victory for the spokesmen for autonomy. Resentment against the government's taking over mission schools and against the measures used in putting down the 1955 mutiny contributed to the election of a large number of men who had been implicated in the rebellion.

Postelection Problems

After the new Parliament convened, the Ummah-PDP coalition formed a cabinet under Khalil. Of fifteen cabinet posts, the Ummah held ten; of these, two were held by southerners. The PDP received five, of which one was held by a southerner. In order to make the cabinet workable the Supreme Commission appointed two PDP leaders defeated in the election, Ali Abd al Rahman and Mirghani Hamza, to the Senate and then to the cabinet.

The two coalition parties disagreed. Both were troubled by internal differences. The southerners agreed with no one. It rapidly became apparent that the cabinet could not exercise effective leadership. Factional maneuvers, vote buying, and personal ambitions dominated the session at a time when crucial issues were raised. A new constitution was proposed in which the future place of the south had to be decided.

Ratification of a technical assistance treaty with the United States aroused bitter conflicts over foreign policy. At the same time the economy was badly depressed because of failure to obtain a good price for the cotton crop, and Sudanese-Egyptian relations had reached a new low. An atmosphere of unrest and tension prevailed in Parliament and among much of the urban population. By July 1958, when Parliament recessed until November, the government had approached stalemate on a number of issues.

Parliament functioned also as a constituent assembly. In considering the draft of the proposed new constitution the southern representatives, led by Father Saturnino Lahure, a priest trained at the Verona Fathers Mission in Waw, appeared to work together more closely and to be more independent than before. The fact that Father Lahure was the major spokesman for the group seemed to intensify the belief prevalent in the north that the missionaries were responsible for southern recalcitrance (see ch. 6).

When Parliament met as a constituent assembly in May 1958, the southern representatives came to the conclusion that the government had no intention even of debating the possibility of a federal system; moreover, the draft constitution was at first published only in Arabic, which many of them could not read. All southerners except the three cabinet members and a few northerners elected from southern constituencies thereupon left the assembly and threatened to boycott future meetings. The crisis was avoided by appointing a committee to study the problem.

The major question before Parliament was the ratification of the technical assistance agreement with the United States. Prime Minister Khalil had signed an agreement in March. In presenting it to Parliament, he found that not only had the NUP decided to make an all-out effort to overthrow the Ummah-dominated coalition on the issue but also many of the PDP delegates were actively working against him under the leadership of Ali Abd al Rahman. Prolonged, heated debate followed, in which the NUP repeatedly charged the Khalil government with being pro-West and with abandoning the neutralist position to make the country an Anglo-American satellite. In this they were motivated by the widespread Arab reaction to the United States military landing in Lebanon in the summer of 1958, which both communist and Egyptian propaganda had succeeded in portraying as a first step in United States efforts to dominate the Arab world.

The move to defeat the aid bill had effective backing from the Anti-Imperialist Front, the overt body of the illegal Sudan Communist Party. The bill was strongly attacked by the Khartoum press and among workers and students, and it was generally thought that a good deal of money was distributed in Parliament to ensure votes against ratification. Nevertheless, the Ummah with the help of some PDP and southern delegates managed to ratify the agreement after some limitations were accepted on the use of the aid.

The spectacle of factionalism and susceptibility to bribery in Parliament revealed by the aid issue increased disillusionment with parliamentary government at a time when concern was already high. In 1958, for the second year in succession, Sudan failed to market its usual quota of cotton, from which most of the country's national income is derived. Restrictions on imports were felt particularly in the towns, where the people had become accustomed to buying a variety of imported goods. The northern tribes also suffered from the quasi-embargo that the UAR had placed upon Sudanese imports, for they depended on the UAR market for cattle, camels, dates, and other products. The ban was indicative of the deterioration of Sudanese-UAR relations after negotiations for a Nile waters agreement had once more failed because, as the UAR saw it, of the intransigence of the Khalil government.

The fall of 1958 brought a series of rumors and covert negotiations among all political factions. The UAR turned its considerable propaganda machine against the Khalil government, and there were constant rumors of an impending pro-UAR coup d'etat. Repeated worker and student demonstrations against Khalil took place in the Three Towns. There were reports that the Ummah and the NUP were near agreement on a new coalition that would exclude the PDP and also Khalil, and at the same time prominent members of both the NUP and the PDP were in Cairo, seeking interviews with Nasser and attacking the Ummah.

On November 17, the day Parliament was to convene, the military coup d'etat took place. Khalil, himself a retired army general officer, leading Ummah members and probably some members of the PDP, apparently planned the coup in conjunction with the two senior generals, Ibrahim Abboud and Ahmad Abd al Wahab. Abboud obtained immediate statements of support from Abd al Rahman and Mirghani.

The Abboud Government, 1958–64

The most important immediate effect of the coup was to remove political decisionmaking from the control of the politicians. The ruling Supreme Council of the Armed Forces contained officers with both Ansar and Khatmiyyah affiliations, and some of the resentment among junior army officers was based on a fear that one group or the other might be on the ascendancy in the supreme council. Abboud belonged to the Khatmiyyah; Wahab was a strong member of the Ansar and a relative of Khalil. Until the removal of Wahab in March 1959, Ansar strength in the government appeared to be the stronger. The government ignored and made no use of the former politicians, even as advisers.

Abboud appointed a constitutional commission, headed by the chief justice, to draft a new constitution for the country, but he consistently maintained that political parties were vehicles for the attainment of personal ambitions and that they would not be allowed to re-form. As early as July 1960 the commission had announced its readiness to make a report to the government, but its report was not released.

The regime benefited during its first year in office from two good years of cotton production successfully marketed. It also profited from the settlement of the longstanding Nile water dispute with the UAR and the marked improvement in relations between the two countries.

Although the coup stabilized a degenerating political situation and Abboud's intention appeared to be the establishment of a paternal government by civil servants, it also opened the door to further military action. Under the military government, the influence of Ansar and Khatimyyah lessened considerably. The strongest of the religious leaders, Abd al Rahman, died in the spring of 1959; his son and successor, the elder Sadik al Mahdi, though he seemed to assume Ansar leadership very quickly, did not enjoy the widespread reverence accorded his father. Moreover, the rapid growth of educational institutions increased yearly the numbers of men to whom religious loyalties were secondary to career and professional interests.

Three officer-group attempts to change the Abboud government in 1959 appeared to arise from a combination of personal ambitions with the desire to form a more "popular government" in which more and presumably less conservative civilians would be included. The leaders of the attempts, Brigadier Muhi-al-Din Ahmad Abdullah and Brigadier Abd al Rahim Shinnan, and some of their supporters and relatives were sentenced to life imprisonment, but they appeared to represent the opinions of a sizable group within the army.

The 1959 coup attempts did not have UAR support, but they had some support from the Sudan Communist Party, the only political organization in the country that was outspokenly critical of the military regime. The Communists were limited in number, but they gained support as the only effective organization covertly opposing the government.

From the first the Abboud government aroused strong opposition among many elements because of its lack of dynamism and by its failure to satisfy or placate political demands. The military government's failure to place capable civilian advisers in positions of authority, to launch a strong program of economic and social development that might have created the conditions essential for future political stability, and to achieve agreement within the army, created an atmosphere of considerable political turbulence and antigovernment sentiment.

The ban on political activity had left southern tensions without an outlet. The Abboud government sought to impose an end to southern restiveness through the use of military force and the expulsion of the Christian missionaries, who were blamed for the resistance of the government's attempts to arabize the region. Several hundred southern soldiers, who had fled after the 1955 mutiny, remained in hiding and staged sporadic attacks on government security forces. By 1964 guerrilla warfare enveloped the south (see ch. 9).

During the Abboud regime Sudan's foreign policy was one of isolation from outside contact, a reaction to demands for rejection of closer relations with the Western countries, distrust of communism, and fear of being engulfed by the UAR. The government sought above all else to demonstrate complete independence of the UAR. Although Sudan remained a member of the Arab League, the military government's leaders came to realize that most other Arab states still regarded Sudan as an historic appendage of its northern neighbor and one that remained within its sphere of influence. The Sudanese felt they would receive little support from the other league members in any dispute with the UAR.

Despite the coup leaders' promises to return the country to civilian constitutional rule, the proposals of the constitutional commission headed by the Abboud government's strongest civilian supporter, the chief justice of the Supreme Court, were not released until November 1962. The commission's stated objective was to build up gradually an adherence to democratic institutions from the grassroots upward; the group's proposals consciously copied the so-called Basic Democracy program of the Muslim military government of Pakistan.

The first step to institute the program consisted of local council elections in April 1963, the first held in the country since 1958. A total of 1,580 local municipal councillors were elected to ninety-four local councils, where they were joined by an additional 800 councillors appointed by the military. The local councils in turn elected members to the nine provincial councils. Finally, each provincial council chose six of its members to fill fifty-four seats in the Central Council, which was eventually to function as an advisory national legislature. The government appointed an additional eighteen members, and all ministers held seats in the Central Council as ex officio members.

Return of the Politicians, 1964–69

The army, finding itself unable to cope militarily with the increasing revolt in the south, began a search in 1964 for alternate methods to bring an end to the crisis. Openly admitting failure of its own resources, the government invited civilians to submit proposals for ending the conflict and granted freedom of expression on the southern problem.

Although the problem of relations between Arabs and black Africans was of historic origin and was unique among the country's difficulties, the north-south animosity had been aggravated during the military regime by the same things that aggravated opposition to the Abboud government within the north. Its approach had been authoritarian, and it had failed to provide the leadership necessary to face economic as well as sociopolitical problems. Moreover, it had refused to allow outlets through which the population could voice legitimate complaints (see ch. 11).

As a result, freedom to express opinions and opposition to government policy quickly spread beyond the southern issue into accusations against the military regime on all counts. Government attempts to cut off the debates, which centered on the university, resulted in a widespread popular reaction; it was not limited to the students but included workers and civil servants in the Three Towns. A ten-day general strike, which began on October 21, 1964, spread quickly to the rest of the country. The leaders of the students, workers, and civil servants called themselves the Professional Front. Along with a grouping of former politicians they formed the United National Front (UNF), which apparently made contact with groups of junior army officers.

On October 26, 1964, after five continuous days of rioting, President Abboud announced the dissolution of the ruling Supreme Council of the Armed Forces and the Council of Ministers. Power positions within the army itself were changed, and the UNF leaders met with army leaders to plan the end of military rule.

On October 30, 1964, a civil servant was named prime minister, although Abboud remained head of state until November 15, 1964. Plans, apparently begun by younger military officers, to form a joint civilian-military government were aborted by renewed popular resentment against the army, which resulted from an incident in which soldiers opened fire on a crowd demonstrating outside the president's residence.

A cabinet was formed from representatives of all political groupings, including one southerner and one Communist. The UNF demanded a program that included a restoration of personal freedoms, a reorganized and independent judiciary, freedom for all political prisoners, and a foreign policy free from close ties to either the Western or the Arab countries.

The new system of government was again to be based on the 1956 interim constitution. At first, however, the political factionalism that had brought the country to a standstill in 1958 was obscured behind a common front government under the UNF. There was a continuing popular hostility to the reappearance of political parties because of their divisive effects. Although all parties (including the Sudan Communist Party) were allowed to function openly, only five of the fifteen cabinet posts went to party politicians. Two posts were given to nonparty southerners. The other eight were drawn from the Professional Front and included a number of Communists. Opposition on the grounds of religion and foreign policy as well as rural opposition to control of the government by town dwellers and modernists contributed gradually to the regrowth of support for the old political parties.

The new government had announced that national elections would be held in March 1965 and that a major task of the new legislature would be the preparation of a permanent constitution. It soon became apparent, however, that the security situation in the south would prevent elections from being conducted among the southern third of the country's population. The resurgent political parties split on the issue of whether elections should be held in the north as scheduled or be postponed until the whole country could vote together. The PDP and the Communists, both fearful of losing ground at the polls, called for postponing the elections, as did southern elements. The cabinet was dissolved over this issue.

The president of the Supreme Commission, which had replaced General Abboud as the country's titular executive, directed that elections should be held where possible. The PDP, but not the Communists, rejected his decision and chose to boycott both the interim cabinet and the elections.

The 1965 elections lowered the voting age to eighteen and gave women their first opportunity to vote. A unique feature of the election was a special fifteen-seat national graduates constituency created to give an added voice to the educated elite. Some 17,000 secondary-school graduates registered to vote in this special constituency without losing their right to vote in the regular territorial constituencies comprising 158 seats in the north and sixty in the south.

Less than a quarter of those eligible voted, reflecting in part considerable antipathy toward elected government. In addition, the parties were unable to get out the vote because most of the organizational structure had been severely damaged by their suppression during six years of military rule. During that period only two groups had been able to retain much of their organizational base: the Communists, through their underground organization, and the Ummah, with its strength in the Mahdiyyah religious brotherhood.

The NUP leadership had been too involved in the power struggle within the cabinet to leave time for organizational matters, and the organization's party base had been traditionally weak. Many of its followers among the urban population and the country's workers resented NUP's establishment of close ties with the Ummah party in the 1965 preelection period.

The Khatmiyyah-oriented PDP had been weakened by changes in the Ummah party, the Khatmiyyah members being less afraid that an Ummah victory would open the way for Mahdiyyah domination. PDP leadership was also indecisive in organizing its boycott of the elections. The Sudan Communist Party—over the objections of some of its internal factions—had entered the campaign openly for the first time, although in some constituencies its candidates ran as independents or as members of the Tenants and Workers Party front.

The 1965 election results were inconclusive. In addition to the low turnout, there was a multiplicity of candidates. The Ummah party, for example, ran two or more competing candidates in sixty-six constituencies. As a result, few of those elected had a majority of the votes cast. Ummah, however, scored a major victory by capturing nearly half of the regular constituency seats —seventy-five out of 158—whereas its NUP ally won fifty-two of the remainder. Three candidates of the PDP ran and won despite their party's boycott, as did the newly formed modernist Muslim Islamic Charter Front (ICF), whose objective was the creation of an Islamic state. Two local groups favoring regional autonomy —the Beja Congress and the Nuba Independents—won ten and eight seats respectively; the remaining seven northern seats went to independent candidates. Finally, although elections had been cancelled throughout the south, twenty-two men—most of them northerners who had filed to contest some of the southern constituencies—claimed victories as unopposed candidates. Their claims were upheld by the courts, and all were seated.

The communist candidates for regular constituency seats were all defeated. They and their sympathizers, however, won eleven of the fifteen graduate constituency seats. The other four were split by the ICF and the NUP.

The elections were followed by efforts led by Ummah to form a multiparty government under a restored national united front, but agreement could not be reached. Instead, Ummah and the NUP formed a coalition cabinet, the NUP leader, Azhari, being given permanent presidency of the Supreme Commission.

The cabinet formed in June 1965 was headed by the Ummah leader, Muhammad Ahmad Maghoub, as prime minister. It had two major mandates: achievement of some major advance toward solving the southern problem and removal of the Communists from positions of power. In December 1965 the assembly achieved the second of these objectives by passing a decree that both abolished the Sudan Communist Party and ejected all communist members from their assembly seats.

The Ummah-NUP coalition was formally ended in October 1965 over a disagreement regarding which party's leader—M.A. Mahgoub as prime minister or Azhari as president—should have control over foreign relations. Maghoub held on in office for another eight months but was forced to resign in July 1966 after a parliamentary vote of censure. His loss was brought about by a split within the Ummah party. One wing led by M.A. Mahgoub was composed of traditionalists under the spiritual leadership of the Imam al Hadi al Mahdi, who had become the Ansar head. This faction was opposed by the modernists, who were led by the Imam's nephew, the younger Sadik al Mahdi. The modernists also had traditionalist supporters in some areas, notably Kordofan and Darfur provinces. Sadik was selected as the new prime minister by a vote of his own wing of the party supported by NUP allies.

The Sadik government, at first backed by a sizable majority in the assembly, sought to widen the political appeal of the central government, to organize the economy so that regional differences were lessened, and to use Sadik's personal rapport with southern leaders as a steppingstone toward bringing the separatists to the conference table. This rapport resulted from Sadik's demands for an investigation into the charges of brutality by members of the security forces after massacres at Waw and Juba in July 1965 and his attempts to replace the less effective Supreme Commission with a president and a southern vice president. He had also demanded the granting of a considerable degree of autonomy to the south.

Despite its break with the traditionalists, Sadik's government continued to face strong opposition from the educated elite and certain portions of the army because of its gradualist approach to social and economic problems. Students and the unions demanded the installation of a socialist state. Although they were only a small minority among the population as a whole, they represented a major element among the educated and were efficiently organized in the capital city.

Resentment against Sadik was provoked further in December 1966 by the assembly's refusal to honor the decision of the High Court of Justice that overturned the assembly's decision to outlaw the Sudan Communist Party and remove its members from the assembly. In late December a poorly organized coup attempt failed. The Communists were accused of supporting the small army unit involved, and a number were arrested.

Elections were held in thirty-six constituencies in the south in

March 1967. The Ummah, with Sadik as its spokesman, won fifteen seats; the Sudan African National Union (SANU) won ten, and the NUP, five. Despite this apparent increase in his support, Sadik's position had become tenuous. The conservative wing of the Ummah was disturbed primarily by Sadik's support for constitutional guarantees of religious freedom and his objections to declaring Sudan an Islamic state. The conservatives and the NUP withdrew their support, and Sadik's government fell. In May M.A. Mahgoub was chosen prime minister again at the head of a coalition cabinet with members of his wing of the Ummah, NUP, PDP, and three southerners. In December 1967 the PDP and the NUP amalgamated to form a large new party— the Democratic Unionist Party (DUP)—under the leadership of Azhari.

By early 1968 the division within Ummah was the dominant split in the Parliament. The close division of assembly votes prevented any government action. Afraid that Sadik had assembled enough votes to bring his cabinet down, M.A. Mahgoub dissolved Parliament. Sadik's followers, including a majority of the members of the assembly, refused to recognize the legitimacy of this dissolution, and at one point two governments functioned in Khartoum; one met in the assembly building, the other on its lawn. The army commander had to request clarification from the Supreme Court regarding which faction had the authority to issue orders. The ruling civilian Supreme Commission, after some indecision, backed the dissolution. New elections were called for late April 1968.

Voter turnout at the polls was much greater than in 1965, as many as 85 percent of the electorate voting in some constituencies. Elections were held thoughout most of the south for the first time since 1958. The apparent calm during the elections was shattered by the assassination of the leading moderate southern leader, William Deng—apparently the work of southern extremists. The election results gave the new DUP a surprisingly strong showing —101 of the 218 seats—but again no single party held the majority of the seats, and governmental stability could not be assured. Thirty-six seats went to the conservative wing of the Ummah, thirty to the Sadik wing, and twenty-five to the two southern parties—SANU and the Southern Front. One seat was won by the secretary general of the Sudan Communist Party, Abdal Khalig Mahgoub, who became minister of health in the postelection government. In a major defeat, Sadik lost his own seat to a conservative Ummah rival.

In order to form a government, the DUP needed eight more votes. The cost for these was heavy; the party was forced to form an alliance with the conservative Ummah wing, which demanded and got the prime ministership for its leader, M.A. Mahgoub, along with four other posts. The DUP held five posts, and the Southern Front was given two.

The new coalition seemed stronger than any of its predecessors. Its program, which won strong assembly approval, included plans for governmental reorganization and strengthened ties to the Arab world and major development efforts, particularly in the hostile south. Sudanese troops were to remain in the UAR, where they had been sent to defend against a renewal of Israeli attacks.

Sadik's supporters in the assembly formed an opposition front and refused to take part in efforts to complete the draft constitution. The government retaliated by closing the opposition's newspaper and curtailing demonstrations among university students. Sadik was particularly critical of the dissolution of the assembly before final approval of the vital new constitution, already ten years overdue. He and his supporters also opposed the new government's adoption of nationalization and socialism as the keys to policy. Over their objections the new cabinet created a government monopoly over the importation and distribution of certain basic consumer commodities; forced the management of foreign banks to accept Sudanese government participation; and accepted military, technical, and economic aid from the Soviet Union.

By late 1968 the two wings of the Ummah had begun to draw back together, particularly after both agreed to support the conservative Imam al Mahdi in the presidential campaign expected during 1969. At the same time the coalition government was weakened by the DUP's announcement that it would seek to install Azhari as president. The Communists and other leftists began to align themselves behind Chief Justice Babikir Awadallah. Although not a Communist, he was viewed by the Communists as an ally since he had supported the party in the government's attempt to have them outlawed during the 1966–67 period.

The Numayri Era

The reunification of Ummah had gone far enough by April 1969 that Sadik was expected to replace M.A. Maghoub as prime minister. At that point the army intervened decisively for the second time. On May 25, 1969, in a quick and bloodless effort, the younger and more radical officers of the army seized power. The coup leader was Colonel Jaafar al Numayri, commander of the national capital's defense forces. Numayri had been implicated in the plots to turn the Abboud government toward a more radical course in 1958 and since then had been secretly involved in building up a political following within the army. His political activities apparently continued while he attended a six-month military training course in England and a nine-month course at the Army Command and General Staff College in the United States.

The coup leaders included only one civilian, former Chief Justice Awadallah. Shortly after assuming control, Numayri suspended the interim constitution, abolished all existing organs of government, and outlawed all political parties. Sixty-three politicians were arrested, and twenty-two senior army officers were forcibly retired. Rule was entrusted to the Revolutionary Command Council (RCC), led by Numayri and with Awadallah as its only civilian member. Awadallah was also appointed prime minister, and a twenty-one-member cabinet was formed. Only two of the new ministers were military officers. Three ministers appointed by the RCC were Communists; several others—including a few of the military members of the RCC—were avowed Marxists although not members of the Sudan Communist Party.

Despite the granting of positions of power to individual members of the Sudan Communist Party and sympathizers, the RCC made clear that its stance was strongly nationalistic and that its good relation with the Communists was one of convenience. The Communists were expected to add useful expertise in turning the country toward a socialist economy, but they were expected to obey the dictates of the RCC. Within a few months Awadallah was demoted to deputy prime minister after delivering a speech that gave too much credit to communist influence. Numayri assumed the additional position of prime minister.

CHAPTER 3

GEOGRAPHY AND POPULATION

The Democratic Republic of Sudan covers about 967,500 square miles in northeastern Africa (see fig. 1.). Most of the country— the largest in Africa—is an immense, sparsely populated plain, with plateaus or mountainous areas near the borders in the west, the southeast, and along the Red Sea coast in the northeast.

The most prevalent landscape is semiarid savanna—a mixture of short grasses, scattered brush, and short trees. Daytime temperatures are high throughout the year, and the dry season ranges from three months in the relatively humid south to nine months in Khartoum, the capital city.

Two contrasts, both associated with the availability of water, are descriptive of Sudan. The southern provinces of Equatoria, Bahr al Ghazal, and Upper Nile receive thirty to fifty inches of rain during the six-to-nine-month wet season and produce a rich variety of tall grasses, shrubs, and trees. Permanent swamps in these provinces cover about 50,000 square miles, and there is an excess of water for most of the year. The lush vegetation in the south contrasts sharply with the deserts of Northern Province, where the occasional rains vanish in the parched sand and broad areas are devoid of either vegetation or people.

Narrow belts of irrigated cropland, no more than a few miles wide, bisect the northern savanna and desert along the main Nile River and along the White Nile, the Blue Nile, and the Atbarah rivers. They contrast sharply with the arid savanna or barren desert just beyond the limits of irrigation.

Settlement patterns and human activities along the Nile River system and a few other perennial streams contrast with life on the open plains (see ch. 7; ch. 13). Since ancient times people have cultivated the gently sloping riverine areas and have used various techniques to bring irrigation water to the rich soil of the flood plains. Elongated villages of closely spaced houses were built on ridges or levees above the average annual flood level. Front doors opened toward the irrigated fields and river; the opposite walls faced the relatively empty savanna or desert.

The population in 1972 was about 16.2 million, or about sixteen per square mile for all of Sudan. Beyond the riverine cities and farms, the average density was lower. The location and size of most settlements had been determined by the availability of a year-round supply of water for human use, for livestock, or for irrigation.

In terms of population the confluence of the Blue and White Nile rivers was the heart of the country. The three largest cities, including Khartoum, the capital, most of the industry, and numerous small agricultural towns had developed in a relatively small area near this juncture. Population density had been increasing in Al Jazirah, the broad wedge of land between the rivers just south of Khartoum. This area was developed in several steps spanning half a century into an irrigated project for commercial and subsistence agriculture that has assumed major importance in the national economy. Meanwhile, accelerated urbanization doubled the population of the three largest cities between 1954 and 1972, and smaller towns also grew rapidly.

Nevertheless, 85 to 90 percent of the population was still rural. The majority were sedentary farmers, many of them growing both subsistence crops and at least one cash crop. Most others were nomadic herdsmen or transhumant cattle keepers who combined tillage farming with seasonal herding (see ch. 7; ch. 13).

Sudanese officials estimated the overall population increase during the decade after the 1955/56 census at about 2.8 percent per year and after 1968 at a somewhat slower rate of about 2.5 percent. About 45 percent of the population was under fifteen years of age. The relatively young population and the availability of potentially productive land—assuming further expansion of irrigation programs—indicated a potential for continuing population growth.

PHYSICAL SETTING

Boundaries and Political Subdivisions

The country has extensive borders with eight other African nations and a 300-mile-long coast on the Red Sea. Most of the northern and western boundaries pass through desert or savanna regions, which offer few impediments to travel by persons accustomed to such terrain. The southwestern border areas receive considerable rainfall and produce lush grasses and forests but have few natural barriers to overland movement.

Only the southernmost boundary, with Uganda, is marked by rugged mountains, some peaks near the border reaching above 10,000 feet. Much of the eastern border lies among the foothills of the Ethiopia mountain complex, but most of the border area is below 4,000 feet. Beacons or pillars mark some border segments, but others have few markings. Some boundaries have never been fully demarcated, but none were actively disputed in early 1972. The total length of all borders, including the Red Sea coast, is over 5,000 miles. Long segments are without guard posts, patrols, or official crossing points.

Most of the 792-mile boundary with the Arab Republic of Egypt is a straight line along the twenty-second parallel. It crosses open desert along its entire length except in the center, where it meets the Nile River flood plain and Lake Nasser, which extends into Sudan from Egypt. In the easternmost part of this border, a separate administrative boundary line, about 222 miles in length, follows a circuitous route north and south of the political border. By agreement, each country administers certain tribal groups in areas between the political and administrative borders without claiming full sovereignty over the land involved. Some small-scale maps show only the administrative boundary.

Sudan adjoins Libya in the northwest for 238 miles along straight lines surveyed across open desert during colonial days and retained when Egypt, Chad, Libya, and Sudan became independent. The northern segment is 138 miles long. The central section is sixty-five miles long; and the southern segment, next to the Sudan-Libya-Chad tripoint, fifteen miles in length.

From this tripoint in the desolate Libyan Desert, the border with Chad extends southward for 261 miles along the twenty-fourth meridian to Wadi Howar. Southward from this watering place for another 584 miles, it follows natural features, such as the crestlines of ranges of hills in some segments and streambeds in others.

In the southwest much of the 725-mile border with the Central African Republic is drawn along the low divide between the Nile and Congo watersheds. The southern borders, with Zaire—until late 1971 Congo (Kinshasa)—and Uganda, follow ridgelines or streams in some areas, but some segments are artificially drawn straight lines. Each of these borders is 300 to 400 miles in length. The short 150-mile border with Kenya in the southeast consists of straight survey lines. As in the north, a separate administrative boundary was drawn in this area, pending eventual final agreements.

More than most of the other boundaries, the long eastern border corresponds with a change in geographic conditions, following the foothills as the land rises from the broad plain of Sudan to the plateaus and mountains of Ethiopia. Cultural or economic exchange across this border area has been minimal. The meandering border line is much longer than the 1,000 air miles from the tripoint with the Kenya border in the southeast (near Lake Rudolf) to the

51

point at 18° north latitude where the border intersects the Red Sea. In 1972 Sudanese and Ethiopian officials were discussing a program for better delineation of this poorly marked border.

At independence the country was divided administratively into nine provinces: Northern, Kassala, Khartoum, Darfur, Kordofan, Blue Nile, Bahr al Ghazal, Upper Nile, and Equatoria. The provinces were further divided into a total of eighty-four administrative districts. The six northern provinces covered almost two-thirds of the country and contained most of the urban centers.

Although these units approximated the administrative boundaries established during the period of Turko-Egyptian rule (1821–81) or the Mahdiyyah (1881–98), most internal boundaries reflected divisions made by the condominium government, which came to power in 1899, and retained by the Republic of Sudan after independence (see ch. 2).

In February 1972 the national government agreed to grant a measure of autonomy to the southern provinces of Bahr al Ghazal, Upper Nile, and Equatoria. They were subsequently combined to form a new administrative division known as the Southern Region. Information was not available to indicate whether provincial designations would be retained within the regional concept.

The Land

The Plains

The topography of the country outside the mountains and the Nile valley is generally devoid of contrast, and the flat plain making up most of its huge area distinguishable more by range of vegetation than by peculiarities of terrain (see fig. 3). The plain, extending some 500 to 600 miles from east to west and more than 1,000 miles in its north-south axis, is a part of the broad savanna belt that begins at the southern edge of the Sahara Desert and extends across the African continent. For thousands of square miles, the only features relieving the monotony of the Sudanese plain are low rolling hills—sometimes referred to locally as mountains—or extensive sand dunes created thousands of years ago and partially or entirely fixed by vegetation.

Soils are composed mainly of clay, much of which is impermeable and difficult to cultivate, or sand that contains little clay or humus. Vegetation is a typical savanna mixture of grasses, thorny shrubs (sometimes called scrub), and scattered short trees. The vegetation varies from a lush mixture in the south, where rainfall is relatively heavy for as much as nine months of the year, to sparse grasses and shrubs on sandy soils in the vicinity of 15° to 16° north latitude, near Khartoum. In the east both the plains area and the northern desert are bisected by the Nile River system.

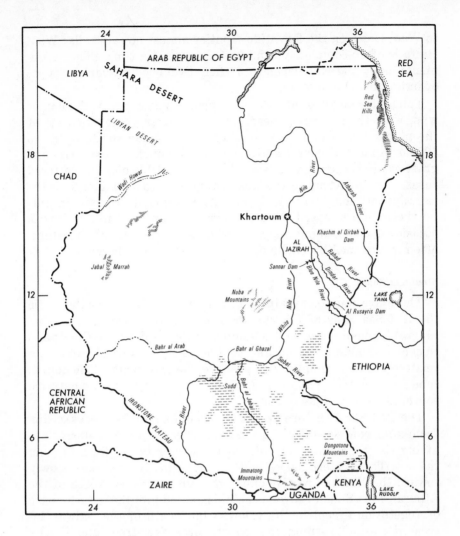

Figure 3. Physical Features of Sudan

The Northern Desert

A line running east to Atbarah and Port Sudan from the western frontier at 16° north latitude defines the approximate southern limit of desert, which covers the northern quarter of the Sudan. Northern Province lies almost entirely within the Libyan Desert, which extends into Sudan from the northwest; to the northeast the Nubian Desert covers part of Northern Province and northern Kassala Province.

From the confluence of the White and Blue Nile rivers, the Upper Nile winds northward through this desert area for a distance of 800 miles inside Sudan and provides the only water for the narrow strips of cultivation along the riverbanks. In the area from Atbarah

53

to Wadi Halfa on the Egyptian frontier almost no rain falls; Wadi Halfa is often completely rainless for years at a time. The settlements along the Nile depend for their livelihood on various types of irrigation or inundating.

The hinterland west of the Nile supports only a few Arab nomads who, with their camels, sheep, or goats, cover great expanses of the parched country in search of grazing, usually south of 18° to 19° north latitude, where a little rain occurs during most years and grass or browse springs to life. Water is available only in scattered oases, such Al Atrun in the western desert and Well No. 6 on the railway between Wadi Halfa and Abu Hamand. Terrain in this northern desert consists of broad areas of sand and flintrock with occasional hills and outcroppings of basalt, granite, and limestone, often surrounded by banks of sand deposited by the wind.

Mountain Zones

There are four mountain or upland zones. To the northeast lie the Red Sea Hills of Kassala Province; in the west is the Jabal Marrah, a mountain complex sloping to the border with Chad; and in central Sudan in Kordofan Province are the Nuba Mountains, a relatively minor complex rising above the clay plains. The fourth zone includes the Immatong and Dongotona ranges in the extreme south, along the Uganda border.

The Red Sea Hills are eroded outcroppings of base rock rising from a narrow coastal plain, the abruptness of their eastern slope giving rise to gushing torrents during winter rains blown in from the sea. The western slopes of the mountains incline more slowly toward the Nile and receive only light summer rains. North of the Atbarah-Port Sudan railway, the hills extend into the desert—bare of vegetation except in the valleys—but south of the railway increased rainfall permits the growth of a few trees and thorny shrubs.

The area is inhospitable and supports only seminomadic herders, who also cultivate hardy varieties of millet in the wetter valleys. They move their flocks laterally across the mountains or to higher or lower altitudes, depending upon the vagaries of the rainfall at various altitudes. The highest of the Red Sea Hills are above 7,000 feet.

The only major mountain range in western Sudan, the Jabal Marrah, stands in Darfur Province. Rising above 10,000 feet in elevation, this range forms part of the watershed between the Nile River and Lake Chad drainage basins. The Jabal Marrah is of volcanic origin, and its valleys are relatively fertile. The upper elevations receive a slightly higher rainfall than the surrounding plains, and the relatively richer soil of the valley is more productive.

54

Some of the rocks and peaks have a sculptured appearance resulting from the action of the rains upon the soft volcanic rock. Much of the eroded rock is deposited by streams on the desert floor below, but on the higher hillsides manmade terraces of ancient origin retain topsoil and water. Although cultivation is generally dependent upon the seasonal rains, some small valleys and terraces are irrigated with water from small perennial mountain streams.

The Nuba Mountains of southern Kordofan Province are scattered granitic masses, rising as much as 3,000 feet above a flat clay plain. They are covered in many areas by variations of savanna vegetation. Some slopes were once terraced and then abandoned by subsistence farmers. Water is not as scarce in the mountains as in the surrounding plains. Wells are numerous in the open valleys, and a few short mountain streams continue to flow throughout the year.

The Immatong and Dongotona mountains stand in southern Equatoria Province, the lower Didinga Hills flanking them to the east. The Immatongs are the highest mountains in Sudan, with peaks above 10,000 feet. The Dongotona Mountains, lying east of the Immatongs, reach a maximum height of about 8,300 feet. Both mountain chains have a considerable coverage of rain forest. Below these ranges and the Ironstone Plateau of the southwestern border, foothills and lower plateaus slope generally northward to the Sudd, a vast region of swamps and marshes covering an area of about 3,000 square miles and extending from eastern Equatoria Province several hundred miles northwestward to the Bahr al Ghazal in Upper Nile Province. The vast swamp and marsh area is as monotonous as the featureless plains farther north, but there is considerable variety of terrain and vegetation in the uplands south of the swamps, particularly near the Uganda and Kenya borders.

Drainage

As the most distant and southernmost source of the Nile River, the White Nile—known in southern Sudan as the Bahr al Jabal—derives much of its water from the lake plateau of east-central Africa. These headwaters include the watersheds around Lake Victoria and Lake Albert, lying on or near the equator, where rainfall exceeds fifty inches per year. Much of this water is lost to evaporation before it reaches the Nile tributaries, but a large volume is carried into the swamp areas, including the Sudd, a region of swamps and floating vegetation in south-central Sudan. Losses to evaporation are also heavy in this area. Partially for this reason, the annual input from the White Nile into the upper Nile at Khartoum is only one-fifth of that from the Blue Nile, but it is important because much of the White Nile water arrives during the months when the Blue Nile input is very low.

The Blue Nile rises at Lake Tana in the Ethiopian highlands and makes its way through the mountains for about 500 miles before entering Sudan. Torrential summer rains draining into the fast-flowing Blue Nile from these highlands cause the seasonal flood on the lower reaches of the Blue Nile and on the upper Nile—floods upon which half of the people of Sudan are dependent. During floodtime the Blue Nile and its two major tributaries, the Dindar and the Rahad, contribute 70 percent of the water of the upper Nile. During floodtimes the flow of the Blue Nile may be sixty times that of its low water period, and 300 times its low stage during short periods of heavy flooding. During the low water stage on the upper Nile, however, the Blue Nile and the other eastern tributaries may contribute only 20 percent of the total flow.

An important tributary to the upper Nile is the Atbarah River, similar in seasonal behavior to the Blue Nile and also originating in the mountains of Ethiopia. It traverses southern Kassala Province and empties into the Nile at the town of Atbarah.

The gradient of the Nile from Khartoum to Wadi Halfa on the northern border of Sudan is considerably steeper than that of its 900-mile course south of Khartoum. Along this lower reach are five of the Nile's six cataract areas of swift, rough water.

All perennial streams of significant size in Sudan are part of the Nile system. There are also numerous wadis, or intermittent streams, which flow only part of the year. Some drain into the Nile during the rainy season and stand empty at other times. Others drain into swamps that have no outlet to a river or disappear into the sands of an inland basin during the dry months. For example, the Wadi Howar and the Wadi al Ku, both originating in western Darfur Province, disappear into the desert. Of similar origin, the Wadi Azum eventually reaches the Lake Chad drainage system to the west.

Some of these intermittent streams carry large amounts of water during the rainy season and support local areas of agriculture. The Qash and Barakah rivers flow into Kassala Province from the northern Ethiopian highlands during the months of July, August, and September. The Qash River provides water for important irrigation schemes north of Kassala, and the Baraka feeds the Tawkar delta near the Red Sea coast. The Bahr al Arab in southwestern Sudan is another important seasonal river.

Climate, Soils, and Vegetation

Most of the country has a tropical continental climate. Dry airmasses from the deserts of Egypt, Libya, and the Arabian

Peninsula flow southward over Sudan most of the year. Humid southerly airmasses from the equatorial regions prevail in southern Sudan during the spring and summer months, pushing northwards as far as Khartoum during late summer. Rainstorms develop along the front between these huge airmasses. Rainfall exceeds fifty inches annually in southern Equatoria Province, reducing to between fifteen and thirty inches in the central area (see fig. 4). The storms are much weaker by the time they reach the region around Khartoum, where rainfall varies between five and ten inches during most years. Much of the area above 15° north

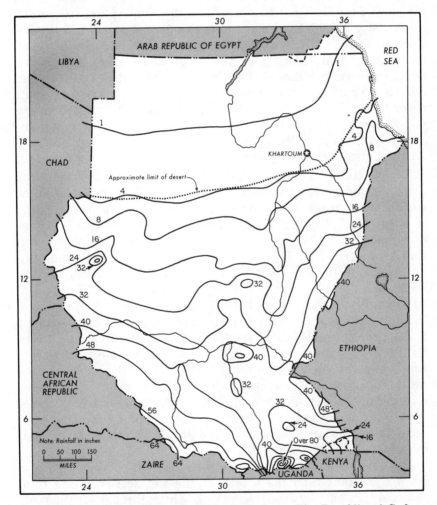

Source: Adapted from Kenneth Michael Barbour, *The Republic of Sudan: A Regional Geography*, London, 1961, 47.

Figure 4. Mean Annual Rainfall, Sudan

latitude receives only a few scattered showers each year, and rain is almost entirely unknown in the northern border areas.

Mean temperatures and daily maximums are high throughout the year. The northern desert area is relatively pleasant during the winter months, when winds from the north bring in cool, dry air. By April or May, however, the sun and the desert wind are uncomfortably hot throughout northern and central areas. By then the rainy season is well established in the south, where the short winter dry season is the hottest time of the year.

By mid-summer the tropical rain clouds have advanced into central Sudan. Cloud cover and rain squalls lower the temperature for part of the time, but between rains the temperature frequently soars above 100°F. Even the approach of a rainstorm has its unpleasant aspects. High winds may precede the rain clouds by as much as an hour, stirring up huge dust clouds. Most squalls are localized; some localities may suffer from flying dust and then get no rain. If rain does fall and settles the dust, the period of cloud cover is usually brief. When the sun reappears, the surface layers of soil dry quickly, and dusty conditions again prevail, especially around villages or wells, where the sparse natural cover has been stripped away by grazing animals or by people collecting firewood.

Temperatures in the Khartoum-Omdurman area are typical of those throughout central and northern Sudan. January, the coolest month, brings mean minimums of about 60°F. and mean maximums of about 90°F. The highest January maximum recorded in Khartoum was 104°F. Maximums for the other eleven months of the year range from 104°F. in December to 117°F. in April and May and 118°F. in June. In the south mean maximums are only slightly lower, held down by more frequent cloud cover and rainstorms, but the humidity is higher than in the central and northern provinces.

As in most arid climates, temperatures in central and northern Sudan drop noticeably after sundown. Mean minimums range from 60° to 80°F. at most weather stations throughout the year. Nighttime temperatures are somewhat lower during the winter in the northern desert, and absolute minimums as low as 34°F. have been recorded at Wadi Halfa. Freezing temperatures are either extremely rare or unknown at all Sudanese weather stations, but they may occur in the upper elevations of the Jabal Marrah or other high mountains.

In terms of human occupancy, the length of the dry season is more significant than the length of the wet season or the total seasonal rainfall. The evaporation rate is high throughout the year. In central and northern Sudan most surface water disappears before the dry season is well advanced. The typical clay or sandy soils become dry and hard, and the streambeds are empty. The need for drinking water for humans and their livestock dominates all other problems until the next rainy season. Various forms of storage are used—tanks, dams, hollow trees, hollows in natural rock formations, natural clay formations, and artificial basins (hafirs), which usually are constructed in areas of impermeable clay. Villagers may carry water for several miles when nearby supplies are exhausted, but the family or village usually moves when the round trip is ten miles or more.

Since 1920 major dams and irrigation projects have been built at Sannar, Khashm al Qirbah, and Al Rusayris. Thousands of large and small storage units have been completed in various areas, boreholes and wells have been put down, and pump irrigation schemes have been initiated or expanded.

The long annual drought and the variability of rainfall—characteristic of arid regions—have generally led to overgrazing, incautious cultivation, and other misuse of the land (see ch. 13). Some observers believe that improper land use is the main cause of increasing aridity. Although average rainfall was heavier from 1910 to 1970 than the average from 1880 to 1910, the desert conditions of Northern Province were reportedly creeping southward, and government officials expressed concern over the loss of formerly useful land.

Central Sudan is an area of alkaline clay and low elongated ridges of sand deposited by the wind. The limited rainfall—about fifteen inches annually in the area of 13° north latitude and less farther north—quickly passes downward through the loose sands in some areas or is held on or near the surface by impermeable clay in other areas. On flat land, shallow surface layers of clay become waterlogged. On sloping areas of clay, rainwater may run quickly off the surface, resulting in very little penetration. Wherever they occur, mixtures of sand and clay provide a useful balance of water-holding capacity.

Natural vegetation consists of sparse savanna grasses dotted with thorny shrubs and short trees, primarily varieties of acacia (see fig. 5). In this central area rains totaling from twelve to twenty inches per year fall within a few summer months, and "rainland" (unirrigated) agriculture is common. Natural savanna vegetation is removed; crops are planted quickly as soon as the soil has been softened by the rains. There are many crop failures, but in good years the crops mature by depending on ground water after the rains have ended. When crops are planted in areas averaging as little as twelve inches of rain per year, there are more failures than successes.

Soils are exhausted after a few years of cropping, and the farm family or village clears and plants a different area. Much of the original savanna has been modified by this shifting cultivation. Other areas of savanna have been degraded by overgrazing, which tends to kill off the grasses, leaving only the thornbush and other shrubs.

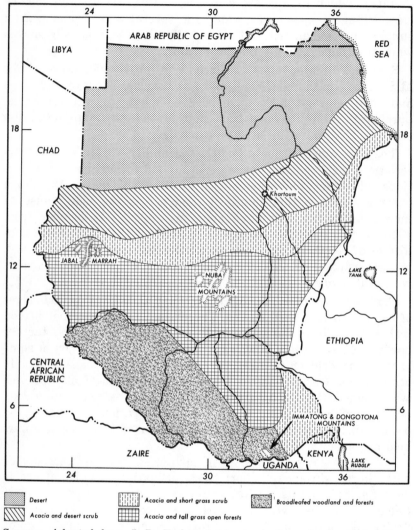

Source: Adapted from J. D. Tothill (ed.), *Agriculture in the Sudan*, London, 1948.

Figure 5. Vegetation in Sudan

South of about 10° north latitude, the central area savanna shades into wooded savanna—a mosaic of forest areas and grasslands in the southwestern area of the country, especially prevalent in Bahr al Ghazal Province. In the south-central region waterlogged clays and flat terrain hold the extensive swampy grasslands of the Sudd. From these broad swamps the land rises gradually to rolling plateaus and foothills. The tall grasses and scattered trees of the marshes shade into numerous combinations of savanna trees, shrubs, and grasses, according to variations of elevation, slope, rainfall, and soil. Fires, both natural and manmade, and shifting agriculture have also affected the mixture of plant cover. A variety of rain forest, similar to that in the equatorial forests of neighboring Zaire, covers the land in a narrow belt close by the southwestern border, where rainfall may exceed fifty inches per year. Although the south has a three-month dry season, the climate is usually uncomfortably hot and humid.

Soils in the more important agricultural areas—the riverine deposits along the Nile, the clays of central Sudan, and the qoz (a broad east-west belt of sandy mixed soil)—were originally deposited by wind or water. Good soils of volcanic origin cover lesser areas, for example, on the slopes of the Jabal Marrah in western Darfur Province.

The qoz is a region of elongated sandy dunes and hills, adjacent to, or interspersed with, the area of impermeable clays in central and western Sudan. The sands are covered in some areas by very thin surface layers of clay. Fertility is low, and in most areas the loose sands do not hold surface water, which escapes into underground channels. Nevertheless, some considerable areas of this soil are used for agriculture. Northward this mixture shades into sandy desert where true soils are almost nonexistent.

Adjacent to the qoz, the clay plains of central Sudan form a narrow wedge in western Darfur Province, widening eastward in central Sudan—the sandy qoz emerging on its northern flank and the ironized red soils of Equatoria Province to the south. The wedge extends northeastward beyond Khartoum and the Nile to Kassala and eastward into the foothills near the border with Ethiopia. The Sudd, region of swamps fed by tributaries of the White Nile, covers broad areas of this clay. Beyond these swamplands, the heavy clay soils extend southeastward to the foothills of the mountains along the border with Kenya and Uganda.

The iron-bearing or lateritic soils of the southwest, like the clays in central Sudan, absorb little water. Much of the southwest is hilly, and rainwater flows over sloping surfaces, carrying the weathered particles of the typical sandy red loam into the valleys. The elevated area along the southwestern border known as the Ironstone Plateau has an extensive coverage of concrete-like layers of red stone at least ten feet thick. Where surface rock has weathered into soil components, it contains little plant food. Nevertheless, vegetation in the lower areas of the southwest ranges from grass and shrubs to tall gallery forests. In the foothills of this plateau region, soils are rich enough to produce subsistence crops (see ch. 13).

Minerals

Many useful minerals are found in Sudan, but none were known to be available in unusually rich concentrations. Relatively small quantities of gold had been extracted over a period of several centuries, mostly in the Red Sea Hills and in Northern and Equatoria provinces. Iron ore deposits are located near Wadi Halfa, along the northern border, and in several other locations. Known ore deposits also include chromium, manganese, lead, zinc, molybdenum, graphite, sulfur, and gypsum. Common salt, limestone, pumice, asbestos, marble, and various useful sands and clays are also available (see ch. 13).

Mineral and general geological surveys had sometimes been integrated with the study and development of underground water supplies. Mineral surveys and study projects had shown little likelihood that major petroleum or coal deposits existed. Continuing mineral research in 1972 included a survey of resources in Darfur Province by a British company.

Wildlife

Wildlife is most plentiful in the south, but varieties of animals and birds are found throughout all areas except the northwestern desert. In the wetter southern areas tall grasses, brush, and trees provide cover and food for large animals for much of the year. Major species include buffalo, elephant, rhinoceros, hippopotamus, giraffe, wild ass, wild sheep, zebra, and several varieties of antelope. Carnivorous animals include lion, wolf, cheetah, leopard, wildcat, jackal, and hyena. In dry areas preferred game animals include oryx and addax (types of desert antelope) and ibex. Land birds include guinea fowl, partridge, quail, ostrich, several types of scavenger birds, and various small birds, including tropical species in the forests along the southern border.

River and swamp areas support storks, cranes, ducks, geese, and other waterfowl. The Nile River system also contains perch, carp, and many other varieties of fish. Fishing areas are especially rich in the White Nile.

Wild animals and natural vegetation are protected in three national parks, fourteen game reserves, and three wildlife sanctuaries. The largest national park, near the southern border, covers 6,500 square miles.

Transportation Features

The road between Khartoum and Wad Madani had been macadamized before 1967, but in 1972 this was the only modern hard-surfaced road extending more than a few miles out of the capital city. About 1,550 miles of road had gravel surfaces (see fig. 6; ch. 12). Another 5,000 miles of roads, or improved tracks, were reasonably useful during favorable weather. Unimproved roads or tracks in areas of clay soils were usually firm during the dry months but became sticky and impassable with the first rains. Conversely, roads and trails across very sandy regions could be most treacherous for vehicles when the sand was completely dry. In the southwest, where the lateritic soils could be compacted into road surfaces that usually remained firm when wet, heavy flooding often prevented travel.

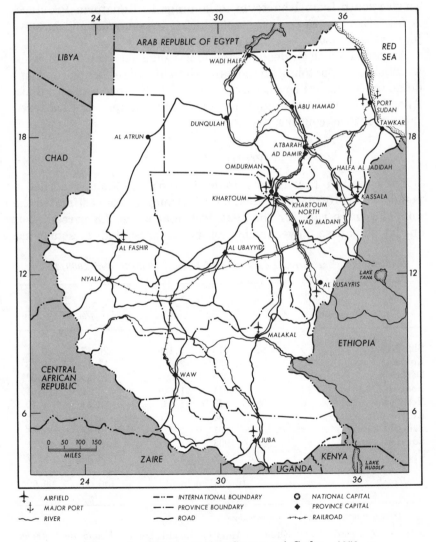

Figure 6. Transportation System of Sudan, 1972

Road problems have made railway construction in Sudan especially important. Work on a line from Wadi Halfa to Khartoum began in 1897. A few years later a branch was extended from Atbarah on the first line eastward to Port Sudan. Between 1906 and 1962 lines were extended southward and westward into Blue Nile, Kordofan, Darfur, and Bahr al Ghazal provinces. The system included about 2,950 route-miles of trackage in 1972, all government-owned.

The main Nile is usually navigable northward from Khartoum into Egypt. The White Nile and Bahr al Ghazal are navigable for hundreds of miles in central Sudan, and river steamers provided service south from Khartoum to landings in Equatoria Province. A few other rivers are navigable during the summer and autumn high-water season.

Airport facilities adequate for long-range jet transports were available at Khartoum. Important airfields were located at Dunqulah in Northern Province and Al Ubayyid in Kordofan Province. About thirty-six smaller airfields and landing strips were scattered throughout the country.

POPULATION

The country's first census, taken in 1955 and 1956, recorded a population of 10,263,536 (see table 1). Demographers estimated the annual growth rate for the next decade at about 2.8 percent, but official Sudanese government estimates presented a somewhat

Table 1.   Estimated Population of Sudan, 1955/56 and 1969/70

Province	Population (in thousands)		Percentage of Total Population	
	1955/56	1969/70	1955/56	1969/70
Blue Nile...................	2,070	3,156	20.17	20.61
Kordofan...................	1,762	2,811	17.17	18.36
Darfur.....................	1,329	1,694	12.95	11.06
Kassala....................	941	1,629	9.17	10.64
Northern...................	873	1,133	8.51	7.40
Khartoum...................	505	877	4.92	5.73
Bahr al Ghazal.............	991	1,427	9.65	9.31
Equatoria..................	903	1,303	8.70	8.51
Upper Nile.................	889	1,282	8.66	8.37
Total..................	10,263	15,312	100.00	99.99*

* Does not total 100 because of rounding.

Source: Adapted from Sudan, Ministry of Planning, *Economic Survey, 1969*, Khartoum, 1970, 10.

slower rate of 2.5 percent for 1968 through 1970. The growth trend estimated by the United Nations during the fifteen-year period from 1955 to 1970 increased the population by more than 350,000 per year. Projections based on Sudanese and United Nations studies indicate a 1972 population of approximately 16.2 million.

Nevertheless, Sudan remained among the least densely populated countries in the world, with an estimated sixteen persons per square mile in 1972. Half the population lived on 15 percent of the land surface. The largest area of high density, centered on the confluence of the Nile, extended southeastward to the Ethiopian border and southwestward into the Nuba Mountains and the farms around Al Ubayyid in central Kordofan Province. There were other localized areas of moderate density, particulary along the various rivers of the Nile system, but most of the population was thinly scattered across the Sudanese plains. Two areas were completely uninhabited: the northwestern desert and the Dindar game reserve near the border with Ethiopia.

The major towns grew rapidly during the period from 1955 to 1970 (see table 2). The three largest urban centers, Khartoum, Khartoum North, and Omdurman—known collectively as the Three Towns—form a single conglomerate at the confluence of the Nile in Khartoum Province. All three towns more than doubled their population during this period, Khartoum replacing Omdurman as the largest urban center. This growth, however, did not indicate an extremely high degree of urbanization; in 1972 these three largest centers still held no more than 3 percent of the total population. Although smaller centers also grew rapidly, the nominally urban population still constituted only about 11 percent of the total. Only a few of the largest towns had developed a strong central administrative structure or were providing the services usually associated with modern towns or cities (see ch. 7).

In both large and small towns much of the population was still directly or indirectly dependent upon agriculture. In several areas the expansion of irrigation schemes brought more land into production (see ch. 13). People migrated to a local town but cultivated the farms located nearby or provided services related to agriculture. Similarly, thousands of people who lived in the Three Towns left their urban home for several months of the year to work on farms in the nearby Jazirah area.

The Three Towns area was the place of residence for most of the highly educated Sudanese as well as skilled or educated people from Europe, Mediterranean countries, or West Africa. Omdurman was formerly the headquarters for political, as well as business and religious leadership (see ch. 2; ch. 6). More recently, Khartoum became the center of government; and Khartoum North, an upper income residential area and a center of light manufacturing (see ch. 9; ch. 13).

Most foreign residents lived either in Khartoum or in Northern Province. The majority were Egyptians; most others were Greek, Italian, Cypriot, or Maltese.

Table 2. Estimated Population of Major Towns in Sudan,
1955/56 and 1969/70

Town	1955/56 (in thousands)	1969/70 (in thousands)
Khartoum (capital)	93.1	246.9
Omdurman	113.6	245.5
Khartoum North	39.1	118.2
Port Sudan	47.6	105.9
Kassala	40.6	85.8
Wad Madani	47.7	73.3
Al Ubayyid	53.4	67.5
Atbarah	36.3	54.5
Qadarif	17.5	60.6
Al Fashir	26.2	48.5

Source: Adapted from Sudan, Ministry of Planning, *Economic Survey, 1969*, Khartoum, 1970, 176.

Population Dynamics

Crude birth rates ranged from a low of about forty-one per 1,000 in Khartoum Province to reported rates of sixty-nine and eighty-four per 1,000 in Upper Nile and Bahr al Ghazal provinces. These latter rates probably reflected errors by people interviewed during the census sampling process; the actual crude birth rate in these southern provinces was probably under sixty per 1,000. The balance between birth and death rates (gross reproduction rate) ranged from a reported low of 2 percent in Equatoria Province to 2.7 percent in the other two southern provinces of Bahr al Ghazal and Upper Nile. The average rate for the entire country was 2.4 percent.

In general terms, the south had high crude birth rates and a relatively high percentage of children from birth to five years of age. From age five to puberty, however, the death rate was higher than in most of the northern provinces; these statistics probably reflected poor diet, unhealthful climate, and an almost total absence of medical care (see ch. 7).

The crude death rate for all ages was also higher in the three southern provinces. Reported annual death rates per 1,000 persons ranged from twenty-seven to 32.6, compared with an average of about fourteen in the north and 18.5 for the entire country. Reported infant mortality rates were also highest in the south. Rates ranged from about sixty-seven per 1,000 live births in Northern Province to 144 in Upper Nile Province. Official estimates published in 1964 indicated a life expectancy at birth of approximately forty years, up from an estimate of less than thirty years at the time of the census (see ch. 7).

There were about 102 men per 100 women in the entire country. The ratio varied from a low of ninety-one in Darfur Province to 118 in Khartoum Province. These figures reflect a pattern of movement that has been established for many decades; men from the subsistence farms and grazing areas of the west go to the cities and irrigated areas near the confluence of the Nile to look for work. Men from Kordofan and Northern provinces also seek jobs in the Three Towns area or Al Jazirah.

Migration

The search for jobs is part of a broader pattern of migration. The 1955/56 census indicated that the northeastern provinces—Khartoum, Blue Nile, and Kassala — were gaining population through migration from other provinces; the largest influx came from the west. Darfur, Kordofan, and Northern Province were losing population. Much smaller numbers were coming to the northeast from the southern provinces of Bahr al Ghazal, Upper Nile, and Equatoria. This south-to-northeast movement continued during the 1960s but in 1972 still involved relatively small numbers of people.

The movement from the arid western and central areas and from farther west, in central and western Africa, had, on the other hand, been going on for centuries and continued in 1972. The migrants came for religious or economic reasons or both. The confluence of the Nile and the old city of Omdurman were on the route to Mecca for Muslims from areas in central and western Africa. Some men making this pilgrimage passed through with little delay; some found it necessary to work for a time before they could continue; and some eventually stayed permanently and reared families there.

Other so-called westerners, as they are known in the Three Towns area, came from Sudanese provinces and from countries to the west specifically to work in the area. The majority of people living in the Three Towns and Al Jazirah in 1972 consisted of immigrants or the descendants of immigrants from somewhere to the west.

Historically, this influx of people to the Nile area was usually slow. Between 1955 and 1972 the development of additional irrigation projects in Al Jazirah and a modest increase in employment in the cities accelerated the movement. Growth of the Three Towns, primarily through migration from other Sudanese areas, was rapid during this period.

Although no specific figures were available, other forms of migration—some following patterns or customs established centuries ago—were an integral part of Sudanese life. Most moves, however, covered only moderate distances. People moved to seek better economic conditions; others moved because economic conditions had taken a turn for the worse in their previous homes and their survival was at stake, as, for example, when water supplies ran out. Others practiced shifting cultivation as their usual means of livelihood. Added to this was migration incidental to marriage; in many Sudanese groups, custom requires that the young men select brides from other villages or other ethnic groups (see ch. 5).

When the Aswan Dam, located on the Nile River in Egypt, was raised to a new height during the 1960s, the enlarged reservoir extended for more than 100 miles into Sudan. About 34,000 people were displaced. With government help they were resettled 800 miles to the southwest on the Atbarah River in Kassala Province. Thousands of others also moved into the province during the 1962–72 decade as more land came under irrigation there.

Elsewhere, millions of nomadic or seasonally nomadic families moved from place to place, usually within fixed patterns over short distances (see ch. 7). About half of all native-born Sudanese live in a locality (such as a village or district) other than the one in which they were born. Only a small minority moved to distant places or to locations outside the province of their birth (see ch. 4; ch. 13).

Many borders in the south and west cut through ethnic territories. Most borders are open and have had little meaning to nearby settlers, who continue to make seasonal migrations, to trade, and to intermarry across national boundaries.

Permanent emigration from Sudan usually has occurred on a limited scale. Small numbers of Sudanese—the actual total was not known—emigrated each year to Egypt, Libya, or other countries, in most cases to find employment as laborers or domestic servants. In the south civil conflict caused more than 250,000 people to flee over the border in 1965. Most of them were believed to have gone to Uganda. In 1972 the Sudanese government, with assurances of safety, was urging them to return. No other major movement out of the country had occurred since the time of the civil war. Permanent emigration was probably still a minor factor in population dynamics in 1972.

Settlement Patterns

Settlement patterns have evolved from a combination of natural and historical forces. Such people as the Fur and the Nuba settled in the hills after being driven from the plains by invading Arabs (see ch. 4). The main factor determining settlement in general, however, has been the limitation imposed by a hot and arid climate in the north, swamps or forests in the south, and the availability of water supplies.

Sedentary agriculture remains the life-mode for the majority of the population, but millions of primarily sedentary farmers move seasonally. In the southern clay plains, which are partly swampland and marshes, tending livestock is as important an occupation as in the semiarid central and north-central zones. The pattern and direction of movements by people and their herds vary, but seasonal movement is usually necessary. In Bahr al Ghazal and Upper Nile provinces, up to one-third of the gainfully employed population are animal owners or herders, compared with about one-fourth of the population in the central and western provinces of Kordofan and Darfur. This is similar to the figure reported by the census for all of Sudan, indicating that about one-fourth of all people gainfully employed in the area in 1955 and 1956 were primarily animal owners or herders (see ch. 13).

The terms *nomadic* and *seminomadic* have been defined differently by various observers. In one narrow interpretation used by Sudanese census analysts, only 14 percent of the population was listed as fully nomadic. It has been generally agreed, however, that more than 40 percent of the population moves either seasonally or at regular intervals. Some of this group are primarily sedentary farmers, but they also raise livestock and find it necessary to move with their animals for part of the year. Others practice shifting agriculture; they abandon their land as it wears out after a few years of cultivation and clear new land elsewhere.

Analysis of the census indicates five major patterns of settlement: large urban centers; small towns; rural sedentary groups (mostly members of cohesive village groups); rural nomads; and rural dwellers in separate homesteads or clusters lacking cohesive village organization (see ch. 5). The last group, with its near absence of community structure or central authority, is prevalent in the wooded southern and southwestern provinces.

According to the 1955/56 census only sixty-eight towns contained populations of 5,000 or more. There were no urbanized centers with over 20,000 persons in Equatoria, Bahr al Ghazal, or Upper

Nile provinces and only one—Al Ubayyid—in Kordofan Province. By 1970 there were only ten urban centers with populations that exceeded 45,000.

Villages usually consist either of elongated rows of huts and storage buildings along rivers or roads or of random clusters of similar buildings on plains or hilly areas; populations range from several dozen to several hundred. Riverine villages are usually built on ridges or levees above the level of the annual flood. Along major rivers or in areas of fertile flood plains, many of them have been extended along the ridges until they join neighboring villages.

Away from the major rivers, most villages are small, unplanned clusters of houses or huts that are usually isolated from other settlements. Except for a few newly built settlements laid out in grid patterns by government officials, no particular internal arrangement predominates. Families or groups who keep livestock usually establish a fence or wall around groups of huts, to enclose an area in which stock can be penned and guarded at night.

The few villages with populations of several thousand contain a few retail shops and craftsmen. Some are centers of local government in which administration is a more important function than commerce, which is usually limited (see ch. 9).

CHAPTER 4

ETHNIC GROUPS AND LANGUAGES

About one-third of the people of Sudan are Arabs. Their historical position as conquering invaders and their present concentration in the most highly developed regions have made them, as a group, overwhelmingly dominant in the nation's affairs (see ch. 2; ch. 11). The Sudanese educated class, including professional men, higher civil servants, and military leaders, consists almost entirely of Arabs or thoroughly arabized people. They also dominate the important sectors of the economy (see ch. 13). The remainder of the population—heterogeneous groups of varying size—shows no degree of self-conscious unity corresponding to that of the Arabs, participates in commercial exchange to a negligible extent, and cannot compete for the leadership of the country (see ch. 5).

The 1955/56 census, which was the latest undertaken as of early 1972, listed fifty-six separate ethnic groups, subdivided into 597 subgroups (see table 3). In many parts of the country these population groups were well defined; in others they were scattered or mixed to such a degree that their precise affiliation was difficult to determine (see fig. 7). Some groups were often known by several different names, which made indentification difficult.

The census results indicated that 115 different languages, including twenty-six major ones, were spoken (see table 4). Some of these languages are unrelated to any other spoken in Africa, and many are known to linguists only as short wordlists. No single language is understood by all Sudanese. Arabic is the language of slightly more than half of the population and since 1956 has become the official language, although at that time only 1 percent of the southern people indicated that they spoke it.

Economic development, better communications, the growth of towns, and population migrations tend to blur some ethnolinguistic distinctions. The seventeen-year civil war had sharpened the traditional division between the Arab-dominated, largely Muslim north and the non-Arabic, non-Muslim south, which physically, linguistically and culturally is a part of the surrounding world of black Africa. The accord that ended the struggle in March 1972, among other concessions, recognized English as a working language in the south.

71

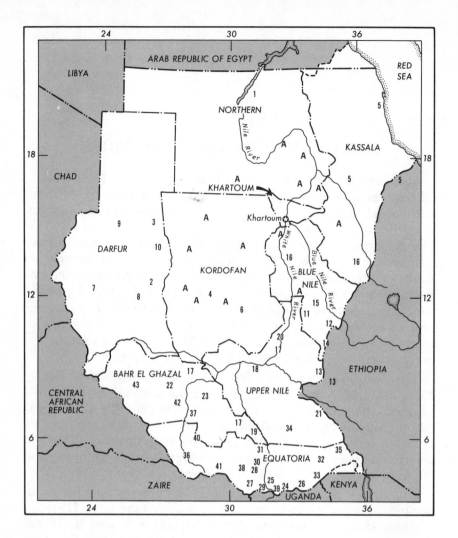

A	Arabs	15	Gule	30	Nyangbara
1	Nubians	16	West Africans	31	Mandari
2	Berkid	17	Dinka	32	Toposa
3	Midob	18	Nuer	33	Didinga
4	Hill Nubians	19	Atuot	34	Beir
5	Beja	20	Shilluk	35	Murle
6	Nuba	21	Anuak	36	Azande
7	Fur	22	Thuri	37	Belanda
8	Daju	23	JoLuo	38	Moru
9	Zaghawa	24	Acholi	39	Madi
10	Berti	25	Bari	40	Bongo
11	Ingassana	26	Lotuko	41	Baka
12	Berta	27	Kakwa	42	Ndogo
13	Koma	28	Pojulu	43	Feroge
14	Uduk	29	Kuku		

Figure 7. Principal Ethnic Concentrations in Sudan, 1972

THE NORTHERN REGION
The Arabs

The term *Arab* is used in Sudan in a variety of ways. Sometimes it means ethnic or linguistic affinities, but more often it refers to cultural characteristics.

Arabs began to arrive in the area from across the Red Sea before the first century A.D. (see ch. 2). The firstcomers were absorbed by the existing population, principally the Beja of the coast, whose languages and cultures they adopted. After the fall of the Nubian kingdoms in the thirteenth century, Bedouin Arabs in large numbers entered the region from Egypt, from which they were driven both by the policy of the Mameluke government and by the unsuitability of the country for a nomadic way of life (see ch. 2). In Sudan some groups remained nomadic, occupying the northern part of the grassland; others intermarried with the Nubians and settled near the Nile River.

By exploiting the existing custom of descent through the mother, the Arabs inherited chieftainships within a single generation. The conversion of both Nubians and Beja to Islam, descent through the father, and claims to Arab ancestry rapidly followed. At the end of the fifteenth century the fall of the Kingdom of Alwa opened the way for Arab expansion to the south; nomadic tribes began to occupy the remainder of the grasslands north of the Sudd marshes (see ch. 3).

Many of the tribes that migrated from Egypt were of Berber (North African) origin, though largely arabized. After the Egyptian invasion of Sudan in 1821, Hungarian, Turkish, and other troops settled in the north, mingling with the existing population. In modern times distinctions between Nubians, Arabs, Berbers, and others found in various combinations in the settled area between Dongola and Khartoum are often difficult to make and in practice are influenced by social attitudes and aspirations.

In many areas Arab penetration was peaceably effected by settlement, trading, and intermarriage. During the nineteenth century, however, the export of slaves to other parts of the Arab world became the principal commercial activity of Sudanese Arabs. The Arab stock—already mixed—became much more so, whereas the original population of the North, often called Negro for want of a better term, was greatly reduced. As a result the Arabs of Sudan are actually of heterogeneous origin.

During the period of the Mahdiyyah movement (1881–98) many people migrated from their former territories to other parts of the Sudan (see ch. 2). Large numbers of cattle-owning Arabs who joined the Mahdi were stationed in northern and eastern areas far from their home territories and subsequently formed expatriate colonies no longer predominantly nomadic. Habbaniya and Taaisha Arabs from Darfur in the west, for example, were employed as garrison troops in the north and subsequently established colonies in the east. After restoration of peace individual leaders appeared,

Table 3. Major Ethnic Groups in Sudan, 1955/56 Census

Ethnic Group	Principal Location (by province)	Number of Persons	Percentage of Total Population
Northern Region			
Arabs	Blue Nile Northern Khartoum Kordofan Darfur	3,990,000	38.8
Nubians	Northern	330,000	3.2
Beja	Kassala	646,000	6.3
Nuba	Kordofan	573,000	5.5
Fur	Darfur	170,000	1.6
Zaghawa	do..	60,000	0.6
Darfung peoples	Blue Nile	173,000	1.6
West Africans[1]	Kassala Blue Nile	602,000	5.8
Other	Various	936,000	9.0
Southern Region			
Dinka	Bahr el Ghazal	1,152,000	11.2
Nuer	Upper Nile	460,000	4.5
Shilluk	do	100,000	1.0
Bari[2]	Equatoria	211,000	2.0
Lotuko	do	116,000	1.0
Toposa[2]	do	120,000	1.2
Didinga	do	51,000	0.5
Azande	do	212,000	2.0
Moru[2]	do	110,000	1.1
Bongo and Baka	Bahr el Ghazal-Equatoria	47,000	0.5
Ndogo[2]	Bahr el Ghazal	71,000	0.7
Other	Various	133,000	0.1
Total		10,263,000	98.2[3]

[1] Africans originating in countries west of Sudan.
[2] And related peoples.
[3] Does not total 100 because of rounding.

Source: Adapted from Sudan, Ministry of Social Affairs, Department of Statistics, *First Population, Census of the Sudan, 1955–56*, Khartoum, 1958.

Table 4. *Provincial Distribution of Principal Languages of Sudan, 1955/56 Census*
(in percent)

Language	Bahr al Ghazal	Blue Nile	Darfur	Equatoria	Kassala	Khartoum	Kordofan	Northern	Upper Nile
Arabic	0.9	86.4	54.5	0.6	36.3	96.9	68.0	81.0	1.7
Beja	...	...	...	...	50.2	...	...	...	...
Nuba	...	0.2	0.1	...	0.4	0.4	26.8	...	...
Darfurian	0.1	0.1	41.7	...	0.5	...	0.4	...	...
West African[1]	...	7.9	2.5	...	11.1	0.8	2.7	0.1	0.1
Nubian	...	...	...	...	0.2	0.2	...	18.9	...
Fung	...	4.8	...	...	0.6	...	...	...	1.6
Zande	0.4	...	...	23.8	...	...	...	...	...
Bongo–Baka	1.5	...	0.6	3.0	...	...	...	...	...
Ndogo–Sere	2.9	...	...	2.5	...	...	...	...	...
Moru–Madi	...	...	0.6	10.2	...	...	0.1	0.1	0.1
Dinka	87.4	...	...	0.3	...	0.1	1.8	...	25.4
Nuer	...	...	...	...	...	...	...	...	52.2
Luo	4.8	0.4	...	4.9	...	...	0.1	...	13.8
Lango[2]	0.1	...	...	31.3	...	...	...	...	...

[1] Includes a variety of related languages of countries west of Sudan.
[2] Includes Bari, Lotuko, and Toposa.

Source: Adapted from Sudan, Ministry of Social Affairs, *First Population Census of the Sudan, 1955–56*, Khartoum, 1958, 8–15.

and many of the great tribes of the past regained their importance; others virtually disappeared, and many regroupings took place.

According to the 1955/56 census, the Arabs constituted 73.7 percent of the population of Blue Nile Province, 66 percent of Northern Province, 60 percent of Khartoum Province, 56 percent of Kordofan Province, and 28 percent of Darfur Province. Ingenious genealogical trees attributed the ancestry of most Sudanese Arabs either to the Guhayna or the Gaaliin, a division corresponding very roughly to that between nomadic and settled tribes. The names are also used in a specific sense for particular groups of Guhayna in the Al Jazirah area and the Gaaliin near Shendi.

The purity and nobility of a family's descent is a matter of great pride but not purely an ethnic matter. Within the Arab community, claims to direct descent from the Prophet are more important than claims to Arab nobility. In consequence, Gaaliin ancestry is considered to be superior to Guhayna. The Gaaliin claim to be descended from Al Abbas, the uncle of the prophet Muhammad. They include several tribes of predominately Nubian extraction in the Dunqulah region and the majority of the settled Arabs in northern Kordofan and the Nile River valley from the fourth cataract to south of Al Jazirah. The genealogical and political association between the various tribes is very loose, and many so-called Gaaliin have little Arab blood.

The Guhayna claim descent from a certain Abdalla al Guhani from southern Arabia. Those of the central region may be divided into the Jamala camel nomads in the north and the Baggara cattle nomads in the south. The Jamala include the Kababish of northern Kordofan Province, who have assimilated a number of other groups, and the Shukriyyah of southern Kassala Province.

The principal tribes of the Baggara include the Rizaygat and the Taaisha in Darfur Province and the Homr, Hawazma, Messiriyyah, and Selima in southern Kordofan Province. The Hawazma and Selima are mainly settled peoples, differing in various ways from the nomadic Baggara. The Homr and Rizaygat move southward during the dry season where they overlap with Dinka, Nuer, and Shilluk of Upper Nile and Bahr al Ghazal provinces. The characteristic Baggara weapon is a long-bladed spear of extraordinary length. They still occasionally wear chain mail for ornamental purposes; at one time it was an essential part of their war equipment. They were active slave raiders until the practice was suppressed. During the Mahdiyyah period they were prominent in support of the Mahdi and his successor the Khalifa, who was himself a Taaishi (see ch. 2).

Although Sudanese Arabs belong to either the Gaaliin or Guhayna tribes, some lineage groups claim descent from other

Arabian ancestors. One of the most important of these is the Kawahla, who entered the area from the Red Sea and to whom the Beja tribes are said to be related. Before the Mahdiyyah period the Kawahla led a large and wealthy nomadic confederacy, which has since broken up; some remnants are settled south of Khartoum.

Slightly over half of the population uses Arabic as a primary language (see fig. 8). It is a Semitic language related to Hebrew and several other Asian Semitic languages and remotely to the African Semitic languages of Ethiopia, chiefly Amharic.

It is the official language of the country, and its use is spreading rapidly, particularly in the northern provinces, where the indigenous non-Arabic speakers are now found only in isolated and relatively small groups.

The language as used in all serious writing and for all official purposes is essentially a modified form of the classical Arabic of the Koran. This modern standard literary Arabic is the language used in Sudan by the educated on all formal occasions, such as radio broadcasts, in print, or in schools. Colloquial Sudanese Arabic differs from both the classical form and modern standard literary Arabic notably in the simplification of grammar by the elimination of case endings on verbs and adjectives. If the colloquial form is written at all, it appears in comic strips, jokes, plays, and folksongs. Educated Sudanese, nonetheless, use both colloquial and modified classical Arabic.

Even in areas where local people have no real command of Arabic it is common for everyone to know enough words and phrases for ordinary dealings with traders and strangers. Returning soldiers and policemen contribute to the spread of Arabic, as do chiefs and headmen who increase their knowledge through contact with the administration.

In many parts of the north, the acceptance of Islam and a degree of arabization have taken place in communities that still speak non-Arab languages but have adopted Arabic personal names. Most Arabic names have a simple and readily apparent meaning, frequently consisting of little phrases. One of the the commonest forms consists of *abd* (slave), followed by one of the many epithets of Allah, such as Al Kadir (the powerful) or Al Hakim (the wise). One element of a man's full name usually indicates who his father was, but the use of family names in the Western manner is not widespread.

The Nubians

The valley of the Nile River historically provided an avenue for migrations northward from the vicinity of the great lakes of East Africa. Among the modern descendants of early Nilotic invaders,

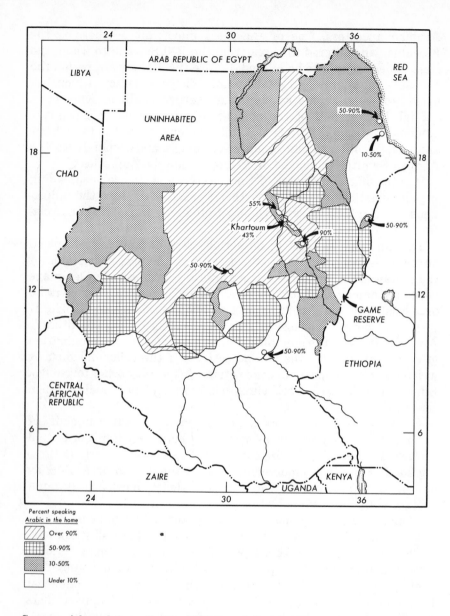

Source: Adapted from Sudan, Ministry of Social Affairs, Population Census Office, *21 Facts About the Sudanese*, Khartoum, 1958, Appendix 1, No. 50.

Figure 8.   Use of Arabic Language in Sudan, 1972

who probably arrived in the area of Sudan between the first and fourth centuries A.D., were the Nubians, whose culture was extensively modified by subsequent contact with neighboring peoples. In fact, their language is now so different from the main body of

Nilotic languages as to be regarded by them and even by some linguists as entirely independent.

The term *Nubian* in common usage refers only to the Nile Nubians, whose homeland is Nubia, the narrow river valley partly in Egypt and partly in Northern Province of Sudan (see ch. 2). Among them the northern, more isolated Mahas are different to some extent in physical appearance and are distinguished by dialect from the Dongolawin or Danagla, who live farther south.

Partly as a result of Arab pressure, the Nubians spread to Kordofan and Darfur provinces, which were once connected to Nubia by well-traveled routes. In northern Kordofan Province they were gradually exterminated by the Arabs, the last of them disappearing during the Mahdiyyah in the late nineteenth century.

In Darfur the Gerkid and the Midob speak Nubian languages and retain traditions of Nubian origin; their numbers are uncertain. In the northwestern Nuba Mountains of southern Kordofan Province, in the vicinity of Dilling, are several groups called Hill Nubians. They are sometimes grouped with entirely different people—the Nuba, whom they resemble culturally.

The Nubians always have been a settled people, living in towns and villages, cultivating irrigable land near the Nile River, and subject to a certain degree of administration. The poverty of their region, however, encourages emigration; Nubians (Nubiyyin) are found as domestic servants, teachers, civil servants, and traders in many cities and towns of Egypt and the Sudan, where they usually form small, tightly knit expatriate communities. Formerly they showed a great love of their homeland, to which they returned after a period of travel, but the inundation of parts of the Nile valley as a result of modern dam-building and an increase in economic opportunity elsewhere have led to the permanent resettlement of many of them.

The 1955/56 census indicated that 10,000 Nubians lived in Kassala Province and 73,000 in Khartoum Province. After the flooding of the Wadi Halfa area that resulted from the construction of the Aswan High Dam in Egypt, more than 34,000 Nile Nubians were evacuated in the mid-1960s and resettled near the Khashm al Qirbah Dam on the Atbarah River southwest of the city of Kassala. The resettlement area was quite different in physical, climatic, economic, and social conditions.

Nubian is an eastern Sudanic language belonging to the Nilo-Saharan language family. During the Christian period the clergy used the Coptic alphabet in writing Nubian, since it had no written form of its own (see ch. 2). The Mahas dialect is considered most closely related to Old Nubian. Nubians, who often claim Arab ancestry, speak Arabic outside their homes.

The Nubians have been Muslims longer than any other non-Arab group. Their eagerness for religious and secular education has earned them many positions of influence in the government (see ch. 8; ch. 11).

The Beja

The nomadic Beja may have lived in the Red Sea Hills of Kassala Province for 6,000 years. In appearance they resemble the ancient Egyptians, although in the last 2,000 years large numbers of Arabs have been absorbed into the Beja population.

The 1955/56 census showed that most Beja lived in Kassala Province; a few thousands more were in Kordofan and Darfur provinces, apparently indicating a recent migration. In the Red Sea Hills they were found scattered in groups of two or three families, which moved about more or less independently in search of pasture.

The majority of the Beja belong to one of three Bedawiye-speaking groups: the Bisharin, Amarar, and Hadendowa, who emerged as distinct units during the fifteenth and sixteenth centuries. By that time they had been converted to Islam. The Hadendowa have been gaining in strength since the nineteenth century, absorbing several small Beja tribes. They are the largest, most powerful group and are influential in the flourishing agricultural development of the Tawkar delta along the Red Sea coast (see ch. 13). The Bisharin cover the largest territory and are divided into two groups—the largely settled tribes on the Atbarah River in the south and the nomadic tribes who live in the bleak northern ranges of the Red Sea Hills (see fig. 1). The Amarar live between the Bisharin and the Hadendowa.

The majority of the Beja are nomads, keeping sheep, goats, camels, and cattle. Because grazing land in the hills is found only in small patches, the herding unit is small, consisting usually of a single household, whose head wields considerable authority. Territorial rights are strictly observed; grazing within another tribe's boundaries is permitted only by prior arrangement. The essential feature of the traditional organization is the practice of compromise, by which the interests of all are reconciled after protracted discussions.

Bedawiye (to-Bedawie), a northern Cushitic language, belongs to the Afro-Asiatic language family. The adoption of Islam introduced a number of Arabic terms into Bedawiye, and personal names have generally been arabicized to suit the Arab ancestry now claimed by the Beja. The word *Bedawiye*, itself an Arabic formation, is sometimes used to designate the people as well as their language.

In conservatism and pride—characteristic of all the nomads—the Beja are extreme. Less gregarious than the Arabs, they are aloof even toward other Beja, extremely reticent with strangers, and elusive regarding governmental authority. Although they have superficially adopted the Muslim religion and Arab ancestry, they do not follow Arab ways in general.

The Nuba

The term *Nuba* covers a variety of sedentary people who live mainly in the scattered hills of southern Kordofan Province. The Nuba retreated to this area after the arrival some 500 years ago of the Arabs who now occupy the plains. Despite their diverse origins, there is some physical resemblance among the various peoples of this group; in general they are tall, big boned, and robust. Men of this type were portrayed in the art of Egyptians of the Middle Kingdom, and skeletal remains of similar people have been found in Al Jaziarah. It is possible that the ancestors of the Nuba were formerly spread throughout Kordofan Province and the Nile valley to the north and east, forming the basis of the Meroitic population (see ch. 2). Nuba villages are rare; scattered settlements are the rule. Whatever unity may be discerned is largely a matter of ritual association in connection with such matters as rainmaking.

Since the beginning of the twentieth century the Nuba have been increasingly leaving their hills to cultivate in the plains or to work elsewhere. They make excellent soldiers and policemen and are ready to adapt themselves to new ways and to learn the Arabic language. Nuba groups have increasingly shown a tendency to become more like each other and to refer to themselves collectively as Nuba. Their primary loyalty, however, still belongs to their community of origin.

The Nuba speak a great variety of languages or dialects, most of which are grouped for convenience under the term *Kordofanian*. Belonging perhaps to as many as seven or more separate language families, these variations are not closely interrelated and are apparently unrelated to any other African language. About 15 percent of the Nuba speak Arabic as a primary language.

Peoples of Darfur

The Fur

The Fur, for whom Darfur Province is named, are considered to be indigenous to the mountain range of Jabal Marrah. A ruling dynasty of partly Arabic origin arose during the seventeenth century and established a sultanate that lasted until 1916. The Fur, whose language represents a separate branch of the Nilo-Saharan language family, are Muslims, but they are not heavily arabized.

They are industrous farmers living in villages. Inherited property in land is the basis of social rank among them. Fur women have a high degree of economic independence and are fairly free to select their own marriage partners.

The Daju

The Daju, who may have come from the Nile River valley during the thirteenth century, form a linguistic, but not a social or geographic, group. Communities of Daju are found in southwestern Darfur Province, in the western Nuba Mountains of Kordofan Province, and in isolated pockets of the neighboring Republic of Chad. They are said to be dying out, but figures included in the 1955/56 census indicate that earlier estimate of 14,000 may have been much too low. They are farmers and cattle breeders. Nominally they are Muslims, but their religious observances include vestiges of earlier traditional religious forms. They speak a version of Arabic in addition to their own Eastern Sudanic language, which belongs to the Nilo-Saharan language family.

Zaghawa

After the Nubians and the Beja, the seminomadic Zaghawa are the third major pre-Arab group of the north. They have long occupied the deserts of northern Darfur and Kordofan provinces. In ancient times they raided Nubia and more recently fought with the Arabs, but they are now largely arabized. Very little is known of them; in Sudan there may be 60,000 Zaghawa, including related people such as the Berti, who are settled in small scattered communities in eastern Darfur and western Kordofan provinces.

The Saharan languages of the Zaghawa and related groups are dying out, and most of them now speak some form of Arabic. They profess Islam, but many remains of their former religion survive among them.

The Darfung Peoples

The Fung, of mixed ethnic origin, formerly ruled over most of what is now Blue Nile Province. In the nineteenth century their sultanate, Dar Fung, was destroyed, and the country was ravaged by Turks. The term *Darfung* was used in the 1955/56 census to designate the heterogeneous population living in the area of this former sultanate. Like the Nuba in Kordofan Province, the Darfung peoples live in isolated hill communities surrounded by the sparse Arab population of the plains. As of the early 1970s little anthropological research had been done in this region, and only tentative classification was possible.

To the north of the town of Baw in the hills named after them live about 14,000 Ingassana, also called Tabi. They may be descendants of Nilotic people who migrated there during the early Christian Era and thus may be distantly related to the Nubians. The Ingassana maintained their independence throughout the Fung era. Since then they have had long history of raiding the Arabs, who call them "the thankless ones." They speak Ingassana, an Eastern Sudanic language belonging to the Nilo-Saharan family.

South of the Ingassana, on both sides of the Ethiopian border, live about 92,000 Berta. They live in scattered groups and have no common name for themselves, identifying only with those occupying the same hill community. They speak various related dialects.

South of the Berta are 10,000 Koma, a name which refers to several groups, including the Uduk and Gule. The Uduk and Gule groups have no sense of belonging to a Koma community, however, and may indeed be quite unrelated both in language and origin. Berta and Koma dialects belong to the Nilo-Saharan language family. These dialects are slowly giving way to Arabic.

West Africans

Since Sudan is on the pilgrimage route to Mecca, great numbers of West Africans pass through the country either on their way to or from the holy city. Many remain permanently in Sudan. Improved communications and the expansion of cotton growing have combined to vastly increase their numbers in the twentieth century. The majority are settled in agricultural areas in Al Jazirah between the Blue Nile and White Nile rivers, in Kassala Province, and in smaller groups in almost every other province. Some of them rapidly adopt Arabic and local customs, but small, tightly knit communties, constantly reinforced by new arrivals, continue to speak their own languages and to retain their own cultures. Those from a common area of origin tend to live together on the edge of Sudanese villages.

Ascertaining the number of West Africans presented a difficult problem for the census takers in 1955 and 1956 because they were dealing with new arrivals as well as with fifth-generation descendants. Grouping together peoples from countries west of Darfur, they arrived at the impressive total of 602,000. This figure included 97,000 from French-speaking equatorial Africa, 298,000 from Nigeria, and 207,000 from West Africa proper. The total figure represented 5.8 percent of the population, and thus Africans originating in countries west of Sudan were by far the largest group of foreign inhabitants and the third most numerous group after the Arabs and the Dinka.

THE SOUTHERN REGION

The Nilotes

The Dinka, Nuer, Shilluk, and some of the other peoples of southern Sudan are called Nilotes because of their association with the Nile. All Nilotes in southern Sudan appear to have arrived in their present territory during the last 1,000 years, some as recently as the eighteenth century, although the order in which the movements took place is uncertain. Formerly pastoral, many Nilotes have become settled agriculturists, but cattle continue to play an enormous, largely symbolic, role in their societies. The Dinka, Nuer, Shilluk, and some Luo designate themselves as Jii, which means "people." They are known for their unusual height and slender build.

Nilotic languages and some elements of Nilotic culture in northern Sudan were introduced through the migrations of the Nubians between the first and fourth centuries A.D. The resemblance, however, between northern and southern Nilotes—never close—has been reduced by subsequent events and is too remote to constitute any bond between them.

All Nilotes in the Sudan, including the Nubians and Ingassana in the north, speak Eastern Sudanic languages belonging to the Chari-Nile group—itself a member of the still larger Nilo-Saharan language family. The majority of the languages spoken in Upper Nile Province and the eastern parts of Equatoria and Bahr al Ghazal provinces are called Nilotic, including those formerly designated as Nilo-Hamitic. Closely related, they constitute one of the ten branches of the Eastern Sudanic language subgroup.

The Dinka

The Dinka are the largest Nilotic group, constituting slightly more than 10 percent of the entire Sudanese population and 41 percent of the Southern Region. Their region stretches from Bahr al Ghazal Province northward beyond the Bahr al Arab to Kordofan Province and southward up the White Nile to about 6° north latitude. Nuer advances in the last 150 years separated the northern, or Padang Dinka from the main element of the ethnic group.

The Dinka are divided into a number of independent groups, each headed by a chief who is the religious leader of the community (see ch. 5). He makes rain, offers sacrifices, and settles feuds. He is always a member of a prominent clan and is frequently the son of the preceding chief. Dinka villages often spread over large areas since each homestead is surrounded by its own farming area. Predominantly cattle people, the Dinka also cultivate extensively. Each village is independent, but during the dry season the requirements of herding bring the inhabitants of several villages to common cattle camps.

Because of their numbers and the extent of their territory, the Dinka have been in closer contact with different peoples and cultures than other Nilotes and have shown more willingness to adopt new ways. Mission schools have had some success among them. The first southern member of the Council of Ministers in the late 1950s was a Dinka and a Roman Catholic.

The Nuer

The Nuer, who are closely associated with the Dinka in language, culture, and territory, are the most homogeneous of the Nilotes, occupying a compact territory within which there are no extensive culture variations and no major differences in dialect. The principal division among them is between the Nuer of the east bank of the Bahr az Zaraf and those of the west bank, who include many conquered Dinka.

Until about 1920 a major activity of the Dinka and Nuer was raiding one another for cattle and captives. Such fighting had its rules and did not result in wholesale slaughter; captives were treated virtually as members of the family and frequently founded lineages of their own that became indistinguishable from those of the conquerors.

South of the Dinka live the Atuot, who speak Nuer dialects. In other respects they resemble the Dinka.

The Shilluk

The Shilluk, who are well known for their highly developed divine kinship, live north of the Nuer and west of the northern Dinka in a compact unit on the west bank of the Nile River near its confluence with the Sobat River (see ch. 5). The Shilluk occupied this long narrow strip in the early sixteenth century, defeating outposts of the nascent Fung sultanate of Al Jazirah. They are settled agriculturists, and their migrations consist only in moving close to the river during the dry season and onto higher grounds during the rains. Their settlements consist of a number of villages or hamlets built on high ground about 100 yards apart. Each village is occupied by an extended family or small lineage and has its communal cow house to shelter the cattle and serve as the public hall.

Shilluk men and women are easily recognized by the characteristic row of bead-like scars above their eyebrows, made by rubbing ashes into a series of incisions. Other characteristic mutilations, particularly the removal of teeth, are made for decorative purposes.

The Shilluk are renowned for their handicrafts, particularly spears, with which they kill game ranging from fish to hippopotamuses.

The Bari and the Lotuko

In central Equatoria Province the Bari group includes the Bari proper on both banks of the Nile River near Juba and Bari-speaking people to the west of them, such as the Kakwa, Pojulu (Fajelu), Kuku, Nyangbara, and Mandari. The Mandari's social organization and economy resemble those of their northern neighbors, the Dinka. Bari is the principal language spoken near the Nile River in Equatoria Province and is spreading rapidly, absorbing related dialects to the west.

East of the Bari live the Lotuko, whose language is also spreading. Because of common cultural characteristics the Bari and the Lotuko are sometimes grouped with the Dinka.

The Toposa

East of the Lotuko in a swampy plain live the seminomadic Toposa (Topotha). Their society is organized on the principle of age-grades, which have a strong military character.

The Anuak

The institution of kinship and of a royal clan are also found among the Anuak, who live near the Sobat River in Upper Nile Province. Their villages are close enough together to allow the development of wider groupings. They are cultivators rather than herdsmen because of the prevalence of tsetse flies. There are estimated to be 10,000 Anuak in Sudan and 35,000 more in Ethiopia. Some Anuak are also found in Equatoria Province, where they live in isolated stockaded villages housing 200 or 300 people and are economically and socially independent from other villages.

Because the national boundary divides the Anuak territory, administration in the eastern part of Upper Nile Province has been particularly difficult. Fighting between Anuak and Nuer, which began at the time of Nuer expansion in the nineteenth century, recurs sporadically.

The Luo

The term *Luo* appears as the name of many peoples of Sudan, Uganda, and Kenya, all of whom share the tradition of a common migration during which several groups broke off from a parent body. In Sudan small groups of Luo speakers, including the Thuri and JoLuo, are found in Bahr al Ghazal Province.

Of several Luo peoples, collectively known as the Southern Luo, only the Acholiare represented in Sudan. They live near the town of Opari not far from the Uganda border.

The Didinga, the Beir, and the Murle

The three groups have little or no contact with each other, but their language is sufficiently related to form a distinct branch of the Eastern Sudanic language family. The Didinga live south of the Toposa, forming the slopes of the hills named after them. The Beir live southwest of the Anuak on the Pibor River. The Murle live mainly in Ethiopia, but small groups have arrived recently in Sudan's Boma plateau. They participate to some extent in the border trade in ivory and other wild animal products.

"Sudanic" Peoples

The heterogeneous peoples of Equatoria and western Bahr al Ghazal provinces are sometimes grouped under the geographic term *Sudanic*. The majority relate linguistically and culturally to larger groups in adjoining counties.

The Azande

The Azande (singular form, Zande) conquered and absorbed many ethnic groups of the Congo River basin in the eighteenth and nineteenth centuries with their military prowess and sophisticated political organization. At the end of the nineteenth century they advanced into southwestern Sudan, absorbing the Bongo, the Moru, the Ndogo, and other small groups, but their main home is still the Republic of Zaire [until late 1971 Congo (Kinshasa)]. They speak Zande, which belongs to the Adamawa branch of the Niger-Congo language family.

In the 1920s the administration resettled most of the Azande along roads in an effort to combat sleeping sickness. In 1946 an experimental development scheme designed to convert primitive agriculturalists into modern farmers required a new dispersal of the Azande. Homesteads were sited on individual plots linked by straight bicycle paths. When the Zande Scheme broke down after a few years, Azande society began to disintegrate. Symptomatic was their declining birth rate, one of the lowest in Sudan.

Other Sudanic Peoples

Ethnic and linguistic confusion among the approximately 217,-000 people who live between the Dinka, the Bari, and the Azande in Equatoria and Bahr el Ghazal provinces in such that no territory can be assigned to any one group. Languages, cultures, and ethnic affiliation no longer coincide; most people speak at least two languages. Several different languages may be spoken at any one marketplace. The Belanda found south of Waw, for example, actually include two groups of different origin, one Nilotic and the other southwestern, who still speak languages that belong to separate language families. Yet the two groups are much intermarried and for practical purposes must be considered as one.

In the east the Moru and related Madi were subjugated by Nilotes perhaps 1,000 years ago and are now found dispersed among Bari, Lotuko, and Acholi. Madi dialects, closely related to some Moru dialects, are spoken in the Opari District. The Moru-Madi languages, which are Central Sudanic branches of the Nilo-Saharan family, are spoken by 103,000 people in Sudan.

Farther west Bongo and Baka peoples predominate. They are ethnically and linguistically related to the Madi and, like them, are also represented in Uganda and in Zaire. The Bongo, whose name means men, cultivate small plots in the wet season and spend the dry season hunting and fishing. The leaders are the hereditary rainmakers.

The Ndogo, Sere, Mundu, and Biri peoples are related to the Azande in language and ethnic origin. Many are now scarcely distinguishable from the Azande, except that they lack the social organization based on a royal clan.

In the west large areas are uninhabited, but small communities of Banda and Golo are found in Bahr al Ghazal Province and in neighboring parts of the Central African Republic. The Banda and Golo, altough still constituting distinct ethnic groups, now speak Zande or Moru languages. Interspersed among them are communities of former slaves, collectively known as Mandala (or Fertit), and other minor groups, including the Feroge; members of the Feroge aristocracy claim to be Arabs.

CHAPTER 5

SOCIAL SYSTEMS

Sudan's people live in a number of different social systems, each largely independent of the others. Despite this heterogeneity, however, major adaptations to the environment over a long period of time have produced four basic types of social systems: the nomadic societies of pastoral peoples in the semidesert plains of the north; the village societies of cultivators settled in the more fertile and accessible northern areas; the homestead societies of cultivators scattered through out the south and certain inaccessible regions of the north, such as the Nuba Mountains; and the semisedentary societies of the southern Nilotic peoples living in the flood plains of the White Nile basin (see fig. 9; ch. 4).

The development of a fifth and more recent urban type of society is closely related to that of the modern sector of the economy and to the progress of modern education and technical training. Urban society includes wage earners, a small middle class composed mainly of merchants and clerks, and the educated elite, who are closely identified with the national government.

The concept of a nation-state is new for the majority of the people, who understand political issues only in parochial terms and whose primary loyalty is to the immediate kinship group. Their knowledge of other groups is usually limited, and interethnic relations are generally characterized by distruct and often hostility. The aggregate of local divisions—modified by ethnic, geographic, and economic considerations—has appeared on the national level throughout history as opposition between two groups: northerners and southerners (see ch. 2; ch. 9).

In the north Arab culture and Islam have provided the major unifying influence. The only feelings shared by the people of the more fragmented south have been hatred and suspicion of the northerners, which exploded into rebellion in 1956. By early 1972 it was not yet possible to tell to what extent the ravages of civil war had changed traditional social structures in the south and whether the experience of a common fight against the north had created a lasting southern consciousness that would prove stronger than the interethnic rivalries of the past.

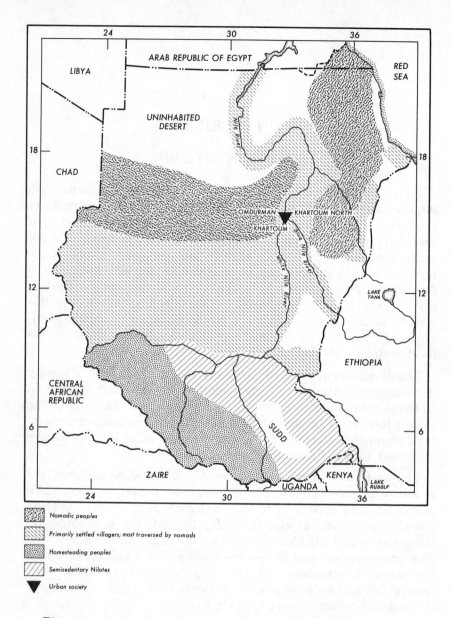

Nomadic peoples

Primarily settled villagers; most traversed by nomads

Homesteading peoples

Semisedentary Nilotes

▼ Urban society

Figure 9. Predominant Patterns of Social Organization in Sudan

NORTHERN ARABIZED SOCIETY

The northern part of Sudan has been penetrated to such an extent by the culture and religion of the Arabs that it is possible to speak of an arabized society, although it encompasses a variety of ethnic groups. Within this society major differences in social organization, deriving from differences in ways of living, exist between nomads and settled agriculturists.

90

Nomads

Sudanese nomads, mainly Arabs but including also the Zaghawa and the Beja, depend for their livelihood on their animals and are required by a difficult environment to move from place to place during the year. Those in the far north are camel raisers and grow no crops at all, whereas the cattle herders farther south usually do some cultivating during the rainy season; but the societies of all of them are organized in a similar manner.

In principle, patrilineal descent provides the basis for the formation of all structural units—from the smallest to the largest— among the nomads. The members of the largest entity, the tribe, are putatively descended through males from a remote male ancestor. The tribe is divided into smaller units, and each of these, into still smaller ones. The process of subdivision is such that there may be as many as five or six levels between the largest group, the tribe, and the smallest, which is likely to consist of a man, his sons, their sons, and those of their daughters who have either married within the group or have not yet married. Whatever the level of a tribal section, each unit claims descent through males from a common male ancestor.

The Homr, one of the tribes of Baggara Arab cattle herders, who moved to their present site in the southwest corner of Kordofan Province at the end of the eighteenth century, present a good example of this societal pattern. The tribe, called *gabily*, is believed to be descended from a founder called Heymir, who is reckoned to have lived ten to twelve generations back from those living.

The tribe has two main sections, also called *gabily*, each subdivided further into five sections. Traditionally tribal sections at this level were called *gabily* as well but became known administratively as *omadiya*, a word the Homr have also been using since 1911. An *omadiya* varies in size from about 2,000 to 9,000 people. The *omadiya* is divided into a number of primary sections, each called *khashm bet* (literally: threshold of a house or tent), indicating the common descent of its members.

Nearly every one of these is subdivided still further—sometimes at two levels, sometimes at three. Each subsection is also called *khashm bet*, except for the smallest, which is called *surra*. Members have a common ancestor five or six generations back. A *surra* comprises a number of smaller groups, in which the youngest male is at most three generations removed from the group's founder. Such a group, together with those who have married into it, constitutes an extended family. Each Homr thus belongs to a series of lineages each reaching further back into the past. In theory, the exact relationship between any two Homr can be worked out. Actual kinship, however, is usually reckoned only between

91

members of a *surra*. Beyond that the genealogy of ancestors is largely theoretical.

Tribal divisions are most readily apparent in connection with the exploitation of economic rights, principally to land and water. For grazing purposes all Homr have rights to all Homr tribal territory as long as they stay clear of land under cultivation; however, tribal sections acquire, through frequent use, rights to specific areas for the cultivation of gardens. Members of a *surra*, for example, return year after year to the same land, which they regard as their home. Within this area, land rights to specific plots become personal and are often handed down from father to son.

The constant subdividing of lineages gives great fluidity to Homr society. Tribal sections secede, move away, join with others for various reasons. The composition of even the smallest units of local cooperation constantly varies in size and composition according to the season of the year and the natural environment. Individuals, families, and larger units move about with considerable freedom to seek a more favorable social environment; the moves are usually induced by quarrels, crowding, or personal attachments. Most lineages, therefore, are represented over a wide area within the bounds of their tribal territory and sometimes ouside it. The size and composition of various groups, and ultimately of the tribe itself, depend on such things as the amount of grazing land available and the policy and personality of the leaders.

Cooperative obligations are strongest within a *surra*, as compared with more comprehensive lineage segments such as a *khashm bet* or a *gabily*. All *surra* members are considered brothers. They address each other as such and are expected to show a united front. The name of the *surra* usually includes a form of the name of its founder.

Ideally, *surra* members belong to one camp (*ferig*), whose members migrate and herd together. The achievement of this ideal, however, is often thwarted by economic necessity or for personal reasons. Men and women are constantly on the move. They go on visits, get jobs elsewhere, and quarrel. When the grazing herd becomes too large, a camp splits up into two or more camps. Despite its shifting size and composition, a camp always retains an identity through its association with one particular *surra*. No camp exists of which the regular male members belong to more than one *surra*.

The fluid character of Homr society has a bearing on political power. Each camp has an accepted leader called *reis al ferig* (head of the camp), usually the wealthiest cattle owner. When there are no splinter camps with their own leaders, the *reis al ferig* is identical with the *reis* (head) of the *surra*. Each *khashm bet*, at whatever segmentary level, is headed by a sheikh; and each of the two main divisions of the Homr tribe, the *gabily*, by a *nazir*. The leaders are always members of a wealthy family.

Wealth is a way to power among the Homr, and wealth among nomads means cattle. A man rich in cattle is sure to attract followers and thus has power thrust upon him. Industry, thrift, and hardiness, needed to build and increase a large herd, are considered highly desirable qualities. At the same time, a rich man is expected to be generous. If he lives up to that expectation, his fame will spread, and he will attract more followers. To uphold his reputation he will need more cattle. Thus the urge to own cattle is paramount.

In the traditional system the offices of *reis*, sheikh, and *nazir* carried prestige but little authority. The power of one of their leaders depended largely on the strength of his personality. Leadership was limited to situations in which his tribal section acted corporately. Moreover, his power rested on consent. No one was forced to follow a particular leader, and the size and composition of his following were constantly changing.

The establishment of the Anglo-Egyptian Condominium in 1899 had a profound influence on Homr society by stabilizing the floating power positions in the traditional system. For purposes of taxation, justice, and the maintenance of public order, the new government needed representative authorities over identifiable groups. Locality could not serve as a basis in shifting nomad society. Thus it settled on the traditional leaders of patrilineal descent groups and gave them a formal power they had previously lacked.

Before the condominium era the tenure of a *nazir*, as traditional leaders of *gabily* were known, was short lived. Their position subsequently became permanent because of government backing, and thus the division of the Homr tribe into two main sections was made rigid. In the same way, the five subdivisions of each *gabily* were "frozen" for administrative purposes. They were from then on called *omadiya* and headed by an *omda*.

The government did not fix leadership positions of sheikhs below the *omadiya* level. Sometimes members of a *surra* followed two different sheikhs; in other cases more than one *surra* were grouped behind one sheikh. The government did not care whether a sheikh led ten people or several hundred, but it wanted to make sure that every Homr was responsible to one sheikh, as far as the payment of his taxes was concerned. A sheikh who was able to collect the entire assessment was allowed to keep one-tenth. He also assisted the *omda* in locating people wanted by the police or administration and gathered his followers for a cattle census or inoculations. It was not a popular position but often a first step toward an omda-ship.

Surra leaders were given no official function. The administration regarded them as notables through whom *surra* members could sometimes be reached directly.

After independence the general trend was toward elimination of the traditional system from the political scene as more and more power devolved on the national government (see ch. 9). All local offices were abolished in 1970. As of 1972 it was not known to what degree the national government had been able to replace traditional leaders with modern cadres.

Villagers

Village societies exist where conditions permit relatively dense settlement, intensive agriculture, and marketable surpluses, as in the riverine regions of the Blue Nile and the White Nile rivers and in parts of Darfur and Kordofan provinces. For centuries the Nubians, settled Arabs, the Fur, and other groups in the north have been used to living within large-scale territorial units under centralized administrative authorities who regulated the exploitation of natural resources and provided protection in return for the payment of taxes. Their ideal is not the warrior but the patriarch, the man of means and influence who dispenses patronage.

In each settled region, control traditionally emanated from an urban center located on one of the principal trade routes, such as Al Fashir in Darfur, Al Ubayyid in Kordofan, Sannar in Dar Fung, and Dunqulah in Nubia (see ch. 2). For the sedentary people of most of the northern area, the national government is the successor of these previous centralized administrations. The settled people of this area live in villages that constitute the smallest political unit. Divisions in village society thus are territorial and not tribal as in nomadic society.

Within the village, kinship remains important. A man inherits land and social position from his father and farms near his brothers and other kin. If he must move, he will probably choose an area in which he already has relatives—perhaps his wife's or his mother's family. As a result the inhabitants of a village are generally linked by a complex network of marital and kinship ties. Often the majority of people within a settled area, encompassing several villages, belong to a single descent group, whose members share certain ritual observances and recognize some obligations toward each other.

In contrast to the segmentary lineages of the nomads, descent lines may also be followed through females, and the generational links to a common ancestor are not traced beyond three generations. Descent groups larger than the three-generation set are of little practical importance. When ancestors are remembered beyond the grandfather of the present elders, it is done for religious and social reasons. Nomads who adopt a settled way of life eventually replace loyalty toward the lineage with that toward the village community.

The village headman is usually either the head or the representative of the leading family and related to most of the council members who elect him. He is also the lowest ranking official in the central government hierarchy. In an economy based primarily on settled agriculture, seasonal cooperation between villages is not required as it is between groups of nomads during certain parts of the year. Thus the importance of a village headman lies less in his actions with neighboring communities than in his dealings with the central government. He collects taxes, takes care of local administrative matters, and settles disputes. In much of Darfur and Kordofan provinces where land is plentiful, the headman apportions the communal holdings among individual users, who are then accepted as members of the village.

The formal religion in the north is invariably Islam, and a village is also to some extent a religious community. Thus the characteristic institutions of village society include kinship groups, hereditary leaders, a corporate relationship to the land, a religious community, and the headman, who is at once an official and an intermediary. These various elements combine to establish a system of patronage that becomes the principal social link between village-based society and the urban elite responsible for national policies. The coordination of the several aspects of community leadership at all levels is illustrated by the meanings of the honorific title sheikh that is given to headmen and higher officials and is used as a general term of politeness in addressing any man of political, religious, or social importance. Primarily it designates an old and experienced man and hence one who is the head of a family and who is important in the community. It is also the specific title of the head of a religious order, a position that is itself often hereditary.

SOUTHERN SOCIETY

Homesteaders

Autonomy, isolation, and heterogeneity characterize homestead society, which occurs wherever the economy is limited to subsistence agriculture and communities are separated from each other, as in the southern regions of dense vegetation. No formal secular authority exists within the community, and each homestead is an independent sociopolitical unit. Neither are there permanent links with neighboring communities other than those of language and culture and the personal ties of individual families. The social organizations of the Madi, Moru, Bongo, Baka, and many other southern groups are examples of this pattern.

Homestead societies also occur in the less accessible areas of the north. There, however, they are close to the village societies of more prosperous neighboring groups, which provide the models for the development of modern local government institutions, a process closely related to the arabization of the entire north.

The homestead often includes a man's married children and his grandchildren. Each adult member has formal rights to living space, food crops, and animals. The senior male may also have more than one wife, maintaining a seperate household for each within the homestead, which is an economic as well as a sociopolitical unit. The head of a prosperous homestead may become a Big Man in the neighborhood. When that happens, his position is usually given formal recognition by a special ceremony of investiture, upon which he is expected to distribute most of his livestock and grains in feasts and gifts. Thereafter the Big Man is a respected local figure, whose advice is accepted. He may attract some of the poor and un-attached of the neighborhood to become his clients—that is, to give their services and allegiance in return for protection, help in emer-gencies, and sometimes sustenance. A Big Man, however has no clearly defined authority outside his own homestead.

Other local figures become Big Men by virtue of their tenancy of ritual offices. The offices may include those of chief of the path (ambassador), cattle welfare supervisor, maker of war magic, and many others connected with particular community activities. Most important and most nearly universal are those of father of the land and of rainmaker, who is sometimes a woman. In some com-munities one of these offices is given paramount importance; in others all of them may be filled by one man. None of them carries any inherent secular authority, but occasionally individuals have been able to exploit the prestige of their position. The various offices are nearly always hereditary, restricted to particular clans or families who are said, for example, to "have rain."

Rainmakers attempt to control the water upon which all families of the area depend. Unlike the rainmakers of the Dinka and the Shilluk, who are chiefs or kings at the same time, those of the Bongo, Bari, and other southern peoples do not personify their group's guardian spirit. The rainmaker's influence, like that of the father of the land, is confined to his community. In the past a sentence of death was sometimes imposed for failure to produce rain. In modern times the rainmaker may be arraigned before the local court. On the other hand, a successful rainmaker might acquire considerable influence over a wide area and become, in effect, a political leader.

The father of the land is usually the descendant of the pioneer settler in the area. He apportions land to those who want it, sometimes receiving a token payment in return. Rights to the use of a lot remain with a family for as long as they assert them, after which they revert to the community. There is no shortage, and land is usually neither sold nor rented. The main function of the father of the land, a religious figure father than a chief, is the conduct of propitiary exercises to assuré good harvests.

In some southern areas the clan from which the father of the land is drawn bears much the same relationship to other members of the community as do the dominant lineages in nomadic societies but without the elaboration of political ties between them. For example, among the Bari-speaking peoples are serf clans that constitute an inferior class. Though not physically distinguishable from other Bari, they are apparently the remains of conquered peoples. The serf clans specialize in such economic activities as hunting and ironworking; some are ritual experts. They are attached as clients to prominent families, who have recognized rights and obligations in regard to them. Some of them, because of their detachment from the main agricultural economy of the Bari, have become wealthier than their masters in the changed conditions of recent years.

In the indigenous social organization of homestead societies the concept of religious or secular order does not imply a universally applicable system of rewards and punishments. Homicide and incest, for example, are considered crimes if committed by a member of the community and are punishable by expulsion or death. The same offenses committed by someone not belonging to the community, however are not regarded as crimes but as private misdemeanors for which compensation may be paid to the injured party. In circumstances in which compensation is expected but refused, a feud usually develops between the two groups. When an offender is considered to have unintentionally incited the guardian spirits of the area to inflict disease and misfortune, the father of the land or the rainmaker may conduct expiatory ceremonies.

The efforts of former British administrators to make secular chiefs out of rainmakers and fathers of the land were generally unsuccessful during the period of condominium rule (1899-1952). In some areas the informal council of Big Men was converted to a court of arbitration and subsequently into an executive body.

The Azande represent a special variation of homestead society because of the existence of a distinct aristocratic clan, the Avungara, who traditionally furnished chiefs for various rival Azande kingdoms. Within each, young men were drafted into service for a specific period during which they worked the chief's fields, producing the grain that enabled him to provide lavish entertainment and thus secure the loyalty of his followers. They also constituted the military forces needed in incessant border skirmishes that each chiefdom had with its neighbors. Territorial boundaries and local groupings were permanent, however and there never was a unified Azande state. Chiefs of the Avungara clan rose and fell depending on the personal followings they were able to attract; lesser chiefs and headmen, some of them non-Avungara commoners, became Big Men and collected their own followers.

During the period of the condominium the British gave artificial rigidity to the Avungara political system by stopping the process of conquest and treating the chiefdoms as permanent political and territorial units (see ch. 2). At the same time, the chiefs were deprived of their right to maintain the squads of young men on which they depended for wealth and prestige, but they were given new authority as government tax collectors and administrators of economic programs. Many Azande began to resent this new power, but the courts of the chiefs continued to be regarded as centers not only of influence but culture and sophistication.

Conflict and competition among the Azande are regulated not as much by chiefs or other individuals specifically charged with the responsibility as by the institution of witchcraft with its elaborate rituals of accusation, divination, and prophylaxis. All misfortunes, and in particular all deaths not the direct result of violence, are considered to be caused by witchcraft, which emanates from rivals. It is divined through the use of oracles; every Zande has access to an oracle of some kind, but the most important ones are owned by the Avungara chiefs as adjuncts of their power. All judicial proceedings depend on evidence obtained from the oracle procedure; the Avungara themselves, however, are never subject to open accusation.

A witch is not thought to direct his malign influence maliciously and, if he is not being deliberately antisocial, he will remove it when requested by making a simple ritual gesture. Witches are not usually ostracized or punished. When any misfortune occurs or is anticipated, various divination procedures are used to identify suspected witches among the neighbors.

98

The Semisedentary Nilotes

The social organization of Nilotic peoples is not uniform, but certain systems or principles, varying in importance from one people to another, are found everywhere. They include: segmentary lineages in which relationships are traced in terms of descent in a single line from a common male ancestor; identification with a king who has largely ceremonial functions; a system of age-sets that groups the entire male population according to age, each age-set having specific duties and prerogatives and each individual passing from one to the next throughout his life together with his contemporaries; and hereditary offices for certain specialized ritual activities. The importance of each of these elements and the size of the group within which they are effective depend partly on history and partly on environmental and economic factors that have influenced settlement patterns (see ch. 2; ch. 3). In addition, wealth and personal qualities sometimes produce leaders whose positions are largely their own creation and not part of the formal structure.

Most of the Nilotes are semisedentary cattle keepers who move twice each year over relatively short distances from small, permanent villages on higher ground (May to December) to dry-seasonal cattle camps near the permanent marshes and streams (January to May) and back again when the floods begin. They share a preoccupation with cattle that far exceeds the devotion of the Arab to his herds. Cattle for the Nilotes are not merely a means of subsistence; they are intimately related to the entire system of social and spiritual values, the whole amounting to a "cattle culture."

In the most developed form of this culture, as exemplified by the Nuer, the ancestors of a lineage are thought of as having owned a herd of cattle, the decendants of which continue to have a constant relationship with the decendants of the orginal owners. Cattle are always being redistributed, but in Nuer thought the clan or lineage and its herd is an enduring collectivity. To the herd the clan owes everthing: its sustenance, much of its equipment, and above all the means to contract marriages. The herd is thus the immediate manifestation of the goodness of God.

The Nilotes are noted for their self-sufficient pride, their disinclination to defer to anybody, and an aloofness approaching arrogance. Convinced of the morality of their own way of life, they have generally remained indifferent to alien cultures.

The Shilluk

The only Nilotic people among whom centralized authority and an administrative structure have developed to any extent are the Shilluk. The distinctive feature of their society is a highly developed divine kingship. The king (*reth*) is thought to be the incarnation of the spirit of Nyikang, the semidivine hero believed to have brought the Shilluk to their present territory. He is elected from the sons of previous kings by a council of elders, receives tribute as spiritual and temporal head, dispenses justice, and intercedes with Nyikang. His personal health is thought to affect the rains, the crops, and the general material and moral welfare of all the Shilluk. In earlier times the king was killed ritually at the first sign of feebleness.

The kingdom is administratively divided into two provinces— north and south—a division believed by the Shilluk to have been created by Nyikang. In each province a chief formerly acted as the king's direct representative. Modern administration introduced subdivision chiefs who occupy intermediate positions.

The actual political power of the Shilluk king is uncertain. According to the people, his powers are absolute, although they admit that the existence of a national government makes their full exercise impossible. It seems likely that at its greatest the royal power was compounded from the prestige of his office, the support of his retainers and of royal clan, his comparative wealth in cattle, and the many marriage alliances be contracted. Certainly he ruled by consent rather than by force and, though the king was acknowledged to be supreme, Shilluk communities traditionally managed their own day-to-day affairs, confining the king's authority in practice to spiritual matters.

The Dinka

In contrast to the Shilluk, the Dinka have never had a paramount chief. They are divided into a number of tribes, bound tenuously together only by language, customs, and religious beliefs. In fact, Dinka tribes have a long history of fighting with each other.

Each tribe is headed by a chief who, in some aspects, resembles the Shilluk king, although his authority is slight. He belongs to one of the clans that have the monopoly of ritual power as symbolized by their possession of sacred fishing spears. The Dinka believe that every tribal segment should have its own spear master. No tribal segment can establish itself independently without a spear master, who sometimes initiates a move to break away.

The spear master is the religious head of the community. He makes rain and offers sacrifices. He has some worldly power because he resolves feuds. Formerly, if he became ill, he was buried alive by some tribes lest the guardian spirit believed to be incarnate

100

in him suffer from his physical deterioration. The office of spear master is not hereditary, although in actual fact he frequently is the son of a preceding chief. His powers rest entirely on his reputation as a man of peace who is skillful in conciliation and successful in prayer.

The Nuer

Nuer social organization resembles that of the Dinka, except that there are no chiefs whatever. Nuer tribes are divided into number of sections, each having rights to its own pastures and water resources. They again are split into further sections, the smallest being a cluster of homesteads. Members of tribal sections sometimes cooperate in warfare and settle feuds among members by adjudicating the amounts that must be paid in compensation for an offense.

The most important position among the Nuer is held by the *kuuarmuon*, a ritual officer whose advice may be solicited and followed but who has no authority to command. He carries a leopard skin over his shoulder as a sign that he may assist in settling feuds and in regulating age-grade ceremonies. His position is based on his wisdom, not on political power.

In the villages elders of the prominent lineages and others who are heads of families and managers of herds may offer their advice, although without the assurance that it will be heeded. Rhetorical ability is recognized and appreciated, however, and may earn its owner the title of spokesman for his group or even his tribe.

Nuer men are organized into age-sets; this limits the activities in which each man is entitled to participate at a given age. Formal initiation into an age-set makes boys adults at the age of about sixteen. During the ceremonies six deep cuts are made from ear to ear across the forehead of the initiated. The scars take two to three months to heal.

Sets are arranged in grades and are promoted as the set in the highest grade is retired to inactive old age. Members of a set—as "brothers"—have certain social obligations to one another; for example, they go to dances, funerals, and weddings together and may not marry each other's sisters. Relations between grades are formalized similarly in kinship terms; all members of a father's set are addressed and respected as "father" and all of their wives, as "mother." Every Nuer has his place in the age-grade hierarchy, and his conduct towards other Nuer is prescribed accordingly.

Age-grade systems are found in less developed form among other Nilotes, particularly among the Dinka and Shilluk. In recent years they seem to have declined in importance, although initiations are still conducted.

101

Among both the Dinka and Nuer, prophets have arisen from time to time, possessed by "sky spirits" and credited with supernatural powers. At the end of the nineteenth century, when Arab and European pressures developed, the influence of some of these prophets exceeded tribal boundaries and was instrumental in the organization of military opposition. The administration therefore suppressed the prophets, regarding them as subversive.

URBAN SOCIETY

Among the small urban population, whose growth is closely related to that of the modern sector of the economy, distinctions of race and tribe are decreasing in significance. The majority live near the confluence of the White Nile and the Blue Nile in Khartoum, Khartoum North, and Omdurman—the Three Towns—which are the political, military, commercial, and administrative hub of the country.

In the Three Towns live the administrators, lawyers, teachers, technicians, business managers, and college students; the minor employees of government, business, and development agencies; and increasing numbers of unskilled workers who try to escape dependence on agricultural and pastoral occupations and who like the choice of different alternatives offered. Indicative of a modern outlook is the fact that a greater proportion of girls in urban areas go to school than those in rural areas of the country.

Khartoum is the seat of the national government and of the university. Its cosmopolitan population includes the largest number of the country's professional and managerial personnel, including many foreigners. Khartoum North, a high-income residential area, is also a center for light manufacturing industries.

Of the three cities, Omdurman is the oldest. Its culture is markedly Arab. It is subdivided into wards dominated by close-knit clan and family groups of various orgins who are linked by innumerable personal ties to every part of the country. Their influence on the national government springs from their leadership of regional and sectional interests.

The citizens of Khartoum, Khartoum North, and Omdurman do not form a closed and cohesive group. An important division exists between the older and the younger generations. The senior group includes the older civil servants and the leaders of religious orders, both representative of conservative Arab Muslim values. The younger group consists largely of Western-educated men, including some southerners. They are modern and often radical in outlook and demand bold economic and social changes in a generally secular setting.

Another gulf divides all urban inhabitants from their rural counterparts. Living at the seat of the national government, participating in modern political activity, and constantly exposed to cross-cultural contacts, urban dwellers have come to think of themselves as Sudanese. The country's 1955/56 census reported an important minority among the people in the Three Towns, Wad Madani, Port Sudan, Al Ubayyid, Kassala, and Atbarah who disclaimed all ethnic or tribal affiliations.

THE FAMILY

In Sudanese societies the family is an important unit of social organization. Family connections and obligations regulate many social activities that in Western countries are the function of other institutions.

The Sudanese family, except for the modern elite, is a cooperative economic, social, religious, and often political unit. The rare person who remains unmarried is excluded from many social roles. Forms of marriage vary considerably between Muslims and non-Muslims but show, nevertheless, certain similarities. These include the slow firming of the marriage bond, lasting many years from the first negotiations until several children are born; the close tie that a woman retains with her own family; the formality observed toward parents-in-law; the internal organization of polygamous households; and the part played by the community in witnessing the marriage.

Marriage in both Muslim and non-Muslim, communities is a contractual arrangement between established families rather than between two individuals, and procreation is its principal objective. The main division in family life is not between generations but between the sexes. Companionship between husband and wife is exceptional. Men and women do not eat together, and both rather seek the company of their own sex.

For almost all Sudanese polygamy is the ideal form of marriage, although only about 15 percent of all married men had more than one wife at the time of the 1955/56 census. A Muslim is permitted four wives, and a non-Muslim, as many as he can afford. Since the sexes are approximately equal in numbers, many men, competing for women with older and wealthier men, remain bachelors until the age of twenty-five or thirty. Girls usually marry much earlier. Thus there is often a considerable difference in age between a wife and her husband or between her and other wives of the polygamous marriage. In the women's sphere the dominant figure is the senior wife or, more often the husband's mother. When more than one wife lives in the same domestic group, each has her own establishment. Divorce is easy and frequent in both Muslim and non-Muslim societies.

In Muslim communities family organization is theoretically governed by religious law as defined in the Koran and other holy writings; however, pre-Muslim elements often survive. For example, many non-Arab Muslims retain the conventions of their former social order and forbid marriage within the kinship group.

Among the Arabs there is much concern with social distinctions and purity of lineage. An Arab prefers marriage with his father's brother's daughter, since no question of social disparity arises. Such a marriage has the added advantage of keeping the property that is transferred to the bride within the family. This marriage preference amounts in some areas to a preemptive right, especially in the case of a first marriage. Lacking a paternal cousin, the Arab male seeks a bride who is related in some other close fashion. In this respect Arab practice contrasts strongly with that of other Muslim or non-Muslim Sudanese, most of whom are less concerned with preserving the purity of their lineage than with establishing widespread family ties and social connections.

Non-Muslim forms of marriage vary considerably from one ethnic group to another but show common differences with orthodox Muslim practices. The most striking is the prohibition of marriage between people who are related or considered to be related. Within the kinship group all men of the same generation are thought to be brothers, and relationships are ordered between them as though they were actually born of the same mother. Where age-sets are part of the social system, they take up the family pattern: a Nuer must not marry the daughter or mother of a member of his set whom he calls "daughter" or "mother," although there may be no blood relationship.

Another characteristic common to non-Muslim forms of marriage is that obligations of contracting families do not lapse, even after the death of the marriage partners. If the wife dies—especially if she has not borne any children—her family may be expected to provide a substitute. If the husband dies, the woman usually joins the household of one of his brothers or a son by another wife. Future children count as offspring of the deceased.

Also contrary to Muslim usage is the custom making marriage payments not to the bride but to her family. A family reserves its corporately owned wealth generally for precisely such payments. Among cattle-raising people, for example, each of the men has rights in turn to a share in the family herd, to be used in providing a wife for himself or one of his sons.

The chief source of wealth for a family is therefore the marriage of women relatives. It is used only to arrange for the marriages of male relatives. Through a succession of marriages—each of which ultimately earns a material return—a family strengthens its social and political influence. An equal number of sons and daughters is considered ideal because the payments received for the daughters provide the marriage payments for the sons' wives.

The introduction of a cash economy has meant the introduction of new forms of marriage payments, such as national currency or imported manufactured goods, especially in areas where cattle are less important. This has had far-reaching effects. For example, although older Azande question the validity of a marriage in which spears are not conveyed, as used to be the tradition, young men have been able to earn cash with which to acquire a wife without waiting for the accumulation of family property. This has reduced the size of the family as an economic unit and has increased the social independence of younger men. In most southern areas, however, the economy remains at the subsistence level. A Dinka or a Lotuko who acquires money will exchange it for a cow, which traditionally represents real wealth and increases his chances of getting a wife.

The government generally leaves the regulation of family life to local and religious courts. Marriages between members of different ethnic groups usually present serious difficulties because of different customs. This practical difficulty prompted the Islamic prohibition of marriage with non-Muslims, a prohibition that is, however, disregarded by some Sudanese groups. The Homr Arabs sometimes take Dinka wives but without recording it in their genealogies. Generally, however, people marry within their own group. Nubians, for example, rarely marry Arabs, and nomads rarely marry villagers.

INTERGROUP RELATIONS

The various components of Sudanese society have long had emotionally charged attitudes toward one another. Within the northern region nomads and settled people distrust each other. The nomad is basically a man of strife fighting for existence in a hostile environment. He relies on himself and his relatives for survival and for the maintenance of his flocks and of his standing. He is contemptuous of the villager whom he used to raid and rob. The villager values peace above all, feels a mixture of resentment and fear toward the nomad, and counts on the support of his local patron and thus ultimately on the government for his safety. Usually there are few marriages between nomads and villagers, and contacts between them are limited to disputes caused by straying animals and to the exchange of produce in the markets.

Nomads and villagers of the northern region generally have in common an attachment to Islam and to Arab culture. They also use the same criteria for ranking, which—apart from such personal qualities as hospitality, generosity, piety, and honesty—include being male, being old, and belonging to a prominent lineage, especially one claiming descent from the Prophet Muhammad or some other noted religious personage.

Both groups share a disdain for manual labor, which gives rise to another fission in northern Sudanese society. The bulk of Sudan's agricultural labor has traditionally been performed by non-northern, non-Muslim people of either southern or West African origin. They used to be slaves or serfs who depended socially and economically upon their master. At present they work for wages or as tenants under modern contractual arrangements; however, the social relationship appears unchanged. A West African or a southerner who becomes a tenant for a northerner helps him maintain his status as traditionally defined.

The effects of the legacy of slavery are most obvious when economic development forces changes, as in the Jazirah and other government agricultural schemes (see ch. 13). Many northerners will not perform the labor needed in export-oriented agriculture. When economic necessity forces them, they do it unwillingly and feel frustration and shame at having to compete with those whom they consider socially inferior people. Whether their property consists of a single holding or tenancy or of many, their ideal is to pay others to work their land while they assume the leisured dignity of property owners. Their actual income may, however, be no more than that of a laborer, and a marked difference between wealthy absentee landlords and landless peasantry is not a feature of Sudanese social structure.

Nomadic and settled northerners, especially those living outside the Nile River valley, also share a dislike for city people. Whatever local government they may acknowledge is not necessarily seen as an extension of the national government. They see emissaries from Khartoum as representatives of a foreign power. They do not use the term *Sudanese* to designate themselves. For the majority of rural inhabitants, city people are agents of unwelcome interference with traditional ways. Urban dwellers in turn have often turned their back on the customs and occupations of rural people, considering them backward, primitive, and ignorant.

Thus within the northern region divisions exist between nomads and villagers, between patrons and laborers, and between urban and rural people. The major sociopolitical division, however, is between the north and the south (see ch. 9).

This breach is frequently presented as a distinction between Arab and Negro, although the latter term is ambiguous and imprecise. Also, there is no clear-cut division because of the considerable ethnic mixing that has occurred for many centuries.

Ideally, the Arab sees himself as a light-skinned man with an undisputed claim to direct descent from the family of the Prophet, who knows the Koran, follows Islamic laws, and is eloquent in classical Arabic—a man who wears white robes and keeps his women in seclusion. To the Arab the southerner's beliefs, his eating and clothing habits, and the freedom of his women are proof of his disregard for the social and moral integrity of family and lineage. Therefore the Arab considers the southerner as physically, morally, and economically inferior. He does not understand that a southerner may have different standards; he assumes that he has no standards at all.

No such single image is available to southerners, who are more aware of their immediate differences than of an overall community of interests. They have only one bond in common, and that is fear and distrust of the northerners, whom they see as unscrupulous and treacherous exploiters. They remember former slave raids and impressment into the army. Although organized slave raiding on a commercial scale was put down at the beginning of the twentieth century, southerners have bitterly resented the northerner's contemptuous attitude toward them. Most northerners have regarded progress and unification of the country as implicitly synonymous with arabization. The southerners have viewed it as an extension of the process of conquest.

After independence in 1956, when the government began promoting Arab values in the interest of nationwide sudanization, the resentment flared up into armed rebellion (see ch. 2) During the seventeen-year civil war most southern communities were destroyed, and an estimated 500,000 people died either in the fighting or from war-related causes, such as starvation and unchecked diseases. This number was arrived at by concluding that nearly every family in the region had lost at least one member. A more accurately estimated figure of 750,000 fled—500,000 into the inaccessible bush area, the rest into neighboring countries. The prevailing tendency was to seek a familiar milieu. Azande, Acholi, Bari, and Lotuko fled in large numbers to their ethnic brothers across the border in Uganda and Zaire—until late 1971 Congo (Kinshasa). Nuer, Dinka, and Shilluk took refuge in the hills of Ethiopia and with kindred Nilotic people in northwestern Kenya.

The war also had the effect of forcing cooperation between once hostile groups. The isolation and fragmentation so characteristic of traditional southern society, however, had been largely caused by ecological conditions. Their effects might conceivably be tempered if the large-scale agricultural projects planned after the conclusion of the peace pact in early 1972 are implemented (see ch. 12).

CHAPTER 6

RELIGION

The country is divided into a large northern region where Islam predominates and a small southern region where most of the inhabitants, except for a small Christian minority, adhere to an indigenous religion. According to unofficial estimates in 1968, about 66 percent of the total population were Muslims and about 4 percent were Christians. The remainder subscribed to traditional African religious systems. Despite these estimates, clear-cut divisions are difficult to make because of the widespread survival of pre-Islamic and pre-Christian beliefs and practices throughout the country.

Most if not all, Sudanese peoples express belief in a remote and all-powerful God, the creator and ultimate governor of the universe, but strict monotheism is characteristic only of small minorities of highly orthodox Muslims and Christians. In the religion of most people, intermediary divinities such as saints and spirits are, in effect, independent objects of worship, although their power is attributed to God. Religious observances consist of prayer and supplication intended to incline them toward favorable actions.

Religion is pervasive and permeates all aspects of Sudanese life. The religious and social communities are identical. A special reverence is accorded to ancestral spirits in all Sudanese religions except Christianity. In general, beliefs in an all-powerful God and in magical processes for controlling the supernatural are always present, but in some areas religion is reduced to a traditional preoccupation with mysterious powers attributed entirely to human agents.

After independence in 1956 a vigorous policy to Islamize was begun. In 1972 Islam was the religion of the urban classes and the governing elite. It played an important role in the formation of national policy, and its strength was likely to increase as government-sponsored educational and economic improvements occurred.

All Christian missionaries in the southern area were expelled during 1963 and 1964 and were replaced, beginning in 1968, by non-Europeans. The declared ultimate goal was the africanization

109

of the Christian church. Although freedom of worship for all religious persuasions continued to receive governmental guarantees, an estimated half of the Christian membership had been driven into exile in neighboring countries during the civil war of the 1960s (see ch. 9).

ORIGINS OF ORGANIZED RELIGIOUS FORMS

The ancient indigenous religion of northern Sudan consisted of many small local cults associated with particular stones, trees, and caves, some of which still function as shrines. In the relatively complex civilizations of the Nile River valley, however, highly developed theologies introduced from the Mediterranean region were closely associated with autocratic systems of government. In Nubia, under Egyptian and later under Meroitic government, massive stone temples to Osiris, Isis, and other Egyptian deities were constructed in Egyptian style (see ch. 2).

The Nubian kingdoms, which eventually developed in the Nile valley, were converted to Christianity in the sixth century by emissaries from the Byzantine court. This new religion, even more than the Isis worship and sun worship that preceded it, was a religion of the kings and of the courts rather than of the majority of the people and was closely associated with the Greco-Roman culture adopted from Egypt by the upper classes. The clergy was Egyptian, and the liturgy was in Greek. Nubian Christianity as the state religion was, nevertheless, strongly influenced by former Egyptian and Meroitic concepts and even more by the tribal values of Nilotic immigrants from the south. Some of the kings, if not all, were also priests; moreover, the land and all its people were said to belong to the king, who personally represented the corporate rights of his subjects.

The decline of Nubian Christianity began in the seventh century with the Arab conquest of Egypt. In Nubia, Christianity remained the nominal religion of the majority until the fourteenth century, when large numbers of nomadic Arabs occupied the northern kingdoms and began to invade the central grasslands. Alwa, the southernmost kingdom, retained its independence until the initiation of the Fung dynasty in 1504.

The Fung claimed to be both Arab and Muslim. They ruled over some large Muslim-Arab groups and over a still larger number of Nubian peoples of heterogenous culture and indeterminate belief, as well as many others whose religion followed the ancient pattern of local cults. The kingdom was far from being a Muslim community; in particular, it lacked a school system. In the sixteenth century the Fung dynasty invited

110

Islamic missionaries to the country and to the royal court; most of these missionaries were Sufis from Arabia. They established Muslim enclaves, many of which developed into full-scale religious orders.

Christianity disappeared in Nubia during the fifteenth century, leaving its only traces in the superstitious use of the sign of the cross and a few red-brick churches converted into mosques. The Beja of the eastern hills, who had already abandoned their zeal for Isis, renounced Christianity for Islam. The successful spread of Islam among these non-Arab people was attributed generally to economic, political, and social factors rather than to a missionary zeal among the Arabs who had invaded their territory.

For a time Christian practice survived in northern Darfur, where in all probability it was introduced from Nubia by the Tungur (see ch. 2). The Fur dynasty, which may have been founded by partly arabized immigrants from the northwest, displaced the Tungur and gradualy formed a state on the Muslim model, which lasted until 1916. Religious teachers were imported from the east, and trade contacts with the Muslim world were strengthened. Islam, however, influenced the laws of the state more than it did the daily lives of the people, many of whom still show great reverence for the sacred trees and caves of the ancient cults.

Western Christian missionaries reappeared in Sudan in 1848. The first were Roman Catholics who worked in both the northern and southern areas with varying success, until their stations were overrun by the Mahdists and abandoned between 1882 and 1885. After the Mahdists were defeated and the Anglo-Egyptian Condominium was established in 1898, the British administrators were at first reluctant to let the missionaries come back for fear of Muslim fanaticism. They were eventually allowed to return but only to the southern area where, in 1905, each missionary society was allotted a specific area. They were to engage in educational and medical work rather than in proselytizing activities and were strictly forbidden to set up stations north of the tenth parallel. In the northern region Coptic, Greek, Armenian, and Ethiopian orthodox churches were allowed to establish themselves and serve their respective communities, although their sizes remained relatively small.

Until independence the dominant influences on administrative control and modern economic development were Christian and European. In the Nuba Mountains and in the three southern provinces ("closed districts" under the British, which northerners could not enter without official permission) direct Muslim influence was extremely limited, and Christian missionary influence was closely associated with programs of educational and social development (see ch. 2; ch. 8). Even in the Three Towns—Khartoum, Khartoum North, and Omdurman—the heart of the Arab world in Sudan, the high proportion of British administrators afforded Christianity a more prominent role in society than the number of its adherents warranted. Since independence, however, Christianity as an organized religion diminished under a continuing governmental policy to Islamize (see ch. 2; ch. 9).

ISLAM

Islam is the religion preached by the Prophet Muhammad, who was born in Mecca in A.D. 570. During his lifetime Muhammad was both spiritual and temporal leader of the Muslim community, and he established the concept of Islam as a total and all-encompassing way of life for man and society. Muslims believe that Allah revealed to Muhammad the rules governing decent and proper behavior, and it is therefore incumbent upon the individual to live in the manner prescribed by this revealed law and upon the community to perfect human society on earth according to the holy injunctions. Islam traditionally recognizes no distinction between church and state. Religious and secular life merge as do religious and secular law. In keeping with this concept of society, all Muslims have been traditionally subject to the *sharia* (religious law), which covers most aspects of life, as interpreted by religious courts.

Tenets of Islam

The fundamental article of Islamic faith is the *shahadah* (testimony), which states: "There is no God but God (Allah), and Muhammad is his Prophet." This simple profession of faith is repeated on many ritual occasions, and its recital in full and unquestioning sincerity distinguishes one as a Muslim. The God preached by Muhammad was not one previously unknown to his countrymen, for Allah is the Arabic term for *God* rather than a particular name. Rather than introducing a new deity, Muhammad denied the existence of the many minor gods and spirits formerly worshiped and declared the omnipotence of the unique creator, God. The word *Islam* means submission to God, and he who submits is a Muslim. Muhammad is the "seal of the Prophets": his revelation is said to complete for all time the series of biblical revelations received by the Jews and Christians. God himself is believed to have remained one and the same throughout all time, but men had strayed from his true teachings until corrected by Muhammad. Prophets and sages of the biblical tradition, such as Abraham, Moses, and Jesus (Isa), are recognized as the inspired vehicles of God's will. Islam reveres as sacred only Christianity's message, rejecting its deification of the messenger. It accepts the concepts of guardian angels, the Day of Judgment, general resurrection, heaven and hell, and the eternal life of the soul.

According to Islamic doctrine, the Koran sets forth all a man needs to attain salvation. The teachings of the four Gospels are accepted, but Muslims claim that the present texts are not as God revealed them. Other books interpreting the Koran but not regarded as divinely inspired are the Sunna and the *hadith*, which are the traditions and sayings of Muhammad. There is a wide difference of opinion about the Sunna. Sunni Muslims accept the Sunna implicity; the second largest Muslim group, the Shia, reject the Sunna as spurious and adhere to a tradition of their own.

Discipline

The duties of the Muslim form the "five pillars" of the faith. There are *shahadah* (recitation of the creed) ; *salat* (daily prayer) ; *zakat* (almsgiving) ; *sawm* (fasting) ; and *haji* (pilgrimage). The believer prays in a prescribed manner after purification through ritual ablutions at dawn, midday, midafternoon, sunset, and nightfall. Prescribed genuflections and prostrations accompany the prayers, which the worshiper recites facing toward Mecca. Whenever possible, men pray in congregation at the mosque under an *imam* (prayer leader—see Glossary), and on Fridays they are obliged to do so. Women may also attend public worship at the mosque where they are segregated from the men, although they most frequently pray in seclusion at home. A special functionary, the *muaddhin*, intones a call to prayer to the entire community at the appropriate hours; those out of earshot determine the proper time from the sun. Most Sudanese Muslims observe the five pillars to some extent, except the nomads who rarely fast or pray, although they are profoundly convinced of the moral and social superiority of Islam.

The severest test of a Muslim's ability to carry out the dictates of his faith is met during Ramadan, the ninth month of the Muslim calendar. During Ramadan all but the sick, the weak, pregnant women, soldiers on duty, travelers on necessary journeys, and young children are enjoined during the daylight hours from eating, drinking, smoking, or sexual intercourse. The well-to-do usually do little or no work during this period, and many businesses close for all or part of the day. Since the months of the lunar calendar revolve around the solar year, Ramadan falls at various seasons in different years. A fast in summertime im-

113

poses considerable hardship on those who must do physical work. Each day's fast ends with a signal that light is insufficient to distinguish a black thread from a white one. A three-day feast and holiday ends the month of Ramadan.

The pilgrimage to Mecca is regarded as the ideal culmination of every Muslim's religious experience and should be undertaken at least once in a lifetime if possible. Those who are too poor to travel are tacitly exempted, however, since authorities disapprove of a pilgrim's begging his way (although this is often done). West Africans in the thousands pass annually through Sudan on their way to Mecca. Many of them settle in the more fertile regions, creating major social problems (see ch. 5). The returning pilgrim is entitled to the honorific title *Haj* before his name.

The permanent struggle for the triumph of the word of God on earth, the *jihad*, represents an additional general duty of all Muslims. Although this has been used in the past to justify holy wars, modern Muslims see it in a broader context of civic and personal action.

In additional to specific duties, Islam imposes a code of ethical conduct encouraging generosity, fairness, honesty, and respect and forbidding adultery, gambling, usury, and the consumption of carrion, blood, pork, and alcohol. A Muslim has a personal relationship with God needing neither intermediary nor clergy. Those who lead prayers, preach sermons, and interpret the law do so by virtue of their superior knowledge and scholarship rather than because of any special powers or prerogatives endowed by ordination.

Institutions

Mosques are prominent in the towns, and most villages of the northern region have at least a roughly fenced area set aside for public prayer. Often the mosque is also a *khalwa* (Islamic school) conducted by a *fiqi* (pl., *fuqaha*; village teacher), who is the resident *imam*. Education, meaning knowledge of the Koran and the *sharia* (see Glossary) is emphasized much more than worship.

Khalwa education consists of memorizing the Koran by group repetition; the significance and application of its text are not explained. The student rarely learns to write; much of his time is spent waiting on the *fiqi*, perhaps farming his land. Few complete the course, for which the final examination is the recitation of the Koran before another *fiqi*. Where higher standards prevail, the emphasis shifts from the Koran to summaries of theological works and *sharia* law.

114

The acknowledged authorities (*ulema*—see Glossary) reside at the schools and colleges of religious learning, the highest institution of which in Sudan is the Maahad Ilmi in Omdurman, founded in 1901. The full course of study takes twelve years. In the provinces there are other colleges, which give only introductory courses. All are run by the Ministry of Religious Affairs and Religious Trusts. The curriculum consists of the traditional memorization of the Koran and studies in the *hadith* and in jurisprudence; classical Arabic grammar, literature, and composition, with the rules of rhyme and meter; penmanship; arithmetic; and logic.

The *fiqi* is the central religious figure of popular Islam; originally the term meant "one who has knowledge of the law." Usually he belongs to a religious order, but his most characteristic function is to teach the Koran in the village school. His next most important duty is writing texts and magical figures to be used as amulets and cures. He may also act as *imam* of the mosque and be in charge of the tomb of a local saint. His blessing is sought at births, deaths, marriages, and other occasions of special importance. He is asked to practice divination and exorcism and, in some remote regions, he participates in ancient harvest rites. Particularly accomplished *fuqaha* are credited with the ability to fly, to change the shape and substance of themselves and other people and objects, to raise the dead, and to bring rain.

The religious orders that developed in Sudan owe much to the concept of sainthood. The term *wali*, used in the Koran to mean "friend," soon came to mean "friend of God" and may be translated as saint. The body of a saint on earth was given a heavenly counterpart in a hierarchy of invisible saints halfway between God and man. The saints were God's agents; they had *baraka* (power; literally, "blessing") to bring rain, to cure disease, to foresee the future, and to perform other miracles.

In general the living *fiqi* is not as revered as the dead saint, who also is called *fiqi*, or more commonly, *wali*. After death the saint's *baraka* is thought to increase and to inhere in the persons and particularly the places associated with him, such as his birthplace or especially his tomb. He often becomes the guardian spirit and protector of the locality or social group in which he lived, and his intercession is sought on all important occasions. Persons seeking blessings, especially barren women and the sick, visit his shrine to perform rituals and absorb some of his blessedness through osmosis.

Shrines may be a square building (*qubba*) with a domed roof or a mere ring of stones. They are protected zones in which, for example, hair-clippings may be left to keep them from falling into the hands of sorcerers and excess merchandise may be stored that elsewhere would be stolen. A saint's annual holy day is the occasion of a local festival that may attract a large gathering.

Women are often the chief participants in the cult of saints. They also monopolize the *zar* (spirit) cult, which is concerned with the appeasement of spirits that take possesion of a person.

Religious Orders

Groups of disciples have frequently clustered around particular saints, especially those who preached an original *tariqa* (pl., *turuq;* a mystical or devotional "way"). Many early holy men attracted disciples, but it was not until the twelfth century that these small groups became organized and self-perpetuating. The common pattern of the religious orders is the personal relationship between a teacher and his followers; succession is traced through named holy men back to the Prophet Muhammad himself.

The rise of the *turuq* was closely connected with development of Sufism, a mystical approach seeking a closer personal relationship to God through special spiritual disciplines. Escape from the self was aided by poverty, seclusion, and other forms of self-denial; states of visionary ecstasy were brought on by group chanting of religious texts and by dances and gestures. Some Sufis resorted to hashish and hypnotism. Orthodox Islamic ritual is limited to *salat* (prayer), but Sufi doctrine requires more elaborate exercises consisting mainly of the *zikr* (remembrance), which finds its authority in the Koranic text, "O ye who believe! Remember Allah with much remembrance." Recital of prayers, passages of the Koran, and names of God repeated a set number of times are accompanied by physical movements, according to the formula established by the founder of the particular order. Religious songs and poetic accounts of apocryphal episodes in the life of the Prophet are introduced; the entire ritual may last several hours and lead the participants to a frenzied climax of emotional abandon.

As a result of the work of the early Muslim missionaries, Sudan still shows preponderant Sufi influence. Sufism has never been condemned outright, because its chief exponents have been careful to assert the supremacy of the *sharia*. The tendency of the mystics to interpret the Koran allegorically and to see God everywhere, even in inanimate objects, facilitated the assimilation of pre-Islamic local cults.

The principal *turuq* of Sudan vary considerably in their practices and internal organization. The largest and oldest order is the Qadriyyah. Introduced in the early sixteenth century, it is the least centralized and has developed into many virtually independent branches headed by local sheikhs; one of these is the Sammaniyyah. The Qadriyyah is also the most varied in its doctrine and the most receptive to outside influences; at its vaguest it is merely the nominal recognition of its founder, Abd al Qadral al Gaylani, as a patron to whom appeals may be made for protection on journeys.

The Khatmiyyah, the best organized and most powerful *tariqah* in Sudan, was founded by Muhammad Uthman al Mirghani in the early nineteenth century. Muhammad Uthman in turn joined all the best known orders; and when he formed his own it became known as the Khatim al Turuq, the Seal of the Paths. He was, however, primarily a student of the celebrated Ahmad ibn Idris (1760–1837), many of whose pupils became missionaries to Sudan. The distinctive feature of the Khatmiyyah is the insistence of the founder and his successors on the peculiar sanctity, amounting to semidivinity, of the Mirghani family, who exclusively reserve the right to be sheikh and refuse to allow the followers to associate with other orders. Politically, the most important Khatmiyyah leader was Ali al Mirghani (see ch. 2).

Orders historically related to the Khatmiyyah include the Idrisiyyah, founded directly by Ahmad ibn Idris; the Senussiyyah, represented in Sudan but strongest in Libya; the Ismailiyyah, a branch of the Khatmiyyah, strongest in Kordofan Province; the Shadhliyyah or Magdoubiyyah, strongest in the northeast; and the Tiganiyyah, a missionary order strongly influential in West Africa. Adherents of the Tiganiyyah order in Sudan include not only West Africans but also better educated townsmen attracted in recent years by its liberalism, its stronger philosophical emphasis, and the restrained outward forms of its prayer.

The Mahdiyyah religious revolt (1881–98) gave birth to still another *tariqah* in Sudan, although the Mahdi maintained that his movement was not a "path" that could be adopted or rejected at will but a universal regime that challenged every man to either join or be destroyed. By his express command the Mahdi's followers were called Ansar, the name of the Phophet's own followers.

The Mahdist state borrowed its laws from primitive Islam; it was egalitarian and communistic, evangelical, and puritanical. Pedigrees and books of law and theology were ordered to be burned because they supported the former corrupt social order; the only books allowed were the Koran and a devotional anthology compiled by the Mahdi himself. In addition, a new core of law was introduced.

The five pillars of Islam were modified to suit the dogma that loyalty to the Mahdi was essential to true belief. The declaration of faith became, "There is no God but God, and Muhammad is the Prophet of God, and Muhammad Ahmad is the Mahdi of God and the representative of His Prophet." *Jihad* (holy war) replaced the pilgrimage to Mecca, and congregational prayer as an organized drill replaced individual devotions. *Zakat* (almsgiving) became the tax that was paid to the state. Worldly and superstitious adherences to religious observances, including elaborate marriages and funerals, music, magic, and the cults of saints, were forbidden. The seclusion of women was enforced, and users of intoxicants were punished. Like those of the Prophet, all reforms were justified as responses to direct instructions conveyed by God in visions.

After the military defeat of the Mahdi, people generally returned either to the earlier superstituous religion or to orthodox Islam. In the west, including parts of Darfur, the fanatical spirit survived, however, and the Mahdi's son, Abd al Rahman al Mahdi, was so revered that the pilgrimage to see him replaced the pilgrimage to Mecca. Many westerners combined their zeal for the Mahdi with their search for economic opportunity in the east by settling on the Mahdi's vast estates and becoming his tenants as well as his followers. The antagonisms of the Mahdist era gave new vigor to the perennial feuds of the nomadic tribes and established the pattern of disagreement later developed by political parties (see ch. 2; ch. 9).

CHRISTIANITY

Missionary Activity Before Independence

The earliest Christian missionaries in the southern region were the Roman Catholic Verona Fathers, who arrived in the late nineteenth century and eventually developed and maintained the largest Christian organization in Sudan. They were followed by Presbyterians from the United States, who began to work among the Shilluk, and by Anglicans from Great Britain, who settled among the Dinka. Other missionaries followed in later years. The rate of Christian progress varied between different ethnic groups. It was fastest among the Moru, Bari, and Azande and slowest among the Shilluk, Nuer, and Dinka. The early missionaries, far from regarding themselves as spokesmen for the government, were often critical of the administration, which they accused of favoring Islam in order to preserve peace in Sudan.

Faced with a multitude of local languages, the missionaries tried to establish English as a lingua franca. At the beginning of the twentieth century government business was carried on at the lower levels partly in pidgin Arabic and partly in local languages. The missionaries pressured the governors of the southern provinces into favoring English-speaking employees, thus providing people with an impetus to send their children to mission schools. The administration, which for lack of funds had to rely entirely on the

118

missions to supply educational, social, and medical services, finally acceded to these demands. This decision had the far-reaching effect of culturally separating the south from the rest of the country. It also led later generations of northerners to regard the missionaries as tools of British colonialism.

The strict segregation of missionary spheres of influence and the prohibition to move north of the tenth parallel were gradually relaxed in the period between the two world wars. Lack of resources, however, forced most missionary societies except the Roman Catholics to stay in their original areas.

In 1920 the Australian and New Zealand branch of the Sudan United Mission was allowed to open a branch in the eastern Nuba Mountains because the government considered their educational and social work to be a useful civilizing influence. In the 1930s the Anglican Church Missionary Society opened stations in the western Nuba Mountains, but the language of education was Arabic, since that area was administratively and economically part of the northern region.

The Sudan Interior Mission was expelled from Ethiopia in 1938 by the Italians and came to work in the area straddling the border between Upper Nile and Blue Nile provinces. In 1942 clubs, which were at the same time congregations, were opened in Omdurman and Khartoum to take care of the many southerners who had come there to work; similar groups were organized in Wad Madani in 1948. On the whole, Christian influence in the northern region was confined to a few of the larger towns, and none of any kind existed in Darfur Province. In the south large government subsidies accounted for the rapid expansion of mission schools after 1946.

Government Policy Since Independence

The administration that came into office at independence in 1956 was largely staffed by Muslims, yet the government officially remained secular. Christian religious festivals were recognized as government holidays, and non-Muslim faith was not a bar to public office. Leading northerners, however, considered the Christian missions as largely responsible for the creation of anti-Arab feelings in the south, and most of the early leaders of the southern rebellion were indeed products of mission schools. Thus mission activities were curtailed, and vigorous efforts were made to bring together the north and the south in matters of education, language, and religion. The Department of Religious Affairs, a national body set up just before independence, established special training institutes at Juba, Waw, and other southern towns to provide religious guidance.

In 1957 a policy of arabizing and Islamizing was begun. All

schools were nationalized, which led to the confiscation of over 350 mission schools and the expulsion in 1958 of all but thirty teachers of various denominations. Plans were made to establish schools teaching Arabic and the Koran in the former mission schools.

No new missionary personnel were allowed to enter the south, and social and medical activities of the Christian churches were gradually stopped. In January 1959 Sunday was abolished as a weekly holiday and replaced by the Muslim Friday. The Missionaries Societies Act, passed in May 1962, gave the government strict control over all Christian mission activities.

The number of missionaries expelled from the country in 1963 was 143. In the following year those remaining in the south, about 200 Roman Catholics and 100 Protestants, were given notice to leave the country within forty-eight hours. The expulsion order did not apply to those working in the north. In 1965 all Christian churches joined to form a Sudan Council of Churches, which affiliated with the All African Conference of Churches and the Middle East Council of Churches.

Freedom of religion remained the avowed goal of the government, and in 1966 envoys were sent to the Vatican to reestablish good relations. In December 1966 a delegation of the All African Conference of Churches was allowed to visit the southern region and to make concrete proposals.

In succeeding years permission was given to hold seminars and to build new churches partly to replace the many that had been destroyed during the civil war. Priests were allowed to reenter Sudan, provided that they were not Europeans. The first to arrive were two Tanzanians in 1968. In 1971, after a total absence of seven years, Roman Catholicism returned, this time represented by Indian Jesuits in accordance with a condition set up by the government. Long-range goals included the africanization of the clergy, the translation of the Bible into marginal southern languages, and the adaptation of certain Christian rites and ceremonies to those that were already part of African indigenous religions.

The Ministry of Religious Affairs and Religious Trusts was established in January 1972 as part of the reorganization of government. It was responsible for supervising all Christian churches and institutions, including the education of theologians, and for working toward the creation of a Sudanese Christian church for Sudanese citizens.

INDIGENOUS RELIGIOUS BELIEFS

The religious beliefs of Sudanese who are neither Muslims nor Christians differ from one ethnic group to another. All share a belief in the Creator God or Supreme Being, who is omnipotent, timeless, and remote from man. Intermediary powers, such as spirits of dead ancestors or those thought to animate trees, rocks, or water, are considered to be either benevolent or malevolent, intimately involved with everyday happenings, and amenable to prayer and propitiary sacrifice.

Supreme Being

Worship of the Supreme Being is most highly developed among the Shilluk, the Dinka, and the Nuer. Nuer religion has no word corresponding to "God"; the word sometimes so translated means "spirit" and refers not only to the universal governing spirit but also to ancestors, totems, and forces of nature whose spirits are considered to be aspects or persons of God. It is possible to pray to one spirit as distinct from another but not as distinct from God. God is not thought to differ from Allah but to be the same spirit worshiped under another name. There is no equivalent for the expression "I believe," since nonbelief is not entertained as a possibility. The expression "I trust" is often heard.

The Dinka attribute any remarkable happening to the direct influence of God and on occasion recognize the fact with an appropriate ritual. They distinguish by the name of Deng (which means rain) a particular aspect of the universal spirit. Deng is at once the beneficent spirit that brings rain and the progenitor and patron saint of the Dinka; his shrines are all over the country (the word for shrine also means cow house). The shrines house iron spears, which are associated with chiefs of the spears, who after their installation are considered to incarnate the tutelary spirit. The chief's special relationship to this spirit empowers him to make rain by intercession; however, he is not held responsible if it does not fall, as that depends on the mercy of God.

Dinka clans also have tutelary spirits that are represented by totemic animals. Clan members respect their totemic animal rather because it shares the same spiritual tutelage than because it is itself sacred. Spirits of ancestors also are prominent in the Dinka as in the Nuer beliefs.

Nyikang, the god of the Shilluk, is both the universal spirit and the founding ancestor of the people. All prayers to God are addressed through Nyikang, but the two are virtually indistinguishable. All Shilluk kings are his descendants and his incarnations. God may be approached through the present king, who is also the chief priest, or through the spirit of any past king. Nevertheless, distinction is made between the human and the sacred aspects of the king's personality; in particular, the decline of the human aspects must not be allowed to affect the sacred ones, and the king used to be ritually killed when his body weakened (see ch. 5). In various parts of the country there are shrines to Nyikang; these are thatched houses much like ordinary ones. In addition to the cult of Nyikang, the Shilluk, like other Nilotes, make sacrifices to their own immediate ancestors and to the founders of lineages.

The Bari, Lotuko, and some other Nilotes combine a belief in a Supreme Being with magical procedures of rainmaking experts. Among the Didinga, ancestor cults seem to be particularly important, but they also respect a universal spirit associated with rain.

The Daju call their god Allah and claim to be Muslims, although their religious observances resemble those of the Shilluk. They maintain similar shrines and elect a "sultan" from a royal clan, who performs religious ceremonies in which sacred stones and trees are important. Some Ingassana, although not themselves Muslims, have adopted Muslim feasts as occasions for their own rituals in which the sun, as a manifestation of God, apparently holds much the same status as does rain among the Dinka and other peoples.

Possessive Spirits

Cults of demons who may take possession of a person appear in a number of traditional societies. The characteristic religious figure of the northern Nuba Mountains in Kordofan is the *kujur*, a man possessed by a tutelary spirit or demon. A demon is thought to be an independent spirit with a will and character of its own; it may be an ancestor, a nature spirit, or an emanation of the Supreme Being. It manifests itself in dreams, from which its character may be deduced. Some demons are inherited by members of certain families and become permanent divinnities; others appear only once or sporadically.

Possession is manifested in hysterical attacks, fits, and trances, in which the *kujur* speaks with the voice of the demon. The similarity between such attacks and lunacy is recognized by the Nuba. The *kujur* trances, however, are often genuine, and in many cases he is as strongly convinced of the fact of possession as are others.

The powers of the *kujur* include exorcism, rainmaking, regulation of agricultural affairs, and the prevention and cure of diseases and other evils. He gives advice at any time, not only when possessed. In some of the Nuba Mountains a *kujur* hierarchy is recognized; the Great Kujur, who inherits the community's most powerful spirit, holds what amounts to the highest political and religious office. His coercive and executive powers are very limited, and his actual influence depends more upon his personal abilities than upon the character of his office.

Among the Hill Nubians, neighbors of the Nuba who have borrowed many aspects of their culture, a divine king of Nilotic type elected from the royal clan still retains his office in some communities but is overshadowed by a Great Kujur. The Nuer and Dinka have produced several "prophets," who like the *kujur* derive special supernatural powers from spirits believed to be residing in them. Historically, these men have inspired concerted military resistance to foreign powers (see ch. 5). The demon in this case is not considered a distinct spirit but an emanation of the Supreme Being, who has many manifestations.

Natural Forces

The ancient religions of the hunting and cultivating peoples who occupied Sudan before the arrival of the present dominant groups (Nilotes, Arabs, and Azande) were fertility cults, which tried to secure favorable terms from the natural environment. Sacrifices were offered to bring rain, to ensure the fertility of cattle and women, and to avert misfortunes. Such cults centered usually on particular stones, trees, and other natural objects with which they frequently associated a snake as an incarnation of the spirit of the place. In some areas this spirit was an independent demon; in others he was regarded as an emanation of the Supreme Being. Hereditary priests, often women, performed the offices and tended the shrine. Emphasis was placed not so much on the sanctity of the shrine, the priest, or the power of the spirit to give or withhold but on the proper performance of rituals that should compel the desired result. The priest attempted on behalf of the supplicants to manipulate the forces of nature by magical means.

Such cults are now predominant in the religious life of some of the peoples of the southwest and the Nuba Mountains. In other areas they have been combined with belief in a universal spirit or, as in Darfur Province, with Islam.

The Bongo, Madi, and some other peoples of western Equatoria Province treat stones in various ways to bring rain. Rainmaking is only attempted at those times of the year when rain may be expected. The rain stones, which are sometimes called "clouds," are inherited but may also be bought; their guardian is bound to observe certain taboos regarding his movements, his diet, or his sexual activity. His person is sacred, and his house is a sanctuary; it is not clear whether this sanctity is derived entirely from the stones or whether the rainmaker is considered also to have a special relationship with a rain spirit or the spirit of a rainmaking ancestor.

In eastern Equatorial Province, among the Toposa and other peoples, fire rituals are more important than rainmaking. The peoples are not fire worshippers, however.

Magic and Witchcraft

Belief in various forms of magic is widespread, and witchcraft and sorcery are used to explain misfortune in personal terms, as the consequence of acts of witches and sorcerers. The "evil eye" is especially feared almost everywhere in Sudan. Any person expressing undue interest in the private concerns of another may be suspected of inflicting deliberate harm by his glance. In the north, blue ornaments are considered effective against the "evil eye", devils, and other dangers and are worn in profusion by children, brides, and bridegrooms. Everywhere, holy men of all kinds provide charms to be worn or displayed about the house.

The Azande and such related neighboring people as the Ndogo think of witchcraft as both a psychological and a psysiological attribute. Witchcraft is held responsible for all illnesses; a large number of plant preparations and other drugs considered to be beneficial are prescribed by witch doctors and the others, but it is more important to discover the source of the witchcraft and to counter it. The case is diagnosed either by a magic oracle, of which there are several varieties, or by a witch doctor, who through taking certain medicines has himself acquired power over witchcraft. Witch doctors do not form a tightly organized professional body, although they often act in groups. They receive fees for their services and may have some local influence.

Witchcraft and the "evil eye," which are regarded as emanations of the personality, are theoretically quite distinct from magic, which is the knowledge and performance of special techniques, but they do have a similar social value. Magic is of two kinds, white and black, distinguished according to the motives of the operator. White magic, intended to procure personal benefits, may be purchased from local practitioners of mysterious arts, including *fuqaha*, witch doctors, rainmakers, and medicine men.

Black magic or sorcery is intended to harm others. In most common techniques an image, piece of wood, or other object is made to represent the victim and then buried or burned. Sometimes objects closely associated with the victim, such as pieces of his hair or clothing, are similarly employed. Black magic is condemned in most areas; in earlier times sorcerers, if identified, were killed.

CHAPTER 7
LIVING CONDITIONS

In the early 1970s living conditions in the large urban centers differed sharply from those prevailing in the countryside. Indicative was the fact that some 90 percent of the country's motor vehicles were registered in the Three Towns (Khartoum, Khartoum North, and Omdurman) and that almost all imported high-priced manufactured goods were retailed there. City dwellers, however, had felt the impact of sharply rising prices. Their incomes, in terms of purchasing power, had declined. Available statistics indicated that in 1969 the average Sudanese had to spend roughly two-thirds of his earnings on food and drink and could afford only few of such items as home furnishings, clothing, tobacco, and transportation.

In rural areas, except for relatively prosperous regions like the Jazirah, money had only limited circulation. People worked mainly as members of a family—not for cash but for food, shelter, protection, and marriage payments, which were theirs by right of kinship. Many subsistence producers sold or bartered part of their produce (see ch. 12). Except for cloth, a few metal goods, salt, and other manufactured items, rural peoples were self-sufficient in essentials and had little surplus cash with which to buy consumer goods; in remote areas, lack of transport severely restricted trade and the import of goods. Periods of temporary plenty, during which people were content with their lot, were often followed by periods of hunger, which they had come to expect and whose effects they tempered by mutual help.

Tenants in the Jazirah constituted perhaps the most fortunate rural group in the country in terms of prosperity and security of livelihood. Regardless of the amount of profit they received from cotton sales, their irrigated grain and fodder crops were assured and theirs to use as they wished. The manner in which they spent their incomes indicated the standard of living considered desirable by farmers elsewhere. As incomes increased, diet began to include more meat, coffee, tea, and sugar. Mainly, however, they used their earnings to entertain and to hire labor (see ch. 13). A housewife bought charcoal instead of collecting dried dung for fuel and used the services of a flour mill rather than grinding the grain herself. She became unwilling to work in the fields, and so did the young men, although the cost of hiring agricultural workers had soared.

The people of the Southern Region suffered from the effects of seventeen years of protracted warfare (see ch. 9; ch. 14). Many of their houses had been destroyed, and cultivated areas had reverted to bush. Famine, disease, and other circumstances arising out of the war had decimated southern ranks and reduced their standard of living to one of the lowest in Africa.

PATTERNS OF LIVING

For the majority of Sudanese, work and leisure are governed by the seasons of the year. Time is described in terms of activities; the early morning and the evening, when different activities succeed each other quickly, are divided into many named periods.

More than 40 percent of the population is on the move at least part of the year. For the pastoralists these moves are dictated by responses to the availability of water and pasture. The Kababish of northern Kordofan Province, for example, who raise no crops at all, settle during the dry season from January to June near permanent wells. After a short southward movement to meet the early rains, they travel north into Northern Province, scattering into smaller groups as the grazing becomes thinner. The movements of the Beja in Kassala Province follow a less well defined pattern because of the wide distribution of permanent wells and springs and the occurrence of two rainy seasons. The majority of Baggara Arabs (cattle nomads) spend the dry season near perennial streams, such as White Nile and the Bahr al Arab rivers, and go north in the rainy period, when they also cultivate sorghum or millet.

Each group has its customary routes and stopping places within its tribal territory and is careful not to interfere with the routes of others. All tend to be most dispersed in the dry season when wells and ponds dry up one after another, the grass becomes yellow, and the cattle have difficulty finding anything to eat in the pastures. They tend to be most concentrated during the height of the wet season, when more numerous ponds and more abundant pastures support large numbers of animals.

The wet season is the time for marriages, tribal meetings, various social events, and the less pleasant tasks of settling disputes and collecting taxes. Economic and social cooperation become much more extensive; some functions, which at other times are characteristic of the family household, are taken over by larger units—food is more widely shared, and cattle are herded in common.

While they are in the central section of the country, nomads live among the sedentary farmers, sharing their water and pastures. This sometimes leads to quarrels but also to the exchange of complementary goods and services. Cereals, mostly millet and sorghum, and vegetables are bartered for tanned hides, clarified butter, dried meat, and the use of animals for transport.

Sometimes nomads and settled farmers conclude herding contracts because of the prevalence of tsetse flies during the rainy season. The farmer entrusts his cattle to a nomad who drives them northward, getting the milk but bringing back the calves that might be born during the migration. Such an arrangement, usually satisfactory to both, can lead to bitter disputes, the farmer suspecting that his animals have been slaughtered or sold, not killed by predatory beasts or disease as the nomad claims.

Nilotes in the southern provinces move only twice each year over relatively short distances from small villages on higher ground to cattle camps near the permanent marshes and streams and back again. They regard the villages as their permanent homes and stay there in the wet season. During this period, which lasts from May to December, they cultivate two crops and keep their cattle on nearby pastures.

In December when the rains cease they take the cattle further afield but are still able to bring them back each evening. During January and February, however, the pasture and water on the higher ground become so scarce that the cattle are moved to pastures on the edges of permanent swamps or near large rivers. The entire population, except for old people and some of the children, move with the cattle and stay with them until the end of the dry-season.

For the settled farmer the rainy season signifies heavy work. This is the period during which he must prepare his fields and sow, tend, and weed his crops, while his reserves dwindle away. His time of ease and plenty occurs at the end of the rainy season after he harvests and fills his granaries.

HOUSING

In recent times lack of adequate housing and the existence of overcrowded urban slums have been partial aspects of the economic and social transformation taking place in the country. Unskilled workers, mostly young men from western agricultural communities, are drawn in increasing numbers to the urban centers. Since they are without an assured income, they often cannot afford proper housing, and so they crowd in with relatives or put up grass or tin-sided shacks in open spaces. In May 1969, a separate Ministry of Housing was established to handle these problems, which had reached critical proportions. In some cities the population had more than doubled during the 1960s.

To accommodate the flood of rural people into the cities and to relieve the pressure on existing housing, inexpensive settlements called *deim* were built outside the cities. Some tenants critized the house plans, however, for not offering a means of maintaining the customary social divisions between male and female members of the household (see ch. 5). The solution offered by the inhabitants—building a dividing wall down the middle—was turned down by the authorities because it could easily lead to subletting and renewed overcrowding. The *deim,* together with new residential areas and the incorporation of outlying villages, accounted for much of the urban growth. In the Three Towns, satellite markets were built to accommodate residents of these new areas. Each of the cities also set aside areas for use by light industry.

Urban residential houses usually consist of three flat-roofed living rooms and a courtyard enclosed by a high wall. One door leads into the street, and the few windows are small and shuttered. The walls are of plastered mud, and the roof is made of mud and matting placed on wooden beams. Commonly an interior dividing wall separates the women's area from that in which the host receives male guests. Upper class households, however, particularly in Khartoum, often follow European models in architecture and furniture.

In many rural areas, households lack the permanence conferred by continuous residence and a major investment in house and land; houses last only a few years, land is plentiful, and people move either seasonally or as circumstances dictate to join any of several households on which they have some financial or kinship claim. Building materials sometimes include stone but more often are grass and sticks with thorn bushes for fencing. Types of rural houses vary from region to region.

A typical home along the Nile River in rural areas of Khartoum and Northern provinces consists of several single-room, mud-brick, flat-roofed structures, of which one or two are reserved for men and others for women. The structures are not physically connected but stand within a courtyard surrounded by a mud wall, usually built in the shape of a quadrangle. Within this wall, smaller courtyards are often created by the construction of mud walls or woven grass screens. Like the rooms, these courts are functionally divided on the basis of sex. When the family grows, the new court areas are added onto the old family courtyard. Homes are usually set out in long rows along the banks, the front door opening toward the river. Nubians frequently decorate their homes with elaborate designs.

South and southwest of Khartoum patterns change. Villages are no longer strung out in long rows but are compact agglomerations, often grouped around a mosque or an area reserved for prayers. In moderately sized settlements of about 2,000 people, at least one shop supplies such necessities as sugar, coffee, beans, flashlight batteries, spices, tobacco, oil, and kerosene. In large villages of the Jazirah white flags identify beer houses.

Houses are usually cylindrical, with cone-shaped thached roofs; the walls made of either mud or thatch. In the Nuba Mountains such houses are set on a foundation of stone, with small, round, or keyhole-shaped doorways. Floors are often tessellated with broken pieces of pottery carefully arranged in patterns. In very poor areas, as in the southern part of Blue Nile Province, houses are likely to be crudely constructed, often in a simple beehive shape.

The tents of nomads are light, simple structures made of local, easily replaceable materials. Usually they consist of a hemispherical framework of slender poles over which mats are laid and roped into position. The mats are of camel hair, strips of bark, or skins. The dwellings can be dismantled and packed within an hour and reerected in about two. They are always set in a circle with the cattle on the inside. A nomad camp can be moved twenty miles a day.

Household possessions are limited to what can easily be transported on the backs of a few animals. The principal item is the wife's traveling equipage, a decorated frame that is mounted on a bull or camel to carry the women and their household goods.

After a tent is set up, the first thing Homr (Baggara Arab) nomads put inside opposite the entrance is the bed, consisting of a wooden frame crisscrossed with split cane or rope and covered with cowhide and mats. Next to it a large tripod supports the possessions of men and women. Outside the door, forked sticks are stuck into the ground to hold up calabashes and cooking pots. When they stay longer at one site, the Homr build a square grass structure to use as a shelter and kitchen.

Some cultivators of the southern area live in substantial dwellings made of thatch over wooden frames, with narrow doorways to prevent sudden attack. Primarily the responsibility of men, their construction is often a community effort for which the householder supplies food and drink.

Within a compound each adult woman has her own house, shared also by her young children. Besides her house she has one or more granaries, good-sized structures raised on stilts, in which she keeps the produce of her own plots. The husband has a separate granary. Skins are used to sleep on and to store things; gourds and clay pots serve for cooking. Iron utensils are rare except where a modern market economy has developed.

A typical Dinka homestead consists of two or three circular huts of wattle and daub, with conical thatched roofs. The fire over which a woman prepares the food is protected from the wind by a low mud screen and from the sun and rain by a rough shelter made from stakes and millet stalks. She stores her household utensils on top of this shelter out of reach of children and dogs. She uses clay pots for cooking, various gourds for storing and serving food, and skins and reed mats to sleep on. Each homestead also has a wooden mortar in which grain is pounded with a long pestle.

The most important structure of a Nilote homestead is the cow house, constructed of the same material and in the same shape as the other buildings. The dung fire inside provides the focal point for the men, who gather around it whenever they are home. It often also houses the shrine dedicated to the householder's immediate ancestor.

CLOTHING

The common garments worn by men in the arabized regions of the north are baggy trousers under a long robe called *gallabiyyah*. They wear slippers or sandals and cover their heads with a loosely tied turban. Women customarily wear a kind of wraparound called *tawb* that also covers their heads. Urban Muslim women are usually heavily robed in public, but their faces are rarely veiled. In villages and nomadic camps, where women of poorer families have to go to the market and help with the farmwork, they may even go about bare to the waist. Urban men and women with modern education tend to adopt Western dress while working at a salaried job and dress traditionally at home.

Among Arabs and Nubians, especially among the riverine people north of Khartoum, a pattern of large linear scars was traditionally made on both cheeks at an early age. The practice is discouraged by the government and deplored by the younger generation.

The wearing of cotton clothes by southern people—shorts and shirts by men, brightly colored wraps tied above the breast by women—indicates to some extent the acceptance of the social values of outsiders. Many Nilotic men wear a single cloth knotted over one shoulder or go naked altogether. Married women wear a goatskin or sheepskin skirt or bunches of leaves as an indication of their status.

Much attention is given to ornamentation, especially by younger men and women. A variety of iron and other metal ornaments are worn in profusion. On ceremonial occasions people, especially in the southeast, paint elaborate designs on their bodies in colored clay, ashes, and similar materials. Extensive ornamental scarification, raised from the surface of the skin by treating the original incision with ashes, is favored among many ethnic groups.

Men of Nilotic groups devote considerable care to their hairstyle, which is often an indication of their tribal affiliation. The hair is dressed with mud, ashes, and dung and interwoven with animal hair into a mass shaped like a helmet. The Nuer favor an upswept horn pointing forward. Often a special neck rest is used at night so that the coiffure does not get damaged during sleep. Women and older men usually shave their heads. The Beja still wear their characteristic hairstyle, first recorded in Egyptian rock paintings of 2,000 B.C.—a huge crown of fuzzy hair, sometimes stuck through with a pin.

DIET AND NUTRITION

The diet of the average Sudanese is neither ample nor balanced. Isolation and shortage of transport in many areas limit the exchange of foodstuffs. Most regional groups subsist chiefly on local supplies that are limited to a few staple foods. In these circumstances, semistarvation and short periods of famine sometimes occur from catastrophies such as floods or locust invasions. Storage facilities are inadequate, and acute food shortages sometimes mark the end of the dry season, when grain is scarce and cattle, camels, and goats give little milk (see ch. 12).

The food of nomads, derived mainly from their animals and supplemented by grain, is high in protein and fat and low in vitamins, minerals, and carbohydrates. Because nomads are reluctant to slaughter cattle, nearly half of their protein intake is derived from milk and clarified butter.

The diet of Nilotic pastoralists is similar, except that during the early dry season they get nearly all their protein from fish. When swamps and streams are drying up, whole villages turn out to spear or net the fish thrashing around in the mud. Usually fish is consumed fresh, but occasionally it is dried in the sun. Later in the dry season when fish become scarce, milk yields are low, and the grain has not yet ripened, they eat the wild fruits, vegetable roots, and seeds that their children collect and eat all year round but that adults consume only in times of extreme hunger. When families or entire villages exhaust their food supplies before the new harvest, they sometimes move in with relatives in other villages to share their remaining stores.

The diet of settled cultivators, although often more ample, is usually even less balanced than that of pastoralists. Though many keep cattle, goats, sheep, and chickens, the usual diet is sorghum or millet and thus is high in carbohydrates and low in protective proteins. Most people have little surplus grain to trade for animal products. The Azande, unable to raise cattle because of the prevalence of the tsetse fly, live on a variety of cultivated crops and fruits. Their staple foods are sorghum, millet, and—in poor crop seasons—the drought-resistant cassava, a starchy root of low nutritional value. They supplement this diet with groundnuts (peanuts), a variety of other crops, some fish, and various kinds of rodents, termites, and insects (see ch. 12).

In many areas, fresh fruits and vegetables are almost absent from the diet. Dietary deficiencies are more severe because of social customs. Cereals are often not well protected from rodents, so that much is lost. Frequently women are forbidden to eat meat, milk, and eggs during childbearing and lactation. In times of scarcity men customarily are served first; women come next, and children eat whatever is left over. Few people, even among the educated and wealthy, understand the need for a balanced diet.

HEALTH

The high incidence of disease that persisted in the early 1970s was a reflection of difficult ecological conditions, inadequate diets, and insufficient medical care. Also contributing was the large mobile population, which often spread epidemics and escaped medical controls.

Despite these adverse factors, typhus, plague, yellow fever, cholera, and smallpox had been almost eliminated. The average life expectancy, estimated in the mid-1960s to be approximately forty years, represented an increase of more than ten years over that of a decade earlier. The distribution of endemic and epidemic diseases and the severity of malnutrition varied, however, from region to region and from season to season. Mainly, a broad distinction existed between north and south, the death rate being twice as high in the three southern provinces without considering the loss of life caused by the civil war.

Prevalent Diseases

Resistance to disease is generally low, but the incidence of and reaction to disease vary from region to region. Only a few diseases are prevalent throughout Sudan. They are the result of nutritional deficiencies in the average subsistence diet or of generally unsanitary conditions and living habits. Other diseases, because of climatic and geographical conditions or regional dietary deficiencies, are contained within fairly well defined areas (see table 5). Nutritional diseases of the eye, for example, are common throughout the country, but pellagra (skin lesions due to faulty diet) are prevalent only in the north. Similarly, dysentery is widespread, but sleeping sickness is confined to the southwest. Some nonendemic diseases are brought in by immigrant workers or by Muslim pilgrims traveling through the country to Mecca.

In the early 1970s the government considered malaria, tuberculosis, and bilharziasis the major disease problems. Stringent government controls and innoculation had decreased the incidence of some of the more common diseases, especially those that can rapidly reach epidemic proportions. In some areas, disease had been reduced through the application of official programs, such as those for controlling bilharziasis in the Jazirah and sleeping sickness in Zande districts.

The general effect of these diseases, if not fatal, is to sap the strength and alertness of the victims. The debilitating effect varies, however; for example, both the Azande and the Dinka are affected by hookworm, picked up through the foot, but the Dinka generally become much sicker than the Azande.

A major goal of health authorities has been the eradication of bilharziasis, a parasitic ailment that spreads primarily through the passing of human wastes into ponds, irrigation canals, and slow-moving streams. The disease-producing organism, picked up through the skin of the foot, develops in the human liver, reproduces, is passed through the urine into the water, goes through a stage of development in snails, and lives in stagnant water until it finds another human host. Typical symptoms are lassitude, low vitality, and blood in the urine. The permanently irrigated areas greatly favor the disease, but there the government has gradually brought it under control by cleaning and disinfecting canals, by examining migrant workers, and by digging pit latrines.

Malaria is widespread in both the north and south. In fact, almost all of the population are considered potential malaria risks, thus presenting a medical problem of mammoth proportions. With help from the World Health Organization, Sudan embarked in 1963 on a premalaria eradication survey—the first country in the world to do so. Sample surveys showed that malaria infections occurred at considerably higher rates among the mobile element of the population than among settled inhabitants. Only a quarter of the Muslim pilgrims crossing the country's western border at various points were estimated to follow international health regulations. Northern pastoralists, moving through different environmental zones during the year in search of water, encountered different malaria conditions that called for a variety of countermeasures. The southern Nilotes lived in the flood plain of the upper Nile, which harbored a wide range of disease-carrying insects, as did the dense vegetation in most of the rest of the southern region.

In Blue Nile Province not only the irrigation canals but also the temporary thatch shelters often erected by migratory workers represent favorite breeding places for mosquitoes. Officers of a

Table 5. Common Diseases in Sudan, 1972

Disease	Mode of Transmission	Area of Greatest Incidence
Bilharziasis (now called schistosomiasis or snail fever)	Infection acquired from water contaminated with larval forms (cercariae) derived from snails.	Mainly in the north along the Blue Nile and White Nile and in Jazirah, Qadarif, and some parts of Darfur.
Cholera	Ingestion of contaminated water or food.	No major outbreak since 1898.
Diphtheria	Contact with a patient or carrier. Raw milk can serve as a vehicle.	Mainly northern and eastern provinces.
Dysentery		
Amebiasis	Contaminated water.	Prevalent throughout.
Shigellosis	Contaminated food, milk, water; direct contact; spread by flies.	Do.
Filariasis (including loiasis and onchocerciasis)	By bite of mosquito, infected "mangrove fly," or infected black fly.	Nuba Mountains and southern provinces.
Hookworm	Infected larvae on the ground penetrate the bare skin, usually the foot.	Serious in the south, especially Bahr al Ghazal and Equatoria; very moderate in Northern Province.
Kala azar (visceral leishmaniasis)	By bite of infective sandflies.	Kassala and Fung districts, in the southeast, and in Darfur.
Leprosy	Spread (presumably) through close household contact with infectious patients.	Widespread in the south, especially in the southwest.
Malaria	By bite of infective mosquito.	Prevalent throughout.
Meningitis	By direct contact.	Southern half of country, especially Nuba Mountains.
Oriental sore (cutaneous leishmaniasis)	By bite of infective sandfly.	Bahr al Ghazal and Equatoria.
Pneumonia	Direct oral contact.	Prevalent throughout.

Disease	Mode of Transmission	Area of Greatest Incidence
Relapsing fever	By bite of infective louse	Almost disappeared through control measures, but outbreaks occur in Jazirah and along travel routes in Darfur, Kordofan, and Kassala.
Sandfly fever	By bite of infective sandfly	Endemic in widely distributed areas.
Sleeping sickness (trypanosomiasis)	By bite of infective tsetse fly	Limited to southern borders of Equatoria and Bahr al Ghazal.
Smallpox	By close contact with patient	Occasional outbreaks through constant exposure to immigrants along major lines of traffic. Eradication was started in 1962, but according to World Health Organization, Sudan registered five or more cases per 100,000 inhabitants in 1971.
Trachoma	By direct contact with discharges of patient, or materials soiled therewith.	Northern provinces.
Tuberculosis	By contact with infected person	Widespread, predominantly in the north, but increasing in south.
Typhoid and paratyphoid fever	By direct or indirect contact with excreta of patient or carrier.	Prevalent, heaviest in urban areas and main traffic routes.
Venereal disease		
Gonorrhea	Sexual contact	Urban areas, increasing in the south. Prevalent, especially in Darfur and Kordofan.
Syphilis	...do...	South, mainly Bahr al Ghazal and Equatoria.
Yaws (nonvenereal treponematosis)	By direct contact with skin lesions of infected persons.	
Yellow fever	By the bite of an infective mosquito	Endemic in southern half of country, but effectively controlled since last severe epidemic in 1940; rare in urban areas.

pilot malaria eradication project with headquarters at Sannar found that it was difficult to include such shelters in regular cycles of insecticide spraying. When the Sannar project was extended southward toward Ethiopia in the mid-1960s, it was found that the boundary was often crossed by people not under health control.

The Sudanese are found to be highly susceptible to tuberculosis, pneumonia, and other respiratory diseases. The Northern Province has the heaviest incidence of tuberculosis, but the disease is also on the increase in the south, particularly since the outbreak of the war. Inadequate living conditions and diet are chiefly responsible. Control measures are hindered by inadequate facilities for diagnosis and treatment.

The government cooperates with other nations in the control of yellow fever and sleeping sickness by issuing passes and by regulating migration in and through affected areas. Sleeping sickness, which used to be frequent in the south, had been reduced in the 1920s and 1930s by resettling the population in villages along roads, by restricting population movements, and by developing barrier clearings along infested streams and rivers. Since the ending of the Zande Scheme settlement program in the 1950s, however, and especially during the civil war, people have moved away from protected areas back into the bush. In February 1972 the government began a four-year campaign to inoculate children against diptheria, tetanus, and whooping cough.

Modern Medical Services

Sanitation and health services are capable of handling major outbreaks of contagious diseases, but preventive and curative medical facilities are still very modest. In 1969 seventy-seven government hospitals provided 11,504 beds, supplemented by nine private institutions with 201 beds. More than half of these establishments with four-fifths of the beds were in cities. All five specialized hospitals—for tuberculosis, eye disorders, mental illness, maternity care, and radiotherapy—were in Khartoum. Rural areas were served to some degree by seventy-three centers, 605 dispensaries, and 1,161 dressing stations. Some of these were mobile units serving the nomadic population.

In 1969 there were 1,108 doctors in the country (including 206 specialists)—a ratio of one doctor to every 14,500 people. These statistics concealed the fact that doctors, too, were concentrated in the cities. In remote rural areas and particularly in the southern region, people never saw a doctor and only occasionally received visits from a health inspector or medical officer. At best they could consult one of the country's 720 medical assistants if they lived near a health center. After three years of training and three to four years of supervised hospital experience, they were able to diagnose common endemic diseases and to give simple treatments and vaccinations to outpatients. In 1969 there also were 2,444 midwives who had been trained either at the High Nurse-Midwives College in Khartoum, the Midwives School of Omdurman, or one of nine village midwives schools.

Training of doctors is the responsibility of the Faculty of Medicine at the University of Khartoum. Fourteen specialized schools and institutions affiliated with the Ministry of Health provide teaching and training for public health and sanitation officers, medical assistants, hospital administrators, laboratory technicians, nurses, and other medical staff.

The Ministry of Health is responsible for planning and supervising medical services, both preventive and curative. It cooperates with the Ministry of Local Government to administer programs for public health, sanitation, and preventive medicine that are organized by provinces. Some medical services such as local dispensaries are the responsibility of province councils. Dressing stations run by certified male nurses are financed by local government councils. Activities in each of the provinces are supervised by a health officer, who is responsible to the Ministry of Health.

Health problems are aggravated by a general lack of knowledge regarding domestic hygiene. The Ministry of Health takes advantage of radio programs, agricultural shows, gatherings of nomads, and its own network of dispensaries to present simple educational programs on disease prevention, mother and child care, and nutrition. Whenever possible, hospitalized patients are told how to avoid a recurrence of their sicknesses.

The Five-Year Plan of Economic and Social Development, 1970/71–1974/75, made provisions to increase the number of hospitals to 124 with a total capacity of 12.085 beds, but in mid-1971 facilities were not expanding at a sufficient pace because of shortages of funds and personnel. Especially in the southern region, health care was urgently needed. Epidemics of bronchitis, pneumonia, and often tuberculosis afflicted the people, who had been cut off from medicine or health care for years. Foreign doctors who examined southern Sudanese refugees estimated that only one southern child in four reached the age of fifteen—double the mortality rate of any other African region.

Folk Medicine

In the absence of sufficient modern medical facilities, people have recourse to traditional methods of diagnosis and treatment.

The Nuer and the Dinka commonly cover their skin with ashes at night to keep off mosquitoes. Potions and ointments made from plants are widely used to treat physical disorders. Medicine men are consulted as specialists in the treatment of specific diseases, accidents, injuries, or burns. Many ailments are attributed to witchcraft or malevolent spirits, requiring magical acts and sacrifices. People wear amulets or charms as a precautionary measure.

Muslims often carry verses of the Koran written on a piece of paper inside a leather satchel; the selling of such amulets provides Koranic teachers and healers with an important source of income. Drinking the water that has been poured over Koranic verses written on a prayer board is also believed to have curative powers.

Sanitation

Many common ailments are attributable to unsanitary conditions. Rivers, canals, stagnant pools, and wells, which serve for laundering, bathing, and washing of food as well as for drinking water, were polluted with human and animal waste; flies bred in open latrines and in waste disposal sites. Disease also results from improper handling of perishable foods and from congested housing in towns. Although the movement of nomadic people to cleaner, unpolluted areas enables them to escape to some extent the unsanitary conditions of settled communities, they are vulnerable to diseases bred in polluted water supplies, particularly open wells and reservoirs.

In 1965 over 85 percent of the households in the Three Towns and Wad Madani had access to water piped into private or communal outlets. People in the rest of the houses, as well as in 25 percent of the houses in Atbarah, Port Sudan, and Al Ubayyid, had to carry water that was often of doubtful quality from far away. In rural areas women and girls often walked several miles once or twice a day carrying clay water pots that were so heavy that two or three people had to help in lifting them onto their heads.

Modern waterborne systems for sewage disposal were not universal in the country's ten largest towns and existed only where water supplies were reliable. The first such system was operative in Khartoum in November 1959. Six years later it was connected to 13.5 percent of the houses in the more expensive residential areas. More than half of the houses in Atbarah had waterborne systems, partly because of the city's importance as a railway center and partly because of its location by the Nile.

Simple pit latrines are common in northern Sudanese towns, or human waste is collected nightly in buckets and buried outside of the towns. Health authorities had sponsored experimental village sanitation projects in Al Jazirah and other-large scale agricultural projects. In most rural communities, however, no disposal service exists; nearby streams, canals, and wells are heavily polluted.

The Environmental Health Service in the Ministry of Health is concerned with enforcement of public legislation regarding waste disposal and food inspection. Controls are ineffectual at times, however, partly because such services are insufficiently financed by provincial, district, and local governmental agencies. The inspection and control of the supply and the sale of milk, meat, and other foods are the responsibility of local health authorities and officials of the national government's Veterinary Department in the Ministry of Animal Production; regular controls have been attempted only in the largest towns. Even in the large cities few facilities exist for the pasteurization of milk.

WELFARE

Government welfare programs are concerned with new housing for low-income city dwellers, health and sanitation services, social security systems for wage earners, municipal development, community planning, and education. Such programs are implemented to a large degree, however, only in large towns. In the Jazirah a social development program represents a government-guided effort to enable tenants to raise standards of living, of health, and of education through their own efforts. The program is financed by a yearly allotment of 2 percent of cotton profits, with fixed minimum and maximum expenditures.

No comprehensive national social security system existed in early 1972. Measures providing old age pensions and compensation for illness or injury applied only to government workers and possibly to workers in a very few private businesses. Government employees also received cost-of-living allowances, which were adjusted yearly. The extension of social security benefits to all wage earners was prevented by the instability of the labor force, poor supervision of migrant labor, the illiteracy of employers and workers, and the low level of wages in relation to living costs.

Alongside these programs, which are being implemented almost exclusively in the towns, older methods of ensuring individual and group welfare continue to operate in both town and rural areas, sometimes equaling and even surpassing government programs in scope and effectiveness. In the traditional system, the welfare agent was the family or larger kinship group, to which the individual was bound by mutual obligation, to which he could turn for protection or aid, and on which he could rely in old age. Mutual obligations were observed not only among kin but also between employer and worker and between landlord and tenant; the highly personal quality of the relationship is still apparent in modern labor-employer situations in which the employer is viewed as patron.

The system becomes less adequate when the family is no longer a self-sufficient economic unit, as in the city or the market economy. Even in the large towns, however, it continues to function in providing protection for relatives who come to seek employment, in providing housing, and, generally, in cushioning family members against the effects of rapid change. In old residential areas of cities like Omdurman, established settlement patterns based on kin or tribal relationships are still strong and tend to regulate conditions that might otherwise contribute to a high crime or delinquency rate.

Within the Muslim community, the concept of the family as a cooperative economic and social unit is legally recognized, and financial obligations and property relationships as defined by religious law are enforceable. Almsgiving is considered the duty of the donor and the privilege of the recipient. It is also an expression of a devout Muslim's broader responsibility to the whole community of the faithful. *Awqaf* (charitable or family foundations or trusts) exist for a variety of secular or religious purposes—to protect children, to provide comfort for strangers, to relieve the poor, or to endow a mosque. The establishment of *awqaf* occurs mainly in large towns where the wealthy and the most orthodox Muslims reside. Until they were expelled in 1963 and 1964, the work of foreign Christian missionaries in the field of welfare, health, and education had been particularly important in the southern region.

CHAPTER 8

EDUCATION AND THE ARTS AND SCIENCES

A broad distinction can be made between artistic expression in the largely arabized groups of the north and in the Nilotic and "Sudanic" cultures of the south (see ch. 5). Beyond this, however, diversity is the keynote of Sudanese cultural expression, a reflection of the existence within the country of a multiplicity of ethnic groups, each with its own unique cultural tradition. The blurring of certain preexisting cultural differences as a result of ethnic migration, the emergence of new and different trends in urban centers, and the disruptive effect of the long period of civil war in the south complicate attempts to assess Sudanese cultural expression.

Viewing the country's fragmented cultural traditions as a major obstacle to national security and development, the government has set forth the goal of a single, national culture in which all people could participate. Calling for the sudanization of all cultural aspects, the government has proposed a synthesis of northern and southern traditions and has implied that controls will be exerted over Western influences that tend to corrupt indigenous traditions. Although interest in this concept has been expressed by certain elements of the educated elite, the scarcity of private funds has given the government a central role in the creation of this synthesis. Openly expressed suspicion by southern leaders that the synthesis would emphasize Arabic culture over southern traditions was a major factor in the protracted civil war in the south (see ch. 9).

Government efforts to mobilize support for the creation of a national Sudanese culture have extended to the educational system. The government considers that providing modern education to young Sudanese ranks next in importance to expanding the country's agricultural potential. Increased educational efforts, higher literacy rates, and training in modern skills were seen as essential steps toward national development.

Administrative revisions and the requirement to teach in Arabic imposed on southern schools in 1957, as well as other reform policies, have been negatively viewed by southern factions as evidence of the government's intention to perpetuate the Arabic

141

influence felt to be existent in the educational system. The elimination of Christian mission education in the south after 1963 while permitting private education to continue in the north has been another issue of contention between the two sections of the country.

Under the agreement between the government and southern rebels that ended the civil war in March 1972, the south was granted some concessions that appeared to affect at least one basic problem in education. The national government retained authority over educational planning and all higher education, but it relaxed the language requirements in the new Southern Region. Arabic will remain the country's official language, but English will be a working language in the south along with the main local languages. The agreement, however, did not define the degree of control over their schools that southerners might expert to exert.

EDUCATION

For the Sudanese, formal education began with the introduction of Islam in the fourteenth century (see ch. 6). With the invading Arabs came the religious teachers known as *fuqaha* (sing., *fiqi*), each of whom soon established his own small Islamic school, or *khalwa*, wherever the Muslim peoples settled. Until the beginning of the twentieth century formal education thus was dominated by the Islamic tradition of religious and classical learning and was confined to settled areas in the north. The curriculum for the *khalwa* was based on rote memorization of the Koran; pupils learned to read and write Arabic incidentally as an aid to learning the Koran. They listened to the recitation of the *fiqi*, wrote the passages on a wooden tablet, and memorized them. Higher education—available only to a small minority—was concerned with Islamic theology and the mastery of classical Arabic.

The development of modern education, which began during the period of condominium rule (1899–1952), was the result of a purely administrative necessity—the need for Sudanese artisans and junior administrators to replace highly paid foreign government workers, mainly Egyptian and Syrian as well as British nationals. The new system of education, which was confined largely to the capital city area, closely adhered to the British model and standards. In the south responsibility for providing educational opportunities fell on the Christian missions, under some government supervision. Educational facilities expanded, particularly after World War II and the upsurge of nationalism.

After independence the government expressed displeasure with the structure of the educational system, and in 1957 the administration of all schools was transferred in principle to the national government. Because of a shortage of teachers, however, many Christian mission schools were allowed to remain in operation with foreign teaching staffs. In 1963 and 1964 these schools in the south ceased to operate when the Christian missionaries were expelled from the country (see ch. 9). A more flexible attitude was taken toward the private schools in the north. Although a number of these—including some operated by Christian groups—had not yet been incorporated into the public system in early 1972, all followed a curriculum provided by the government's Ministry of Education.

Limited school facilities were recognized by the government as a major shortcoming in the country's development. Fully accredited schools were not evenly distributed, and attendance at institutions above the elementary level frequently required that students leave home and reside nearer their schools. Only a small percentage of the student population, however, was able to continue at residential facilities. Estimates indicated that only about 18 percent of all school-age children were enrolled in general education courses during the 1968/69 school year.

The Ministry of Education had planned construction of some new facilities during the late 1960s, but these were in fact limited largely to classrooms added to existing facilities. Some were temporary, and the ministry planned to rent facilities from private sources.

The scarcity of facilities was especially acute in the south as a result of the civil war. Reports in 1965 indicated that all village schools had been destroyed or occupied by northern troops (see ch. 14). Some schools were reportedly reopened in Equatoria Province in 1968, but security considerations in the area were sufficiently uncertain to force the removal of intermediate schools at Juba and Rumbek to Khartoum and Omdurman; the only schools above primary level in the southern half of the country were in Malakal. In early 1972 the Ministry of Education announced plans for the reopening of southern primary schools and the relocation of secondary schools in the south. The degree to which this policy would be affected by the new southern autonomy was not known in early 1972.

Ethnic or regional origins and sex were factors influencing access to education. Social attitudes, administrative policies, and the structure of the educational system provided channels for or were sources of both intentional and unintentional discrimination. The sincerity of government programs designed to reduce regional limitations had received multiple interpretation and represented a major issue in events leading to the civil war.

The disproportionately fewer educational facilities in the southern half of the country represented in southern minds the first barrier to equal educational opportunities for their children. The adoption of Arabic in all southern schools under the sudanization policy that followed nationalization in 1957 was felt to be another imposed limitation. A greater amount of time was spent teaching Arabic in southern schools than in the north, which decreased the time spent learning other material. Southern children thus comprehended less and performed with less ability than their northern counterparts. The government nonetheless regarded the use of a single language essential to standardization.

The inadequacy of educational facilities has been only one of several factors restricting public school attendance and forcing most of those who do attend to drop out after a short time. Although Sudanese Muslims respect learning in its traditional form (the ability to recite passages from the Koran) and a growing number of Sudanese see in education the means to a nonagricultural occupation of high prestige, not all of them desire a modern education for their children. For some, schools represent government interference in their accustomed way of life. In the subsistence economy, children are important and are productive members of the family or community work force; as such, they are indispensable economic assets during much of the year.

In the remote regions, because schools are inaccessible, it is impossible for children of nomadic tribes to attend classes regularly. In some areas elementary education has been accepted only recently, the incentive being the strong belief that schooling will provide an automatic entry into the civil service.

A few years of primary schooling, however, neither ensures this opportunity nor equips the child with a lasting literacy. Oriented towards academic training, primary instruction fails to teach the child skills that are useful in his community. For the vast majority of southern peoples, learning to read and write requires learning a foreign language that they cannot speak when entering school.

Estimates of literacy in the country vary with the statistical base and definition of literacy selected. On the whole, the number of people able to read and write in any language probably does not exceed 10 percent of the population. Government literacy programs begun in 1948 had grown to include about 60,000 people in 1970.

The government was continuing the standard schedule of literacy projects aimed at teaching reading and writing skills to adults and had initiated a special program designed for school leavers. The major development in literacy advancement, however, was experimentation leading to the adoption of functional literacy programs. Aided by agencies of the United Nations, projects were established in the late 1960s linking simple reading skills, manual skills, industrial safety, agricultural instruction, and hygiene. Total investment in the project was scheduled at the equivalent of US$12 million for the first three years. The program was being coordinated by the Ministry of Education in conjunction with other governmental agencies.

Literacy projects as well as classroom instruction were hampered by the lack of textual materials for beginners. Many of the texts in use were old and followed methods no longer current. In the late 1960s the Ministry of Education appealed to the Arab Regional Literacy Organization (ARLO) for help in revising school texts to fit current needs. ARLO sent an adviser to aid the revision and to help cover some of the costs of printing new texts. Additional aid was supplied by the Arab States Fundamental Education Center. Arabic typewriters and duplicating machinery were also included in the aid provided by ARLO.

The education of girls has lagged far behind that of boys. There were very few girls' elementary schools before 1920; girls intermediate schools were first opened in 1938, and secondary schools, in 1949. Girls and boys are educated in separate schools. There has been some discussion of introducing coeducation. Muslim families are little inclined to sanction primary education for their daughters; the number of girls attending intermediate and secondary schools is even smaller, as it is common practice in Muslim areas to confine a girl to the home after she is about eleven years old. Throughout the country, moreover, girls generally marry at a younger age than boys and are thereafter cut off entirely from educational opportunities.

Experiments by the government before World War II to encourage educational facilities for girls in the north resulted in but a trickle of students. Some private schools were more successful, but it was not until after World War II that comparable institutions for girls were developed to match those that had been established for boys. One of the early specialized courses to become popular was nursing and midwifery. The flow of southern girls into the educational system was limited more as a result of economic considerations; a son, rather than a daughter, usually was sent to the distant school. An increasing number of women were entering university programs and filling professional positions, but the absolute and relative role they played in society was still small.

Of the total number of schools in the late 1960s, the proportion available to girls at the elementary, intermediate, and secondary levels were 32 percent, 30 percent, and 21 percent, respectively. There were no technical schools for girls, but commercial programs were available.

In 1969, the latest year for government information on the country's school systems, there were an estimated 4,630 schools throughout the country. Although the data did not separate public from private institutions, about 82 percent of all general education facilities were believed to be in the public system. Exceptions were known to exist, but private institutions were generally expected to follow the same basic structure and procedures established for public schools.

The total number of students in 1969 was estimated at 783,000 —an increase of about 34 percent over the enrollment during the 1964/65 school year. Of these, about 80 percent were enrolled in elementary schools; 16 percent, in intermediate schools; and 4 percent, in secondary schools. There were an estimated 22,800 teachers. These figures did not include complete information on enrollments in the three southern provinces.

The Public School System

In early 1972 public education was supervised by the Ministry of Education located in Khartoum. The ministry was organized into nine subdivisions—one for each of the provinces; an assistant under secretary for education in Juba administered the three southern provinces. Each province had an education office that was responsible for coordinating elementary and secondary education. Training institutions operated by other ministries usually developed their programs in accordance with the government's educational policy.

After the government assumed control of the educational system, former Koranic and mission schools that were unable to meet government standards were labeled as village schools and placed under the direct administration of municipal councils. In 1969 phased integration of these schools under the Ministry of Education commenced. Information concerning the completion of this program was unavailable in early 1972, but total incorporation of the more than 1,000 institutions classed as village schools appeared unlikely.

For nearly fifty years the public educational system, which had been introduced in the mid-1920s, was divided into elementary, intermediate, and secondary levels. Public education was free but not compulsory. The school year began in early July and continued until mid-March or early April.

Common to all schools was a requirement that access to Islamic instruction would be available to all students. Religious instruction was placed under the separate control of the Ministry of Religious Affairs and Religious Trusts. The ministry supervised Islamic instruction in both religious and general educational institutions, operated special Koranic instruction centers, provided grants for local instruction and religious study abroad, and supervised the selection of the theological teaching staff and students for advanced study.

In 1969 the system of public education was reviewed by the government from the standpoint of its ability to satisfy the needs of social and economic development. Under specifications of the Five-Year Plan of Economic and Social Development, 1970/71–1974/75, extensive reorganization of the educational system was scheduled. The elementary, intermediate, and secondary levels were to be restructured into a six-year primary level program, a three-year general education program, and a three-year higher secondary level program. The higher secondary curriculum would offer a choice of academic or vocational and technical fields. Special programs in agriculture, veterinary science, trade and commerce, technical education, and teacher training were to be developed.

The new educational program proposed to make elementary education compulsory, even in nomadic areas. One authority estimated that compulsory education at any level could not be achieved before 1980 or 1985, but the government expected to speed up this process. Recognizing that a major deficiency was posed by the shortage of school buildings, the program proposed to establish new schools at each level in all of the provinces. Included in the program were plans to diversify the curricula to train more students in technical subjects and thus produce more specialists and technicians so badly needed in Sudanese society. Further features of the new program dealt with an expansion of educational facilities for girls.

Information was not available in early 1972 detailing the extent to which the planned reorganization had been implemented in northern areas. It was also not known whether a similar reorganization would be followed in the separate development plan being prepared for the new autonomous Southern Region (see ch. 9; ch. 12).

Elementary Education

Under the system still in operation for school year 1969/70 children entered four-year elementary schools at the age of seven years. Instruction emphasized the Arabic language, arithmetic, religion, and nature studies. There were an estimated 2,050 fully graded elementary schools.

Village schools not offering an entire four-year elementary program were scheduled for upgrading. Official statistical information listed 1,000 of these schools, but the actual number may have been higher. Provisions existed for the completion of an elementary education at the nearest fully graded institution, but the distance between the schools and the students' homes often made it necessary for them to live in the institution's boarding facilities. The low incomes of many families restricted the number of students at qualified institutions.

Intermediate Education

Students able to pass the intermediate entrance examination were entitled to enroll in a four-year intermediate program. In addition to general academic subjects, seperate curricula were instituted for students planning to pursue technical or vocational programs; students following the specialized curricula also received some general educational training. In 1969 there were an estimated 555 intermediate schools.

Instruction on the intermediate level was in Arabic, but English was a compulsory subject. Other courses included mathematics, geography, history, religion, and physical education. Upon completion of the four-year program students took an examination; those who passed received an intermediate school leaving certificate.

Secondary Education

Students possessing an intermediate school leaving certificate could enter secondary school without any additional examination. At the secondary level separate curricula existed for academic, commercial, and teacher training programs. English was the language of instruction, and the maximum age for entrance was sixteen and one-half years. In addition to the study of the English and Arabic languages and literature, the academic curriculum offered geography, history, mathematics, science, religion, physical and military training, and other general courses.

At the end of the six-year program students were given examinations supervised by the Ministry of Education. Those who successfully passed all requirements were granted a Sudan school certificate; the rest received a general certificate of education.

Private Education

In addition to a number of northern private schools that had not yet been incorporated into the public system, there were a few facilities classified as foreign community institutions. Some twenty-two mission schools in the north, such as the Catholic Mission Sisters School and the Anglican Cathedral's Unity High School for Boys, were being allowed to continue under this classification. The Bishop Gwynne College, founded in 1945, existed to train Sudanese clergy, lay workers, and religious teachers under a joint program of the Episcopal Church in Sudan, the Church of Christ in the Upper Nile, and other Evangelical churches.

Ten schools offered programs similar to those in their home country for children of Greek, Indian, and Armenian residents. Egyptian teachers operated nineteen schools for children of Egyptian expatriates; other private schools followed the Egyptian syllabus. The French government sponsored two schools for students at primary and secondary levels.

Higher Education

Higher education was available at several institutions, the largest of which were the University of Khartoum and the Khartoum branch of the University of Cairo. There were also thirteen training institutes offering postsecondary programs that varied in duration from two to six years. Some institutes, such as the university farm at Shambat, were attached to the University of Khartoum; others, such as Khartoum Polytechnic and the Khartoum Nursing College, were independent institutions. The Islamic University re-formed in 1969 as a college for Arabic and Islamic studies.

Higher education was administered separately from general education in 1972 by the Ministry of Higher Education and Scientific Research. Statistics were not available for the total number of Sudanese students enrolled in postsecondary educational programs. During school year 1969/70 there were 100 students attending the Khartoum branch of the University of Cairo, 4,030 at the University of Khartoum, and 2,950 at various other schools.

The origins of the University of Khartoum date to the founding in 1899 of Gordon Memorial College as a primary school. In 1913 secondary education was added to the curricula, including training programs for teaching, engineering, and administrative skills; postsecondary programs were developed in 1938. In 1945 the college became an institution of higher education; full recognition of this status was granted by the University of London in 1947. In 1951 the college was merged with the Kitchener School of Medicine, founded in 1924, to form the University College of Khartoum; university degrees were offered in affiliation with the University of London. At independence the university became a completely seperate institution, granting its own degrees.

149

In the early 1970s the university offered a bachelor of arts degree and also a bachelor of science degree in economics, the social sciences, engineering, and architecture. Master of arts and doctor of philosophy degrees were available in these fields as well. Degrees at all three levels were available in law, in medicine, and in veterinary science.

The Khartoum branch of Cairo University was founded in 1955. Degrees awarded by the local branch were considered less prestigious than those obtained in Cairo, but its evening program allowed students to continue their education while employed. The branch offered courses under three faculties: the arts, commerce, and law. Since 1969 the university also has offered a two-year postgraduate course in statistics. Most staff members were Egyptian.

Teacher Training

Throughout the 1960s there was a shortage of teachers for the expanding educational system, especially at the elementary and intermediate levels. The restructuring of academic levels envisioned for the educational system included similar plans for teacher training facilities. In the late 1960s separate institutions prepared teachers for southern and northern schools, and a similar separation of training programs for boys' and girls' schools also existed.

Teachers for village schools were recruited from students who had successfully completed their intermediate education. Students preparing for fully graded schools were required to enter a two-year training program. Village teachers were eligible for elementary teaching after completing four years of teaching at the village level supplemented by training during holiday periods. This option was to be terminated when all schools had been upgraded to elementary school standards.

The principal educational facility for the training of elementary and intermediate teachers was operated by the Institute of Education at Bakht al Ruda, founded in 1934 in Blue Nile Province. Separate colleges were maintained to train teachers for later work in elementary and intermediate schools. Branches of the institute provided intermediate teacher training at Mabrouka and elementary training programs at Shandi and Dilling, with varying entrance requirements. Since training at these schools was intended as preparation for teaching in northern boys' schools, the language of instruction was Arabic. A similar program at Maridi in Equatoria Province trained teachers for southern schools; the language of instruction was English.

Until the late 1960s separate facilities were maintained to train teachers for girls' schools. Institutes at Wad Madani, Omdurman, and Dilling provided training for teachers in northern girls' schools, and an institute at Yei provided teachers for schools in the south. Since then, the Institute of Education has also been responsible for training and syllabus planning for girls' education.

In the early 1960s the Higher Teacher Training Institute was founded at Omdurman under a joint program of the Sudan government and the United Nations Special Fund, acting through the offices of the United Nations Educational, Scientific and Cultural Organization (UNESCO). Entrance requires a Sudan school cerificate and leads to a four-year university-level program in secondary education and, since affiliation in 1971 with the University of Khartoum, a bachelor of education degree. The program was coeducational and residential. In 1965 the first graduates entered the school system; by 1968 there were approximately 100 graduates, of which about 10 percent were female.

Ministry of Education data revealed that about 20 percent of all elementary school children repeated at the end of a year and about 40 percent of all intermediate students failed their final examinations. During the last half of the 1960s the annual rate of student increase, except at the intermediate level, exceeded that of increases in the teaching staffs. Attempts to counter this imbalance included the increased use of student teachers.

The qualifications of many Sudanese teachers did not meet the standards established for the public education system, but they were being employed to alleviate the general teacher shortage. The scarcity of science teachers was particularly acute. Although the intermediate-level curriculum stipulated the inclusion of laboratory sessions, the lack of facilities and of adequately trained personnel limited the scope of science programs. A special science-teaching project launched during the 1969/70 school year, with the support of the United Nations Children's Fund (UNICEF), was designed to help alleviate certain aspects of the problem.

Efforts were underway in the early 1970s to augment classroom teaching with closed circuit television and educational broadcasting. The production of video tapes was limited, and overcrowded facilities restricted the quantity and quality of programming. Until separate facilities were available, educational television utilized broadcast services at Omdurman. Some programs were brought to individual schools through the use of mobile television vans, and tapes were available by mail through a central distribution office in Khartoum. A series of training aids developed in 1970 featured English-language instruction and science programs stressing physics and biology.

ARTISTIC EXPRESSION AND SOCIETY

With few exceptions artistic expression has been judged traditionally by the Sudanese as the achievement of functions regarded as essential to the survival of particular social groups rather than in terms of their aesthetic merits. Thus, although evening recitations of oral literature provide a certain measure of entertainment —more so in the south than in the north—their fundamental purpose is to establish guides for social action to both children and adults, to facilitate the transmission of myths and sacred beliefs, and to strengthen group cohesion. Particularly in the south, plot development and thematic variations in oral literature are secondary to these purposes. Similarly, plastic art forms are usually limited to utilitarian objects, such as food and water containers, or ritual objects to which decoration has been added. Particularly well crafted objects may be passed on from one generation to the next, but the name of the craftsman is seldom associated with the work.

Artistic expression is usually a group process. Apart from literary recitations, group participation is more common than individual performances, and few participants are remembered by name for their individual talents. The major exceptions are Koranic readers and specialists in oral recitations, who are held in high esteem.

With the exception of songs and chants related to work, group gatherings for song and dance occur mainly in the evenings. In the north dances and songs frequently are associated with the Islamic religious calendar; those in the south are often specifically related to seasonal events, such as crop planting and harvesting. Some are associated with events in the life cycle of group members: birth, puberty, marriage, death. Particularly in the south, celebrations commemorating personal gains are used to repay social debts or to demonstrate social position or   ealth.

Islamic peoples distinguish far moɩ clearly between sacred and secular artistic forms than southern groups. Sacred forms are usually highly regulated, whereas secular forms are usually patterns within which a degree of variation is allowed. Greater attention to the correct performance of particular dances—usually solo performances by young girls—occurs in the north than among southern peoples, where dancing is usually a group act emphasizing the mystique of the entire dance over the intricacy of steps and movements.

The development of particular forms of Sudanese artistic expression has resulted from an interplay of cultural and environmental factors. The restrictions of nomadic life, limiting the movement of bulky or fragile items, have stimulated the development of oral literary traditions. The introduction of Islam and its prohibition on representational art forms have further limited the development of the plastic arts in the north. Similarly, pottery making is little developed among the nomadic peoples, but leather crafts and basketry are technically advanced. The difficulty involved in obtaining wood or other easily carvable, lightweight materials has provided further restriction on northern artistic development.

Observable changes in Sudanese artistic forms and themes—providing a useful index of social change—can be seen most readily in the literary movements that provide the major cultural bridge between traditional society and the modernizing culture developing in urban areas. Poetic themes were one of the first reflections of growing national identity among the educated elite in the twentieth century and aided the call for self-government. The lyrics of popular songs have become the major form of popular culture and the means of social and political protest among both the literate and the illiterate. The willingness of the government to allow the continued existence of this avenue of dissent will determine the direction of literary developments and popular culture in the 1970s.

Independent development of artistic expression is hindered by insufficient private funds, limited local interests, and dependence upon the central government as a major source of support. The country's low literacy rate has restricted the development of the novel and the short story. There are few private galleries providing sales outlets for the visual arts, and most urban dwellers prefer to hang needlework, photographs, and plaques on their walls instead of paintings. Abstract art forms have little appeal.

Government programs supporting the arts are coordinated within the Ministry of Information and Culture. The ministry maintains the National Theater and the Music and Folklore Institute. It provides funds that permit some Sudanese artists to study abroad, and it underwrites the cost of exhibitions of the works of local artists. The performing arts are largely dependent on the government radio and television services for access to a mass audience.

LITERARY TRADITIONS

Oral literary traditions are the most pervasive literary forms to have developed within the country. Oral literary forms—including legendary histories, sacred myths or rituals, folktales, scenes from family life, riddles, and children's stories—vary in length and seriousness. Proverbs passed in conversation are a common literary tradition. Especially among northern groups, oral forms are frequently sung or recited with rhythmic accompaniment.

Oral forms were not always rigidly memorized, and there has been considerable flexibility and variation in their development. Common themes that cross ethnic boundaries exist among many

153

ethnic groups, although the same tale may be told differently from village to village. Some variations developed to serve particuar social needs and were later incorporated into the larger literary tradition of an individual group. Folktales in the northern part of the country have been influenced by Islamic traditions and vary less than those found among southern groups.

Animals play an important role in many folk traditions. Among the Nubians, for example, the cat is a common figure in oral literature.

The spider is common in the tales told by many southern people. The antagonist of a story may possess the characteristics of a spider or even may be a spider with human qualities; frequently the distinction is not made clear. The spider is generally considered to be a cunning creature, and his use of this ability varies from tribe to tribe. Other tales deal with the search for food, hunting, family rivalries, and spirits.

Written literary traditions are limited to arabized groups located in the northern half of the country. They consist largely of religious works, poetry and, to a lesser extent, chronologies. The most commonly known piece of written literature is the Koran. Other religious works include the litanies of religious brotherhoods, various biographies of the Prophet Muhammad, and assorted hymns and prayers. The two major Sudanese secular histories are the *Tabaqaat of Wad Daifallah* (Generations of Wad Daifallah) and the *Fung Chronicle*. Writing is highly revered by the people, and portions of the Koran or other Arabic inscriptions on paper are regarded by some to possess special power.

Written poetry that developed before the twentieth century was largely the work of a small number of religious teachers (*ulema*—see Glossary), whose works generally detailed the feats of the Prophet. The religious orientation of these teachers, however, restricted the development of free verse and universal, secular themes. Their poems were indebted to external, classical traditions, and stylistically they were decorative, repetitive, and filled with allusions. In most of them greater concern was evidenced for the creation of individually brilliant lines than for the development of a unifying concept or topic. As a meaningful form of artistic expression, written poetry reached only a limited number of people.

The development of modern forms of poetry did not occur until early in the twentieth century, after the establishment of secular education. The young poets from Gordon Memorial College, who founded the New Graduates Club in 1919, relied heavily on traditional poetic forms throughout the 1920s; their works lacked subtle imagery. This group contained a number of romantics whose poetry praised the glories of the past; the rest were advocates of religious reform. None played a major role in the administrative crises that occurred after World War I, and as a group they were only a minor force in the political development of the country (see ch. 2).

During the early 1930s poetry passed through a brief naturalistic period; it then passed on to form the romantic school, Al Fajr. The romantic secular themes that developed in the 1930s and the early 1940s displaced but did not eliminate Islamic themes and traditions. Even in the early 1970s religious imagery and thought survived both independently and in secular works.

After World War II the social realist school of poetry came to the foreground. Picking up earlier calls for national identification and independence, the themes of this school became increasingly socialist in tone, attacking imperialism, capitalism, and the exploitation of the masses. Many of these poems were set to music. Throughout the 1950s and early 1960s themes of poetry became increasingly focused on social, political, and racial injustice; much of the poetry of the realist school was anti-Western and anti-American. By the late 1960s, however, this hostility had ebbed. Since then Sudanese poetry has placed increased emphasis on the problems faced by an individual in an increasingly urbanized, industrialized, and secularized society. Disruption caused by the protracted war in the south was a prevalent theme.

By the 1950s sufficient interest had developed to support sporadic presentations of folk dramas and adaptations of Western plays in facilities provided by the Sudanese Broadcast Service in Omdurman. In 1959 permanent facilities were provided for the newly formed, government-supported National Theater, and tours of foreign performers were augmenting local productions. In the early 1970s the Sudanese theater was still in the early stages of development, but an experimental school was organized in conjunction with the theater arts department at the University of Khartoum. Based on Western allegorical models and short novels by Sudanese writers, a number of plays attempted to combine modern and traditional themes and symbols, employing the stream-of-consciousness style and colloquial Arabic expressions. Some plays were written for mass audiences, and others were for more educated audiences. Original works and adaptations by Abdal Rahman Shibil predominated.

MUSIC AND DANCE

Music has come to replace poetry as the most popular form

of cultural expression. Instrumental music seldom is performed independently and usually serves as an accompaniment to songs, hyms, folktales, or dances. Koranic music in the north is regulated by religious prescriptions. Northern secular music reflects the same rigidity. All northern music is restricted by the use of a five-note scale; southern musical expression is more fluid and varied.

Except for funeral music most songs are designed to celebrate occasions of joy or to pass a period of time in a pleasant atmosphere. Even when a gloomy thought is expressed, it frequently is obscured by a buoyant musical style that seems to disregard the lyrics. Sometimes songs have a topical content, referring to marital problems or moral issues. Southern groups such as the Dinka sing songs about animals or people who possess characteristics associated with a particular animal. Both the Bari and the Azande have rich vocal traditions.

Traditional musical instruments include both gong and membrane drums, simple lute-like stringed instruments, and occasionally simple reeds. Among certain groups special drums and simple trumpets producing a shrill sound are used in various rituals. The Azande and other people of the southwest make and play small harps. Traditional choruses accompany themselves with triangles, tambourines, and castanets. More recently these groups have added drums and synchronized clapping to their musical renditions.

Dance forms between north and south diverge. Solo dances are performed by young girls in northern Sudan, but group dances predominate in the south. Two of the more common forms are the circle dance of the Baggara Arabs and a broad grouping of Nilotic dances composed of stiff-legged jumps that are repeated to the point of exhaustion but executed with little thought to rhythm. Ingenuous and dramatic mimes are sometimes performed, but in general most dances are not complex. Muslim brotherhoods often perform dances designed to induce a trance-like state.

Modern Sudanese music represents an adaptation rather than a rejection of traditional music. Musical sound has been changed by modifications of traditional instruments, including the replacement of gut strings with wire strings and the addition of metal parts to drums. New instruments, such as the violin, guitar, saxophone, and brass trumpet, have resulted in a fuller tone. Traditional rhythms have been influenced by Western classical and jazz forms and by African Highlife styles, but this has produced slower rhythms rather than a modification of form. The traditional scale and tonal intervals still dominate.

The major transformation of Sudanese music has been the changes in lyrics, the refinement of which reflects Egyptian influences. Nationalistic and social protest issues have replaced ethnic topics in songs, and there is increasing use of allusion and words formed by imitating the natural sound associated with the object or action involved. The popularity of love songs and the use of sexual allusion have even affected the traditional wedding ritual. These changes seem to have increased most rapidly after the introduction of modern communication media, particularly television.

THE VISUAL ARTS

Although numerous examples of prehistoric rock paintings are found throughout the northern part of the country, the visual arts did not develop except as an adjunct to architecture. The wall painting used to decorate ancient Egyptian and early Christian structures were not the products of indigenous peoples but were the contributions of external cultures. Even the geometric designs and simple figures painted by the Azande and other ethnic groups on the mud walls of their homes have ritual rather than aesthetic functions.

The indigenous development of sculptural form was largely restricted to early peoples of the southwest, who produced small wooden carvings representing human and animal forms. The few examples that remain are less than twelve inches high. Their use varied, but most were ritual objects and were not valued for their aesthetic merits. The Bongo carved ancestor figures that served as tops for the stakes set around the grave of an important hunter. In the case of the death of a twin, some groups carve ' an effigy to be cared for by the survivor. The Bari made what are ›- lieved to be imitations of Bongo figures to be worn as amulets a for use in ritual observances.

Since World War II interest in the visual arts developed in the West has increased, and a small school of artists has formed in Khartoum; their works follow Western techniques and traditions. Most have been trained at the School of Fine and Applied Arts at the Khartoum Technical Institute. In the early 1960s their works seldom related to the African experience, and they had gained little international recognition. By the early 1970s a fuller exploitation of indigenous cultural themes and artistic forms in their compositions had increased the vitality of the school and had given it a limited but growing role in contemporary cultural expression.

CRAFTS

Archaeological excavations have revealed former cultures in the Sudan area that possessed skillfully produced pottery of highly imaginative design. Except among groups in Darfur and Kordofan provinces, the largely utilitarian pottery produced in modern times does not reflect such traditions. Pottery making is mainly a southern craft and is produced among most ethnic groups by women. It is seldom embellished with more than a few linear incisions.

Basket making is found throughout the country but has been most technically perfected in northern areas. The Beja make baskets of so fine a weave that they can hold milk without leaking. Colored patterns are commonly produced by dying fibers before they are plaited. Baskets are used most commonly as food containers. Leather work is found in the north, but wooden utensils are carved only by a few groups in the south.

The knowledge of metalwork flourished during the Meroitic period between the third and second centuries B.C. but has since declined. Iron smelting is still the common skill of many groups for the production of hoes, spearheads, and ornaments. Among some groups it has become a lost art or is restricted to certain individuals; among other peoples it may be considered a task formerly relegated to slaves or regarded as a sacred religious skill. In the north the manufacture of gold and silver jewelry not only provides a decorative item of apparel for the owner but also offers him a means of saving his wealth.

Many handcrafted items are associated with a particular festival or religious holiday. Small dolls representing characters from folklore and miniature mosques are manufactured of sugar, decorated with brightly colored papers, and sold during the celebrations connected with the Prophet's birthday throughout the northern area.

The manufacture of traditional handcrafted items has been disrupted by changes in the country's economic and social structure. Certain objects have lost their former sacred meanings, and there is less time to produce time-consuming secular items. Many traditional items thus have been displaced by the introduction of new methods and products. Earlier elaborate needlework, for example, has given way to simpler forms of handmade clothing, and shoes are being replaced by readymade items that are produced locally or imported. Pottery and baskets are being replaced by tin and plastic items. Some crafts, however, have been improved through the introduction of new techniques. Traditional fabrics may have lost their former texture, but they have become more competitive as a result of new weaving techniques. Moreover, new crafts aimed at commercial outlets have emerged. Urban centers abound with plaques on which reproductions of historic artifacts have been mounted; some traditional peoples are manufacturing wooden bed legs for the export market.

ARCHITECTURE

Monuments to the civilizations of the Egyptian empires and of the later Egyptian-influenced Cushitic, Meroitic, and Nubian kingdoms survive in the innumerable ruins of temples, palaces, forts, and burial sites found in the north (see ch. 2). Before 1960 few of these sites had been thoroughly examined; many remained uncharted, and the development of archaeology was still in its early stages. Existing research was largely the work of foreign teams operating under the auspices of the Department of Antiquities of the Sudanese Ministry of Education. The department also maintained museum facilities, supervised the protection of excavated sites, and published a multilingual journal, entitled *Kush*, on archaeological developments in the country.

The earliest ruins of Egyptian origin found in Sudan are forts built along the Nile and on islands between the second and third cataracts of the river. The best examples were built at Semna in about 1860 B.C. At the end of the Eighteenth Egyptian Dynasty (1379-62 B.C.) the religious reformer King Ikhnaton founded a new monotheistic religious order whose influence extended into Nubia. The temple to Aton at Sesebi is the only remaining temple of this order, and the temple at Sulb, said to have ranked with the magnificence of the Luxor temple in Egypt, contains the only relief carvings from the Ikhnaton period. A great temple to Amon—the god worshiped before and after the rise of Atonism under Ikhnaton —was built about 715 B.C. by Piankhi, the Cushite ruler whose control extended into Egypt. Of particular note are the four colossal figures carved by Piankhi's successor, Taharqa, at a temple site at Jabal Barkal. These date back to the fifteenth century B.C. and the pyramids and temple complexes that were built at Napata and Mero by the kings and queens of the Meroitic period (see ch. 2).

Threatened submersion of northern historic sites by the backwaters of Egypt's Aswan High Dam stimulated archaeological research during the 1960s. The survey, excavation, and preservation of valuable ruins in Egypt and Sudan became the subject of an international appeal sponsored and coordinated by UNESCO. During the first phase of the operation, site surveys indicated the existence of a larger number of ruins that previously had not been charted. Teams of specialists from foreign universities in cooperation with local officials carried out an exhausting task of excavating, measuring, drawing, and photographing the sites. Several ruins were lifted from their locations and scheduled for reconstruction on higher ground or at a special center located in Khartoum. As a result, all the significant ruins were saved, and the new data recovered from site excavations led to reappraisals and the setting back of the date when Egyptian penetration into the Sudan area was believed to have occurred.

As Egyptian influence declined, the architectural achievements of succeeding Sudanese kingdoms degenerated. Building size decreased, and bricks of mud replaced stone as a building material. Between 500 A.D. and 1300 A.D. Nubian architecture developed as an adjunct of Egyptian styles. The only remaining examples are ruins of Christian churches that fell into disuse after the spread of Islam in the fifteenth century (see ch. 6). Construction of these churches followed a basic basilica-and-dome pattern with granite support columns. Excavations during the 1960s revealed a greater number of these structures than were known to exist, and more than a hundred sections of restorable frescoes were removed for restoration and further study.

Although few structures have survived from the Nubian period, buildings of traditional Nubian design built during the nineteenth and twentieth centuries abound in urban centers of the north. The mud brick walls are covered with plaster and then are whitewashed. Few buildings are more than two stories high; most have one main floor with a second-floor room sometimes reached by an exterior stairway. Existing windows are usually small, and modest courtyards are common protective devices. The corners of buildings often are surmounted by miniature towers. In more recent times plates and ceramic plaques have been inserted over doorways, and the homes of pilgrims who have visited Mecca have been decorated with green panels or inscriptions from the Koran. The local mosque is the most impressive structure in most traditional urban centers.

During the period of British rule (1889–1952) two- and three-storied structures combining the least exciting elements of British and Middle Eastern architecture were erected in some of the urban areas. Although these buildings were larger in size and introduced the use of windows and Western decorative features, construction styles continued to be traditional. By the 1960s the introduction of modern concepts of design and construction included the use of concrete, cement blocks, and modular metal units. The greatest architectural advancement had been in commercial, public, and government buildings. During the 1960s functional design with a minimum of decorative detail was emphasized in most building construction.

LIBRARIES AND MUSEUMS

In 1970 there were ten major library facilities in the country. Most were administered by government ministries or agencies, and all but three were in Khartoum. The library of the University of Khartoum contained 90,000 volumes and received 1,550 periodicals

—the largest collection in the country. It also contained special Sudanese and African collections and was a depository for publications of United Nations agencies, such as the Food and Agriculture Organization (FAO), World Health Organization (WHO), International Labor Organization (ILO), and UNESCO. The Khartoum Polytechnic Library, the second largest facility, contained a collection of 10,000 volumes on technical subjects. The Central Records Office maintained an extensive document service covering Sudanese history since 1870.

The collections of the remaining libraries ranged from 2,000 to 9,000 volumes each. The Ministry of Health maintained the Wellcome Chemical Laboratory Library, of which the Sudanese Medical Research Laboratories Library was a branch. The Ministry of Agriculture operated the Research Division Library and the Jazirah Research Station Library; both were in Wad Madani and specialized in agriculture. The Antiquities Service Library also included the Flinders Petri Library. The Geographical Survey Library published annual reports and bulletins in addition to maintaining its modest collection. Library and research facilities were provided in Khartoum by various cultural centers, including the American Cultural Center, the British Council, the French Cultural Center, and the Soviet Cultural Center.

Although Omdurman had a public library with some 17,000 volumes, library facilities for areas outside Khartoum were largely limited to small collections associated with the various schools. Schoolteachers throughout the country were able to obtain books by mail through the Bakht al Ruda Institute of Education Library, the central office of which was located in Khartoum.

The Sudan Museum, founded in 1905 and located in Khartoum, was the major museum facility. Museum publications included various reports, occasional papers, pamphlets, and the annual archaeological publication *Kush*. Also located in Khartoum were the Ethnographic Museum, which was responsible for the collection and preservation of national treasures, and the Sudan Natural History Museum. Other museum facilities included the Marawi Museum and the Sheikan Museum, which housed general antiquities collections recovered from nearby archaeological sites.

SCIENTIFIC AND CULTURAL ORGANIZATIONS

Organized Sudanese research programs were largely dependent on the central government for financial support and administrative control. In 1970 the government established the National Council for Research, which served as a coordinating agency. The council administered all activities of the various research institutes, most of which were attached to the University of Khar-

161

toum. The Arid Zone Research Unit, founded in 1961, conducted scientific investigations into the problems of fauna, flora, and soils in the arid regions of the country. The Hydrobiological Research Unit, founded in 1951, investigated hydrobiological problems of the Nile River with special interest in inland fisheries. The National Building Research Station was founded in 1962 to explore the problems related to the design and construction of buildings. The Sudan Research Unit was established in 1964 to promote and coordinate interdisciplinary research, and it received support from the university.

The two remaining research facilities of note were government-supported projects assisted by the United Nations. The Industrial Research Institute was founded in 1965 to carry out research on industrial planning and to provide consultation services to the Sudanese government. In addition to providing practical and academic training, the Institute of Public Administration, founded in 1960, conducted studies on administrative problems and policies and published manuals and bulletins on administrative operations.

Cultural organizations varied widely in their size and scope of interest. The Association of African Universities, established in 1967, promoted educational exchanges, conferences, and cooperation between African universities. The Philosophical Society of Sudan served as a major forum for academic and intellectual development. Since its establishment in 1946 the society has assumed responsibility for the publication of the *Sudan Notes and Records*, which was first published in 1918 and temporarily suspended in the late 1950s. The society sponsored annual seminars and conferences between European and African administrations, scientists, and intellectuals on archaeology, ethnography, economics, sociology, and natural history. The proceedings of these sessions were available to the public.

Foreign cultural organizations, such as the American Cultural Center, the British Council, the French Cultural Center, and the Soviet Cultural Center, provided language programs and discussions for the public. There were a number of smaller Sudanese associations whose stated purpose was the encouragement of cultural and education achievement of their members. A number of these maintained limited library facilities. Their main function, however, was to provide a social outlet for members; most offered meeting places for informal discussions, snack bars, and organized sports.

SECTION II. POLITICAL

CHAPTER 9

GOVERNMENT AND POLITICAL DYNAMICS

In early 1972 the country was still suffering the effects of repeated changes in government and protracted civil war between
the Arab north and the black African south. For the first time
a strong, progressive executive had taken power in late 1971, and
an agreement ending the war had been put into effect in March
1972. The political dominance of the traditional forces had been
ended, the powerful communist movement was crushed, and regional hatreds were lessened. In April 1972 these major developments were too recent to permit a determination of the direction in which the country would move, the form of government
it would have, or the permanence of the reform and peace brought
about by the Arab socialist military officers who were its leaders.

The same political parties and forces around which the country's politics had revolved since independence in 1956 had continued to control the government until May 1969, when Arab
socialist military officers staged a successful coup (see ch. 2).
The new government's first move was to officially quash the
political parties, and by 1972 the parties themselves had vanished
from the scene. Nevertheless, the country's sociopolitical divisions
remained largely unchanged. Primary ties continued to be the
same as those in terms of which former political parties had
formed: to family, ethnic groups, and individual religious leaders
rather than to the nation. They were still best understood by
examining the dynamics of the former parties.

Major changes were underway. The government's social and
economic policies had as their aim a total reorganization of much
of the traditional socioeconomic structure of the country. By early 1972, however, these policies had not yet been implemented in
a degree sufficient to have made major lasting impressions.

The government established by the May 1969 coup vested all
legislative and executive power, as well as supervision of the
judiciary, in the ten-man Revolutionary Command Council (RCC).
All but one of the members of the RCC were military officers.

In order to broaden the narrow base of support for its modernist and socialist aims, the RCC initially felt it necessary to depend upon all radical elements in the country, including the 5,000 to 10,000 members of the Sudan Communist Party (SCP) in the late 1960s. The largest and best organized communist party in the Arab and African worlds, the SCP continued to function even though legally disolved. Despite early harmony the basic hostility of the orthodox communist elements that dominated the SCP quickly came into conflict with the Arab nationalist attitudes of the majority of the RCC leadership. The apparent triumph of the Arab Socialists and the idea of the formation of a single, monolithic party—the Sudan Socialist Union (SSU)—had gained the support of many modernists, even those who earlier had given the SCP much of its support. By April 1970 the most significant conservative political elements in the country had been brought under control. Hostility between the RCC and the SCP then came to dominate the country's political development until the communist party was destroyed after its short-lived success in a July 1971 coup attempt.

The corporate leadership of the RCC was succeeded by a single executive in the person of the RCC's leader, General Jaafar al Numayri, who became the country's first president in October 1971. Both the RCC and Numayri sought to create a government that would build a nation on the model outlined by the late Egyptian president Gamal Abdul Nasser, whom they much admired. At the same time they sought to maintain independence from the more powerful nation to the north.

Although largely ignored by the outside world, the Sudanese civil war was one of the six or seven heaviest conflicts of the twentieth century in terms of estimated casualties. The estimated 500,000 dead represented an eighth of the Southern Region's population. The war had lasted seventeen years, consuming a large portion of the national budget and burdening the country with large long-term foreign debts (see ch. 12).

The rebellion pitted the 4 million black African, non-Muslim southerners against the 12 million arabized Muslim northerners. National military forces were engaged by a much smaller rebel force—the Anya Nya—which was fragmented and ill equipped but highly effective as a guerrilla force (see ch. 14).

Thus it was a major achievement for President Numayri to conclude an agreement at Addis Ababa, Ethiopia, in late February 1972 with the southern rebel leadership. The agreement resulted in a cease-fire. In mid-1972 it was too early to tell whether the agreement would bring lasting peace and unity to the country. The rebels seemed satisfied with the terms of the settlement, which answered major southern grievances by granting considerable autonomy to the Southern Region without splitting the country into two separate states.

THE GOVERNMENTAL SYSTEM

The governmental system has been in a nearly constant state of flux since independence; its form has been influenced most by two systems—those of Great Britain and Egypt. Since 1953— three years before independence—when Sudan was granted self-governing authority, disagreement over the form and substance of a permanent constitution remained one of the country's major political problems. In early 1972, despite nearly twenty years of frequent and often continuous debate on the subject, a formal constitution had yet to be approved. Lack of a constitution was both a symbol of the divisions that existed within the country and a strong irritant that made them more difficult to bridge.

Information on the structure of government was sketchy and subject to change at short notice as President Numayri continued to refine his approach to national administration. Major changes in both the national and the regional structure of government would be required to comply with the terms of the February 1972 agreement ending the southern rebellion.

Executive and Legislative Authority

The government in existence in early 1972 was drawn from the one brought to power by the army coup of May 25, 1969, but without any of the SCP elements that had given it their support and had played an important part in its early structure. The RCC had functioned as a ten-member executive body. The country had had a multiple executive since 1954 (see ch. 2). Under this system a prime minister had led a cabinet responsible in varying degrees to the multiple executive body and, in the periods of civilian control, to the national assembly. In August 1971 the RCC announced plans to reorganize the government with an elected president as a single executive who would function as the head of government with a cabinet of ministers responsible solely to him. This refinement was put into effect in October 1971.

Plans called for the eventual establishment of an elected national legislative body, but the strong presidential form of government would be retained. The elected assembly was not to be created until after a monolithic political party, the SSU, had been created and had begun to function nationwide. The party's charter would finally delineate the main points of a permanent constitution for the country.

In the interim the outline of basic constitutional law was pro-

165

vided by Republican Decree Number 5 of August 13, 1971. The decree's significant points specified that the SSU would be the only political organization allowed to function; that the socialist system was to characterize the economic system of Sudan; that ethnic and religious discrimination was banned; and that freedom of religious belief and practice was guaranteed.

Only a single candidate for the presidency—the one selected by the SSU—was to be nominated. He was to be confirmed in office by public referendum rather than be elected; his term was to be for six years. He could appoint and dismiss two or more deputies as vice presidents in addition to having a prime minister if he chose. These and the members of the cabinet were to be responsible to him. He was to exercise the executive power of the government, be supreme commander of the armed forces, and supervise the security forces and the civil service.

The decree authorized the creation of a body to be known as the People's Assembly, whose major task was to be the drafting of a permanent constitution. The number of members as well as the regulations for its work and the work of its committees would be decreed by the president; the ministers were to be ex officio members of the assembly. Until it formed, the president was to exercise legislative authority unilaterally. The assembly would automatically dissolve itself once the constitution became law, after approval by a popular referendum. The president, however, could dissolve the body sooner but had to arrange the formation of a new assembly within sixty days.

The final clause of the basic law specified that the RCC and the cabinet were to be automatically dissolved when the first president took office. Under RCC guidance a referendum was held to confirm General Numayri, then chairman of the RCC and prime minister, in the post of president. The announced results gave him nearly 99 percent of the 3.8 million votes cast. He was sworn into office as the country's first president on October 12, 1971.

President Numayri appointed his first cabinet almost immediately; the twenty-seven ministries were organized into six fundamental groups, reflecting a considerable realignment of responsibilities. The first group, classified as sovereignty ministries, included those of defense, foreign affairs, interior, justice, and public service and administrative reform. Services ministries were those of local government, housing and public works, health, communications, and supply. Grouped together as economy ministries were those of planning, treasury, economy and trade, industry and mining, and transport. Grouped separately as agriculture ministries were those of agriculture, cooperatives and rural development, irrigation and electric power, and animal production. Guidance ministries included those of education; information and culture; youth, sports, and social affairs; religious affairs and religious trusts; and higher education and scientific research. Ministries of state included those for presidential affairs, cabinet affairs, and southern affairs. In January 1972 four deputy ministers were promoted to full ministerial level, increasing to thirty-one the total number of cabinet posts; the new additions consisted of a minister adviser to the presidency, a minister adviser to the Ministry of State for Southern Affairs, and two ministers for SSU affairs.

The new president also promulgated three new decree laws on October 14, 1971. Two specified the organization and functions of the ministries; the third established separate consultative councils to advise the president on economic matters, provincial and urban development, and science and technology.

The Legal System and the Judiciary

The administration of justice is regarded traditionally by arabized Sudanese and a number of southern ethnic groups as the most important function of government. In the old order supervision of justice was solely in the hands of the ruler. In the north most cases were actually tried by an Islamic judge (cadi), who was trained in the precepts of the *sharia* (law based on interpretations of the Koran). Crimes against the government, however, were heard and decided by the ruler with the advice of the grand mufti, a canon lawyer who served as his legal adviser.

Although the Muslim influence on Sudanese law remains important in modern times, the long years of British colonial rule left the country with a legal system derived from a variety of sources. The Commercial Code was copied from that of Egypt. Personal law covering matters dealing with such subjects as marriage, divorce, inheritance, adoption, and other family matters is within the purview of Islamic law throughout the Arab-populated areas. Customary law, as modified in varying degrees by the impact of the *sharia* and concepts and changes introduced by the British, governs matters of personal law in the rest of the country.

The major basis of legislation for the *sharia* court system that administers Islamic law is the Sudan Mohammedan Law Courts Organization and Procedures Regulation of 1916. This act, however, did not set up a static system of adherence to ancient traditions. Instead it provided that changes and modifications could

167

be promulgated by regulations set out in notices by the grand cadi, thus allowing for modernization of the system.

The basis for the application of customary law is the Chief's Courts Ordinance of 1931 in the Southern Region and the Native Courts Ordinance of 1932 in the north. The jurisdiction of the lowest levels of courts is restricted to matters under local law and custom, as long as they do not conflict with codified law, binding legal precedents, or British concepts of justice and equity. In 1966 the nearly 1,000 local courts heard between 55 and 75 percent of all Sudanese court cases. In addition to personal law matters, these courts also often hear cases involving conflicts of rights between local clans and tribes, such as disputed ownership of unrecorded land and grazing rights.

Laymen, generally a chief or a group of elders, preside over local courts. Cases that they are unable to settle or that are appealed go to the civil division of the regular courts. In these circumstances and in other appropriate cases, the civil courts are empowered to apply customary law.

The origin of the general Sudanese civil law includes both legislation and judicial precedents. These were published in an eleven-volume directory, *Laws of the Sudan*, published from 1954 to 1965. Changes and additions since those dates were provided by items in the *Republic of Sudan Gazette*. The volumes do not constitute a code, however, and precedents not reported in them are still utilizable in court.

In order to be accorded major weight, precedents must be drawn from Sudanese law, but particularly during the colonial era much weight had been given to British precedent. The generally used dictum was that the courts were guided but not bound by British legal precedents. Egyptian law and precedent also have considerable weight, and in the late 1960s pressure was being exerted to replace British influences and codes with ones of Egyptian origin.

The primary legal influence remained British, however, in part because most of the lawyers and judges were British trained. The Penal Code, published in 1925, was modeled on the Penal Code of British colonial India. As all early senior judges had been British, early precedents were drawn from British practice if not directly from British precedents.

Those pressing for the remodeling of the Sudanese legal system along Egyptian lines were generally impressed by the merger between the civil and *sharia* systems that had been carried out in Egypt. Such a merger would require a considerable increase in legal education, however, since all judges had to be capable in both systems. In addition, it would result in increasing the major conflict at the practical level between *sharia* and customary practice, since both must be given weight and often conflict radically. The civil courts hearing cases under the *sharia* are required to refer questions of law to the *sharia* courts, but in practice the Muslim judges rarely do so.

At the pinnacle of the judicial system is the chief justice, who serves in a number of capacities: presiding judge of the Court of Appeal and of the High Court of Justice, head of the civil court system, and administrative head of the *sharia* court system.

Below this level the civil and *sharia* systems run in separate but parallel lines. The civil system hears both civil and criminal cases; *sharia* courts are restricted to Islamic personal law and related matters. The highest echelon in the civil system consists of a pair of courts with common membership and national jurisdiction but differing functions. The Court of Appeal serves as the court of final appeal in all cases. The related High Court of Justice serves as the court of first instance in major criminal matters. The Court of Appeal may also hear cases in their entirety, but only in instances when it feels that a case first heard by a lower court has violated the norms of justice. Until the 1969 revolution this highest echelon of the court system also exercised the power of judicial review over acts of the national assembly.

At the next descending level are nine provincial courts that supervise the activities of the district and local courts. In addition to the chiefs' and native courts, the lowest level includes town benches in urban centers, presided over by trained magistrates. In cases of crimes not important enough to be referred to the High Court of Justice, the provincial courts have primary jurisdiction. In such cases the bench is composed of a judge of the High Court of Justice or the provincial court, assisted by two other judges. The conduct of criminal cases and their allocation to differing court levels is governed by the Code of Criminal Procedure, designed by the British colonial government.

The *sharia* system also has two courts at the top level, a court of appeal and a high court; both are presided over by the grand cadi assisted by the grand mufti. Cadi courts function at the district level.

The president, and before him the RCC, in consultation with the members of the appropriate court of appeal had the power to appoint the senior members of the judiciary in both the civil and the *sharia* systems. All lower court judges were appointed by the members of the appropriate high court.

After the RCC came to power, courts at the lowest level were purged of traditional leaders of ethnic units in order to lessen their power. Other judicial bodies called people's courts were created, initially only at the highest level, to hear cases alleging treason and malfeasance in office. The term *people's court* was later also applied to courts at the local level. They, in turn, were purged of their communist members in late 1971 and early 1972. Local committees of SSU members functioned for this purpose under the directives issued by the chief justice.

Local Administration

Until 1969 each of the six northern provinces had a commissioner, who acted as chairman of the Province Authority, a body of officials representing the various ministries of the central government functioning in a particular province. Each province also had a council composed partly of representatives chosen by local government authorities and partly of members of the Province Authority. As the head of both the centrally appointed and the locally designated officials, the commissioners were responsible to the minister of local government in Khartoum.

Local government evolved under successive central governments into a total of eighty-four local councils; these included forty-one first-stage councils, eighteen second-stage councils, and twenty-five third-stage councils. The primary difference was the degree of local authority; third-stage councils enjoyed only limited powers delegated by central government inspectors, whereas first-stage councils had considerable local autonomy. About twenty of these local government units were local councils in urban centers. Levels of authority, duties, and effectiveness varied greatly from one authority to another. All suffered from lack of adequately trained staff, as most skilled men preferred to seek posts with the national government.

One of the early acts of the Numayri government in 1969 was to announce the outright abolition of the existing local and regional government structures at all levels. A further change in the local and regional systems was required by the agreement in February 1972 aimed at settling the lengthy southern rebellion. This required considerable decentralization and the creation of an entirely new level unit, the autonomous Southern Region. The effect of this action on the provincial system was not yet clear in April 1972. Some of the supposedly abolished structures continued to be utilized, however, pending a total reorganization, which had not yet been accomplished in mid-1972. The government's announced objective was to set up the new organs of local government in a structure parallel to that of the SSU. In every village, for example, a village development council was to be created to serve as the basic unit of both party and government.

MAJOR POLITICAL DIVISIONS WITHIN THE NORTH

All political parties except the SCP were officially abolished in 1969. By late 1971 the SCP had also been eliminated, and no vestige of the former parties was observable. Nevertheless, the religious, ethnic, social, and ideological forces that they had represented were still the basis of political alignments and divisions within the northern two-thirds of the country. These forces were still best understood by examining the background of the parties that had been their formal representation for nearly thirty years.

Ansar and Khatmiyyah

The great religious sects, the Ansar and Khatmiyyah, became decisive in political development less because of differing political ideas than because they provided structures whose rivalry made them suitable for use in the creation and sustenance of national political parties. This broadening also had the effect, however, of bringing the rivalry of the two most influential men in Sudan into the political arena.

The Ansar, or Mahdiyyah, constituting about 20 percent of the country's population, were followers of the religious teaching of the Mahdi, who had ruled Sudan in the 1880s and recognized the spiritual leadership of Abd al Rahman al Mahdi. Abd al Rahman's acumen allowed him gradually to amass considerable political and economic power. His political power was applied through an organization similar to the *turuq* (religious orders), which were central in Sudanese religious life (see ch. 6).

The Khatmiyyah, led by Ali al Mirghani, constituted another 20 percent of the population. It was the most important religious group of northeastern Sudan and had been associated with Egyptian influences in Sudan since the early nineteenth century. Throughout the hundred years since the Ansar had first set out to conquer the country, the Mirghani family—as hereditary leaders of the Khatmiyyah—had been the major political and religious opponent of the Ansar (see ch. 2).

During the 1920s and 1930s new leadership had emerged among civil servants and businessmen, particularly in the cities. The first political party, the Graduates' General Conference, was formed in 1936. Beginning in 1942, when the conference sought to increase its numerical strength, membership was extended to the Ansar and the Khatmiyyah. At the same time a split developed over the means of obtaining independence. Two factions formed, the Ansar in one and the Khatmiyyah in the other. They contested the conference leadership in 1943; when the faction including the Khatmiyyah and the more radical members of the

171

urban middle class won, the more conservative faction walked out and formed the first mass political party, the Ummah, or people's party. Shortly thereafter the conference ceased to exist, and the remnant was replaced by a second party, the Ashigga, or blood brothers.

Political Parties in the Colonial Period

The Ummah, led by Abdullah Khalil, vigorously opposed any union with Egypt and believed that independence could come by cooperative negotiations with the British. It was supported by the Ansar and at times by smaller Arab tribal interests.

The Ashigga, later renamed the National Unionist Party (NUP) in 1953, was led by Ismail al Azhari. The party was supported by the more radical secular nationalists who were most antagonistic to the British policy of building up tribal leaders, by some who sincerely desired unity with Egypt, and by others who considered alliance with Egypt the only means of getting rid of the British. The Ashigga-NUP was supported by the Khatmiyyah because of its antipathy for the rival Ummah party's Ansar supporters. At times the Ashigga-NUP cooperated with several other pro-Egyptian factions and leftist groups, including the small, illegal, but effective SCP, in the National Front. Because the Ashigga boycotted elections to the first representative assembly, from 1948 to 1952 the assembly was composed entirely of representatives of the Ummah-led Independence Front.

Before independence Great Britain, under Egyptian pressure, granted Sudan a considerable degree of self-government and set in motion a rapid transition to independence. The popularity of the Egyptian leader General Muhammad Naguib, a Sudanese by birth, and the fear among all non-Ansar that an Ansar victory would lead to the political ascendancy—possibly the kingship—of Abd al Rahman, all contributed to the rising popularity of the NUP. In elections to the new Parliament in 1953 the NUP won an absolute majority of the seats, a feat never again duplicated. Its leader, Azhari, was elected prime minister.

The results appeared to be a mandate for rapid independence and a pro-Egyptian policy. Frictions within the majority party and changes in the Egyptian government undermined this, however. Opinion in Sudan was largely against the goal of complete unity of the Nile valley, but various degrees of association with Egypt were possible. The National Front and the NUP were both divided. The Ummah, backed by the Ansar, with its numerical strength and the support it commanded in nearly every politically important institution, was prepared to go to almost any lengths to prevent any real union with Egypt.

172

Because of a number of factors—particularly the growing indications of Egyptian control attempts as seen in Nasser's dismissal of Naguib and Egyptian intransigence in negotiations over Nile water distribution in 1955—the pro-Egyptian Azhari, with the backing of both Abd al Rahman and Mirghani, reversed NUP's policy toward Egypt, announcing support for complete independence. Conflict over this policy reversal and other differences split Azhari's party. His opponents joined to form a new group, the People's Democratic Party (PDP). These groups—Ummah, NUP, and PDP—plus the Communists and the Muslim Brotherhood formed the political parties of the north throughout the rest of the 1950s and 1960s.

The Ummah

The Ummah was the most united in organization and consistent in policy, because it remained primarily the political voice of the Ansar sect and its leaders; however, it also attracted other traditionalist elements because of its generally conservative policies. The party placed strong emphasis on absolute independence, on economic development in which private foreign and domestic investment should be encouraged, and on the importance of public order. In foreign policy its official position was one of neutrality, but it favored cooperation with Great Britain and the United States and conservative policies in the Arab world.

Largely because of the unique position and the ability of Abd al Rahman, who saw the need to adapt to modern political requirements and who educated the young men of his large family to carry on that work, the Ummah was able to provide educated leaders who could participate in government. The party, however, suffered from its failure to build an organizational structure apart from the Ansar, particularly in urban areas. Its support among the educated came mainly from older and more conservative men; many rural peoples felt empathy with its religious leaders.

The degree to which specifically religious attitudes among the Ansar influenced party policy is obscure, but among the Ansar, as among many Sudanese, there was no separation of political from religious functions, and many favored the creation of an Islamic state. Until his death many of the Ummah also sought to make Abd al Rahman president, thus arousing strong anti-Mahdist emotions among the opposition.

For its political strength, the Ummah relied almost entirely on the Ansar organization among settled farming people and on the adherence of nomad tribes bound by tradition to the Mahdist cause. Members of the Mahdi family traveled extensively dur-

173

ing campaigns, spending most of their time cementing Ansar-Ummah loyalties in the traditional areas of Ansar strength.

The geographic center of Ansar strength was among inhabitants of a central belt stretching from Kusti in Blue Nile Province west to Darfur. The Baggara, the Arab cattle tribes of Kordofan and Darfur, were largely Ansar. Many of the regional leaders of the Ummah were members of the families of the heads of tribal or local administrations. Outside their main territory the Ummah gained support from the ruling families of the Hadendowa and the Bakr from Kassala Province and from the Dunqulah area in Northern Province, from which the original Mahdi came.

The National Unionist Party

Azhari's National Unionist Party (NUP) was pared down to an urban, secular organization by the defection of the Khatmiyyah. It had central offices in Khartoum, regional headquarters in provincial capitals and other large towns, and party workers in the larger northern villages. In domestic affairs the NUP put more stress on rapid, government-directed economic development and on the nationalization of major economic enterprises; to the Ummah in particular this carried the threat of the nationalization of Abd al Rahman's estates and the destruction of Ansar power. The party campaigned extensively against the political power of religious groups, maintaining that they had no proper place in the political life of a modern country. In foreign affairs it favored a defensive alliance with Egypt and neutrality in the cold war, accusing the Ummah of pro-Western leanings.

NUP support came largely from the towns and cities, where probably the majority of professional men, civil servants, and laborers, particularly younger men, backed it. To them the NUP appeared to be the only modern liberal party not bound to old religious ideas or to feudal tribal authority. For many in the cities the choice of political allegiance was between the NUP and the Communists. NUP campaign tactics reflected the difference in its base of support. Although the other large parties relied more on existing ties of loyalty, the NUP made the most use of mass rallies, ward organization in the cities, and efforts to get out the vote.

The party had its greatest strength in Khartoum Province; the NUP was also successful in northern Blue Nile Province, where the Jazirah Scheme brought changes unknown to most of the rural areas. The only large tribe supporting the NUP was the Kababish, historically anti-Mahdist but not allied with the Khatmiyyah.

174

The People's Democratic Party (PDP), despite its Khatmiyyah backing, never achieved cohesion as a political party. Although led by men close to Mirghani, the party was composed of at least two groups, which had been unable to work with Azhari. One section appeared able to cooperate politically with some Ummah leaders and to share their moderate approach to policy questions and their emphasis on the primary importance of stability. It could not, however, support the Ummah because of ethnic and religious factors.

The PDP was vaguely committed to preserving the unitary state, to making Islam the official religion, and to pursuing a policy of neutrality in international affairs, but its president, Ali Abd al Rahman, was known for his close ties with Egypt, his interest in forcefully propagating Islam in the south, and his foreign policy statements critical of the West.

The PDP like the Ummah, relied primarily on religious allegiance—on the Khatmiyyah members of Kassala and Northern provinces. The party's most certain constituencies were in the Beja territory of Kassala (Beni Amir, Amarar, and Bisharin tribes), in the Shukriyyah constituencies of Kassala and the adjacent area of Blue Nile Province, and in Northern Province. The Khatmiyyah, however, was not as well organized a political force as the Ansar, had no leader of the stature of Khalil or Azhari, and suffered also from its position as a religiously oriented party in the Blue Nile towns in which the NUP had made the strongest inroads. The PDP and NUP amalgamated again, as the Democratic Unionist Party (DUP), in 1967 and 1968.

Muslim Brotherhood

The third major politicoreligious body, the Muslim Brotherhood, was totally unlike the Ansar or Khatmiyyah in every way except Muslim religious fervor. The movement spread to Sudan from Egypt in the early 1950s but did not emerge openly until 1964. Like the SCP, it consisted of a small, intellectually elite pressure group. It dominated the larger Islamic Charter Front (ICF), a political party that included many supporters of the Muslim Brotherhood objectives. The most important of their objectives was the creation of a modern Islamic state, which would borrow from non-Muslim cultures only those things that were consistent with Islamic dogmas. As a part of this demand the brotherhood and the ICF called for recognition of Islam as a body of doctrine capable of serving as the basis for a modern state and for the utilization of *sharia* as the sole legal system of the country. The ICF opposed

175

the influence of the government of the United Arab Republic (UAR) because of its forceful purging of the Muslim Brotherhood in the UAR. With regard to the Sudanese southern problem, the ICF had as one of its major tenets the preaching of Islam throughout Africa. It was, therefore, as strongly opposed as the conservative Ummah party to any lessening of ties to the south.

The brotherhood opposed all forms of socialism, viewing Marxism as an atheist doctrine and Arab socialism as a violation of the laws of Islam, particularly those regarding freedom of the individual. This last strongly held tenet brought the brotherhood into direct conflict with the socialist forces that came to power in 1969.

The brotherhood was distasteful to the majority of Muslims because of its demands for strict adherence to religious tenets and the challenge it represented to the leaders of the traditionalist sects. Its primary appeal was among the younger educated Muslims in the universities and the armed forces—the same groups among whom were found the converts to communism and less doctrinaire forms of radical socialism.

The Sudan Communist Party

The leaders of the Sudan Communist Party (SCP)—illegal under both the colonial and postindependence governments until 1964—were largely drawn from the educated middle class. The party's rank and file were generally drawn from the same class or from urban workers, particularly unskilled, detribalized workers. It also drew some strength from the organized agricultural workers of the Jazirah Scheme.

Communism and the party have remained repugnant to the leaders of the Islamic factions and their followers who constitute the vast majority of the northern population. Communist appeal in the south was limited to a small segment within the educated minority.

Sudanese communist advances were made possible by the organization, training, and experience that provided a professional leadership in the trade union movement and by a simplified philosophy that appealed to students and dissatisfied urban professionals. In this philosophy most of the country's ills were attributed to the single cause of Western imperialism; communism in contrast was associated with anti-imperialism, and the communist countries had appeal as models for rapid economic development. The party also gained support from 1958 to 1964 because it actively campaigned for greater democracy in government; as the only political organization that strongly and consistently opposed the government of General Ibrahim Abboud after the coup d' etat, the party gained its greatest strength immediately after his overthrow.

Organized communist activity began in 1946 with the formation among Sudanese students in Cairo of the Sudan Movement for National Liberation. A few individuals of communist leanings took part in the various preindedendence negotiations in Cairo, but the Communists lost face by rejecting as reactionary the Anglo-Egyptian agreement of 1953. Several factions developed, but by 1952 or 1953 the party began to show strength.

In the 1950s communism showed its greatest strength in the Railway Workers' Union, the largest of the trade unions and the spearhead in the formation of the Sudan Workers' Trade Union Federation (SWTUF). Although leaders of the federation usually were Communists, the leaders of component unions often were not. Outside the trade union movement, the Communists had considerable influence in the Student Union of the University of Khartoum, in a number of secondary school students' organizations, and in some of the urban professional associations. Attempts to organize peasants appeared to have only limited success. By taking up the cause of tenant grievances the party gained a following in the Jazirah Tenants' Union. Until 1968 their only electoral successes were in the graduate constituency elections, winning one seat in 1953 and twelve in 1965.

A number of front organizations were sponsored by communist leadership. The Communists tried with varying success to sponsor women's groups, study groups, and other organizations designed to attract the support of the educated elite, both to gain actual adherents and to win the type of support useful in a popular front policy.

Party organization was on conventional lines; cells, called "struggle units," were grouped into "circles," which in turn were under a provincial organization. Directing the whole was the Central Committee, in theory elected by periodic national congresses; a political bureau and organization office carried on direct party activity. The party published several newspapers and magazines.

Party Realignments, 1964–68

The major events of the 1964–68 period, although affecting their political fortunes, had little impact on the alignments of the parties (see ch. 2). The only exception of note was the appearance of a modernist wing in the Ummah, under the leadership of Sadik al Mahdi, the grandson of the party's founder. Sadik's major opponent was his uncle and the titular head of the Ansar, Imam al Hadi al Mahdi.

Sadik's wing of the party included those Mahdists whose education or urbanization had opened their eyes to the need for adapting to changing conditions and for accepting a weakening of divisive

177

traditional barriers in order to achieve a united country. They rejected the use of force as a solution to the southern problem and approved the concept of regional autonomy. Their attitudes toward social and economic matters matched those of the Muslim Brotherhood, whose chief leader was Sadik's brother-in-law. While retaining their traditional faith, however, they rejected the political concepts of the brotherhood and called for the creation of a secular state and equality for non-Muslims.

The modernist wing drew a major portion of its support from nonmodernist sources, particularly from a traditional division within the Mahdist movement. These supporters were primarily from the country's poorer regions, Darfur and Kordofan provinces. The Mahdists in those areas had always been jealous of the wealth of their coreligionists in the traditional Ansar stronghold of the rich farmlands of Blue Nile Province centered on Aba Island, where Imam al Mahdi had his headquarters and center of support. Some others also opposed Imam al Mahdi's wing because of alignments dating from the splits between the three caliphs in the 1890s (see ch. 2).

Two other small political parties made their appearance in the 1965 election campaigns, the Beja Congress and the Nuba Independents. Both had strong showings in their regions, winning ten and eight seats, respectively, in the national assembly. Two of the Nuba elected were Christian clergymen. The parties' strength in the 1968 elections declined but, although the parties may not have been of importance, they reflected the fact that regional autonomy was an issue with broader appeal than just to the south.

This appeal stemmed from the strong ethnic and regional animosity that existed in the north. On one side were the Arab and Nubian peoples of the Nile valley and the Jazirah region between the Blue Nile and the White Nile, who had the most economic and educational advantages and who as a result occupied most of the seats of power. Government policies under the colonial and postcolonial governments had concentrated further economic development among the same people as the best means of improving the national economy.

On the other side were their fellow Muslim peoples of the poorer and remoter areas of the north: the Beja of the Red Sea Hills, the Fur and Massalit of Darfur, other nomadic herdsmen of the north, and the numerous West African immigrants. In addition, the only sizable non-Muslim group of the north, the Nuba of the mountains of southern Kordofan, specifically aligned themselves with the non-Muslim peoles of the southern region (see ch. 4).

Political Dynamics After the 1969 Coup

The bloodless May 1969 coup was carried out without any effective opposition (see ch. 2). The nine young military officers who led the revolt all aligned themselves behind Colonel Numayri. Their proclaimed intention was to carry out the principles set forth in the popular uprising of October 1964 and to end the conflicts among the politicians that had paralyzed the decisionmaking process and prevented effective resolution of the country's many problems.

The army officers around Numayri were popularly referred to as the Free Officer Movement in emulation of the organization within the Egyptian army that had brought Nasser to power. Because of the need for secrecy, however, a formal organization had not existed. Instead those officers of like mind in the army had been drawn together by a common outlook. This included not only the officers associated with Numayri—all those who favored the creation of a modern state with a socialist economy, including the Communists—but also the supporters of the Muslim Brotherhood, conservative officers, and officers of ethnic minorities who favored the creation of a federal state. The move by Numayri and his allies preempted all others. In addition, the lack of counteractions by other groups during the following three years indicated that the socialist-minded officers were either widely supported or very well organized. The steps taken to ensure their own security may have played a major role.

The former government was charged with bankrupting the country through mismanagement and fraud. A hundred or more politicians were jailed; all government services—including the army, the police, and the courts—were purged; and the pay and living conditions of the soldiers were improved. Strong efforts were made to destroy permanently the political power of traditional conservatives, particularly the Ansar and its Mahdist leaders— the only force politically strong enough to resist the Revolutionary Command Council (RCC). Imam al Mahdi was forced to retreat to his estate on Aba Island, and his representatives among his distant followers were removed from positions of local authority. The Muslim Brotherhood was effectively suppressed along with the regular parties; its leaders were jailed.

Local government as a stronghold of tribal and ethnic interests was overhauled or, in Numayri's word, "liquidated." The local sheikhs were deprived of their powers, first over taxgathering and then over local judicial matters. The state was declared to be secular rather than Islamic.

The ten-member Revolutionary Command Council (RCC), with

179

only one civilian member, formed the executive body of the new government. The RCC's stated objectives were the building of a new Sudan with political unity and the placing of social and economic development in socialist hands in order to liberate the country's population from underdevelopment and dependence on Western influence for development.

The RCC's attitudes toward socialism were in some measure influenced by the country's need to find new sources of foreign assistance among the communist bloc nations after breaking ties with its two main creditors, the United States and the Federal Republic of Germany (West Germany), over the issue of their support for Israel. The United States was seen as Israel's major ally and therefore as a major enemy of all Arab peoples, including the Sudanese. Although members of Numayri's group were inspired by the doctrines of the UAR's President Nasser, they were strongly attached to the concept of a genuinely independent Sudan (see ch. 10).

Immediately after coming to power the RCC made clear the basis of its cooperation with the Communists. As so few capable educated men favored radical reforms, the RCC felt that its programs would be impossible to implement without the help of individual members of the SCP. They were regarded as natural allies in seeking to achieve any major transformation of Sudanese society. Since the RCC had neither specific ideological goals nor experience in politics and civil administration, the Communists and their allies were allowed considerable leeway.

The RCC placed the administration of the government in the hands of a cabinet (see The Governmental System, this ch.). The cabinet was under the leadership of the one civilian RCC member, former Chief Justice Babikir Awadallah, who was not a Communist but was popular with the SCP. Numayri, promoted to the rank of major general and named chairman of the RCC and commander of the armed forces, also served in the cabinet as minister of defense. Two other RCC members were appointed to cabinet posts: Major Faruk Uthman Hamadallah in the key slot of minister of interior, controlling both the police and intelligence organs, and Major Muhammad Hassib as minister of communications.

Of the other seventeen posts, all went to civilians, at least four of whom were members of the SCP: the ministers of foreign affairs, southern affairs, labor, and industry and mining. In addition, two of the RCC's ten members, Major Hashim al Atta and Lieutenant Colonel Babikir al Nur, were also members of the SCP. A third officer later aligned himself with them. Although the remaining thirteen ministers included progressive members of the

180

former Ummah and DUP, the majority were drawn from the small Sudan Socialist Party or were Marxists unaffiliated with any party.

Despite providing the Communists with such access to power, the RCC officers had no intention of allowing anyone, particularly the SCP, to take control of the country. From the first the RCC made clear that they sought the help of Communists only as individuals not as a party. They demanded that the SCP dissolve itself in order to allow its members to join the proposed Sudan Socialist Union (SSU), which was to be the sole and all-encompassing political party. Although the SCP—unlike others—was allowed for a time to exist on sufferance, the necessity of its dissolution was made clear from the first.

The RCC was again following the example set by Nasser, who had created a monolithic political party intended to inform and mobilize the entire population and to include persons of all political persuasions. Under considerable pressure the Egyptian Communist Party had disbanded to allow its members to join Nasser's Arab Socialist Union, although not until 1965. Any group that tried to operate outside this union was considered illegal, if not treasonous.

The SCP leadership was itself divided in its attitude toward cooperation with the RCC and ignored the directive to dissolve itself. Moreover, Communists holding ministerial posts took advantage of the expulsion of numerous conservatives and appointed fellow Communists and their supporters to many posts in order to increase the party's strength. Most troublesome for the RCC was the fact that the Communists paid more attention to party ideology and directives than to RCC orders.

The RCC's major preoccupation, however, was with the continuing threat to their control represented by conservative forces, particularly the Ansar. Their leader, Imam al Mahdi, had withdrawn to his stronghold on Aba Island and maintained an attitude of opposition to the government, motivated in part by a belief that the government planned steps to destroy the Ansar movement. In late March 1970 hostile Ansar crowds had blocked a visit by Numayri to Aba Island, and Imam al Mahdi had issued formal demands that the government be returned to democratic rule and the Communists removed from power. A major army force attacked Aba Island, killed Imam al Mahdi, and destroyed the Ansar movement. Violent clashes occurred simultaneously in Omdurman. The dead in the two battles were estimated variously from 300 to 1,600. Sadik al Mahdi, leader of the liberal wing of the Ansar and an expected successor to Ansar leadership, was promptly exiled to Cairo.

With the last overt center of conservative political power at the national level destroyed, the RCC concentrated on planned reform;

181

major cabinet changes occurred in July 1970. The growing tensions between the Communists and the RCC were not reflected in the cabinet changes, which gave more power to the Communists. Those Communists holding important posts, however, were almost all drawn from the wing of the party that favored cooperation with the government and association with the plans for the SSU. RCC members continued to make plain that their basis of cooperation was still one of need. They recognized that the Communists continued to have their own end in mind, namely, the establishment of communist control over the workings of the government. The ideological conflict intensified and became public between the orthodox wing of the party, led by Abdal Khalig Mahgoub, which demanded a united front government with heavy communist influence, and the wing labeled National Communists, which was willing to accept continued control of the executive by the army as a move in the correct direction. The army leaders, despite their proclaimed socialism, were supported by conservatives and businessmen who saw communism as their greatest danger.

Mahgoub wing of the SCP had kept up a constant criticism of any action of the RCC that conflicted with decreed party doctrine and insisted on labeling the RCC "petty bourgeois." Immediately after crushing their rightwing opponents at Aba Island, the RCC moved against the left for the first time, seizing and deporting Secretary General A. K. Mahgoub with the aim of silencing his wing of the SCP. He returned illegally within three months and was promptly placed under house arrest.

The government's blow aimed at the Mahgoub wing had the effect, however, of strengthening it. Those who had earlier favored cooperation with the RCC became fearful of its intentions. Although they remained in their posts, the rift in the party was healed with Mahgoub again at the helm. Communist leaders of the trade unions and other front groups all became more critical of the government's policies. This continued even after the RCC took a major step called for by the Communists. Until 1969 the country's large-scale commerce and industry had remained in foreign hands. In May 1970 General Numayri announced the carrying out of a massive nationalization program (see ch. 12).

Instead of being grateful, the Communists saw the nationalization as an effort to weaken SCP support among nonmembers who were attracted by its program. The SCP leaders were particularly alarmed by the progress of the RCC's plans for a national charter creating a single party, the SSU. At the same time the RCC, whose attitude toward the Communists was influenced by their need for strengthening ties with the European and Asian Communists, had begun to conclude that they did not need to associate them-

182

selves with Sudanese Communists in order to obtain increased Soviet foreign assistance.

In addition to the conflict over abolition of the SCP and the formation of the SSU, a clash occurred over attitudes toward union with the UAR and Libya in the Confederation of Arab Republics (CAR). The move was feared by the Communists because the leaders of both those countries were strongly opposed to Communists within their borders.

Rumors of differences among members of the RCC were obscured for over a year by the body's collective leadership policy. All decisions and announcements were taken after a majority vote that was binding on all members, a method adopted during the movement's conspiratorial years. In mid-November 1970, however, differences within the RCC and between the RCC and the SCP were prominently projected by the expulsion of the two communist officers and their associate Major Hamadallah from the RCC and the government. General Numayri later announced that the three had been expelled because they ignored the collective decisions of the RCC. Instead, he said, they had followed the lead of the Mahgoub wing of the SCP and had set up an opposition group within the security services.

For another six months General Numayri and the RCC again refrained from moving against the party. This inaction was motivated by a continuing belief that their opponents were not the Communists as a group but rather a minority of SCP leaders, old men motivated by a desire to capture leadership for themselves.

In the spring of 1971 steps weakening the position of the orthodox SCP members increased rapidly, culminating in May 1971 in a major speech by General Numayri. He announced major steps to place the trade unions, always a communist stronghold, under tighter government control. Many unions and other bodies, such as the secondary school graduates' and women's clubs, were dissolved; others were ordered to find new leaders. He announced the planned release of a national charter to provide an ideological base for the projected formation of the SSU. This ideology drew very heavily on the Arab nationalist socialism of President Nasser. The SSU would provide Numayri and his fellow RCC leaders with the structure they needed if they were to find a popular basis of support outside the army.

After the speech Numayri had seventy leading Communists arrested, including the party's entire Central Committee. All other important Communists were placed under police surveillance. The SCP, however, had continued to maintain two organizational structures: one overt and the other covert. The covert structure was not crushed by the arrests. Five days after Numayri's speech the

Central Committee met and issued instructions for a coup to be carried out before Numayri could take any further steps against them. The chief plotters were the three army officers dismissed from the RCC in November 1970, along with other Communists, some officers associated with the extreme left wing of the Arab Ba'ath movement based in Iraq, and various officers whose motives remained unclear.

The coup was carried out on July 19, 1971, without casualties. Troops carrying out actions involved in the uprising were not told their ultimate purpose. All members of the RCC and a number of pro-Numayri officers were seized. Almost immediately a reaction among junior and noncommissioned officers began. The senior officer of the army, Major General Khalid Hassan Abbas, was out of the country and was able to rally the support of the UAR and Libyan leaders as well as the Sudanese army brigade stationed on the Suez Canal. Libyan aircraft seized an airliner flying two of the coup leaders back to Khartoum from Great Britain. This external assistance, however, proved unnecessary. The Communists, although at first militarily successful, were unable to rally popular support. On July 22 major army units moved against the newly proclaimed rebel government in order to restore Numayri. He was released unharmed, although the coup leaders had ordered all their prisoners to be shot. Thirty-eight officers were killed by the communist forces despite the swiftness of their collapse.

The restored RCC promptly arrested more than 1,000 Communists and their sympathizers. Twelve officers and three communist leaders—A. K. Mahgoub, Joseph Garang, and union leader Shafi Ahmad al Sheikh—were executed for treason and the murder of the thirty-eight military prisoners. The RCC reacted with particular bitterness toward the Soviet bloc countries which had begun to extend reconition and support to the coup leaders as soon as they had appeared successful.

Having apparently crushed the Communists completely, the government affirmed its major announced policy of establishing a socialist state. It remained hostile to the United States, which it regarded as the leader of the neocolonialist forces in the world (see ch. 10). Major initiatives toward peace with the south and for the actual creation of the mass-based SSU were taken in early 1972.

THE SOUTHERN PROBLEM

Although political divisions existed between Ansar and Khatmiyyah, between modernists and traditionalists, and between the Arab, Beja, and Darfur peoples, none have been as significant as the sharp line that divided the northern and southern Sudanese.

The south began its rebellion in mid-1955, after the country had obtained self-governing status shortly before independence. Ancient conflicts originating in the slave trade, exacerbated by preindependence political developments, had generated such hostility that any small spark might have ignited a conflagration (see ch. 2). At this point rumors that all jobs were to be given to northerners were given weight by a decision to discharge a number of workers at the Zande Scheme's cotton mills, the south's only industrial enterprise. Protesting workers rioted and were fired upon by northern soldiers, aided by local Arab merchants. An unknown number were killed, and rumors inflated the incident to the beginning of an attempt to exterminate southerners. Three weeks later, in August 1955, sparked by the shooting of a black soldier by an Arab officer, the locally recruited Equatoria Corps of the army mutinied. The dissidence was supported by other Africans throughout the region. At least 300 Arab men, women, and children were killed before the British airlifted northern troops into the southern towns to bring the revolt to an end. The entire Equatoria Corps of several hundred men fled into the bush, forests, and swamps, where some were to remain out of reach of the authorities for a long time.

This initial revolt was without organization or leadership, and the government's suppression of the mutiny was effectively carried out with limited bloodshed. The major lasting impact of the brief revolt was the existence of several hundred trained soldiers in the bush who later served as the nucleus of antigovernment forces.

There was no sophisticated leadership in the mutiny or the accompanying raids. Political leaders were concentrating their efforts in Khartoum, where they hoped to win constitutional concessions. Although a number of political leaders made outspoken and sometimes inflammatory statements about the demands of the south, most were opposed to violence. Most southern representatives, however, were fully committed to the cause of southern provincial autonomy and had threatened that failure to win legal concessions would drive them to more extreme methods.

At the time of the independence negotiations the southern representatives were promised that their demands for autonomy would be given full consideration, but in 1957 and 1958 the matter was shelved by the Constiuent Assembly. The government's policy was to use northern officials as leaders of the administration in the southern region, to ignore or suppress demands for federation, and to assimilate the south in administration, education, language, and religion. A policy of arabization and Islamization was pursued vigorously, particularly after the government forced the closing of the mission schools in 1957.

The military regime that took power in the 1958 coup received considerable support among the Arabs because of the belief that it would prove more effective in facing the country's problems, particularly the rising tensions in the south. The Abboud government's policy toward the southern problem was one of suppression of overt expressions of religious and cultural differences. Police power was used to bolster government efforts at arabization and Islamization. The closing of the mission schools was followed by increasing restrictions on the activities of the missionaries, culminating in the mass expulsion of all those in the south in February 1964.

The Abboud government also suppressed the national assembly and freedom of expression, thus cutting off the limited outlets for southern complaints (see ch. 11). Thus forced to seek more forceful means of expressing dissent, the southern leaders turned in earnest to secessionist ideas for the first time. The revolt broke out again in 1962 and spread throughout the entire south during 1963. Heightened dissidence gave rise to the formation of guerilla forces known as the Anya Nya (see ch. 14).

In 1964 the Abboud regime was replaced by a civilian government; some of its leaders expressed a more concilatory attitude toward the south, but the war had already gathered a momentum of its own. Talks between southern political leaders and the northern government resulted in the proclamation of a cease-fire, but this effort was not supported by the guerrillas.

The Ummah-led government under Muhammad Ahmad Mahgoub, which came to power in mid-1965, was in favor of an aggressive policy of Islamization. In addition, its leaders were outraged by the failure of the Anya Nya to honor the cease-fire. Under the Mahgoub government the army launched a major hard-line campaign to crush the rebellion by striking at its supporters. Killing of civilians was carried out throughout the south, the educated elite bearing the brunt of the attacks. It was in this period that most of the heavy casualties and the large exodus of refugees occurred (see ch. 5; ch. 14). The hostility between north and south reached a high point, and the impact of the war was felt directly by almost every southerner. In addition, the loss in lives among northern soldiers and officials and the heavy drain on the country's fragile economy was felt throughout the north.

In July 1966 Sadik al Mahdi, a strong critic of M. A. Mahgoub's southern policy, became prime minister. Sadik, leader of the modernist wing of the Ummah party, was also an opponent of the demands for the creation of an Islamic state and supported constitutional proposals that would have granted a considerable degree of autonomy to southerners. He was unable to pursue his policies, however, because of opposition within the national assembly and his own coalition cabinet. As a result, he was replaced again in May 1967 by M. A. Mahgoub, who renewed the war effort. The chances of rapprochement remained dim from then until after the RCC military coup of 1969. The RCC almost immediately announced plans for a southern policy parallel to that of Sadik.

Southern Political Forces

In the 1950s a number of southern political parties made their appearance. The most significant of these was the Southern Liberal Party, a loose organization formed by the southern representatives in the legislative assembly. By 1958 this group was partially divided between those who were willing to work with the northern political leaders and those who demanded a stronger and more independent voice for the south. All agreed, however, on the essential demands for a secular rather than an Islamic state and on considerable autonomy for the south, preferably through a federal structure.

When political parties made their reappearance after the fall of the Abboud government in 1964, two major allied parties functioned in the south. The Sudan African National Union (SANU), led by Joseph Oduhu, Aggrey Jaden, William Deng, and a Sudanese Catholic priest, Father Saturnino Lahure, was primarily active among refugee groups and guerrilla forces. The Southern Front, whose principal leader was Clement Mboro, functioned openly within the southern provinces. After the collapse of government-sponsored peace conferences in 1965, Deng's wing of SANU and the Southern Front coalesced to take part in the parliamentary elections. SANU remained active in Parliament for the next four years as a voice for southern regional autonomy within a unified state. SANU remained active despite the assassination of its leader, antisouthern race riots in Khartoum, and increased conflict in the south.

SANU leaders who remained in exile or who fled into exile in large numbers after the Juba and Waw massacres of mid-1965 balked at the moderate approach adopted by Deng and accepted by other southerners who continued to live under the control of the Sudan government. Under the joint leadership of Jaden and Oduhu they formed the Azania Liberation Front (ALF), based in Kampala, Uganda. From then on the refugee centers in the five neighboring states of black Africa served as centers for the opposition movements, particularly those in Uganda, whose population is closely related to the southern Sudanese, and Ethiopia, which has a tradition of conflict with the Muslim Arab world (see ch. 10).

The leaders of the Anya Nya units in the field, however, did not join the ALF. During the period between late 1965 and late 1967 the exile and guerrilla groups fragmented under personal, tribal, and religious strains. In 1967 a basis for unity was created with the formation of the Southern Sudan Provisional Government (SSPG) at the prodding of younger, better educated leaders, notably Gordon Mayen and Barri Wanji. The SSPG had Anya Nya support, but ethnic and personal conflicts again broke up the apparent unity. In 1969 at least three separate organizations appeared, the most important being the Nile Provisional Government under Mayen.

Differences had also surfaced within the Anya Nya between the older leaders like Emilio Tafeng who had been in combat since fleeing into the bush as early as 1955 and the younger, better educated men who returned from outside the country to fight after 1964. Gradually Joseph Lagu, a former captain in the Sudan army and secondary school graduate from the small Madi tribe, gained a considerable degree of authority. In January 1971 he proclaimed the creation of a new body, the Southern Sudan Liberation Front (SSLF), also called the Southern Sudan Liberation Movement. The Anya Nya leaders united behind him, and nearly all the exiled politicians gave the SSLF their support. Although the organization did create a governmental structure with a consultative assembly composed of the politicians to consider all major issues, the real power remained concentrated in the hands of the military element, the Anya Nya command, with Lagu, then a major general, at its head. After 1967 the training and equipment of the Anya Nya improved considerably (see ch. 14). The national government insisted that the Anya Nya command was receiving considerable assistance from Israel, motivated by a desire to tie down as many Arab troops as possible in southern Sudan and thus to lessen the Sudanese government's support for the UAR on the Suez Canal.

Despite the improvements in their forces, the Anya Nya efforts against government security forces remained thwarted. As both sides came to realize that a military solution was impossible, a new willingness to negotiate a settlement appeared. In contrast with earlier attempts at negotiation, however, this time the southerners were both united and militarily strong. The national government was also in the hands of a group that had executive power and also a distaste for continuing the conflict. Moreover, its announced policy favored reconciliation, regional autonomy, and a secular state.

Another significant group of southerners was composed of those who had remained active in Khartoum, often in government service and even in cabinet posts but always clearly working for southern interests despite persecutions and jailings. By 1972 the most important among these men was Abel Alier, chosen by President Numayri in October 1971 as one of his vice presidents. Alier served as minister of state for southern affairs and was charged with coordinating the work of all the other ministeries in the south. He was supported by a number of others, including the first southerners to govern a southern province, Hilary-Paul Lugali, Toby Madut, and Luigi Adwak.

Moves Toward Peace

Almost immediately after assuming power in May 1969, Numayri had announced that priority would be given to settling the rebellion and that the route to peace would be sought through the granting of regional autonomy and the economic development of the south. The number of southerners among his active supporters was limited. His choice for the man to implement the program as minister of state for southern affairs was Joseph Garang, a Communist. The mere fact that a southerner was put in charge and accomplished some steps favorable to the south improved southern attitudes toward the government. Garang, however, followed the directions of the SCP rather than those of Numayri's RCC and attempted to use his position primarily to create a basis for a communist-led cadre in the southern administration and development bodies. At the same time Garang was greatly distrusted by other southern leaders, who were unwilling to accept the appointment of southern Communists to positions of power as being in their region's interest. As a result no major steps toward peace were taken in the RCC's first two years of rule. Rather, the scale of the war increased.

This pattern ended shortly after the crushing of the communist coup attempt in July 1971. By October major steps were underway to improve relations with the south and to establish contacts and dialogue with the SSLF. In the initial contacts, officials of the World Council of Churches, which had connections with the refugee leaders through aid programs, served as an intercessor. After considerable consultation within Sudan and among southern exiles, a conference between high-level delegations of the SSLF and the national government met at Addis Ababa from February 16 to February 26, 1972.

In their initial points of approach, the two sides were far apart. Vice President Alier called for making the south a single autonomous region with its own executive council and legislature but giving the national president full control over the council and veto power over acts of the regional legislature. The rebels, led by a former Sudanese minister of communications, Ezbon Mondire,

189

demanded a generally federal state, the south having its own government and its own army,which would come under the popularly elected national president's control only in the face of external threats. They also demanded that the implementation of any agreement be supervised by foreign observers. At a crucial juncture the Emperor of Ethiopia intervened personally, lending his prestige to the mediation effort to ensure that an agreement was reached.

The Addis Ababa agreement was contained in six documents. The first and most important of these required a basic constitutional reorganization granting major elements of southern demands for federal status; because of northern sensitivity, however, the phrase used was regional autonomy. This grant was also in line with the Numayri government's earlier pronouncements on creating decentralized and elected organs of local and regional government.

The national government retained power over national defense, foreign affairs, immigration matters, foreign trade, currency and finance, interregional transport, telecommunications, educational planning, higher education, and economic and social planning. The Southern Region—composed of the three provinces of Equatoria, Bahr al Ghazal, and Upper Nile—was to be responsible for all other matters, including police control and tax collection. An elected regional legislature and an executive council were to be created. The Executive Council was to execute the policies set forth by the regional legislature and to have duties assigned to it by the central government for the conduct of national affairs within the region.

The agreement specified that the chairman of the Executive Council would administer the region as the national president's regional representative. It was intended that the council chairman would be selected by the regional assembly and appointed by the president, although the first incumbent was to be appointed before the formation of the assembly. The assembly was, however, to be elected within eighteen months after the agreement was signed.

This document also asserted that Arabic was the country's only official language. It agreed, however, that English and local languages were to be considered working languages that would be used as needed in public administration.

The other documents agreed upon by the two sides provided for a cease-fire, amnesty, and the resettlement of refugees. The most difficult document was a protocol dealing with the 12,000 members of the armed forces to be stationed in the south. The protocol specified that 6,000 of these troops must be southerners, including returning members of the Anya Nya. The police units were to be completely under regional control. Those Anya Nya members not meeting the standards for the army and not absorbed into the police were to be employed by the government in construction groups.

By March 2, 1972, the SSLF leader, General Lagu, had announced his satisfaction with most parts of the agreement and his plans to ratify the accords formally, although reserving his conclusions on the agreement on the stationing of northern troops in the south. Both sides put an effective cease-fire into operation almost immediately. The national government announced passage of a decree legalizing the agreements and creating an international armistice commission to assure the well-being of returning southern refugees. A broad amnesty, retroactive to 1955, was also announced. The accords officially ending the war were signed on March 27, 1972, by General Lagu and the national government in Addis Ababa.

CHAPTER 10

FOREIGN RELATIONS

In shaping the new state's foreign policy at independence, government leaders began with the assumption that Sudan, as a new and not very strong nation, could risk neither involvement in the political crises of the cold war nor commitment to either side in most regional conflicts. The foreign policy goals to which they devoted most attention were the preservation of sovereignty and the undertaking of any steps that would promote economic development of the country. Primary emphasis was given to relations with the country's most influential neighbor, the Arab Republic of Egypt—from February 21, 1958, to September 2, 1971, the UAR—although Sudan continually sought to establish an identity separate from Egypt that would guarantee expression of its particular national interests.

After each of the several changes of government, Sudanese foreign policy shifted in line with the internal policies of the regime in power: from pro-Western to Arab nationalist to pro-Egyptian or to alignment with the communist bloc. Alignment with the communist bloc accounted for some of the foreign policy positions established after the major deterioration of relations with the United States and the countries of Western Europe that followed the Arab-Israeli War of 1967.

Despite continued hostility toward the United States as a major supporter of Israel, relations with the West improved considerably after mid-1971. This followed a sharp lessening of links to the Soviet bloc countries as a result of their support for the abortive coup attempt against the military government of General Jaafar al Numayri.

In the period after the Arab-Israeli War—and particularly after General Numayri's Revolutionary Command Council (RCC) came to power in May 1969—a trend developed toward increased activity and involvement in regional relations. Major internal political forces actively sought stronger ties to, and even formal association with, the Confederation of Arab Republics (CAR), composed of Libya, Egypt, and Syria.

The establishment and improvement of good relations with neighboring African states also played an increasingly important part in the country's foreign affairs as the government sought—with apparent success—to bring the long civil war in the south to an end by cutting off southern support routes through neighboring countries. Outside the Arab world, and to a lesser extent the African continent, involvement in international affairs continued to be limited by the small number of qualified personnel and the lack of the funds that would be needed for the expansion of diplomatic representation. More fundamentally, however, it reflected a continuing primary focus on relations with neighboring states.

THE FOREIGN MINISTRY AND DIPLOMATIC TIES

According to the governmental reorganization that occurred in October 1971, a secretariat general for the presidency was created within the Ministry of State for Presidential Affairs. The secretariat was charged with formulation of policy and advice to the president on foreign political and economic affairs. The implementation of foreign policy outlined by the government was the task of the Ministry of Foreign Affairs, whose responsibilities included the development of political, economic, and cultural relations as well as the negotiation of foreign assistance programs. The ministry also supervised the affairs of such technical personnel as commercial attachés in coordination with the ministries involved. The Ministry of Economy and Trade, however, was charged with the function of developing foreign economic cooperation.

The minister of foreign affairs was aided in foreign policy implementation by an under secretary and a deputy under secretary for foreign affairs. Assistant under secretaries provided liaison with major ministerial sections, including those responsible for political, economic, consular, and protocol matters. Each one in turn had its own sectional directors.

In early 1972 the government inaugurated a restrictive policy designed to curtail official visits abroad and to consolidate foreign policy declarations. All official travel to foreign countries had to be cleared through the Council of Ministers, and foreign service officers were reminded that their role was implementation rather than formulation of foreign policy. As official representatives of the state, foreign service officers were also warned against misconduct and were encouraged to become familiar with current domestic developments.

In early 1972 forty-three countries maintained diplomatic missions in Sudan at the ambassadorial level; included were all of the neighboring states except Kenya. Uganda, with which rela-

194

tions had long been difficult, was in the process of opening an embassy in Khartoum, raising the number of ambassadors from equatorial Africa to nine. The largest block of embassies belonged to fourteen Islamic countries, including Pakistan and the newly formed United Arab Emirates of the Persian Gulf. Nine West European countries maintained embassies in the national capital, as did the Soviet Union and five Soviet bloc nations. Japan, India, the Democratic People's Republic of Korea (North Korea), the People's Republic of China (PRC), and Yugoslavia completed the list. In addition, Egypt maintained consulates in Port Sudan and Al Ubayyid; Ethiopia had consular representation in Kassala.

Relations with the Federal Republic of Germany (West Germany) and Romania were resumed in late 1971, after having been terminated in 1967 over their alleged support for Israel during the Arab-Israeli War. Diplomatic relations with the United States, also severed at that time, had not been resumed as of early 1972. The offices of the United Nations and of the apostolic nuncio had diplomatic status, and Sudan had nonresident diplomatic relations with eighteen other states, including eight African countries, Albania, and the Democratic Republic of Vietnam (North Vietnam).

MAJOR ELEMENTS OF FOREIGN POLICY

The foreign policy expounded by the Numayri government in 1972 represented a mixture of traditional policy positions and new initiatives. Key points, as outlined in the National Charter of the Sudan Socialist Union (SSU), included support for Arab unity, resistance against neocolonialism, opposition to Zionism, the strengthening of African progressive governments, support for African self-determination, and the elimination of discrimination on the basis of race and color.

Initially the concept of nonalignment provided an umbrella for relations outside Africa. Shifts in policy from a centralist position to the left or the right have complicated this image. The Sudanese have used various opportunities to separate the political and economic aspects of their foreign policy, however, in order to expand their relations with both Eastern and Western states and as a means of bettering their position. Examples of this balancing process included increased relations with the PRC and the encouragement of Scandinavian interest in the development of the southern provinces.

Sudan has generally supported the principles advanced by the Organization of African Unity (OAU), of which it is a member, and has increasingly involved itself in OAU activities. Recent initiatives included proposals for a ban on mercenary activity in Africa advanced by Sudanese representatives—in coordination with the representatives of Nigeria—at the January 1972 session of the OAU Commission of Legal Experts. These proposals were presented in February 1972 at the OAU ministerial council meeting, which also discussed proposals for an African mutual defense agreement.

Sudan has firmly declared solidarity with its northern neighbors and has demonstrated its interest in Arab unity and opposition to Israel. Shortly after independence Sudan joined the Arab League; its initial participation in regional affairs was dominated by the bid for recognition of status separate from Egypt. A foreign policy increasingly independent of its North African neighbors was indicated in early 1972 by the expansion of diplomatic and economic ties with the United Arab Emirates and Kuwait.

During 1970 and 1971 plans for the establishment of the Confederation of Arab Republics (CAR) initially included Egypt, Libya, and Sudan; Syria later expressed an interest in joining. The major immediate task of the confederation was to be the formation of ministerial commissions to study the coordination of transportation, communications, and various economic activities of the members. Because of internal opposition, particularly in the south but also among important northern elements, Sudanese membership in CAR had not been effected by mid-1972. President Numayri had stated that, although the government still supported the concept of CAR in principle, Sudan could not join the confederation until its own political system was unified. It was generally recognized that the membership question would not be supported by the national plebiscite Numayri felt was prerequisite to Sudanese entrance. The government indicated that Sudanese membership could not be brought about in the near future.

Intensely emotional protest against Israel has included charges of aggression against Arab states and of support for rebel forces in southern Sudan (see ch. 9; ch. 14). Sudan has supported the liberation of Palestine by sending Sudanese troops to the Suez and by aiding Arab guerrilla fighters. Sudan advocated the rejection of traditional warfare and supported a pan-Arab policy of lauching guerrilla-conducted popular liberation assaults from all fronts on the Israeli borders.

Since independence in 1956 Sudan has been involved with border problems with most of its neighbors. In some cases the issue has been border demarcations. In the case of southern neighbors, however, there have been disagreements over the movements of refugees, rebel forces, and military pursuit groups crossing the frontiers in both directions. Relations with Uganda, Zaire—until late 1971 Congo (Kinshasa)—and the Central African Republic have been particularly troubled at different times on this account.

In 1972 the Numayri government policy was to affirm Sudan's position as a link between North Africa's Arab cultures and the black societies of equatorial Africa, largely because elements of both lived in Sudan. Linked to this diplomatic position was the government's effort to reduce hostilities between these two cultures. Calling upon neighboring states as "brother peoples," the government urged noninterference in the internal affairs of other countries, exchanges of high-ranking government officials, goodwill visits, and regional cooperation in various functional areas.

The Sudanese government has announced its opposition to all manifestations of colonialism and racial discrimination. It has particularly cited the governments of Rhodesia and the Republic of South Africa as well as the Portuguese colonial administration in Mozambique for violations of human rights and African dignity. In addition to contributions supporting the African Liberation Committee of the OAU, Sudan was also a member of that body's Military Experts Committee, which studied the military requirements of the various liberation movements. Given its position, Sudan has been compelled to reject claims that racial discrimination existed within its own borders.

RELATIONS WITH THE ARAB REPUBLIC OF EGYPT

Beginning even before independence, Sudanese political leaders remained preoccupied with the formulation of foreign policy toward Egypt as well as the establishment on the international scene of an identity separate from Sudan's historical position of subordination to its much more powerful northern neighbor. Until the early 1950s Egypt had sought to incorporate Sudan as part of Egyptian territory. Between 1956 and the mid-1960s relations between the two countries alternately warmed and cooled over such issues as the division of the Nile waters, boundary disputes, and Sudanese relations with the West (particularly the United States). Other major factors were alleged Egyptian programs designed to control Sudan through direct economic and cultural intervention and political actions including large-scale propaganda efforts and close Egyptian association with some Sudanese political parties (see ch. 2; ch. 9).

Egypt was the first state to recognize the government of General Ibrahim Abboud after the 1958 coup d'etat; spokesmen for the new regime stated that the desire for better relations with Egypt was one of the motives leading to the coup. By the end of

197

a year's time a new Nile waters agreement had been reached. The accord provided that Sudan would receive one third of the annual total flow of water instead of one-twelfth as under the 1929 agreement. The issue of the Aswan High Dam was also settled; Egypt agreed to pay for the relocation of Sudanese inhabitants at Wadi Halfa, and both countries agreed to share the costs of other joint projects connected with the rising water of Lake Nasser. Although relations were somewhat troubled by continued Sudanese acceptance of American technical assistance, commercial cooperation with Egypt expanded.

The commencement of hostilities leading to the Arab-Israeli War in 1967 strengthened Sudan's relations with Egypt. The Sudanese demonstration of support for Arab unity included the mobilization of troops and domestic resources to aid Egyptian forces along the Suez Canal as well as the severing of diplomatic relations with the United States, Great Britain, and West Germany. The Sudanese government seemed ready to assume a more active role in Arab affairs and arranged for an Arab summit conference to be held in Khartoum in July 1967. The number of trade agreements with Egypt increased, and in 1968 Sudan joined the Arab Common Market under the terms of the Arab Economic Unity Agreement.

The avowed socialist orientation of the Numayri government, which came to power after the 1969 military coup, facilitated closer agreement and cooperation between Sudan and other revolutionary Arab states. It also set the stage for Sudanese interest in membership in the CAR. This level of rapport was indicated by policy statements depicting the Sudanese and the Egyptians as twin peoples. The firmest Egyptian backing of the Numayri regime, however, appeared publicly in its press support for Numayri's victory against the communist-inspired coup of July 1971. Soviet interference in the domestic affairs of Sudan was implied and was criticized heavily.

Egypt, joined by Libya and Syria, met with the Sudanese in early 1972 in efforts to encourage common solidarity. In March 1972 Egyptian President Anwar Sadat visited Sudan to urge closer ties and cooperation between the two countries. President Numayri, however, continued to emphasize Sudan's need to achieve national unity before attempting any international union.

RELATIONS WITH OTHER AFRICAN NEIGHBORS

Throughout the 1960s relations with neighboring states were complicated by the refugee groups fleeing from civil war in the southern provinces. According to 1970 estimates there were more than 175,000 Sudanese registered with the United Nations High Commissioner for Refugees: 75,000 in Uganda, 55,000 in Zaire, 25,000 in the Central African Republic, and 20,000 in Ethiopia. At least another 75,000 were living unregistered in those countries as well as in Kenya and Chad. Within the country's own borders an estimated 500,000 refugees had been forced to flee their homes.

Hostility toward Sudan had been engendered by the information spread by the refugees among related peoples into whose countries they had fled. More troublesome, however, was the fact that the refugee camps had served as recruiting posts and, in some cases, as covert bases for the Anya Nya guerrillas (see ch. 9). Political leaders among the refugees had found a center of support in the camps and had used the capital cities of the host countries as homes for their political offices.

In early 1972 a conference convened in Khartoum to discuss relief programs for refugee resettlement. International groups expressed hesitancy to become involved in the civil war issue, and most of them limited their commitments to short-term emergency relief. The cease-fire agreement between southern rebels and the central government forces, which was concluded less than a week after the conference closed, increased the willingness of participants to extend longer term development assistance. A follow-up conference for coordination of relief work chaired by the International Council of Voluntary Agencies (ICVA) was scheduled for May 1972.

The refugee problem had the greatest repercussion on relations with Uganda, which had provided shelter to the largest number of refugees. Moreover, the Sudanese government had alleged that Israel was directly aiding guerrilla operations based in Uganda.

Relations improved significantly in mid-1971 when Uganda returned Rolf Steiner, a West German mercenary who had fought with the Anya Nya, to Sudanese authorities. Mutual declarations of support for noninvolvement in each other's internal affairs followed, and by December diplomatic relations at the ambassadorial level had been restored and discussions were underway on reopening the border, which had been closed since May 1969. Minor border violations occurred on several occasions in early 1972, but both states appeared to be sincere in their interest in improved relations.

Chad, which shares 845 miles of border with Sudan, is the African country with racial divisions most closely paralleling those of Sudan. Like Sudan, it straddles the dividing line between the Arab north and black Africa, but in Chad the black

African elements hold power. Western Sudanese have generally had considerable sympathy for their fellow Arabs in Chad, particularly for the impoverished Massalit tribesmen who inhabit both sides of the border along Sudan's Darfur Province. In addition to the Massalit, an estimated 200,000 to 500,000 persons of Chadian origins live within Sudan.

Relations between the two countries deteriorated in 1965 and verged on open conflict as rebels and brigands from the tribes along the border raided Chad from sanctuaries inside Sudan with the apparent compliance—if not the support—of at least local Sudanese officials. Chadian armed forces were accused of reprisal attacks on villages inside Sudan. Approximately 300 raiders from Sudan were killed in Chad during 1965 and 1966. Although the Sudanese government agreed to expel Chadians engaged in subversive activity, the problem continued into 1968. Intergovernment tensions then eased by the mediation of Niger's President Hamani Diori, who arranged for the creation of a mixed Sudanese-Chadian commission.

After the RCC came to power in Sudan in 1969, Chad's President François Tombalbaye established contact and rapport with General Numayri. The two leaders exchanged visits, during which Numayri expressed support for Tombalbaye's peace efforts and toured eastern Chad. In early 1971 Tombalbaye released a number of political prisoners, including some who had family ties in Sudan. Subsequently, Numayri took steps to prevent Sudan's use as a rebel base and granted educational assistance to Chad.

Relations had clearly reached a cordial level in February 1972 when President Tombalbaye visited Sudan. Upon his departure a joint communiqué was released to the press. Direct telecommunication links between the two capitals were resumed, and similar communication links between border towns were to be opened. Extension of the Sudan Railways to the Chadian border was proposed, and the airport at Al Junaynah in western Sudan was opened to Chadian civil aircraft. The presence of large numbers of Chadians in Sudan, however, remained a continuing problem in early 1972.

Sudan shares its longest frontier with Ethiopia. Although there were historical animosities between the Muslims linked to Sudan and the dominant Christians of Ethiopia, relations remained harmonious until after the overthrow of the Abboud government in 1964. Tensions were then raised by conflicting claims to a small triangle of agricultural land under Sudanese control along the border with the Ethiopian province of Eritrea. Relations worsened in 1966 as the Sudanese reacted to the flight of a number of Eritrean Muslims into Sudan. These Muslims, estimated at between 7,000 and 25,000, were refugees from the conflict between the secessionist Eritrean Liberation Front (EFL) and the Ethiopian security forces. Similarly, Ethiopia had provided shelter for southern Sudanese fleeing from the civil war.

Despite diplomatic efforts to mitigate the significance of these irritants, including a visit of Emperor Haile Selassie to Khartoum in 1967 and continuing talks on particular facets of the problems, throughout 1970 the real issues between the countries remained unresolved. These issues involved accusations by each country that the other still allowed its territory to be used as a base for military activities of the various rebel movements.

The two countries attempted to improve relations by insuring the inactivity of the rebel leadership among the refugees on a quid pro quo basis but with little lasting success. Ethiopia accused Sudan of providing a base of operation and a supply route, as well as some military training, to the ELF. The Ethiopians believed that the ELF's continued activity was a sign of at least passive acquiescence on the part of Sudan. The Ethiopian government rejected the Sudanese allegations that Ethiopia was implicated in the insurrection in the south and labeled as completely false other Arab claims that it was allowing Israelis in the country to support the Anya Nya rebels with military training and arms.

Relations between Sudan and Ethiopia improved markedly in 1971, culminating in the reactivation in March of a long-dormant commission to study disagreements over boundary demarcation and an exchange of state visits by Emperor Haile Selassie and General Numayri in November and December. The Emperor provided facilities and support for the negotiations leading up to the Addis Ababa Agreement, which halted the Sudanese civil war in February 1972. Without the help of Ethiopia in preparing for the difficult negotiation and the Emperor's direct intervention when the talks appeared to be failing, peace in the south would have been difficult to achieve. In recognition of this service, relations were amicable in early 1972. A trade agreement had been signed, a consulate was to be opened in Port Sudan, and two customs posts were to be established to facilitate the resumption of border trade.

RELATIONS WITH GREAT BRITAIN AND THE UNITED STATES

One of the goals inherent in the nationalistic movement leading to independence was the reorientation of Sudan's international position away from political, economic, and cultural dependence on Great Britain in order to participate as an equal in the common interests of other Arab and African countries. Sudan rejected commonwealth status and replaced British nationals serving as civil servants in the bureaucracy as soon as qualified Sudanese were available. The fact that most of the nationals replacing British personnel were from the Islamic north was negatively received in the south (see ch. 9).

Practical considerations, however, necessitated reliance on the British on several accounts in the immediate years after independence. The civil service and the army were patterned along British lines, and the governing elite spoke English. More important, Great Britain was a major trade partner, investor, banker, source of economic assistance, and technical adviser.

Diplomatic relations were interrupted during the mid-1960s over British policies toward Rhodesia and South Africa. They were normalized only to be broken in June 1967 after the outbreak of the Arab-Israeli War. Although diplomatic ties were resumed shortly afterward, relations between the two countries were to be complicated in 1970 as a result of the Numayri nationalization program, which included the seizure of British-owned banks and commercial firms in Sudan.

Although the Sudanese foreign ministry indicated a willingness in 1971 to settle the issue of compensation, the treasury lacked funds to make an acceptable offer to the British. Commercial operations between the two countries have been complicated by this unsettled issue, but relations were friendly. The British expressed an interest in increased cooperation in the areas of sports and education, and an easy-term loan equivalent to US$25 million promised in the fall of 1971 was scheduled for approval in early 1972 through the United Kingdom Export Credits Guarantee Department (see ch. 12).

During the early years of sovereignty, Arab involvement—particularly that of Egypt—in internal Sudanese political factionalism and the official posture of nonalignment required the Sudanese government to move cautiously in forming relations with the United States (see ch. 2). In February 1957, however, the government first officially requested economic and military assistance from the United States. Domestic opposition to this step was mirrored in the cool reception received by Vice President Richard Nixon during an official visit to Khartoum in March 1957. A general feeling of distrust towards the United States was orchestrated by communist- and Egyptian-influenced groups, and anti-United States demonstrations broke out.

After the Nixon visit the United States sent a special mission to Khartoum with an offer of economic aid as well as military assistance in the event of attack by a communist-controlled state. The Sudanese government, however, rejected the proposal on grounds that it did not meet the real dangers in the area but would increase them by making cold-war issues more prominent in interregional relations.

Debate over relations with the United States continued into 1958 and almost toppled the coalition government in power at that time. The technical assistance agreement was finally ratified after a compromise was reached limiting the use of available funds. Total aid reached the equivalent of US$103 million by mid-1967 and was concentrated in the fields of transportation, agriculture, and education. The role of United States assistance continued to be an issue in domestic politics.

On June 6, 1967, after the commencement of the Arab-Israeli War, Sudan broke diplomatic relations with the United States over the latter's military aid to Israel. Although the Sudanese attempted to separate their own receipt of economic aid from the political issue of diplomatic relations, the United States discontinued its direct technical aid program. Since 1967 United States aid to Sudan has been limited to that channeled through the United Nations Children's Fund and the United Nations High Commissioner for Refugees. By mid-1971 an estimated US$250,000 had been extended through these agencies.

Initially it was felt that relations between the two countries might be normalized; by late 1967, however, the governmental positions had become too polarized for this to occur. Since then the Netherlands has assumed responsibility for United States diplomatic interests in Khartoum; the United States has maintained a staff of about sixteen as the American Interest Section of the Royal Netherlands Embassy. Through a similar arrangement Sudanese interests have been represented in Washington by the embassy of the Somali Democratic Republic.

After the July 1971 coup attempt the issue of diplomatic relations with the United States was again raised. Although the United States government expressed willingness to resume full diplomatic relations, the Sudanese government indicated that, until the United States discontinued support of Israel, only economic and cultural ties could be improved. Talks were believed in progress through the ambassadors to the United Nations of both countries, and there was some indication that they had been initiated before the coup attempt occurred. By the end of September 1971 the United States had extended to Sudan credits amounting to US$18 million, sold it US$250,000 worth of gold, promised to review Export-Import Bank policy toward Sudan, and proposed a humanitarian food-for-peace program.

In December 1971 President Numayri restated that his government was not contemplating a resumption of diplomatic relations with the United States. Both countries, however, were increasing the size of their respective "interest sections" in Khartoum and Washington. By April 1972 there had been a distinct improvement in bilateral relations, although the Sudanese government continued to criticize the United States position in Vietnam as well as in the Middle East.

RELATIONS WITH COMMUNIST COUNTRIES

The growth of close relations with the Soviet Union was retarded in the immediate period after independence by Sudan's avowed policy of nonalignment, the concern of some political factions that close ties would facilitate the growth of communism within the country, a reliance on economic relations with Great Britain, and the more pressing concern of relations with Egypt. Officially the government declared an interest in economic assistance from any country that was willing to supply aid without making political demands in return. Thus as early as 1958 the government had endorsed in principle the acceptance of technical assistance from the Soviet Union. There was some trade, but no specific agreements were reached until the 1960s.

Pressure for closer relations with the Soviet Union increased in the early 1960s. Concern for this foreign policy move was demonstrated by the Sudan Communist Party and noncommunist groups interested in Soviet aid for pragmatic reasons or out of interest in communist experience with central planning as a model for Sudanese development. Commercial interaction culminated in the 1965–67 trade protocal and subsequent technical and financial aid agreements. The suspension of diplomatic and economic relations with the United States in 1967 increased the economic and political importance of the Soviet Union as a foe of Israeli incursions into Arab territory.

As relations with the Soviet Union progressed, the Sudanese army was largely reequipped with Soviet weapons (see ch. 14). Soviet industrial machinery and farm implements were traded, medical and agricultural development projects were supported, and friendship delegations were exchanged. By 1970 an estimated 2,000 Soviet and East European technical advisers were in Sudan —more than in all the rest of North Africa except Egypt. The Soviet bloc nations had become purchasers of about 25 percent of the country's exports and supplied about 18 percent of all imports. The Soviet Union's share in these trade figures was about half of the imports and two-thirds of the exports (see ch. 12).

Relations with the Soviet Union deteriorated rapidly, however, after the 1971 communist-led coup attempt. The anticommunist reprisals taken by the government upon its resumption of control resulted in a heavy propaganda attack by the Soviet press and Radio Moscow. The Sudanese government initially expressed regret over the Soviet interpretation. Continued Soviet press attacks and the alleged sanctioning of demonstrations in front of the Sudanese embassy in Moscow were regarded by the Sudanese as hostile acts. In August 1971 the Soviet leadership met in the Crimea with representatives of East European countries to condemn the Sudanese government's repression of communist activities (see ch. 9). The Sudanese government immediately withdrew its ambassador to the Soviet Union and requested the departure of the Soviet ambassador from Khartoum.

The respective embassies were not closed, however, and Sudan continued to maintain cultural, economic, and military missions in the Soviet Union. In an effort to normalize relations, the Soviet Union submitted a new ambassador for accreditation in early 1972, but the Sudanese did not accept his credentials. Third-party mediation was reportedly underway in early March, but resolution of the issue remained complicated by internal political factionalism.

It was initially reported that the Soviet Union had terminated its technical and financial assistance programs in Sudan, but Soviet technical advisers remained in the country. Deteriorated relations were reflected in complaints over trade relations, in which the Sudanese attacked the Soviet Union for the terms of trade it offered—allegedly placing the value of Soviet goods at 20 to 30 percent above world market prices—and for dumping cotton stockpiles on the world market. It was not expected that trade would be discontinued, although a substantial reduction was possible. The willingness of the Soviet Union to supply spare parts for military equipment remained an issue in early 1972 (see ch. 12).

During the last half of the 1960s Sudan expanded economic relations with Bulgaria, including trade exchanges of wheat for cotton as well as technical and financial aid agreements. Relations deteriorated rapidly as a result of the 1971 coup attempt. The Bulgarian embassy was reported to have been the planning center for the coup and to have offered refuge to the Sudanese communist leader Abdal Khalig Mahgoub. The Sudanese ambassador to the Soviet Union also had been accredited to Bulgaria; his Bulgarian credentials were withdrawn at the time of his recall from Moscow in August 1971, and the Bulgarian ambassador to

Sudan was expelled as well. Information on the status of Bulgarian technical and financial aid was not available in early 1972.

After the 1971 crisis Sudan attempted to replace former ties to the Soviet Union with improved relations with other communist countries. Relations with Yugoslavia and the PRC were expanded, and new ties with Romania were established.

The Yugoslav mission to Sudan predated that of the Soviet Union and had received heavy publicity designed to show the independent, nonaligned path Sudan was following in the immediate period after independence. Yugoslav aid during the Abboud regime included secondhand naval patrol craft for use in the Red Sea and on the Nile River; relations had remained cordial throughout the 1960s and were not adversely affected by the 1971 coup attempt. Moreover, Yugoslavia was not represented at the Crimean conference and was the only East European country to attend the 1972 relief and resettlement conference in Khartoum. Numayri had personally traveled to Yugoslavia, and Sudan had received Yugoslav radio-transmitting facilities. In early 1972 discussions were underway to broaden economic cooperation between the two countries.

Relations with Romania were disrupted in 1967 over the Romanian attitude toward the Arab-Israeli War and later in 1970 when Romania raised its diplomatic relations with Israel to ambassadorial level. Romania's absence from the Crimean conference signaled the possible resumption of relations as a counterbalance to the Soviet Union, especially in view of the more independent foreign policy Romania itself had adopted in recent years. Diplomatic relations were resumed on December 24, 1971. The two countries agreed to double their trade. Romania offered Sudan an easy-term loan equivalent to US$75 million to finance development projects with Romanian technical assistance. An agreement for joint petroleum exploration was announced. Two representatives of the Romanian Socialist Unity Front visited Khartoum in early 1972, and Romania's President Nicolae Ceausescu visited Khartoum in April.

Recognition of the PRC was one of the first acts taken by the Sudanese government after independence. Nominal relations existed between the two countries until the 1960s, when they began to expand. In 1971 contacts with the PRC increased rapidly. In March 1971 the two countries signed a nine-month trade protocol worth the equivalent of US$12 million. After the short-lived July 1971 coup, relations were further enhanced when the PRC extended its support to Numayri in spite of his retaliatory action against Sudanese communist elements. Numayri made a state visit to Peking in August 1971. At the conclusion of the visit agreements on economic and technical assistance and scientific and cultural cooperation were signed. Similar agreements were concluded with North Korea at the end of the trip to the PRC.

Among the significant features of the agreements with the PRC were offers of medical and veterinary assistance and a proposal to construct two roads, a bridge over the Blue Nile River, a textile mill, and an international conference hall in Khartoum. In late November 1971 the PRC acceded to a request by the Sudanese government to send forty medical specialists to work among the rural settlements. These medical personnel brought the total number of doctors from the PRC practicing in Sudanese rural areas to sixty.

By December 1971 another US$80 million worth of loans had been extended by the PRC to provide financing for an agricultural equipment factory, a chrome ore prospecting program, and development of a fishing industry on An Nubah Lake. The PRC also had expressed interest in aiding the Numayri government in the resettlement of southern refugees. In April 1972 limited military training of various elements of the Sudanese armed forces was offered in accordance with an earlier protocol agreement, and some Communist Chinese military equipment was furnished.

INTERNATIONAL ORGANIZATIONS

Sudan's interest in membership in the United Nations was realized on November 12, 1956, ten months after independence. Since then the country has become affiliated with all thirteen of the specialized agencies of the United Nations except the Intergovernmental Maritime Consultative Organization. Its affiliation has included membership on various councils and boards of the agencies. The country has supported United Nations initiatives in several instances and, although it approached the issue with reserve, Sudan furnished troops for the Congo operation during the mid-1960s.

Sudan holds membership in the United Nations Economic Commission for Africa (ECA), one of the regional commissions of the international body's Economic and Social Council. In 1963, under the auspices of ECA, the African Development Bank (ADB) was established to aid the economic development and social progress of its members on an individual and joint basis. In 1972 Sudán was a member of the bank, and Khartoum was the site of its permanent headquarters.

Various United Nations programs provided the country with financial assistance. Government-supported research projects, such as the Industrial Research Institute and the Institute of Public Administration, were aided by United Nations funds, as were plans coordinating communication facilities between Sudan and its neighbors. Both the World Health Organization and the United Nations Children's Fund were active in the country. The office of the United Nations High Commissioner for Refugees played a major role in coordinating aid from United Nations sources for displaced southern Sudanese and worked in cooperation with the International Council of Voluntary Agencies (ICVA) in channeling the aid of nongovernmental organizations into the country.

Sudan also belonged to the International Atomic Energy Agency and the United Nations Development Program. Although involvement had been somewhat curtailed since nationalization of the mass communication media, Sudan maintains membership in the Pan African Union of Journalists. In addition to membership in the Arab League and the Organization of African Unity (OAU), Sudan participated in various conferences and seminars, such as the Arab Information Ministers Conference in February 1972.

CHAPTER 11

MASS COMMUNICATION

In 1972, despite the existence of several newspapers and radio and television broadcasting stations, traditional modes of communication remained the most pervasive means of spreading information among the masses of the Sudanese people. A variety of interpersonal situations, arising from the living habits of diverse peoples, offered ample opportunity for face-to-face dialogue (see ch. 5). As a source of data on broader topics than local affairs, however, traditional channels were often unreliable mixtures of facts and rumors.

Almost all information disseminated through the modern mass media emanated from Khartoum, and a strong centralism was apparent in all dissemination of the news in its various forms. The central government exercised a high degree of control over all formal channels of mass communication. Since independence in 1956 the national leaders have been aware of the potential for political control offered by the mass media. Radio and television have long been owned and operated by the government, and in August 1970 action was taken to nationalize all elements of the press.

Although efforts had been made to increase the spread of information to rural areas—particularly through the use of radio and films—modern methods of mass communication were only beginning to be applied in the drive for national development. The sources of news and information about the national society were often restricted to the urban centers of the north; the impact of its dissemination through modern channels was strongest among the more educated urban population. The printed word did not easily penetrate the vast rural areas where literacy and income were low (see ch. 8; ch. 12). Assessments of the disruption of communication patterns and facilities by the civil war in the south were not readily available.

TRADITIONAL COMMUNICATION CHANNELS

Traditionally news and information have been communicated by word of mouth to small groups meeting for social purposes or work. The most common examples are gatherings of families

209

and larger kin groups, religious associations, and groups engaged in cultivation and herding. The number of assemblages in which an individual participates varies from one ethnic group or locality to another. Exchange also occurs at marketplaces, wells, coffeehouses, cultural clubs, and waterholes, linking local groups to one another in an informal communications network.

Some nomadic or semisedentary groups always use the same water source; others are more mobile and play a greater role in the dissemination of information. Nomadic herders and semisedentary people often get news from the radio when they come into towns or villages to trade. These reports—or the listener's interpretation of them—are passed along during the performance of the group task at hand, as in the case of herding the community flocks to market, or during religious observances and social occasions after the task is completed. The majority of information passed by word of mouth concerns local matters; traditional communication patterns are further fragmented by ethnic hostilities and cultural dissimilarities separating northern and southern peoples.

Formal groups are usually structured with an opinion leader or a number of elders who guide discussions and interpret all new information received. Individual opinion concerning information usually conforms with that of the group leader and affects an individual's evaluation of new information received outside the context of the group.

The reliability of news and information received into such groups is not usually taken for granted. It is more apt to be accepted as true if it comes from an outside source such as a visiting religious leader, and in some groups it is almost certain to be accepted if it conforms to existent beliefs and if it is presented in accordance with the group's conventional literary style. Introductory pleasantries and the exchange of traditional proverbs often precede the discussion of any news reports.

The need to rely on face-to-face communication makes it difficult for the government to introduce new concepts of national development to the people, not only because information transmitted in this way is often inaccurately reported but also because local ideas and points of view tend to take precedence over the outside ones.

Links between traditional channels and the modern media are insufficient to permit news and other information to reach all segments of the diverse population. Similarly, the government often encounters difficulty in assessing the effect of its formal communication efforts. Among many groups any statement or appeal by the government is regarded with suspicion.

THE MODERN MEDIA

Role of Government

The mass media have served throughout their history as channels for the dissemination of information supporting various political parties or, more recently, official views of the government. Until November 1958, when the military regime of General Ibrahim Abboud came to power, the press was largely controlled by political parties and was heavily subsidized by the United Arab Republic (UAR). Before this change of government, the press enjoyed a considerable degree of freedom but occasionally was warned not to express its opinions too freely. In August 1958, for example, when the government of Abdullah Khalil was preparing to negotiate a Nile waters and trade agreement with the UAR, newspapers were asked to refrain from publishing statements that might strain relations between the two countries. Standing by what they claimed were their legal and constitutional rights, the editors, through the chairman of the Sudanese Press Association, bluntly rejected the government request.

When the military regime of General Abboud assumed control of the government, strict censorship of the mass media was imposed. With the ban on all political parties, the newspapers of the pro-UAR National Unionist Party and those of the Ummah party were forced to stop publishing. Two communist newspapers were likewise suspended.

Strict censorship and the threat of suspension compelled newspapers that survived the change of regime to follow the government line. Any editorial policy that seemed hostile to the Abboud government brought a reprisal either in the form of an indefinite suspension or in the form of warnings.

Shortly after its accession to power, the Abboud government began the reorganization of information services by establishing a guidance office for the regulation of mass media activities. The Central Office of Information, under the Ministry of Information and Labor, included sections devoted to the press, photography, film production, and broadcasting. The information center, a department of the ministry, provided the local press with information about the government's activities.

The information center also distributed government news to foreign news services, foreign diplomatic missions, and a variety of foreign press institutions and organizations. Under the condominium rule the dissemination of information about Sudan had been left almost exclusively to the British. The center issued daily and weekly news bulletins in Arabic and English as well as pamphlets describing the government's development programs.

It also maintained a display room where photographs of Sudan and examples of Sudanese handicrafts could be viewed by the public.

After the fall of the Abboud government in late 1964 and the formation of a civilian coalition government, mass communication activities were reorganized under the Ministry of Information and Social Affairs. Censorship of the media was temporarily suspended by the government, although the Central Office of Information was maintained as the centralized outlet through which national guidance was disseminated to the people. The ministry expanded the services of its information center with the addition of the Regional Information Section, which was responsible for coordinating the dissemination of national and local information to all areas of the country. To achieve this purpose regional offices were established in most of the provincial capitals and a number of the major towns. These regional offices relayed to local inhabitants news releases and other information distributed by the information center in Khartoum. They in turn provided the central ministry with information regarding local happenings in the provinces.

During the mid-1960s the Arab Relations and Magazine Section was established within the information center in Khartoum. This section was responsible for all information concerning the Arab League and its relevant organizations. As part of the program undertaken by this section, the government published a monthly cultural magazine in Arabic for dissemination to readers both at home and abroad.

After the nationalization of the press in 1970, certain sections of the Ministry of Information and Social Affairs were reportedly eliminated. Further reorganization in 1971 redistributed its earlier functions between two new agencies: the Ministry of Communications and the Ministry of Information and Culture. Sources available in early 1972 did not reveal the division of functions between these two ministries or their internal administrative organization.

The Press and Publishing

The country's first newspaper, *Al Sudan*, was published in 1903 through the efforts of Syrian and Egyptian journalists, and throughout the 1920s the press in Sudan was published, edited, and read mainly by non-Sudanese residents. Sudanese participation in the publishing field and the focus of the press on politics increased during the 1930s and 1940s, when the press came to play a major role as a forum for discussion and agitation for independence.

During the 1960s—and especially during the middle of the decade when government censorship was temporarily removed—the Sudanese press passed through a highly fluid stage. In 1960 newspapers in circulation included seven dailies, four semiweeklies, fifteen weeklies, and fifteen publications that appeared at less frequent intervals. In succeeding years the larger newspapers competed to consolidate their positions and to expand their facilities, but many small newspapers closed within weeks after publishing their first issues. By 1968 there were thirteen daily newspapers, two semiweeklies, and thirteen weeklies. All daily newspapers were published in Khartoum, but some weekly and monthly periodicals were published in Al Ubayyid, Wad Madani, Juba, and Malakal. The language of all newspapers was Arabic, except for four that were published in English and one in Greek. Most newspapers had their own printing presses, although the smaller ones often shared a press.

Most newspapers consisted of only eight pages. Editorials, leading articles of international significance, and important domestic or government news items were placed on the front page. Inside pages were devoted to social news, sports, entertainment, and letters to the editor. A daily column featuring commentaries by foreign correspondents or the discussion of an international topic sometimes appeared on the last page of a newspaper. Advertisements, both public and private, provided a large share of newspaper revenue, and circulation accounted for very little of their income.

The largest dailies, such as *Al Ayam*, obtained news either from foreign correspondents or from three domestic news agencies. The Sudan News Agency, the Sudanese Press Agency, and the African News Agency—all with home offices in Khartoum—published daily bulletins covering local and international news and excerpts from the local press. The Sudan News Agency had correspondents in each provincial capital. The Sudanese Press Agency maintained correspondents in all major Sudanese towns, in Cairo, and in London. The press received news of governmental activities through weekly press conferences designed to publicize governmental accomplishments and to counter what the administration considered to be seditious rumors.

After the fall of the Abboud government in 1964, government censorship of the press was relaxed for a time. Mounting dissatisfaction within the succeeding civilian coalition governments over press objectivity, however, led to the reestablishment of official censorship on October 1, 1968.

Further restrictions were imposed in the aftermath of the 1969 military coup d'etat. Through the government-owned radio, the ruling Revolutionary Command Council (RCC) accused the press of distorting government policy statements, of practicing excessive commercialism, and of propagating foreign ideologies instead of participating in nation-building. In August 1970 the RCC nationalized all privately owned Sudanese newspapers and news agencies and concurrently announced the suspension of all publications except those of the government. Four Arabic-language dailies and one English-language daily were among the newspapers that initially survived the nationalization decree.

The nationalized press was placed under control of an agency designated as the Sudanese Press Corporation, which directed the operation of two publishing companies, the Al Rai al Amm Printing Company and the Ayam Printing Company. Although the corporation was advanced as a short-term mechanism to coordinate and integrate rather than directly control all phases of press operations, it held diverse and far-reaching authority. Two of its major functions included acting on all new newspaper and magazine requests for registration and certifying the membership of journalists in the press union. Favorable action by the corporation was dependent upon an ideological framework considered appropriate to the goals of national and social development.

Improvement of newspaper distribution, expansion and improvement of press facilities, and the training of personnel were major responsibilities of the corporation. Additional projects included the listing of the assets of former owners of nationalized papers and recommendations to the RCC of regulations for political supervision of the press. By early 1971 the RCC indicated that the overall goals of the corporation had been satisfactorily realized.

On September 6, 1971, the RCC placed the administration of the press directly under the Ministry of Information and Culture and dissolved the previous press control mechanisms. The internal administration of publishing houses was reorganized by the ministry. The authority of the director of each publishing house was transferred to a managerial council composed of the chief editor, who served as chairman of the council; management and printing directors; and worker representatives. Although the structuring of concise press regulations was still under consideration in early 1972, specific guidelines had not been published by the government.

In early 1972 two daily newspapers—*Al Ayam* and *Al Sahafa*—remained in circulation. Both were in the Arabic language, and each had an estimated circulation of about 25,000 copies. The last English-language daily to survive the nationalization and suspension decree ceased operation in December 1971, leaving the bulletins issued by the local news services as the only daily source of news in English. Two former dailies, *Al Sudan al Jadid* and *Al Rai al Amm*, appeared weekly in Arabic. The first of these was published under government direction by the Ayam Printing Company, which also published the daily *Al Ayam*, a few provincial newspapers that appeared less frequently, and a women's journal. Under similar government contract, the Al Rai al Amm Printing Company published the daily *Al Sahafa*, the weekly *Al Rai al Amm*, and a monthly magazine, *Al Khartoum*. A new English-language weekly, *Nile Mirror*, devoted to news on development plans for southern Sudan, began publication in September 1971. Published by the Office of the Minister of State for Southern Affairs, it was edited by the office's information adviser.

Domestic news was provided to the press and the Broadcast Service by the Sudanese News Agency (SUNA), which was established in mid-1971 to replace the news agencies that formerly operated throughout the country. SUNA maintained its own radiophoto and teleprinter equipment to receive news from various parts of the world. Telegraphic links provided news to local Sudanese subscribers.

In addition to its domestic responsibilities SUNA provided news of Sudanese achievements to various foreign nations. In mid-1971 SUNA began broadcasting its news file to the Middle East News Agency in Cairo, as discussions began on increased cooperation and possible merger of SUNA with the news agencies of the other Tripoli Charter States of the UAR, Libya, and Syria (see ch. 10). As of late 1971 Sudanese journalists affiliated with SUNA were assigned to the capitals of various Middle Eastern and African countries, and several were stationed in Peking.

In early 1972 the generally low literacy rate in rural areas and the concentration of newspaper publishing in the larger urban centers limited the role of the press as a medium for disseminating information to the public. Although circulation of newspapers and periodicals in rural areas was gradually increasing, most issues were distributed directly to a few newsstands in the towns and villages and to subscribers in the capital city of Khartoum. Delivery of daily newspapers by air to southern towns was initiated during the 1960s, but they were usually received several days after publication. Improvement in this service, resulting in delays of but a few hours, was claimed by the government in 1971 after nationalization of the press.

In 1972 the publishing industry, which formerly had circulated some books and locally produced printed materials, was entirely under the control of the central government. The ministries and other governmental agencies in Khartoum provided

215

reports, guides, and statistical information, such as the *Sudan Almanac* and *Radio and TV Magazine,* for publication by the Government Printing Press. In addition to the official printer, eight publishing facilities that had been nationalized were indirectly administered by the government. Their major publications consisted of short descriptive periodicals and pamphlets on such subjects as irrigation, agriculture, education, health, and other features connected with the programs of national development. They often reflected accurate appraisals of the problems confronting government planners; although they functioned as endorsements of government programs, their technical or educational worth was often considerable. Government-supported research programs and museums also printed material for general public distribution. In early 1972 expansion of the publishing sector remained a stated governmental goal.

Radio

The most effective modern medium of mass communication, which at times reached even some remote nomadic tribesmen, was the radio. It was of particular importance because of the limited impact of the printed word. Much of the potential of radio was restricted by the shortage of radio sets, especially in rural areas. The introduction of low-cost, battery-powered transistor radios, however, had increased the value of radio as a communicatoin tool. In addition, the government had installed radios in popular meeting places, such as cafés and village squares. Generally these installations consisted of loudspeakers that amplified newscasts, Sudanese music, and information the government had chosen as relevant to local needs and interests.

In early 1972 all radio broadcasting was under government direction; the Broadcast Service of the Ministry of Information and Culture arranged all programs. Radio Omdurman, the central station, maintained studios and transmitters at Omdurman and additional shortwave transmitters at nearby Feteihab. All technical servicing was accomplished by the Postal and Telegraph Service of the Ministry of Communications.

The facilities were modern, and the Broadcasting House at Omdurman could transmit two programs simultaneously. Transmission equipment included two mediumwave band transmitters with peak powers ranging from sixty to 100 kilowatts and five shortwave band transmitters with peak powers ranging from twenty to 120 kilowatts. Two standby transmitters provided backup power for both shortwave and meduimwave broadcasts. Radio services were to be expanded under the Five-Year Plan of Economic and Social Development, 1970/71–1974/75. The program included the procurement and installation of more modern equipment at Omdurman and the installation of additional broadcasting stations in Khartoum, Malakal, Kassala, and Nyala.

Daily domestic broadcasting was divided into the standard Home Service in Arabic for the northern area and the Southern Service in English and Somali. Broadcasting schedules varied for each transmitter, but in most areas radio transmissions were received from 4:00 A.M. until 10:00 P.M. In addition to music and other entertainment features, programs featured such items as recitations of the Koran, religious talks, world and national newscasts, programs for women and children, instructive programs on health and personal hygiene, and subjects related to national development programs.

In January 1972 Radio Omdurman initiated a special program for Sudanese living in foreign countries. Broadcast in the shortwave band six days each week, the new program was designed to inform Sudanese expatriates of the changes occurring in Sudan and of the government's plan to bring progress and modernization to the homeland. Included in the hour-long Arabic language broadcast were a daily newscast, a résumé of other items appearing in Sudanese newspapers and magazines, and Sudanese music interspersed with messages from local citizens to their relatives abroad.

In 1960 about 6,000 registered radio receivers were in use by the public; a single set located in a public place, however, often served an entire village. By 1970 the number of receivers in use had increased to an estimated 180,000, largely through the introduction of inexpensive transistor equipment. In the larger towns radio broadcasts could be heard in many public buildings and commercial establishments, such as hotels, bars, and coffeehouses.

Television

An experimental pilot program conducted in 1962 led to the establishment of the country's first television station in 1963. By the mid-1960s regularized programming had been established. In late 1971 two broadcast channels were operated by the government-owned Sudanese Television Service in Omdurman. All television staff members were Sudanese. Transmitter sites were located in Omdurman and Wad Madani in the Jazirah area of Blue Nile Province; additional sites were planned for Atbarah and Port Sudan. Construction of a station at Wad Madani was expected to be completed and to begin transmission by mid-1972.

Daily broadcasts were transmitted between 4:30 P.M. and 8:30 P.M., providing a total weekly program time of twenty-eight hours. Programs of both live and taped performances included music, interviews, panel discussions, religious programs, women's topics, and cultural features. An educational series was broadcast once a week in cooperation with the Ministry of Education.

Television was popular among viewers, who consisted largely of people in the capital complex with sufficient income to afford receiving sets and those who watched receivers placed in public buildings and in commercial establishments. The number of receivers in use had grown from an estimated 10,000 in 1965 to about 50,000 in 1970.

A protocol agreement was reached between Sudan and Czechoslovakia in July 1970 for two additional television transmitters, a mobile radio transmitter, and equipment for monitoring foreign broadcasts. Construction of an industrial facility for the assembly of television and radio receivers was also under consideration in 1971.

Films

Films have always been popular with the Sudanese people, and motion picture theaters have continued to be well attended wherever they have been accessible. In 1970 there were forty-five film theaters in the country, principally in the major urban centers. This number included a variety of open-air facilities; as a result, estimates of the total seating capacity ranged from 42,000 to 75,000. Although motion picture theaters were included in the government's nationalization plans, most of the facilities in early 1972 continued to be privately owned and operated.

The Film Vans Section of the Ministry of Information and Culture operated a fleet of forty-five mobile vans throughout the provinces. At least one van was stationed at each provincial capital, and periodic film showings were scheduled in many areas. Mobile film units also traveled the railways, making periodic stops at villages and railroad stations en route. Attendance at mobile film showings was excellent, with most of an entire village usually attending. Physical conditions of the roads prohibit access to some areas, and consequently a large number of Sudanese had never seen a film.

Sudan did not produce feature-length films but imported them largely from the Arab Republic of Egypt, India, and the United Kingdom. Newsreels were regularly shown, supplemented by newscasts produced by the Sudan Film Center of the Ministry of Information and Culture. The center produced both sixteen-

and thirty-five-millimeter documentary films in monochrome and in color for government agencies and for newsreel and television presentation. The unit did its own photoprocessing and sound recording, and the films it produced recorded government accomplishments in such fields as agriculture, health, and education. The unit also produced a weekly summary of official news to be shown at the principal film theaters. In 1970 the annual production of government educational and documentary films was estimated to be about thirty short-length features, many of them — particularly newsreels — designed for showing both in Sudan and abroad.

POSTS AND TELECOMMUNICATIONS

Communication services were provided by the central government through the Postal and Telegraph Service of the Ministry of Communications. In addition to standard letter and parcel delivery, postal services included the sale of money orders and postal checks and a postal savings system. In the late 1960s there were approximately 370 postal facilities, of which about half were listed as government postal offices. The remainder were commercial agencies operated independently by private merchants. Commercial agency services were more limited than those of the government postal offices; facilities frequently were in buildings with insufficient space and generally were poorly suited to the services they were to perform. The majority of government postal offices and commercial agencies also provided varying levels of telephone and telegraph services. Postal services were also provided by river steamers operating on the Nile River and by the Sudan Railways.

In late 1969 there were about 45,000 subscribers to the government-owned telephone service as compared to about 34,000 in 1960. During the late 1960s the capacity of postal and telegraph services increased by 24 percent. An increase of 41 percent in telephone services during the same period reflected major expansions in rural telephone networks.

Expansion of the national communications system, under a £S3 million (1 Sudanese pound equals US$2.87) allocation of the Five-Year Plan of Economic and Social Development, aimed at improving the technical quality of communications facilities and personnel and expanding the number and kinds of postal and telegraphic facilities. An automatic telephone exchange linking Khartoum, Wad Madani, Atbarah, Singi, Dunqulah, Qadarif, and Port Sudan was established in February 1971. Installations of automatic telephone exchanges were scheduled for Port Sudan,

Al Dueim, and Qadarif. Radio links between Khartoum and southern towns were scheduled for expansion from eighty-one channels in 1970 to 116 in 1975.

Under the five-year plan projects were introduced for the improvement and expansion of radio links with Addis Ababa, Nairobi, Tripoli, Beirut, Moscow, East Berlin, and Jaddah. During 1970 and 1971 progress was made in the expansion of radio facilities linking Sudan with Ethiopia and the Central African Republic, and communications improvements with the Democratic People's Republic of Korea (North Korea) were discussed. Plans were also underway for coordination of future developments of microradio networks and satellite facilities with neighboring states. The United Nations had contributed US$500,000 for the implementation of the first stage of the project, and a number of Norwegian experts arrived in mid-1971 to begin its development.

In late 1971 an agreement was concluded with Saudi Arabia for laying a marine cable in the Red Sea to strengthen communications between the two countries. In early 1972 negotiations were in progress to implement the project as soon as possible.

SECTION III. ECONOMIC

CHAPTER 12

CHARACTER AND STRUCTURE OF THE ECONOMY

The modern economy is based largely upon irrigated cotton growing which is government controlled from field to export; the traditional economy is based upon independent herding and summer rainfall cultivation of drought-resistant food grains. One axis of population density and maximum economic activity follows the Nile River in a north-south direction; another lies along the railway from east to west through the center of the country. Where the two meet is the hub of productive and commercial activity, in Al Jazirah and the Three Towns (Khartoum, Khartoum North, and Omdurman).

In 1972 it was said that roughly one-fourth of the population lived in the modern sector and three-fourths were in the traditional sector. More than 85 percent of the population derived its livelihood from primary activity—herding or cultivation. Most of these were in traditional agriculture, relying upon scarce rainfall or upon hand- or animal-operated irrigation. The distinction between modern and traditional activity is chiefly one of scale, methods, and conditions of production. In agriculture, for example, the modern sector is distinguished by the use of diesel-pump or gravity-flow irrigation or, when reliant on rainfall alone, by the use of mechanized implements.

The division between subsistence and commercial production is less clear cut. Most of those engaged in herding or cultivation produce primarily for their own subsistence, but many subsistence cultivators market their surplus whenever the occasion arises, and much of the agricultural output produced in the modern sector is used for subsistence. Some groups that farm or herd primarily for their own subsistence rely upon regular sale of such products as gum arabic, groundnuts, or sesame to supplement their livelihood in kind. In central Sudan there is considerable seasonal movement from traditional cultivation or nomadic herding to wage employment on the government irrigation or mechanization schemes.

221

Diversification of the productive structure had barely begun in the 1960s. Cotton still provided between 60 and 70 percent of merchandise exports and largely determined the level of economic activity, money incomes, and fiscal revenues. Other agricultural exports were on the increase but depended largely on varying climatic conditions from year to year. Mineral extraction was still negligible, and industry was in the embryonic stage, employing about 6 percent of the active population and providing about 13 percent of gross domestic product (GDP). About 8 percent of the economically active were engaged in tertiary activity, such as commerce and services.

A notable characteristic was the dominant and growing role of government in economic activity. Because of the dearth of private savings, the government had always been the prime mover in agricultural investment, primarily in irrigation schemes. At independence in 1956 it took over operation of the cotton marketing boards, a crucial sector of the economy. In the 1960s the government also became fairly active in industrial investment through its Industrial Development Corporation. Since mid-1969 the government has been committed to socialism, and since the inauguration of the nationalization policy in mid-1970 it has taken over all commercial banks as well as the medium-sized and large firms that dominated the modern sector of manufacturing and trade. Foreign trade became government directed. It was estimated that by 1972 the public sector was accounting for about 55 percent of gross output. It had taken over all the private pump irrigation schemes, so that virtually all of the modern sector of agriculture was in government hands. Traditional agriculture, handicrafts, and small-scale trading and manufacturing, however, still remained in private hands.

In these circumstances the role of public finance and planning —already crucial—has taken on added importance. The lack of appreciable real economic growth from 1965 through 1971 was attributed to the relatively low level of public investment after completion of the major irrigation projects of the early 1960s. The relatively depressed cotton earnings of the mid-1960s, among other factors, led to a decline in private investment as well. The public sector was unable to muster enough investment financing to match foreign assistance received for the Ten-Year Plan of Economic and Social Development, 1961/62–1970/71, and the plan had to be virtually abandoned after the first five years. Some of its proposed agricultural projects were later included in the Five-Year Plan of Economic and Social Development, 1970/71–1974/75.

In the meantime current government expenditure on military

and other requirements was mounting (see ch. 14). Consumption outstripped savings at an alarming rate, and the government was obliged to borrow heavily from the banking system. Money supply increased dramatically. The rising rate of inflation cancelled out most or all of the nominal yearly growth in GDP of about 5 percent a year between 1960 and 1969; and since the population was growing at about 3 percent a year, the purchasing power of per capita income had actually declined. In 1969 per capita income was estimated at about £S36 (1 Sudanese pound equals US$2.87), the equivalent of about US$103.

Inflation and mounting consumption had also put pressure on the balance of external payments and, despite improved cotton exports from 1969 through 1971, there was a continuing shortage of foreign exchange for the imports needed for development. The burden of foreign debt was considerably increased by the end of the 1960s. Thus the country was in a precarious financial position, and it appeared that implementation of the five-year development plan would depend heavily on commitments of foreign assistance on favorable terms.

The potential for greatly increased production through adequate investment was judged basically good, given the requisite political and financial stability. The economic potential of the Southern Region had as yet scarcely been tapped, and the central rainlands, where the bulk of proposed investment was to take place, were also thought to promise a favorable return. Two developments that tended to improve the country's credit worthiness as an applicant for international loans were the termination of the war with the southern rebels in March 1972 and the achievement of increased yields and stability of output in cotton growing. The peace settlement was the first step toward creating conditions that might permit some stabilization of public finances and a possible diversion of expenditures from current to development needs. The improvement of cotton output was attributed to increased use of fertilizers and pesticides and other improved methods. By the 1971/72 season the plateau of high stable production and improved yield had been maintained for five years without the radical year-to-year fluctuations that had previously characterized cotton output. It thus offered encouraging evidence that planned investment in organized and irrigated cotton growing could yield real returns for the grower and for the national treasury.

PATTERN OF ECONOMIC ACTIVITY

Whereas most of the active population is engaged in herding or cultivation as the primary economic activity, only about 38 percent of total domestic product is thought to be derived from agriculture (see table 6). This is the result of the low average productivity per man-hour in agriculture and the modest imputed value of most subsistence production.

Manufacturing had shown rapid growth during the 1960s, while agriculture was relatively stagnant. Industry had expanded from so low a base, however, that its share of economic activity was still slight. In 1972 total employment in the modern industrial sector was estimated at about 80,000 persons, of whom some 60,000 were employed in establishments of ten or more persons. Commerce and the services, including government, had expanded most notably. In 1972 there were thought to be from 100,000 to 120,000 people in government employment.

Table 6. Sudan, Active Population, 1956, and Gross Domestic Product, 1966–68, by Economic Sector

Sector of Economic Activity	Percentage of Active Population 1956	Gross Domestic Product[1]			
		1966	1967	1968	1968
		(in millions of Sudanese pounds)[2]			(in percent of total)
Agriculture, forestry, and fishing...............	85.6	173.0	190.2	199.9	37.9
Manufacturing...........	5.0	38.5	42.0	43.8	8.3
Mining.................	n.a.				
Electricity..............	n.a.	16.6	16.3	16.7	3.2
Construction............	0.6	23.9	21.7	24.3	4.6
Commerce..............	2.1	104.8	113.7	127.0	24.1
Finance................	n.a.				
Transport and communication........	0.6	31.8	31.4	33.8	6.4
Government services.....		40.6	46.3	51.5	9.8
	4.6				
Services, other.........		27.8	28.2	30.0	5.7
Inadequately described....	1.3	.....	.....	.....	.....
Total................	100.0[3]	456.9[3]	489.9[3]	527.0	100.0

n.a.—not available.
.... not applicable.
[1] At factor cost.
[2] 1 Sudanese pound equals US$2.87.
[3] Does not total because of rounding.

As in many developing countries, the statistics on origin of GDP were derived from approximate estimates and were somewhat unreliable, particularly for measuring trends over time. The calculations for 1966 to 1969 were thought to be a considerable improvement over previous estimates, however. The growth of commerce and finance may have been inflated by the inclusion of the profits of public entities, such as the sugar monopoly, which in fact were a form of indirect tax. The valuation of agricultural production may have been slightly overestimated. The estimates for other sectors were thought to be approximately correct.

Because 1969 was a poor crop year, the share of agriculture was disproportionately low, and the share of other sectors was correspondingly inflated. Making due allowance for year-to-year fluctuations, however, the contribution of agriculture to domestic product had shown a decided drop since 1960, an increasing share being generated by commerce and services, including public corporation profits. The portion of GDP shown as derived from agriculture is equivalent to value added in herding and cultivation—in other words, the return to the producer. The share of export proceeds on cotton and other agricultural products retained by the Jazirah Board and other trading agencies may probably be included under commerce. The share retained by the government, although actually an indirect tax may be included on the same principle as sugar profits, thus inflating the share reported for commerce and finance. Thus the breakdown of GDP by sector of origin tends to minimize the importance of agricultural production to the economy as a whole.

WORKING FORCE

Unemployment is thought to be a less severe problem in Sudan than in many developing countries. Like most developing countries, it has a chronic problem of thinly disguised underemployment in rural or urban subsistence production, with too many people producing just enough on which to live. Unlike most developing countries, however, it also suffers a chronic seasonal shortage of labor in the modern sector of agriculture, which tends to drive up wages and to attract considerable migration from elsewhere in Africa (see ch. 3; ch. 4). Until about 1965 a major problem was shortage of skilled urban labor, and a high proportion of skilled jobs and managerial and executive positions was filled by foreigners of Greek or Armenian descent. The financial reverses and the decline in public and private investment in the late 1960s reduced the rate of demand for skilled and managerial workers, and by 1965 the graduates of newly established institutes of technical education and training centers were available to fill such jobs (see ch. 8). Consequently unemployment among skilled urban workers began to increase, and there began to be a net outflow of teachers, clerical staff, and skilled labor to the Arab countries.

Estimates of the economically active population for 1971 were made by applying ratios from the census conducted in 1955 and 1956 to the estimated population for 1971, giving a working force of 7.4 million out of a population of 15.8 million. This included 66.6 percent of males and 26.4 percent of females. A comparison with the Arab Republic of Egypt, where similar religious traditions prevail, suggests that the number of economically active women in northern Sudan may have been substantially underreported for reasons of traditional propriety.

There is no legal minimum wage. Except for a very few large modern firms, wages are higher in the public sector than in the private sector. The minimum monthly wage paid in permanent employment in 1971 was £S14 in the public sector and as much as 30 percent lower in the private sector. For skilled employees, however, salaries in the public sector reached £S35 or £S40 a month, and in private industry, 5 to 15 percent higher. In 1970 the daily minimum wage ranged between 25 and 50 piasters (100 piasters equal £S1), depending on season and region. In Al Jazirah during the cotton-picking season, when heat is severe and labor scarce, the daily minimum might rise as high as 50 piasters. Wages and salaries have lagged behind the increase in the cost of living over the twenty years from 1950 to 1970, bringing a net decline in average real earnings (see ch. 7).

At the beginning of 1972 there were 562 trade unions (see ch. 9). A new law was being drafted that would consolidate them into only thirty comprehensive trade unions. The objective was to make labor benefits more uniform in their application and to permit coordination of planned vocational training programs.

ECONOMIC REGIONS

In early 1972 it was possible for convenience to divide the country into nine fairly distinct economic regions (see fig. 10). Within some of these regions great diversity was found in ethnic affiliation, living conditions, and agricultural practices of the inhabitants as well as in crops, livestock, and such crucial factors as access to water, transport, or markets. In preponderant range of climate, vegetation, and soils, however, the economic regions were more conveniently defined than some of the provinces or districts, and they permitted the separate treatment of the more developed urban or irrigated areas.

Of the nine regions, six supported rural economies engaged predominantly in subsistence activity and utilizing chiefly traditional implements and methods of production. The other three regions—the Three Towns region, Al Jazirah, and the economic

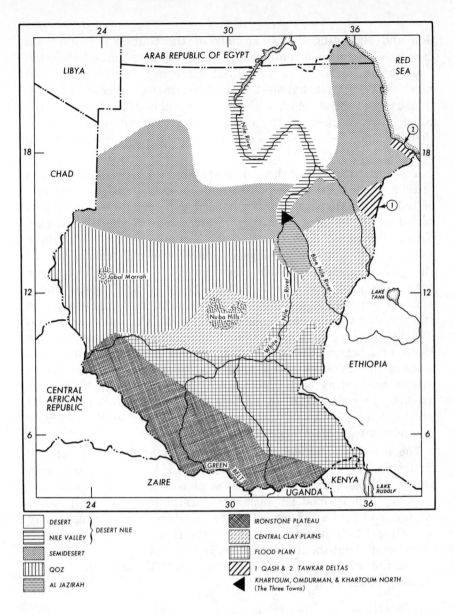

Source: Adapted from Rolf Güsten, *Problems of Economic Growth and Planning: The Sudan Example: Some Aspects and Implications of the Current Ten-Year Plan.* (No. 9 in the series Africa-Sudien of the IFO-Institut für Wirtschaftsforschung, West Berlin, 1966.

Figure 10. Economic Regions of Sudan

"region" including the geographically separated Qash and Tawkar deltas—included among them most of the modern sector of agriculture, employing more efficient tools and methods of produc-

227

tion and supplying the great bulk of the country's commercial exports. They also included much of the rather limited industry and tertiary activity in organized commerce, government, and services. They attracted most of the investment and capital formation. They absorbed most of the imports and employed most of the wage labor. Almost all the persons who received part or all of their income in cash, as opposed to subsistence goods, were living in these three regions.

The work of defining the nine economic regions was undertaken in 1959 on the basis of the population census and national accounts of 1956. Since that time there has been some progress in mechanization of agriculture in a very limited area of the central clay plains as well as in small-scale cash-cropping schemes elsewhere (see ch. 13). Moreover, groups with access to rail transport have long sold a portion of their crop surplus for cash in good crop years. The gum arabic gatherers of the *qoz* (sand) region make a fairly significant contribution to exports, and inhabitants of other regions may make seasonal trips to the more developed regions in search of wage labor. If development plans for the 1970s and beyond are realized, the three heavy investment regions of the 1960s may come to have a progressively less exclusive role in generating cash incomes and in monopolizing skills and literacy. In many African nations the gap between urban and rural incomes, however, has tended to widen rather than narrow as early development efforts have progressed.

The most common and widespread form of economic activity is the cultivation of drought-resistant food grains—durra sorghum or dukhn millet—which takes place both in the traditional economy and in modern mechanized rainland farming. Production of food grains occurs wherever moisture is adequate. It may be assumed that summer rainfall cultivation of food grains takes place throughout the livestock zone, in the southern tsetse fly zone, and in the northern desert zone along the Nile or in the beds of seasonal streams (see fig. 11).

The Northern Area

The Three Towns—the contiguous urban agglomerations of Khartoum, Omdurman, and Khartoum North—form the country's only urban complex of any size. Khartoum is the center of government activty and the modern component of commercial enterprise; Khartoum North is a light manufacturing and high-income residential center; Omdurman is a traditional sprawling African city (see ch. 3).

Primary activity—in agriculture, forestry, fishing, or mining—

is negligible in the Three Towns, although the rural area immediately surrounding them is relatively highly developed in production of dairy products, vegetables, and other supplies for the urban market (see ch. 13). Secondary activity—manufacturing and crafts—accounted for only about 5 percent of the region's output in 1956. Much of this sector's activity at that early date consisted of cotton ginning located near the cotton fields, cement production, and the railway workshops, which were in Atbarah.

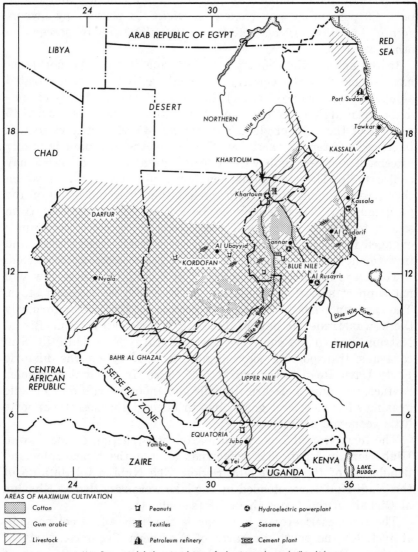

Figure 11. Economic Activity of Sudan, 1970

Limited consumer goods industries, however, were concentrated in the Three Towns even then, since the market as well as the necessary water and electricity were to be found there. Industrial development in the 1960s led to greater concentration of manufacturing and crafts in the Khartoum area.

The tertiary sector—commerce, transport, and services—accounts for the bulk of economic activity in the Three Towns. In 1956 about 95 percent of estimated local GDP was generated by the tertiary sector: about 32 percent by distribution and transport, 26 percent by government services, 13 percent by ownership of buildings, 12 percent by construction, and 10 percent by other services.

In the desert Nile economic region, constituting the northernmost segment of the country, economic activity is concentrated along the Nile, where the old traditional forms of hand- or animal-driven irrigation survive. Agriculture generates about 45 percent of the local product, and another 45 percent is estimated to come from tertiary activity. The role of the merchant is highly esteemed, and any man with a little capital at his disposal may aspire to it. The merchants commonly practice *sheil*, in which they advance money on a crop for less than it would bring on the open market. These debts may be carried on indefinitely from season to season. In general, there tend to be more individuals engaged in commerce than the volume of trade can support, and investment in more productive activity is consequently neglected.

There are few oases in the desert of Sudan, and those few will not support a settled population, serving only as caravan stops. The caravan trade had gone into decline by the 1950s; formerly there was trade in natron (sodium bicarbonate) from Bir al Natrum, and in the early twentieth century there had still been caravans transporting slaves, gold, and ivory on the historic Forty Days' Road to the markets of Cairo. In a few depressions, ravines, or wadis there are silt soils and enough scrub for nomadic grazing of camels and goats, but in general the desert supports little economic activity.

The formation of Lake Nasser after construction of the Aswan High Dam in Egypt has somewhat altered the topography and population of the desert Nile region. The Nubian inhabitants of the Wadi Halfa area flooded by the lake were resettled at Khashm al Qirbah in the Butanah plain (see ch. 4).

The semidesert economic region is the home of camel nomads. It includes the southern parts of Northern Province, parts of northern Darfur Province, and most of the northern part of Kordofan Province. It affords sparse grazing for camels, goats, and sheep, but they must move over a very large area. Within six months a nomadic tribe may travel more than 1,000 miles in search of grazing and water for the animals. In good years they may wander as far north as 18° or 19°N. The period of nomadic wandering is generally from May or June through December. The dry winter season is spent in the nomadic home camp.

Every two or three years the rains may be heavy enough in the semidesert to produce a special combination of vegetation known as *gizu*. In such years the young men of the tribe can stay on with the camels, living mainly on milk, while the rest of the group returns to the home camps. The nomads supplement their milk and meat diet with grain purchased from the cultivators or occasionally by the durra or dukhn they sow in casual fashion in riverbeds or areas flooded by the seasonal rains.

The desert has been encroaching gradually southward into the savanna. At a meeting of the United Nations Food and Agriculture Organization in February 1971, the delegate of Sudan joined with the delegate of Chad in asking for help to halt the advance of desert sand on arable land. He declared that ten years earlier a third of the country was already covered by desert. If the current erosion process continued, he said, by the early 1980s half of Sudan would be invaded by sand.

The central area of the country, comprising the *qoz* and central clay plains economic regions, traditionally supports migratory cattle herding combined with some summer grain cultivation, chiefly at a subsistence level. For purposes of income definition, Al Jazirah, which lies within the central clay plains, has been designated as a separate economic region. If Al Jazirah and the Three Towns were included, this central belt would clearly emerge as the economic heartland of the country, containing four of the five principal towns and receiving by far the greatest share of investment in agricultural improvement. Since the completion of Al Jazirah's Manaqil extension, most investment has gone into the central clay plains economic region, but limited areas within the *qoz* sands are also being developed.

The *qoz* economic region extends from the White Nile River westward across central Kordofan and southern Darfur provinces. Soils are fairly uniform, and settlement has depended in large part on the availability of water and the location of transport. The chief area of settled cultivation is the central belt, with nomads to the north and south. The principal groups of settled cultivators are of Nubian origin. Nomadic or semisedentary Arabs graze their cattle across the southern *qoz*, moving northward from July through September and spending November until May near the Bahr al Arab watercourse. In the central belt the Arabs al-

231

ternate summer grain cultivation with the harvesting of gum arabic from wild gum trees.

A separate economy within the *qoz* region is found in and around the Jabal Marrah area of western Darfur Province, where the Fur cultivate a range of temperate crops. The traditional isolation of this region may be modified in the 1970s by a planned railway extension and by an ambitious agricultural improvement scheme for the Jabal Marrah region.

The region of the central clay plains, including Al Jazirah, is so important to the economy of the country that one prominent geographer has ventured that, had this region been no more productive than the *qoz* or the Red Sea Hills, Sudan as an organized state could not have come into being. Even the economic region excluding Al Jazirah and the Three Towns is of vital importance as the chief area of rainland cultivation and hence the granary for much of the country. The region extends across much of southern Kordofan Province, Blue Nile Province south of the Jazirah triangle, and Kassala Province south of the Tawkar delta. It is not a rich area; the climate is often harsh, and the heavy clay soils are unfavorable for many crops and a deterrent to the needed improvement of road connections. Yet in this region a variety of peoples live peacefully in close contiguity; the so-called westerners, who have migrated from western Darfur Province and other parts of Africa, are on the way to assimilation economically, if not socially (see ch. 5). Here also there has been a very gradual trend toward settlement among the nomads, and sedentary and nomadic peoples have worked out an economic accommodation.

Settled populations of cultivators are to be found on the central clay plains wherever there is a permanent water supply. In the 1960s there were very few settled villages in the western part and practically none on the waterless plains west of the White Nile. Many of the settled peoples of the central clay plains are relatively recent immigrants, and they come from a wide variety of tribes. The eastern area around Qadarif lost much of its population during the Mahdiyyah era of the late nineteenth century and has been largely resettled by western Sudanese and by immigrants from areas west of Sudan.

A distinctive local economy within the central clay plains is found around the Nuba Hills in southern Kordofan, west of the White Nile. In the early years of the condominium the Nuba people were brought down from the more remote reaches of the hills and resettled in the foothills and on the adjoining plains. The clay plains between the hills were not settled but provided extensive grazing for several Arab tribes.

Southern Sudan

The south comprises two economic regions: the Ironstone Plateau region—the western parts of Bahr al Ghazal and Equatoria provinces—and the flood plain region, which includes most of Upper Nile Province and a portion of Bahr al Ghazal Province. Even before the rebellion this area was characterized by its isolation from the rest of the country, and there was a striking disparity in the relative degree of development between the south and the northern part of the country.

The southern clay plains are subjected to heavy rainfall every summer, and the Nile overflows its banks for a considerable distance. The flood plain proper remains inundated for from four to six months, and there are permanent papyrus and other swamps along the river that remain flooded all year (see ch. 3). Penetration of the Sudd, or swampy portion of the Nile, is difficult and time consuming and has long served to cut off the south from the rest of the country. In the rest of the area there are various degrees of flooding, with areas of intermediate land that are flooded for a month or two by rainfall rather than by the river and with smaller areas of high land that usually escape the flood.

Semisedentary cattle herding with seasonal cultivation is the pattern of economic activity in the flood plain region. The area is inhabited by Nilotic tribes. Most of the terrain in the flood plain is ill suited to crop production, and the prevalent land use is unimproved grazing, either of the perennially moist riverine grassland or of the seasonally wet grassland away from the rivers. The rainy season cultivating villages are located on the unflooded higher ground of the plains or on the adjoining Ironstone Plateau (see ch. 13).

The Ironstone Plateau differs fairly radically from the rest of the country in climate, soil, vegetation, and other environmental factors. Not only is it isolated from the north, but also communications within the region are difficult—a factor that has contributed to the great diversity of peoples within a relatively limited area (see ch. 4). Over most of the plateau the prevalent land use at the end of World War II was shifting cultivation (see ch. 13). Different systems are used by the various ethnic groups. In some areas the pattern of shifting cultivation may have been modified as population increased.

Along the southwestern edge of the plateau near the border with Zaire—until late 1971 Congo (Kinshasa)—lies the most humid area of woodland, known as the green belt. The densest population on the plateau—mainly the Azande—was found on the relatively fertile soils around Yambio. On the northern outer margins of the belt are areas of more limited potential for cultivation. On most of the Ironstone Plateau the tsetse fly is found, and cattle can be kept only in certain limited areas. The people therefore depend heavily upon cultivation for subsistence; but poultry, goats, and a few sheep may be kept.

Some foreign observers have called southern Sudan the least developed region in Africa; yet there seems to be general agreement that its potential for economic improvement over the long term is superior to that of the north. In 1952, for example, a British economic survey team reported that, given the money, the technical proficiency, and experts, southern Sudan could easily become one of the richest areas in Africa. Southerners have maintained that national funds have in the past been allocated to development of northern Sudan for political reasons (see ch. 9). National investment has tended to concentrate on projects that can be expected to yield an early monetary return to the national treasury, which in practice has meant primarily irrigated cotton production. Proximity to transport and cost of clearing the land have also made it easier to establish remunerative projects in the central part of the country. Lack of understanding of local ethnic attitudes and economic and social practices have hindered successful administration of development projects in the south, notably in the ill-fated Zande cotton-growing and resettlement scheme of the 1960s (see ch. 13; ch. 5).

During the years of the rebellion the south became still more isolated from the rest of the country, and wartime destruction and the abandonment of cropland by the flight of refugees resulted in the cessation of most cash crop production and a severe decline in food supply. By 1972 what little development had previously taken place in the south had been almost entirely swept away by the war. Equatoria Province in particular had been badly depopulated. Many roads had reverted to bush, and there were no longer any sizable plantations in production.

A new approach to economic development for the south had been promised as early as June 1969, when the newly created government of Jaafar al Numayri proclaimed that the south would be accorded regional self-government (see ch. 9). A council for planning and coordination was granted the necessary authority to plan, supervise, and follow up local development projects for the southern provinces. Given the continuation of the rebellion and the disruption of transport, however, no practical steps could be taken. In January 1971 the Council of Ministers authorized a development fund of £S1 million for exclusive use in the south, and in April a number of agricultural projects were approved by the Ministry of Planning.

The land was scheduled to be cleared for cultivation by the beginning of the planting season at the end of March 1972.

It was not until late March, however, that the final political settlement with the rebels was concluded. It appeared unlikely, therefore, that planting could get underway on the proposed projects until the following year. At an international relief and resettlement conference held at Khartoum at the end of the February 1972, the government announced that the allocated £S1 million for the south would be treated as an interim development fund and that an additional list of projects for the south would be incorporated in a separate five-year development program for the Southern Region, to be carried out by a separate southern economic planning board.

The foreign press estimated that the proposed southern development program would require an annual expenditure of at least £S5 million; with the continuation of previous subsidies to the south for normal current expenditure, the total financial requirement would be on the order of £S13 million a year. This would be considerably less than the financial drain on the treasury caused by the rebellion. With the country in a tight financial position, however, it appeared that the development plan for the south would depend upon fresh allocations of assistance from foreign countries or multilateral organizations. In the interim, the United Nations High Commissioner for Refugees and voluntary aid organizations were assisting with the repatriation and care of refugees, and the United Nations Food and Agriculture Organization had authorized food assistance equivalent to US$10 million for programs previously agreed upon with the Ministry of Local Government.

The interim agricultural projects coming under the £S1 million interim development fund would reportedly include five that would rely on the surplus of the government's Mechanized Agriculture Organization. These would be at Kapoeta in the Didinga Hills of southeastern Equatoria Province; at Akobo and Nasir on the Sobat River and Pibor Post on the Pibor River, all in Upper Nile Province; and at Bentiu. Another project planned for Upper Nile Province would involve tomato growing at Malakal. Projects for Bahr al Ghazal Province would involve pineapple and vegetables at Khawr Tembere near Raga; a sawmill in Al Rawal; and other projects at Waw, Raga, Yirol, Rumbel, and Gogrial. Another sawmill would be erected at Lukka in Equatoria Province.

The ensuing five-year program would comprise projects involving the farming of some 30,000 feddans (1 feddan equals 1.038 acres) in all three southern provinces; the maintenance and improvement of some 3,000 miles of principal and secondary roads; and the digging and maintenance of 412 water wells. Other projects would involve the restoration of river transport and the improvement of health, education, and town planning. Industrial projects would include a paper plant to use papyrus reed and bamboo as raw materials, a sugar refinery, and a factory to make sacking of locally grown kenaf fiber. Agricultural projects would include the rice scheme at Uwayl in Bahr al Ghazal Province; restoration of a previous pineapple plantation and of old tobacco, tea, and coffee plantations in Equatoria Province; production of tomatoes at Juba; and the growing of kenaf fiber at Tonj.

A very important project not mentioned among special plans for the south, but agreed upon between the central government and Egypt in December 1971, was the proposed Jonglei Canal, to be constructed in the Sudd marshlands of Upper Nile Province. A primary purpose was to increase the annual allocation of Nile irrigation water to be shared between Sudan and Egypt, but the canal should also relieve congestion in the Sudd and drain a considerable expanse of flooded land for grazing.

FOREIGN ECONOMIC RELATIONS

The country's foreign economic relations were in a state of transition in early 1972. In moving to diversify its markets and sources of assistance after 1969, the Numayri government had made the country's trade somewhat overreliant on bilateral barter arrangements with the communist countries. Official dissatisfaction with these arrangements was reportedly mounting even before the abortive communist coup of July 1971 resulted in the elimination from government of the faction most strongly in favor of close ties with the Soviet bloc countries (see ch. 9). Although still trying to maintain good relation with the communist countries, the government was seeking to obtain more favorable terms for trade and for aid with no strings attached. It also sought to expand trade with Western Europe, the wealthier Arab countries, and the Far East and had even arranged to import wheat on credit from the United States to the value of about US$10 million, the first such import since diplomatic relations with the United States had been broken off in June 1967 (see ch. 10).

The government was also negotiating for a loan of US$100 million to US$130 million from the International Bank for Reconstruction and Development (IBRD, commonly known as the World Bank), which had been denounced as an agent of imperialists in the early days of the Numayri regime. It was expected that the negotiations would have a favorable outcome, perhaps by mid-1972, making it possible to proceed with massive new irrigation investment (see ch. 13).

In the 1950s the country's imports had been modest enough to be fully covered by merchandise exports. With the growth of development expenditure in the early 1960s, however, imports of capital goods increased, and a deficit appeared on the merchandise trade balance. Since that time the balance of payments has been almost continually in deficit, drawing down the comfortable reserves of foreign exchange that had been built up before 1960.

Throughout the 1960s the deficit on trade was supplemented and sometimes even exceeded by a sizable deficit on current services (invisibles) (see table 7). The heaviest debit items under services were debt servicing, travel expenditures, and "other governmental expenditures." The last item included local currency payments for technical assistance, which were offset by receipts from foreign governments under "transfers."

From 1960 through 1965 there was a steep decline in official convertible foreign exchange reserves as they were used to finance the balance of payments deficits. Consequently, beginning in 1966 the deficits had to be largely financed by drawings on the International Monetary Fund (IMF), by resorting to short-term borrowing from the commercial banks, or by using up the balance owed by bilateral trading partners. The foreign exchange holdings of the Sudanese monetary authorities, which stood at US$166 million in 1960, were down to US$7 million by the end of 1966 and by the end of 1971 amounted to only about US$40 million, the equivalent of less than two months' 1970 imports. The value of four months' imports is generally considered the minimum safe level for reserves.

The problem of heavy imports in the 1960s was exacerbated by a generally declining level of cotton prices from 1958 through 1968 (see fig. 12). Marked variations in price and volume of cotton exports from year to year have from time to time led to sharp annual fluctuations in the country's foreign exchange earnings. These fluctuations derive from a combination of factors, including seasonal conditions in Sudan, the country's marketing policies, and world market conditions (see ch. 13). The United States has generally supported the world price of short-staple cotton by banning exports below a stated price, which usually somewhat exceeds world market price. This has meant that stockpiles accumulate in the United States, and other countries can sell at world price or above. In practice, Sudan's export is more directly affected by the marketing practices of Egypt and Peru, which are the only other important producers of long-staple cotton. Cutbacks in Egypt's production in the late 1960s favored higher export prices in crop years 1968/69 and 1969/70, so that the large crops produced by Sudan in those years did not result in the usual fall in prices. The result was a highly favorable trend in export value.

In recent years cotton fiber has accounted for about 60 percent of

Table 7. Balance of External Payments, Sudan, 1964–70
(in millions of U.S. dollars)

Balance of Payments	1964	1965	1966	1967	1968	1969	1970
Goods and Services							
Trade balance	—55.7	—9.8	—27.8	—20.7	—29.3	2.3	—13.8
Investment income	—6.3	—7.2	—9.4	—8.6	—10.3	—14.7	—14.9
Other	—23.8	—23.2	—17.0	—19.2	—11.8	—15.5	—13.5
Total	—85.8	—40.2	—54.2	—48.5	—51.4	—27.9	—42.2
Transfers							
Private	—3.7	—1.7	—0.9	—0.6	—0.6	—0.6	—1.2
Central government	2.6	3.7	2.6	2.3	—1.2	—1.1	1.5
Capital n.i.e.[1]							
Private	15.5	2.0	2.9	—0.3	—0.6	0.8	0.9
Central government	21.8	16.9	41.0	26.4	22.9	35.9	8.0
Commercial Banks							
Assets	—2.0	—1.1	0.3	—1.1	...[2]	...[2]	...[2]
Liabilities	2.9	—3.7	0.6	0.3	13.2	—12.9	—1.2
Allocation of SDRs[3]	...[2]	...[2]	...[2]	...[2]	...[2]	...[2]	9.6
Monetary Authorities							
Monetary gold	...[2]	...[2]	...[2]	...[2]	...[2]	...[2]	...[2]
SDR[3] holdings	...[2]	...[2]	...[2]	...[2]	...[2]	...[2]	—0.1
IMF[4] general account	5.2	11.3	12.0	12.3	1.3	—0.6	—9.0
Other assets	42.2	10.2	—2.8	9.3	8.3	12.6	22.5
Other liabilities	0.8	...[2]	—1.4	3.5	6.3	—5.6	12.6
Total	48.2	21.5	7.8	25.1	15.9	6.4	26.0
Net errors and omissions	0.5	2.6	—0.1	—3.6	1.8	—0.6	—1.4

[1] Not included elsewhere.
[2] Nil.
[3] Special drawing rights.
[4] International Monetary Fund.

Source: Adapted from International Monetary Fund, International Financial Statistics, Washington, March 1972.

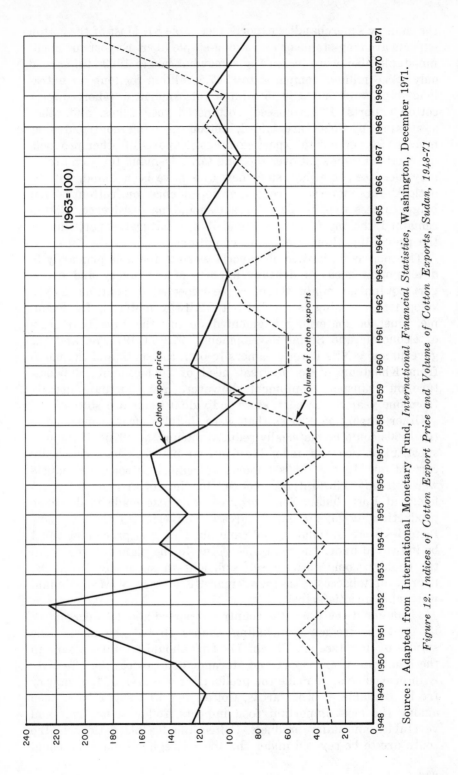

Source: Adapted from International Monetary Fund, *International Financial Statistics*, Washington, December 1971.

Figure 12. Indices of Cotton Export Price and Volume of Cotton Exports, Sudan, 1948-71

the country's merchandise exports (see table 8). Most of the cotton exports are long-staple or extra-long-staple fiber. Exports of medium-staple-fiber were increasing somewhat but in 1969 still earned only £S3.6 million, compared to £S47.8 million for long- or extra-long-staple and only £S0.35 million for American (short-staple) cotton exports. If cottonseed, cottonseed feed cakes, and other associated products are added, cotton growing contributes as much as 70 percent to export earnings. Exports of other products have gained somewhat over the long term. Demand for gum arabic may increase somewhat, since new uses have been found, but the outlook for materially reducing dependence on cotton is not bright unless exploitable minerals should be discovered. Cotton remained the most remunerative of agricultural exports under the prevailing climate and soil conditions.

The increasing burden of imports was attributable primarily to development needs, and heavy imports of machinery and transport equipment might therefore be expected to continue as development planning is carried out. Railway matériel, for example, must be materially augmented during the Five-Year Plan of Economic and Social Development, 1970/71–1974/75, and the government's Nile River steamers to both the south and the north from Khartoum were in great need of replacement. Expenditure on transport equipment, however, may fluctuate greatly from one year to the next, since individual items are so costly.

Other import categories that were unduly burdensome during the 1960s could be materially reduced during the 1970s, if import-substitution projects under the five-year plan can be successfully carried out. In the 1960s imports of refined petroleum products were already substantially reduced by the construction of a refinery at Port Sudan. Some progress was also made in domestic production of sugar; but sugarcane deliveries to the two new factories were unreliable, and cane planting and processing must be improved under the plan. According to the planners, the country could become entirely self-sufficient in sugar by 1975. Deliveries of tobacco to the new cigarette factory at Wad Madani were also unsatisfactory.

Throughout the 1960s the country imported about 15 percent of its food requirements, including almost all but the most basic staples of diet (see ch. 13; ch. 7). This should be unnecessary in the long run, if transport and storage facilities can be effectively improved so as to make the products of one area of the country freely available in other areas. Coffee, tea, and sugar have been among the most important food imports, followed by fruit and vegetables and dairy products. Coffee and tea plantations in the south are to be revived under the special regional plan and could

240

Table 8. Sudan, Foreign Trade in Principal Commodities, 1969–70
(value in millions of Sudanese pounds)[1]

Commodity	Quantity[2]	Value 1969	Value 1970
Exports			
Cotton fiber	172	51.8	63.7
Gum arabic	47	8.6	9.1
Sesame	113	7.1	6.5
Groundnuts (peanuts)	82	5.0	5.5
Cattle and sheep	234	2.7	n.r.
Hides and skins	7	1.9	1.7
Cottonseed	65	2.8	3.1
Oilcakes	n.r.	3.0	5.6
Other products	...	3.3	8.7
Total		86.2	103.9
Imports			
Foodstuffs		7.6	12.0
Beverages and tobacco		5.2	8.9
Crude materials and fuels		7.9	5.6
Chemicals and related products		8.2	9.9
Textiles		15.4	12.5
Machinery and equipment		9.3	14.5
Transport equipment and parts		13.1	13.8
Other manufactures		22.6	22.9
Total		89.3	100.1

n.r.—not reported.
.... not applicable.
[1] 1 Sudanese pound equals US$2.87.
[2] Cattle and sheep in thousands; others in thousands of metric tons.

Source: Adapted from *L'Economie des Pays Arabes* [Beirut], XIV, 36/162, July 1971.

readily be expanded to replace imports, as could local tobacco production. In the south and other areas, such as the Nuba Hills and the Jabal Marrah, a wide variety of fresh fruits and vegetables could be produced on a commercial scale.

Imports of textiles, notably from India, and of footwear and clothing were an important category of foreign exchange expenditure throughout the 1960s. The architects of the five-year plan were convinced that Sudan could achieve virtual self-sufficiency during the plan period in yarns, textile fabrics, knitwear, footwear, and readymade clothing.

Until 1969 the direction of the country's foreign trade was determined primarily by the market for long-staple cotton fiber and, on the import side, by a decided consumer preference for British goods, bolstered by the operation of London-based importing firms, banks, insurance agents, and retail houses. The Manchester cotton mills took only a fairly modest share of Sudan's cotton, so that trade with the United Kingdom was highly unbalanced (see table 9). Imports from Japan and India had gained as a result of their strong role as cotton purchasers. The European Economic Community (EEC, known as the Common Market) was also an important market for cotton fiber. The direction of total exports tended to conform to that for cotton exports, except for Egypt and the United States, whose chief imports from Sudan consisted of goods other than cotton. The United States is a major importer of gum arabic.

After mid-1969 the Numayri government moved to expand its trade relations with the centrally planned economies and somewhat restrict its trade relations with Western countries. This trend was reflected in the trade statistics for 1970, when the Soviet Union and several other communist countries took 25 percent of the country's exports and supplied 18 percent of imports. The Soviet Union alone took one-quarter of cotton fiber exports in 1970. In the 1971/72 cotton season the communist world was expected to take more than half the cotton available and also more than half the country's total exports.

Table 9. Sudan, Trade with Principal Foreign Countries, 1969–70 (in millions of Sudanese pounds)[1]

Country	Imports		Exports		Cotton Fiber Exports	
	1969	1970	1969	1970	1969	1970
Soviet Union...............	4.5	8.6	3.9	16.3	2.5	16.3
Italy.....................	4.5	2.0	11.2	10.7	7.8	7.0
Federal Republic of Germany[2].	5.9	7.8	10.1	10.6	5.6	3.8
India.....................	8.9	13.3	10.5	10.3	10.5	9.3
Japan.....................	7.6	5.9	7.4	9.3	4.1	4.6
People's Republic of China...	5.0	4.2	6.4	6.2	4.6	5.4
United Kingdom............	17.8	20.1	5.8	6.2	4.2	3.9
United States..............	2.7	3.1	2.9	3.8	0.3	0.5
Other countries............	32.4	35.1	28.0	30.5	12.2	12.9
Total.................	89.3	100.1	86.2	103.9	51.8	63.7
Communist countries[3]......	12.6	18.3	15.4	25.6	11.5	24.3
EEC[4] and United Kingdom..	36.9	36.9	33.8	35.4	19.2	17.0

[1] 1 Sudanese pound equals US$2.87.
[2] West Germany.
[3] Bulgaria, Hungary, and the German Democratic Republic (East Germany) were not reported in source for imports; Bulgaria and Hungary were not reported for exports. Yugoslavia is not included.
[4] European Economic Community.

Source: Adapted from L'Economie des Pays Arabes [Beirut], XIV, 36/162, July 1971.

In August 1971 the Sudanese minister of finance and economics publicly criticized the terms of the bilateral exchange with the Soviet Union. He claimed that the Soviet Union had charged from 20 to 30 percent above world market prices for the goods it shipped to Sudan under the agreement and had undercut Sudan in its traditional markets by dumping Sudanese cotton at 10 percent below the prevailing price. As a result, Sudan had lost between 25 and 30 percent on every £S1 million in its trade with the Soviet Union.

Despite these complaints, the trade agreement with the Soviet Union remained in force, and the Soviet economic advisers who had formulated the five-year development plan were asked to stay on in Khartoum. Moreover, the authorities made it clear that some other communist countries—notably the People's Republic of China (PRC), the Democratic People's Republic of Korea (North Korea), and Yugoslavia—were explicitly exonerated from any blame for such trading practices as those criticized. A new trade and aid agreement was concluded with the PRC, which pledged to double its trade with Sudan and to provide "unlimited" economic and financial aid for approved projects. Earlier an interest-free long-term loan of about the equivalent of US$45 million had been negotiated with the PRC in 1970 and was to be used for several projects including a hospital, an international meeting hall in Khartoum, and the segment from Wad Madani to Qadarif of the planned road from Khartoum to Port Sudan. The road had originally been surveyed by an Italian firm, but the PRC offered to build it at below the estimated cost, presumably by the use of low-cost Chinese labor. Imports of raw materials from the PRC, financed by the 1970 credit, were materially increased in 1972.

Sudan also turned for aid to the Western countries, the wealthier Arab countries, and the multilateral organizations. The United Kingdom responded with a US$26-million loan on soft terms, Kuwait and Libya also came up with assistance, and the World Bank offered a US$15-million loan for agricultural development and roadbuilding.

The resumption of normal trade relations with Western countries in 1971 and 1972 was complicated by the countrywide changeover to a new variety of long-staple cotton with which buyers were still unfamiliar (see ch. 13). This development coincided with the nationalization of the cotton-marketing system in June 1970 and the elimination of auction sale. More resentment was caused by the nationalization of the foreign-owned banks, insurance agencies, and importing companies, which disrupted long-established trading channels, notably with the United Kingdom. Relations remained friendly, however, and there was talk of eventual payment of compensation to the expropriated British firms. The Sudanese wanted the settlement to be accompanied by a British government loan on easy terms. Trade with the United Kingdom was also continuing at the normal level in 1971, but because of Sudan's rather precarious foreign exchange position its British imports had to be supported by government-guaranteed British credits.

Despite the difficulties experienced with bilateral trade agreements after 1969, the balance on merchandise trade improved, mainly because of the favorable trend in world cotton prices and in the level of cotton exports. The shortage of foreign exchange also restricted imports, and the issuance of licenses for nonessential imports was tightened. The deficit on the current balance of payments—on goods and services—remained heavy, however. The chief causes were an increasing burden of debt servicing and a flight of private savings abroad attributed to uncertainties arising from the nationalization measures of 1969.

The nationalizations had also affected confidence among prospective foreign investors and official lenders, and receipts of both private and official capital declined. Official assistance from the United States had already dropped off after the rupture of diplomatic relations in mid-1967. Ties with countries of Western Europe somewhat loosened after 1969, and the country's precarious foreign exchange positon, heavy debt burden, and inflationary trend of government spending had adversely affected its credit standing and made it inadvisable to contract further debt except on easy terms, which were more difficult to obtain.

The inflow of capital slowed down, until by 1971 it did not exceed the amount required in servicing old foreign debts. In 1971 foreign debt servicing requirements were running at about 10 percent of the country's total foreign currency earnings. Unless outstanding debt could be rescheduled, payments were expected to rise to 20 percent of total earnings during the ensuing five years.

By the end of the 1960s Sudan was depending somewhat more heavily upon foreign aid than it had in the past, when its own public savings and foreign exchange availabilities had permitted the Sudanese to finance a greater share of their development requirements. Nevertheless, in its relative dependence upon foreign aid, Sudan ranked very low on a list of ninety-four developing countries. From 1968 through 1970 annual average aid receipts from the multilateral agencies and the members of the Development Assistance Committee (DAC) of the Organization for Economic Cooperation and Development (including the West European countries, the United States, Canada, Australia, and Japan) totaled only US$17.36 million, or US$1.18 per capita—placing Sudan eighty-fifth on the list in per capita receipts and seventy-seventh in receipts as a share of total imports of goods and services (6 percent). The "grant element" of aid received during the same period was 62 percent, indicating easier terms for interest and term of repayment than in the past.

As of mid-1969 Sudan had received the equivalent of US$156.2 million from the World Bank Group, including the World Bank, the International Development Association (IDA), and the International Finance Corporation (IFC). It was thus the third largest recipient in Africa, after Nigeria and the Republic of South Africa. For the years 1960 through 1968 it had received US$219 million from the multilateral organizations and the DAC countries. From 1964 through 1967 the communist countries had furnished the equivalent of US$49 million, of which US$22 million came from the Soviet Union and US$27 million came from East European countries.

During 1969 Sudan received aid commitments totaling US$63.6 million, of which 52 percent was for agricultural improvement and 17 percent was for regulation of the Nile waters. The largest commitments were from Bulgaria, Egypt, the Soviet Union, Japan, and the German Democratic Republic (East Germany). Of the Western countries only Sweden and the United Kingdom made commitments of relatively small amounts in 1969. Of larger scale aid projects for Africa in 1968, Sudan was the recipient of US$24 million from the World Bank for expansion of electric power; in 1969 it received the equivalent of US$11.2 million from the Soviet Union for regulation of the Blue Nile waters.

PUBLIC FINANCE

There are two major budgets: the first including recurrent, or ordinary, expenditures of the central government administration; the second covering development, or capital, expenditures. In addition, there are separate budgets for the local governments and for each of the government boards or enterprises, which before the nationalizations of 1969 numbered twenty-one. The development budget of the central government includes most of the development expenditures of these self-financing public entities, but the ordinary budget of the central government includes only transfers between the central government and the public entities. Detailed information on the budgets of the local governments and public entities is not published.

The fiscal year begins July 1, and the ordinary and development budgets are usually prepared for approval in May or June.

The Ministry of Finance and Economics is responsible for the preparation of the budgets. The development budget is coordinated with the Ministry of Planning and with the current development plan. As far as possible, the development budget is financed by public saving, defined as the excess of central government recurrent revenue over central government recurrent expenditure or, in other words, the budget surplus. Such a surplus was regularly maintained on the ordinary budget until 1957. In fiscal year 1957/58 financial reverses were suffered, but a surplus was again attained the following year, and public saving reached a peak of £17.8 million in 1963/64. Thereafter it declined, and in 1968/69 there was net dissaving.

In 1968/69 and 1969/70 the public entities also had a net deficit, so that deficit financing by bank borrowing had to be used to cover not only much of the development budget but also a portion of the ordinary budget and the public enterprise budgets. Whereas deficit financing of the ordinary budget was a new development, deficit financing of the development budget had already been a well-established practice. Of total development expenditure in the years 1965 through 1970 amounting to £S138.1 million, £S49.1 million had come from bank borrowing, and only £S16.8 million had come from budget surpluses, the remainder being provided by foreign loans.

When the Numayri government came to power in mid-1969, it was conscious of the inflationary bias of the economy created by deficit spending and pledged to balance its budgets so that a surplus of revenue could contribute to development. In practice, however, in the years since 1969 actual recurrent expenditure had considerably exceeded the government's preliminary budget estimates. The southern rebellion was a major drain on financial resources (see ch. 14). In the five years from 1967 through 1971 overall appropriations for military requirements more than doubled; military operations in the south cost an average of £S15 million a year for matériel alone. About 20 percent of the budget went for this purpose, and some reports maintain that budget data do not reflect the entire military expenditures in the south.

In consequence of the increasing resort to deficit financing, the government's internal debt—like its foreign debt—was growing fast in the late 1960s. By mid-1971 it had reached £S96.6 million, against £S63.2 million in mid-1969. There was a legal ceiling on central government borrowing of 10 percent of each year's anticipated revenue. The state-owned enterprises, such as the Sudan Railways and the managerial board of the Jazirah agricultural improvement program, had no such limitation, however, and in the 1960s they were sometimes obliged to borrow to cover their operating deficits instead of earning a surplus to be turned over to the central government account. The debt of the government corporations was £S27.6 million in mid-1971, against £S0.4 million in mid-1969.

The statute of the Jazirah Board provides that the central government should receive annually an amount equivalent to 36 percent of annual gross receipts from cotton sales. From fiscal year 1963/64 through 1966/67, however, the board was operating at a deficit, and the central government budget suffered accordingly. Thereafter the board's transfers to the central government increased rapidly as a result of improved cotton exports, contributing to a steep increase in central government revenue from 1966/67 through 1970/71 (see table 10).

The budget for 1971/72, presented in July 1971, contained an estimate of £S13 million in revenues from "unconventional sources," which would amount to more than 5 percent of total revenues. This item reflected the anticipated receipts from nationalized and confiscated organizations, and the treasury minister stated that it was hoped the contributions from this source would increase in future years.

Other sources of the increase in central government revenue were an increased volume of foreign trade, higher import and excise taxes, and improved administration and tax collection. Taxes on foreign trade, particularly on imports, are the most important source of revenue, followed by excise and consumption taxes, sugar monopoly profits, and other indirect taxes. Through most of the 1960s direct taxes provided only about 4 percent of total revenues, but in 1969/70 the proportion was increased to 10 percent, largely as a result of a special emergency tax imposed in that year and of an increase in the rate of the tax on salaries.

In the last half of the 1960s government expenditures rose at a rapid rate, averaging about 15 percent a year. All of this increase was attributable to recurrent, or consumption, expenditure; development spending remained fairly stable. Government spending on development investment had marked a record high of £S59 million in 1963/64 because of spending on the Rusayris Dam and the Khashm al Qirbah resettlement scheme (see ch. 13). It declined to a low of £S25 million in 1966/67, however, and remained at a low level until the five-year plan was launched in 1970/71. Actual development expenditure has had a tendency to lag behind the budget projections, whereas the opposite tendency has prevailed for recurrent expenditure.

Table 10. *Sudan, Principal Sources of Central Government Revenue, 1966/67 to 1971/72*
(in millions of Sudanese pounds)[1]

Revenue Source	Actual[2]					Budget 1971/72
	1966/67	1967/68	1968/69	1969/70	1970/71	
Tax Revenue						
Taxes on net income and profits	4.1	5.0	5.8	11.8	15.1	22.9
Pension contributions	0.9	1.2	1.1	0.9	0.7	1.5
Taxes on production and consumption	25.1	29.6	31.0	33.5	39.5	41.1
Excise duties	(8.6)	(11.4)	(10.6)	(15.3)	(20.7)	(23.8)
Sugar monopoly profit	(16.5)	(18.2)	(19.3)	(18.0)	(18.7)	(17.3)
Taxes on international trade	34.7	42.4	54.3	64.7	77.8	71.2
Import duties	(26.2)	(30.2)	(39.2)	(43.1)	(51.3)	(49.8)
Consumption duties	(2.4)	(2.5)	(3.9)	(4.7)	(5.6)	(5.2)
Export duties and royalties	(6.1)	(5.8)	(5.2)	(6.3)	(8.1)	(8.2)
Jazirah Board profit transfers	(...)[3]	(3.9)	(6.0)	(10.7)	(12.8)	(8.0)
Stamp duties	0.5	0.8	1.0	1.4	1.2	2.0
Total tax revenue	65.3	79.0	93.2	112.2	134.3	138.7
Nontax Revenue						
Fees, fines, and charges	6.5	6.5	7.3	8.1	9.0	14.1
Proprietary receipts	2.8	1.3	2.2	1.1	1.3	4.1
Participation in agricultural schemes	(0.1)	(0.2)	(...)[3]	(0.1)	(0.2)	(0.5)
Rents, interest, and dividends	(2.7)	(1.1)	(2.2)	(1.0)	(1.1)	(3.6)
Profits received from Bank of Sudan	1.8	3.3	3.4	2.6	4.4	3.4
Other profits	...[3]	...[3]	...[3]	...[3]	1.8	14.0
Other revenues	1.2	2.2	2.3	4.7	2.4	4.9
Reimbursements and interdepartmental services	7.1	6.9	7.4	7.9	7.6	7.4
Total nontax revenue	19.4	20.2	21.5	24.2	26.4	47.9
Total revenue	85.9	99.2	114.6	136.4	160.7	186.6

[1] 1 Sudanese pound equals US$2.87.
[2] Figures as found in source.
[3] Nil.

248

In contrast to development expenditure, ordinary expenditure by the central government was rising rapidly in the second half of the 1960s. This was primarily because of spending on defense and security, but requirements for local government and economic services also showed a rising trend. The stabilization effort succeeded in cutting back the growth in ordinary expenditure from 23 percent in 1965/66 to 11 percent in 1966/67 and 8 percent in 1967/68. Thereafter, however, the rate rose again with an increase of 28 percent in 1968/69 and 17 percent in 1969/70. Actual expenditures persistently exceeded the budgeted amounts in this period, partly because of underestimation of the cost of wage and salary increases for public servants.

BANKING AND CURRENCY

In May 1970 the country's banking system was completely revised by the Banks Nationalization Act, which provided for the strengthening of powers of the Bank of Sudan and for complete government takeover of the seven commercial banks with their sixty-two branches. The Board of Directors of the Bank of Sudan was given control of the newly nationalized commercial banks, and the chairman of the board was upgraded to ministerial rank.

Of the nationalized commercial banks, five had been foreign based. These were (with their new names given in parentheses): Barclays Bank, British-owned (The State Bank for Foreign Trade); National and Grindlay's Bank, British-owned (Omdurman National Bank); Bank Misr, Egyptian-owned (People's Cooperative Bank); Arab Bank, Jordanian-owned (Red Sea Commercial Bank); and Commercial Bank of Ethiopia, Ethiopian-owned (Juba Commercial Bank). The Sudan Commercial Bank (retaining the same name) had been owned by Sudanese private interests, and Al Nilein Bank (retaining the same name) had been owned 60 percent by the Bank of Sudan and 40 percent by the Credit Lyonnais of Paris.

Besides the central bank and the seven nationalized commercial banks, there are three special-function banks: the Agricultural Bank, the Industrial Bank, and the Estate Bank. The Agricultural Bank was founded in 1959. It supplied loans and advances to private agriculture, chiefly on a seasonal basis. Its short- and medium-term loans carried interest rates of 7 to 9 percent. It was heavily involved in cotton financing; but since the government's Agrarian Reform Corporation took over the private cotton estates, its activity has been negligible, and the outlook for its future was uncertain.

The Industrial Bank, established in 1962, provided loans and technical assistance to private industrial firms. It occasionally participated in share capital but for the most part provided short- or medium-term loans for from two to fifteen years. Its interest rate on medium-term loans of two to six years was 8.5 percent; on longer-term loans, 9.5 percent. It usually tried to persuade the firms to get suppliers' credits, which the bank then guaranteed. The bank had encountered problems because of its very limited funds and because of arrears in repayments, which at the end of 1969 constituted 40 percent of repayments due.

The unit of currency is the Sudanese pound, which is divided into 100 piasters and 1,000 milliemes. Bank of Sudan notes in circulation have denominations of £S10, £S5, £S1, 50 piasters, and 25 piasters. Coins are cupronickel pieces of 10, 5, and 2 piasters and bronze pieces of 10, 5, 2, and 1 milliemes.

Before the introduction of the Sudanese currency on April 8, 1957, the currency in circulation was the Egyptian pound, which had been established on September 19, 1949, with the same par value of US$2.8716 to the pound. In other words, as of 1972 the par value of the Sudanese currency, expressed in United States dollars, had not changed since 1949. When the United Kingdom or other trade partners had devalued their currency, therefore, the Sudanese pound had been revalued upward in terms of that currency.

Sudan is a separate, independent monetary area. Most of its foreign transactions are settled in British pounds sterling at the "external" rate; it is not part of the sterling area. Because of chronic inflationary pressure and the drain on foreign exchange in the 1960s, the Sudanese pound—if smuggled out of the country—brings only about half of its par value. Because of this official overvaluation, it was decided to let the Sudanese pound float with the United States dollar in late 1971—an effective devaluation in terms of the currencies of most trading partners.

TRANSPORTATION

In 1972 the country's transport system relied principally on the government-owned railway (see ch. 3). Roads had not been very extensively developed as an alternative to rail transport. More than three-fourths of the country's roads consisted of tracks impassable in the rainy season, but some were getting heavy use. The only asphalt-paved road was the stretch between the vital traffic centers of Khartoum and Wad Madani. Outside the towns, there were only about 250 miles of hard-surfaced roads in 1968.

The country's leadership was conscious that transportation is the chief potential obstacle to expansion of commercial production and trade, and there has been recurrent debate in the press and government circles over the relative merits of road and rail transport. The Ministry of Transport was reportedly strongly railway oriented, and the railway workers' union is politically the most powerful in the country. On the other hand, according to press reports, the government has been highly critical of railway management.

Rail Transport

In the late 1960s the railroad was carrying 80 percent of the freight traffic, more than 95 percent of exports, and 60 percent of all passenger traffic in the country. About 73 percent of the railway freight capacity was taken up by the movement of imports and exports. The railway line is the longest in Africa. It was started in 1897, and most of the track was constructed before 1930 under the Ango-Egyptian Condominium (see ch. 3). The latest additions were the line to Nyala in the west, reached in 1959, and to Waw in the south, completed in February 1962. In the mid-1960s a seventy-mile extension was run out from Kassala the length of the Khashm al Qirbah resettlement scheme (see ch. 13).

Because priority had been given in the past to extension of the line, the railway suffered during the 1960s from obsolescent matériel and inefficient operation. In 1971 only about 6 percent of the trains arrived on time, and in holiday season passenger cars were so overcrowded that people were riding on the roof. Exports suffered from lack of freight capacity during the harvest season as well as from traffic delays.

The single track was narrow gauge and unballasted, so that in rainy weather the trains had to move very slowly. During flood seasons the track often washed away altogether. Although large sums were spent during the 1960s on the purchase of 103 diesel locomotives, speeds did not increase. Rolling stock was underutilized, and maintenance was poor. Even the busiest freight line, from Khartoum to Port Sudan, was operating at only 60 percent of capacity. During the late 1960s Sudan Railways was operating at a deficit that had to be made up from the central government budget. This was primarily because of the obsolescent Nile steamer traffic, but the profitability of the railway itself had also declined. The airlines were diverting first-class passenger traffic, and the railway management complained that by keeping down freight charges the government was using the railway to subsidize export crops and the very cheap third- and fourth-class passenger traffic.

Railroad investment under the five-year plan focused on improving maintenance and matériel rather than on extending the track. In 1971, however, the Ministry of Planning decided to add two new extensions from Nyala to the cash-cropping schemes at Jabal Marrah and in the Nuba Hills (see ch. 13).

Once the TanZam railway linking Zambia with Tanzania is completed, the only missing links in the rail connection from Capetown to Cairo will be largely on Sudanese territory—from Waw in Bahr al Ghazal Province to Gulu in neighboring Uganda and from Wadi Halfa in Northern Province to Aswan in Egypt. Extension of the line to Aswan has long been under discussion but has received low priority, as the two centers are linked by lake steamer operating on Lake Nasser.

Roads

Automobile registrations are among the lowest in Africa. At the end of 1969 they numbered only 26,624 passenger cars (including 4,264 taxis), 17,778 trucks, 5,318 vans, 2,080 buses, and 1,811 motorcycles. More than 40 percent of the total was registered in Khartoum Province.

As automobile and truck ownership increased, there had been growing public demand for some improvement in the road system. It was also urged that the building of more roads would provide much-needed competition for the railway and relieve some of the overflow in peak seasons. A major problem was that, although the railway and steamer systems were badly overstrained at certain seasons and in certain directions, their cost structure suffered from the highly uneven traffic pattern, and there was severe underutilization in off-seasons or on return journeys, such as the steamer trip from south to north. Thus increasing the use of roads and motor trucks for goods shipment, according to some critics, would not only be far more costly in terms of maintenance and repair but also would reduce traffic on the railway to the point where its operation would be even more uneconomic.

The five-year plan had accorded high priority to investment in railway transport and relatively low priority to road construction. The only major road project outlined was from Kaduqli in the Nuba Hills to the railway near Al Ubayyid, to move the cotton from the Nuba cash-cropping project (see ch. 13). There was much public dissatisfaction over the plan's failure to provide for work on the long-projected road from Khartoum to Port Sudan. In addition to the railway, the Wad Madani to Port Sudan segment of this vital traffic route was served only by a bad track, usually impassable between July and September. Nevertheless, trucks were carrying about 4,000 metric tons of goods a month by this route; at peak seasons some goods could not move at all.

The Khartoum to Wad Madani section of the projected road had been paved before 1967 with United States aid. In 1972 the PRC agreed to undertake the next segment from Wad Madani to Qadarif. The entire 700-mile road, however, would cost more than £S30 million to build, and some Sudanese maintained that it would be more efficient as well as cheaper to double the railway track to the coast instead.

Air Transport

Given the state of the roads and the enormous distances to be covered, domestic air transportation was a vital necessity. The country's international airline, however, served primarily a prestige function and had heavy operating losses amounting to about 20 percent of expenditure. Until 1972 both domestic and international flights were operated by Sudan Airways. In that year the company divested itself of the troublesome international flights and prepared to concentrate on the development of domestic connections, which were used to a higher percentage of load capacity. A new company to be known as Sudan International was to inherit the international traffic rights of Sudan Airways, and it was hoped that it could exploit them more profitably by cutting down on prestige flights and concentrating on the rapidly expanding Middle Eastern market. Sudan International was to be owned 51 percent by the Sudan government and 49 percent by Kuwaiti interests.

In 1971 Sudan Airways served sixteen airfields within the country (see ch. 13). None had night landing facilities. The fleet in operation at the end of 1971 consisted of two De Havilland Comet 4–C's, four Fokker F–27s, three Douglas DC–3s, and three DHC–6 Twin Otters. Three Ilyushin IL–62s were on order.

CHAPTER 13

AGRICULTURE AND INDUSTRY

Land is the country's only abundant resource, and agriculture and herding are the main source of livelihood for more than 85 percent of the population. In 1968 they were thought to contribute about 38 percent of the gross domestic product (GDP). Although rainfall and ground water are deficient over a sizable portion of the land surface, the ratio of population to arable land is so low that in an average year the country is self-sufficient—although at a low average level of nutrition—in essential foods such as cereals, edible oils, and meat (see ch. 7). In addition, surplus agricultural products constitute all but a small fraction of the country's exports. Cotton exports in particular earn important quantities of foreign exchange and furnish a major share of government fiscal revenues.

Government intervention and investment in economic development go back more than fifty years but have been concentrated almost entirely on agriculture and transport as the key sectors of the economy. Efforts to develop industry date chiefly to the early 1960s, and industrialization is still in the incipient stage. Manufacturing and construction occupied about 6 percent of the active population at the last census in 1955 and 1956 and, with handicrafts included, these activities were thought to account for about 12.9 percent of GDP in 1968. Mineral extraction furnishes only about 0.4 percent of GDP. Mineral exploration is continuing, but as of early 1972 only copper had been found in large enough quantity to justify commercial exploitation.

Government investment and activity in agriculture have been focused on alleviating the country's principal problem, the scarcity of reliable rainfall and surface water, by harnessing its most precious resource: the flow of the Nile River network (see ch. 3). Since construction of the Aswan High Dam in the Arab Republic of Egypt and the conclusion of the revised Nile Waters Agreement of 1959 with Egypt, the irrigation potential has enormously increased. Investment in irrigation development was heavy in the early 1960s, but diminished cotton earnings and other factors subsequently placed a strain on financial resources (see ch. 12). Of the potential of 6 million total irrigable feddans (1 feddan

255

equals 1.038 acres) permitted by the terms of the 1959 agreement, a little more than half were under irrigation in 1971, and not all of this land was being cropped. Under the Five-Year Plan of Economic and Social Development, 1970/71–1974/75, there were ambitious plans to further accelerate the rate of irrigation development with the help of loans from multinational agencies.

Cultivation practiced without benefit of irrigation is known as dryland or rain-fed cultivation. Those portions of the central clay plains and *qoz* (sand) regions where annual rainfall is high enough to permit permanent cultivating settlements are often referred to as the rainlands. Only about 40 percent of the country's population lives within reach of the Nile Waters. Of the rest, about 3 million live in areas of adequate rainfall; but for the remaining 4.5 million, water is a scare and carefully hoarded resource that governs their cycle of movement and entire way of life (see ch. 4). Surviving ethnic and social divisions tend to militate against the transfer of population to more productive areas of higher rainfall and have also retarded the settlement of nomads. About 15 percent of the population is thought to consist of true nomads and another 25 percent of seminomads who move with their flocks during part of the year.

The irrigated and rain-fed land placed under development by the government or private entrepreneurs by 1971 was providing a livelihood in the modern sector of agriculture for more than 500,000 people. At least 75 percent of the population, however, was still occupied in the traditional sector. Although characterized by low average yields and laborious and unscientific methods, the traditional sector was not entirely devoted to subsistence production. It harvested the entire supply of gum arabic—which grows wild throughout central Sudan and is the largest export after cotton—as well as most of the sesame exports and in good crop years supplied an exportable surplus of other crops as well. It also furnished most of the country's food supply for local or urban markets as well as for subsistence consumption. Dependent on rainfall or on *saquiyah* (animal-driven water wheel) or *shaduf* (counterweighted pole-and-bucket) irrigation, the traditional sector probably exercised a retarding effect on the growth of overall agricultural production—notably food production, which fluctuates considerably from year to year in response to variations in rainfall and other factors.

In the late 1960s most of the land employed in the modern sector of agriculture, including almost all of the land under irrigation, was devoted primarily to cotton or other export crops, although other crops were employed in rotation to restore the soil. Cotton provided employment for about 15 percent of the active pop-

256

ulation, furnished more than half the country's exports, and was the source of an important share of government revenues. Its indirect influence on the level of economic activity through processing, transport, and trade was also significant.

The heavy dependence of the modern commercial economy on exports of a single raw material in declining world demand has produced considerable financial uncertainty, in view of the strong year-to-year fluctuations in world cotton prices and in domestic cotton yields. Efforts to diversify cash crop production were pursued during the 1960s and were to be intensified under the current five-year plan. The bulk of new investment, however, will continue to go into irrigation development and cotton growing, since no comparably remunerative export crop had been found as of early 1972.

In 1970 the principal crops in terms of estimated area planted were: durra, a drought-resistant sorghum; dukhn, or bulrush millet; sesame; cotton; and groundnuts, in that order. The principal exports, after cotton, are gum arabic, sesame, and groundnuts.

The modern sector of agriculture is characterized by government ownership of the land and pervasive government intervention and supervision of tenant growers. The country has no class of enterprising or innovative peasant cultivators. Although private entrepreneurs have sponsored pump irrigation schemes as well as mechanization schemes for the irrigated rainlands, they usually disdain participating in cultivation themselves, and the incentives to innovation, investment, or improvement among cultivators have remained extremely limited. Since 1968 the government has espoused a policy of taking over private pump schemes with the tentative intention of eventually forming them into cooperative ventures.

Social divisions between peoples of cultivating tradition, who are in an ethnic minority, and the majority of Sudanese, who traditionally disdain cultivation, have reportedly not only survived the abolition of slavery but also have actually been reinforced by economic development trends (see ch. 5). The consequences are reflected in recurring labor shortages in agriculture, a trend toward progressive withdrawal of effort and declinig productivity on government irrigation schemes, a serious deficiency in the level of agricultural education, a certain entrenched cultural resistance to resettlement, and a consequent dearth of population on potentially productive land.

AGRICULTURAL POTENTIAL

It is generally agreed that the country's vast land surface in-

257

cludes enough arable soils to permit considerable expansion of cultivation even with the use of traditional farming methods but that the potential for increased production with improved scientific methods is tremendous, if some of the factors that retarded growth in the 1960s can be overcome. Despite the drawbacks of many of the soils, there is thought to be a sufficient variety of good soils to permit large-scale mechanized production of such hardy, quick-growing food grains as durra and dukhn, as well as a wider range of other crops than have been grown in any quantity in the past.

Statistics on arable land cited in different sources vary quite radically, but one figure given in Sudanese government sources is 200 million feddans. If the population is taken as 15 million in 1971, this gives a ratio of about 13 feddans per capita. Other sources, however, suggest that 200 million feddans is the total area suitable for agricultural use; of this total, about 80 million feddans are better suited to livestock raising, and only about 100 million feddans, to cultivation.

The official land use statistics of the United Nations Food and Agriculture Organization (FAO) give the following data for Sudan in 1968: total land area, 587.1 million feddans; unused but potentially productive land, 93.9 million feddans; arable land and land under permanent crops, 17.5 million feddans; grazing land, consisting of short grass with scrub and acacia, 59.3 million feddans; forested land, 226.1 million feddans; and built-on area, wasteland, and other, 190.2 million feddans.

In most regions of the country the main factor limiting expansion of agriculture is water rather than land. The season of summer rainfall increases in duration from north to south (see ch. 3). In the northern half of the country the low annual amount and the uncertainty of this summer rainfall make irrigation ensential to cultivation through the year, except where an occasional wadi permits collection of some rain and seasonal cultivation in good years. In the southern third of the country, where rainfall is more plentiful, forest growth, seasonal floods, and tsetse fly encumber the land, and isolation and popular disaffection have contributed to retarding agricultural development (see ch. 12).

In certain exceptional regions, such as the desert deltas of the east, the Jabal Marrah, and the Nuba Hills, accumulations of silt from the streams afford especially propitious conditions for intensified production of diversified crops. By far the most valuable potential for expansion and modernization, however, is offered by the vast expanse of central clay plains that extend across the Blue Nile and the White Nile rivers from east to west for more than 600 miles in a belt up to 400 miles deep. Rainfall in this area ranges between five and ten inches a year in the northern portion to fifteen or twenty inches a year in the southern part. The growing season is short, but with mechanization and improved quick-growing varieties of durra or duhkn it is possible to make the most of it. The characteristic vegetation cover can be burnt off or easily removed, and the soils tolerate deep plowing.

The land is sparsely populated because the dearth of drinking water has discouraged permanent settlement. Hence there are no serious tenure problems, and in the 1970s the government owned most of the land. This is true of much of the central rainlands. Moreover, much of the central clay plains area also has the advantage of being served by the railway and of containing four of the five largest towns to provide markets.

Thus the agricultural potential already noted includes vast areas with adequate rainfall to permit a very substantial increase in food and cash crop production by rain-fed methods alone, independently of irrigation development. The highest hopes for accelerated agricultural development in the near future, however, are tied to the planned expansion of irrigated areas in the Nile valley. The water allocated to Sudan under the Nile Waters Agreement of 1959 can potentially supply an estimated 6 million gross irrigable feddans, or about 4.5 million crop feddans. An additional area can be supplied by the annual floodwaters of the Qash and Barakah rivers in eastern Sudan; and if plans to drain the swamps of the Sudd by means of the proposed Jonglei Canal are successful, they will increase the total of naturally watered grazing land and cropland.

In January 1970 about 3.5 million feddans were under irrigation in the country as a whole, but not all of this land was being cropped. In 1968, of the country's total area under crops of 9.8 million feddans, 7.9 million feddans were rain fed, 200,000 feddans were under natural flood irrigation, and 1.6 million feddans were artificially irrigated. Investment in gravity-irrigated agriculture, which in 1970 was used in roughly two-thirds of the area of irrigation, came entirely from the public sector.

At the end of the 1960s about one-third of the population was living either in towns or in settlements along the Nile, in areas of pump-irrigated or gravity-fed cultivation. The remainder of the sparse population was distributed fairly evenly over the two-thirds of the country to the south of the northern desert. Of the factors impeding more rapid growth and development in agriculture during the 1960s, this distribution of population was one of the more important. Nomadic cultivators and pastoralists alike flock to the Jazirah and other cotton-growing areas in the picking season to supplement their meager subsistence by wages that are driven upward by the persistent labor shortage. Because their own subsistence production absorbs their primary interest, however, they are a rather unreliable source of labor, and they lack stamina in the grueling heat of the picking season. There is cultural resistance to the free movement of population into the more productive areas and the remunerative forms of labor (see ch. 5).

Other important factors retarding growth and development in the 1960s were deficiencies in the freight capacity and timing of railway transport and the lack of adequate storage facilities to offset the fluctuations of production from good to bad years. In 1971 there were only two grain silos in the country, which had storage capacity of 150,000 metric tons. The country is basically self-sufficient in foodstuffs in good crop years, importing in quantity only sugar, tea, coffee, spices, and dairy products. In the 1960s, however, rising incomes meant that the country was importing about 15 percent of its food needs, and in the not infrequent poor crop years the government is obliged to import sorghum and other grains. In addition, cultivators and herders in areas of marginal rainfall may experience localized famine even in generally favorable crop years.

CROP PRODUCTION

Available quantitative information on agricultural output is extremely unreliable, except for data on cotton production and on exports of agricultural products, which are thought to be reasonably accurate. Statistics reflecting area planted and quantity produced of most other crops are arrived at by informed guesswork by tribal leaders and sheikhs, supplemented by rough estimates by Ministry of Agriculture officials. It is known that there are extreme year-to-year fluctuations at times in the output of rain-grown food crops (see fig. 13). It is thought that the full extent of these fluctuations is not always accurately reflected in the statistics. Cotton, on the other hand, has shown a fairly steady expansion in output but is subject to annual fluctuations in price and export volume.

After showing a remarkable rate of growth during the 1950s, agricultural production grew somewhat more slowly than population during most of the 1960s. As far as the underlying trends can be discerned, they seem to indicate a rate of growth in agriculture of somewhat less than 2 percent a year. Through much of the 1960s there was no perceptible increase in yields, and the level of production from year to year therefore depended largely upon area planted—largely a function of the previous year's price and

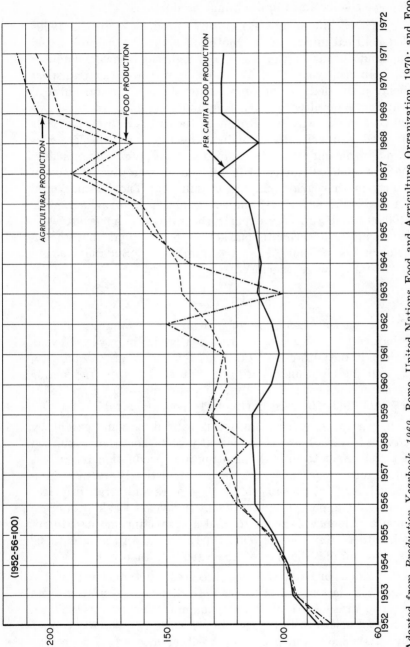

Source: Adapted from *Production Yearbook, 1969*, Rome, United Nations Food and Agriculture Organization, 1970; and Food and Agriculture Organization, *Monthly Bulletin* [Rome], XXI, No. 1, January 1972.

Figure 13. Indices of Food and Agricultural Production of Sudan, 1952-71

of subsistence stocks on hand—as well as upon weather conditions. Labor supply at the time of harvest and at other crucial points in the crop cycle sometimes limited final production.

Other factors influencing agricultural production in the 1960s included political unrest in the south since 1965, which disrupted planting and output in Equatoria and Bahr al Ghazal provinces beginning in crop year 1966/67. Difficulties in railway transport have delayed the delivery of supplies for the modern agricultural sector and interfered with marketing and exporting from the traditional sector. Railway investment in the 1950s and early 1960s was devoted primarily to extending the line, and obsolete matériel and inefficient operation impeded freight movements during the late 1960s. Priority in freight space was given to cotton shipments, so that grain shipments suffered. The bumper crop of durra in 1967/68, for example, should have provided more than 400,000 long tons for export; the railways, however, were unable to move the crop to marketing points, and foreign exchange earnings of some £S2 to £S3.5 million (1 Sudanese pound equals US$2.87) were sacrificed.

Food Crops

With the partial exception of wheat and groundnuts, crops other than cotton are grown on rain-fed land; their year-to-year fluctuations in output are in large part dependent on the quantity, timing, and distribution of rainfall. For all three of the major subsistence crops—durra, dukhn, and sesame—the crop years 1966/67 and 1968/69 were particularly poor (see table 11).

The zigzag trend in crop output is caused to some extent by fluctuations in prices, which apparently have not been regulated by the government to provide planting and production incentives for cultivators. A bumper crop characteristically results in a withdrawal of effort by subsistence producers and a fall in prices culminating in a poor crop the following year. Cash producers also have a tendency to work toward a target income and to relax their effort after a good year. Durra output in the late 1960s affords an example of some of the variables involved.

Durra, which provides the staple cereal diet of most of the population, is the crucial food crop. High prices resulting from a poor crop in 1966/67 produced a bumper harvest in 1967/68, which caused prices to fall. Accordingly the area planted declined sharply in 1968/69, and poor crop weather also affected production. Only about 700,000 metric tons of durra were produced of an estimated national consumption requirement of 1.25 million metric tons. Apparently some of the previous year's surplus had

Crop Year	Durra Sorghum Area Planted	Output	Dukhn Millet Area Planted	Output	Sesame Area Planted	Output
1956/57	2,492	1,067	1,269	321	793	153
1961/62	3,516	1,434	759	205	981	232
1962/63	3,517	1,266	1,066	291	776	142
1963/64	3,277	1,348	1,410	373	1,184	174
1964/65	3,158	1,138	1,427	354	1,116	184
1965/66	3,200	1,095	1,447	253	948	160
1966/67	3,182	850	1,297	252	925	134
1967/68	4,700	1,980	1,452	369	1,234	187
1968/69	2,780	710	1,516	278	1,090	122
1969/70[3]	4,160	1,417	1,510	427	1,333	202

Crop Year	Cotton Area Planted	Output	Groundnuts Area Planted	Output	Wheat Area Planted	Output
1956/57	736	405	460	146	30	18
1961/62	1,133	612	472	149	41	29
1962/63	1,066	476	694	229	54	31
1963/64	1,049	310	847	289	56	37
1964/65	1,068	443	779	280	136	56
1965/66	1,050	449	935	305	137	69
1966/67	1,158	537	926	314	173	78
1967/68	1,149	527	847	297	213	88
1968/69	1,118	656	782	197	296	152
1969/70[3]	1,264	684	1,042	383	299	n.a.

n.a.—not available.
[1] Area planted in thousands of feddans (one feddan equals 1.038 acres).
[2] Output in thousands of metric tons.
[3] Tentative estimate.

Source: Adapted from Sudan, Ministry of Planning, Research and Statistics Section, *Economic Survey, 1969*, Khartoum, 1970.

been retained at the subsistence level, however, for although there was a rise in prices on urban markets, acute shortages were averted. The improved price in turn led to a doubling of area planted in crop year 1969/70. The cycle was somehow broken in 1970/71, when the area planted increased again by 18 percent to a record high.

Cotton

As a commercial crop dependent on year-to-year decisions in foreign industry and as the most dynamic element in the country's agricultural production, cotton presents a changing picture from one year to the next. Pessimistic prognoses concerning crop yields or market outlook may give way abruptly to more favorable forecasts—or vice versa. At the end of 1971 the situation was predominantly favorable in production but somewhat uncertain in marketing.

Whereas in the mid-1960s there had been expressions of discouragement at the failure of cotton yields to keep pace with expanding area planted, in 1971 there was general satisfaction after five years of yields stabilized at a higher level. The growth of production to a record high in crop years 1968/69 and 1969/70 was thought to be the result of improved yields rather than of the limited increase in area planted. The gain was attributed to better management, improved water supply, improved plant varieties, increased use of fertilizers and insecticides, and better cultivation practices, such as watering before sowing and earlier and more rapid sowing.

Cotton marketing was nationalized in June 1970, when eighteen private export firms were reorganized into four firms controlled by a newly established government-owned body, the Cotton Marketing Corporation. With the nationalization of the remaining private cotton estates in May 1970, the government thus controlled both production and export. Cotton had formerly been sold at auction, but the auctions were now eliminated, and the former link with European importing companies through their local commercial representatives was broken. The new system had not yet hit its stride in early 1972, and some initial difficulties with clients over grading and sorting standards remained to be resolved.

Two problems in the marketing of cotton were being encountered in 1971, and the outcome was not yet certain (see ch. 12). After the political crisis of July 1971, the government of Jaafar al Numayri was attempting to reestablish trade links with Western Europe but had lost bargaining power and flexibility as a result of several years of policy commitment to barter agreements with the Soviet Union, other communist countries, and India. Another problem involved the conversion of long-staple cotton plantings from the sakel variety to a superior new derivative called barakat. Established plant varieties of cotton tend to show unexplained degeneration after a period of time, and it is important that new varieties be continually developed. The results of barakat in production in the 1970/71 season were most encouraging, but some deficiencies in grading and sorting produced an initially adverse reaction in consignees. The deficiencies were remedied, but it was feared that sales of Sudanese cotton might suffer in the vitally important quality market of Western Europe, where sakel had been popular with fine-yarn manufacturers and in the production of poplin.

Predictions regarding the long-term market for cotton have varied. The long-staple variety has long commanded a premium on quality markets over the short-staple American varieties, which are produced by some seventy countries. Egypt, Sudan, and Peru are the only significant producers of the long-staple Egyptian types. Since 1964 there had been dire predictions that the quality market was disappearing and that long-staple cotton would have ceased to command a premium by 1970. In the late 1960s this theory appeared to have been disproved, and the Sudanese government appeared justified in gearing its investment to the production of long-staple. In late 1971, however, there were some signs of alarming weakness in the long-staple market.

In crop year 1969/70, 81.9 percent of cotton production consisted of long- or extra-long-staple; 13.8 percent, of acala medium-staple; and 4.5 percent, of short-staple. The share of medium- and short-staple had been increasing, principally because of the decision to grow acala at the Khashm al Qirbah resettlement scheme on the Atbarah River. The output of short-staple cotton goes to domestic cotton mills; when the supply falls short of requirements, it is supplemented by medium-staple deliveries. Otherwise, the entire medium- and long-staple crop goes for export. Acala has the advantage that it can be picked mechanically. Labor shortages in the cruelly hot picking season are a recurrent problem in Jazirah and elsewhere.

In the second half of the 1960s long- and extra-long-staple varieties were being grown on Jazirah, the private estates, the White Nile Scheme, and the Malut Scheme on the southern clay plains beside the White Nile in Upper Nile Province (see The Modern Sector: Government Agricultural Schemes, this ch.). Medium-staple acala cotton was being grown at Khashm al Qirbah on the Atbarah River, on the Qash and Tawkar delta schemes in eastern Sudan, at the Az Zaydab Scheme, and on the Junayd Scheme on the Blue Nile. Short-staple was grown on the Nuba Hills Scheme and in the Qadarif rain-fed area.

TRADITIONAL AGRICULTURE

Livestock Herding

The country's animal wealth is thought to be one of its most plentiful and most neglected resources. Herding of cattle, camels, sheep, and goats is largely a nomadic occupation, although north of the tsetse zone most sedentary cultivators try to keep some livestock. It is usually necessary to move with the herds in search of fresh grazing and drinking water during at least part of the year.

Estimates of livestock numbers are the least reliable of statistics, but relative orders of magnitude are suggested by the data cited in the government's 1969 economic survey, which reported about 12 million head of cattle, 10 million sheep, 7 million goats, and about 2.5 million camels. Some pigs are kept by the Nuba and other non-Muslim peoples. No data are available on poultry. Except for camels, which do not penetrate the three southernmost provinces, some of each type of animal were found in all of the provinces in 1969. Khartoum Province was thought to have only about 375,000 head of livestock, chiefly goats that are commonly kept in the towns for their milk. Northern Province had only about 900,000 head, largely sheep and goats; and Equatoria Province had only 1.5 million head of cattle, goats, and sheep. The largest population of sheep and goats was thought to be more or less evenly divided among Darfur, Kordofan, and Blue Nile provinces. Cattle were probably concentrated in Darfur Province, with an estimated 4.1 million head, followed by Kordofan Province, with 1.7 million, and Upper Nile Province, with 1.6 million.

In 1971 it was estimated that herding provided about 10 percent of the GDP and 6 percent of the country's exports. Cattle on the hoof are shipped to Egypt, Saudi Arabia, Aden, Libya, and Kuwait; camels are exported to Egypt. The lack of grazing stations to fatten cattle on their way to export has led to poor quality. In general livestock are kept for their numbers rather than their productivity, and selection, breeding, grazing management, and veterinary supervision are still at a rudimentary stage. The government maintains a veterinary program of inoculation, but the nomadic habit of most herders makes control difficult.

The expansion of livestock numbers in recent years has not been paralleled by a corresponding increase in suitably watered grazing area. About £S2 million was allocated to the development of animal resources under the Ten-Year Plan of Economic and Social Development, 1961/62-1970/71, and it was only in the late 1960s that the program of drilling deep bores and excavating artificial reservoirs (hafirs) got underway. Some of the land around these watering points has become overgrazed.

Sudan is predominantly a land of savanna, and unimproved grazing is the principal form of land use from the northern desert to the southern frontier (see ch. 3). In the north the chief grazing animal is the camel, which can go long distances without water and is therefore able to use all the available grazing land. In the central areas and in the south cattle are the main grazing animal. They are more limited in their movements away from sources of drinking water, and there are therefore extensive tracts of unused grazing land in the central and southern parts of the country that are either unsuitable for grazing during the rainy season or too remote from water supplies during the dry season. The program for draining of swampland and the anti-thirst campaign for establishing watering points in the arid regions could therefore create sizable tracts of new grazing land; but unless social understanding of scientific range management can be promoted, such new areas could quickly become overgrazed.

The chief ecological regions of the country differ so radically that livestock breeds from one zone may not be able to survive in another (see ch. 3). There are two principal indigenous types of cattle; the northern, or Arab, variety and the southern, or Nilotic, breed. Nilotic cattle seldom survive for more than one generation away from the flood plain, and the Arab cattle will quickly die if left in the flood region. The Arab cattle have large humps and short horns and are thought to be descended from zebu. They are hardy and can withstand shortages of both water and grazing. The largest group are the white type with red or black marking kept by the Baggara tribes of southwest Kordofan and southern Darfur. Nilotic cattle have small humps and large horns and are thought to be descended from an earier, Paleolithic strain of long-horned zebu. Unlike the Arab cattle, they are never trained for work. They are well adapted to the marshy habitat of the southern swamp grasslands.

There are considerable local variations in types of sheep, but all are kept for meat rather than wool. The desert sheep of the west is the predominant breed and the best in weight and milk yield. This variety is kept by the nomadic pastoral tribes both east and west of the Nile in northern Sudan; they number about 4.5 million. The Nilotic sheep, occurring south of 12°N, are less numerous and very small.

There is no private ownership of grazing land; men graze their cattle, camels, or sheep by right as members of a tribe. Most tribes have their traditional migration patterns, which may be extremely complex. In general the northern, or camel-owning, tribes roam in a territory stretching across the country from the Red Sea to northern Darfur Province. Southward of the northern axis of rainland cultivation from Qadarif to the Wadi Azum is the zone of the cattle-owning Baggara tribes. Most cattle entering the market economy come from the western Baggara. In the mid-1960s Sudan Railways had a carrying capacity of about 30,000 head, which were conveyed to the Egyptian frontier at Wadi Halfa. Many of the cattle for sale or export were driven across the country on foot, stopping at government water yards but usually arriving in depleted condition. The extension of the railway in the 1960s was designed in part to permit cattle to arrive at market in better condition, but in 1970 the planners were aware that far more needed to be done to meet this objective.

The primary objective of a Sudanese herder is to maximize the number of animals in his herd, not to maximize their milk or meat yield or the number sold. Only bulls surplus to this objective are sold. The object of animal husbandry is the subsistence of the group; and men must keep as large flocks as possible, partly as insurance against losses from drought, disease, or lack of grazing, partly for status reasons, and partly because they are traditionally used in social transactions such as marriage (see ch. 5). In a sense, cattle are not really regarded as being owned by the individual, although they contribute to his status in the group.

In central Sudan sheep are killed from time to time for meat, and milk—either fresh or in the form of *semn* (clarified butter)—is a dietary staple. The hides, wool, horns, and other parts of the animals are also used in the nomadic way of life. There is a limited sale of male camels, sheep, or cattle not required for breeding; female animals are never sold. Among the Nilotes male animals are not sold, but it is thought that large numbers may be used in ceremonial slaughter.

The pastoral economy is skillfully adapted to support the maximum number of people in a near-subsistence system by minimizing the rate of takeoff for slaughter and by emphasizing milk rather than meat production. Although timing in the use of pasture is skillful and the varying mobility of the different kinds of livestock is minutely exploited, the use of grazing is very uneven. Near all perennial water sources in the central and northern areas in the mid-1960s there was local overgrazing, creating an area of virtual desert for several miles around water points during the dry season. Consequently camels, cattle, and sheep were all at the limit of their endurance by the time the rains began.

Under the Five-Year Plan of Economic and Social Development, 1970/71–1974/75, the government has launched an intensive Freedom from Thirst campaign calling for the construction of twenty barrages and the drilling of 6,000 wells. It is designed to provide adequate drinking water for both people and livestock so as to permit settlement through the central belt of the country and thus more intensive cultivation. Except for the small areas bordering the Nile, all the country north of 12°N is regarded as a "thirst zone" in which there is available only five liters of water per person per day (not all potable) in contrast to the twenty liters considered by the World Health Organization as the essential minimum. Moreover, this does not take account of the water needed for animals. It is estimated that the "thirst zone" as a whole contains only about 60 million cubic meters of available water, about one-fourth of the amount required. The average man there works at only about 30 percent of his capacity, and his animals lose 70 percent of the weight they put on in good pasturage by having to journey to water points as far as forty miles away.

The government has for some years been building reservoirs and drilling wells to help alleviate these conditions (see ch. 3). The planners are aware that a far more intensive effort is needed, however, and the Freedom from Thirst campaign has been launched to help meet the objective. Because of its heavy cost, the country appealed for international aid; by early 1972 the countries that had responded with assistance included the United Kingdom, Czechoslovakia, Denmark, Italy, Sweden, and Egypt.

Traditional Cultivation

The country's vast territory stretches over the most diverse zones of vegetation and climate, and the forms of land use are correspondingly varied: infinite combinations of animal husbandry and cultivation; nomadic, seminomadic, semisedentary, or sedentary way of life of the inhabitants; subsistence production or varying degrees of production for market; and differing forms of irrigation or rain-fed cultivation.

Along the Nile, particularly in Northern Province where modern irrigation development is more limited, the old traditional forms of irrigation survive. Such cultivation takes place along the river between the Egyptian frontier and Khartoum. The Nile in this desert stretch is so deeply incised that the valley is too narrow to be distinguished on a scale map without exaggerating its width. Most of the cultivated land along the river is perennially irrigated, either by natural flood, by diesel pumps, or by *shaduf* or *saquiyah* irrigation. North of 14°N cultivation is generally impossible without irrigation of some kind. Unlike the perennially irrigated land farther south, however, the irrigated land in the desert Nile economy was producing chiefly for subsistence rather than for commercial use in the 1960s.

The area most readily irrigated by traditional *shaduf* or *saquiyah* is the alluvium terrace, or natural level, at the river edge, which is consequently known as *saquiyah* land. As the longest cultivated and most valuable land, this has been so parceled out through Islamic inheritance that it is now subdivided into minute holdings. In the enlarged reached of the Nile valley, three other categories of terrain are found. Alluvial terrace that is well above the level of the highest floods was formerly beyond reach of irrigation but can now be irrigated by means of diesel pumps. Pump projects have proliferated along the desert Nile region since the 1950s, and more are planned. Slightly lower alluvial areas, or basins, are divided into much larger units of holding and cultivation than the older *saquiyah* lands and usually have but one crop a year, whereas the *saquiyah* lands have an elaborate succession of crops. There is also a category of alluvial land that forms part of the Nile channel but is exposed during the low-water season. This is known as *seluka* land.

Date palms are very numerous along the Nile in this region, declining in number and date yield toward the south. They are so little cared for by the inhabitants as scarcely to qualify as a cultivated crop. When the date harvest takes place in October, the transport facilities of the area are strained to capacity, including the government-operated barges and steamers, traditional boats, camels, and trucks. At other times most of the traffic may be carried by the truck route from Dunqulah to Omdurman.

The doum palm also springs up naturally on the cultivated lands in this region and is used both in subsistence and in commerce. The nuts are used for carving buttons and other ivory substitutes. The leaves are woven into useful matting, and the trunks are used in building houses. The acacia leaves are used as fodder for livestock; and the seeds of the sunt tree, for tanning.

For the most part, traditional cultivation is rain-fed cultivation. Before the inauguration of large-scale cotton growing, much of the grain was produced in the Jazirah area. Since the 1940s, however, most of the country's food crops are grown away from the Nile by rain-fed cultivation. Rain cropping without irrigation is generally most important south of an axis stretching from Qadarif in the east (at about 14°N) to the level of Al Junaynah in western Darfur Province. North of this line, rainfall averages about four to fifteen inches a year, and settled agriculture cannot be undertaken without irrigation. The semidesert is used chiefly for nomadic herding of camels, goats, and sheep; but some of the nomads plant durra in river beds or in areas flooded by the seasonal rains, returning later in the hope of finding a crop.

The traditional forms of rain-fed cultivation are practiced largely in three or four of the nine economic regions of the country (see ch. 12). These are the central clay plains, the *qoz* regions, the Ironstone Plateau, and the flood plain. The flood plain proper is used chiefly for grazing after the waters retreat; but there are villages of sedentary cultivators on higher ground in parts of the southern clay plains included in the flood plains economic region, and some migrate to cultivate on adjoining portions of the Ironstone Plateau.

Contrary to frequent assertion, shifting cultivation, in the narrower and more accurate sense of shifting village location, is for the most part practiced only in the southern provinces. Even there, a village is abandoned only after all the surrounding fields have been exhausted, perhaps after ten or twenty years. The predominant form of sedentary land use in the central economic region is that of rotating fields within walking distance of the permanent village, use of a field being resumed after the land has rested for several years. This is sometimes referred to as shifting cultivation but more accurately as land rotation.

The principal crops in the central economic regions are the drought-resistant durra sorghum and dukhn, or bulrush millet, along with sesame and beans. Maize is grown where sufficient moisture is available. In the southern provinces eleusine millet and cassava are also commonly grown, and the climate and soils permit a far greater variety of supplementary crops. Within the central regions the Nuba Hills and the Jabal Marrah, with their silt-depositing streams and more varied temperatures, form separate economies with a greater range of crops, including some temperate-zone crops.

The chief granary of the country in the early 1960s was the eastern portion of the central clay plains. Settlement here, as in the qoz sands, tends to be more dense along the railway line, which coincides roughly with the area of higher rainfall. Cultivated land has been expanded in this area by the promotion of rainland mechanization projects, but traditional cultivation has also been assisted by the excavation of reservoirs by the government. The prevalent land-use system is rotation with unimproved grazing, and hariq (the burning of grassland for cultivation) is widely practiced. Quantities of grain—chiefly durra and millet—and of sesame are exported from the region to the rest of the country or even abroad in good crop years.

Hariq cultivation is practiced extensively in Kordofan, Blue Nile, Kassala, and Upper Nile provinces, in areas of well-watered clays, wherever almost pure stands of certain dense grasses occur. A thick mat of coarse dead grass is allowed to accumulate for two to four years, protected by fire lanes, and is then fired after the first rains have fallen and the grass seed has germinated. The burning enriches the soil and destroys the young seedlings, leav-

271

ing the ground almost weed free and clear for the sowing of crops.

Most of the food grain is produced by sedentary cultivators, both for their own subsistence and for trade with the nomads or with the towns; but throughout the central rainlands many semi-nomadic groups take advantage of the summer rains to sow crops of dukhn or durra in patches of cultivation near their temporary settlements. There are also a number of semisedentary groups who prefer cultivation but must leave their villages during part of the dry season in search of water and grazing for their herds or flocks.

Even south of 14°N, cultivation occurs only where the soil is good and where rainfall collects easily. Although it involves less hard work than irrigation agriculture, raincropping in the savanna of central Sudan is an uncertain and risky source of subsistence; there are often years of drought when the seeds do not sprout or when the crop is suited only for cattle fodder. This is why so many must have an alternative or supplementary source of livelihood: a few animals, a grove of wild gum trees, a proficiency in hunting or in gathering honey or other wild foods (see ch. 7). Many seek temporary wage labor in cotton picking or other seasonal activities, often traveling many miles in search of work in years of drought or crop failure.

In localities of low and uncertain rainfall, the only practicable system of land use is that of embanked fields with flush irrigation, rotated with unimproved grazing. Low earthen banks called *terus* are thrown up around fields to impound the water after thunderstorms. This is the practice of the nomads in the northern belt of the central clay plains, for example, where annual rainfall is less than sixteen inches. They cultivate scattered patches of quick-growing millet called *feterita* in this manner in the wadis after heavy rainfall or transient floods. Cultivation is quite casual, with little weeding, and the patches are cultivated only when the rainfall has been heavy enough. There are a few such patches in the Butanah plain, but they occur mostly farther north and west and west of the Nile in the Wadi Muqaddam.

Embanked fields are used more systematically by cultivators in the unirrigated parts of Al Jazirah and from Khartoum to south of Manaqil. They also occur east of the Blue Nile, from Rufaah to beyond the Khartoum-to-Kassala road. By maintaining several such embanked fields in widely scattered locations and keeping a stored reserve of grain for use after seasons of low rainfall, it is possible to maintain a permanent cultivating population in these areas of low and unreliable rainfall. Most of these cultivators produce a surplus for cash sale, with the object of increasing their herd of livestock.

Land rotation is the commonest form of land use. There are also a few areas where crops may be rotated or fallow land is left to grow wild gum trees, as through the central belt of the *qoz* sands. For example, northwest of Al Ubayyid semisedentary Arabs maintain cultivating villages where there are temporary wells or enough rainwater to permit a stay of six or seven months. During July and August the rains soak into the sand, which retains the moisture, and dukhn is sown as the staple crop, interplanted with groundnuts and sesame for oil and watermelon to satisfy the thirst of those animals that remain in the village during the drought.

In this area the patches of cultivation are usually of about three or four acres and are dotted about at some distance from the villages. Crops and gum trees are alternated on the land. The wild gum seedlings take root among the crops and are carefully left intact. When the cropland is exhausted after a few years' cultivation, the farmer will move to another patch but maintain rights over the old land with its collection of gum trees. The gum is collected during the winter months, until about May, and taken into the gum market at Al Ubayyid, whence it is shipped to Obdurman or Khartoum and then to Port Sudan for export. After years of tapping the trees are exhausted, and the land is cleared for renewed crop cultivation.

Other distinct cultivation practices prevail among the Nuba and among the Fur of the Jabal Marrah area (see ch. 7). A government-sponsored cash-cropping scheme for the growing of cotton has been operating in the Nuba Hills for some years, and an elaborate regional development scheme is under preparation for the Jabal Marrah. The lowland Fur raise durra, dukhn, groundnuts (peanuts), maize (corn), sesame, and bamia (okra) as well as cash crops, such as tobacco, wheat, and barley. The upland Fur have a long tradition of terrace agriculture and practice traditional irrigation from the streams from considerable distances to water their fruit orchards and barley fields. Fruits include mangoes, guavas, limes, Italian lemons, apricots, and mulberries.

The Nuba, who once maintained an extensive system of terrace agriculture on the hills, are sedentary cultivators by tradition. Around the Nuba Hills, the alluvial soil of mixed sand and clay brought down by the streams creates a belt of fertile soil that produces high-quality crops of durra. Short-staple cotton was introduced by the government as part of a cash-cropping scheme for the Nuba Hills and has proved to be of excellent quality. In the late 1960s it was transported to the cotton mill at Nzara in Equatoria Province, originally constructed to process the cotton of the ill-fated Zande Scheme of the 1950s. There has been some criticism of this procedure as highly uneconomic.

In the 1960s the Nuba were growing durra, bamia, tobacco, and vegetables. Although the cotton crop had been introduced for their benefit, there were some reports that it was cultivated largely by the Arabs of the vicinity, who are in the transitional stage between their traditional cattle nomadism and sedentarization. Another report held that the Nuba cultivated the cotton for the benefit of the Arabs, perpetuating a tradition lingering from the former days of slavery. Increasing investment in cash cropping and a rail line for the Nuba scheme were scheduled under the five-year-plan.

Most of the flood-plain economic region is ill suited to cultivation, but the Nilotic inhabitants maintain their permanent cultivating villages from May to October on the areas of high ground or on the edge of the adjoining Ironstone Plateau (see ch. 12). The lands are prepared for crop cultivation by cutting and burning the grass during the dry season.

Except along the northern edge, the prevailing form of land use in the Ironstone Plateau economic region is that defined as shifting cultivation in tropical rain forest or high woodland savanna. This pattern may, however, be merging into simple land rotation in many places, especially where an economy of land abundance has given way to denser population. Along the northern edge of the plateau the Dinka cultivate during the summer months, and the land use is the Nilotic type of land rotation with grazing.

The highest incidence of shifting cultivation is in the western part of Equatoria Province, between Yei and Yambio, an area of closed savanna woodland. It is also practiced in the western part of Bahr al Ghazal Province, which is very sparsely populated. Outside the Ironstone forest region, shifting cultivation was also being practiced in the 1960s by a few small tribes or subgroups in the high woodland savanna of the Fung district of Blue Nile Province and the adjoining district in Upper Nile Province.

The densest population on the plateau is found on the relatively fertile soils around Yambio in the green belt (see ch. 12). Most of the population here are Azande, and an elaborate form of shifting cultivation is traditionally practiced. The staple crop in most of the area is durra sorghum, but an indication of the potential for diversification offered by the climate and soil is suggested by a partial list of other crops: eleusine millet, cassava, maize, groundnuts, sesame, sweet potatoes, pulses, dukhn, cotton, to-

274

bacco, cucurbits (members of the squash-gourd family), chilies, mangoes, bananas, yams, papaya, tomatoes, pineapples, rice, coffee, castor beans, and shea nuts. The Zande Scheme after World War II was accompanied by the compulsory addition of cotton to the crops grown. This diminished the time available for food crops and led to increased reliance on cassava.

The Moru people northwest of Juba in Equatoria Province have a similar cycle of land use but have traditionally practiced a distinctive form of shifting cultivation known as *katiri*, in which each kin group engages in communal clearing of a circular area of land, which is then assigned in wedged-shaped portions to the women, who do most of the cultivating. The traditional *katiri* system is rather wasteful of land and may lead to soil erosion, but it has been modified in recent years. The Jur people, around Waw in Bahr al Ghazal Province, have the most advanced form of cultivation. Other methods are practiced by other groups on the plateau.

THE MODERN SECTOR: GOVERNMENT AGRICULTURAL SCHEMES

Since the 1920s government planning and expenditure have accorded priority to the country's two central problems: water and transport. Linking the enormous distances to bring some of the more remote areas of cultivation into communication with centers of trade and export has been of vital importance and has absorbed a sizable share of available financial resources. First priority, however, has been given to harnessing the Nile water, the country's key productive resource.

Irrigation and cash cropping have been the two fundamental features of government plans for the improvement and expansion of agricultural production since even before the days of the condominium, for only cash production of a commodity in world demand can financially repay the costly investment in civil engineering required for most of the irrigation schemes.

Cash cropping has continued to be more or less synonymous with cotton growing. In the 1960s increasing areas or rotation periods of other crops—notably groundnuts and other oilseeds, but also cane sugar and forage crops—have been added to the major improvement schemes, and allotments of acreage for food grains such as durra have always been used to attract tenants. Groundnuts are the most profitable of the alternative crops and provide the advantage of leguminous rotation with cotton to restore soils. Both existing and proposed areas of irrigated agriculture, however, are reserved for cotton up to the limit considered agronomically feasible, since it is by far the most profitable of the exportable cash crops that can be grown on a large scale outside the southernmost area of the country. Although Sudanese planners and foreign advisers of every persuasion tend to agree that it would be desirable to diversify commercial production so as to avoid excessive dependence on a one-crop export economy, by 1972 extensive experimentation had not yet disclosed any equally rewarding alternative export crop.

There has been some criticism of this orientation of agricultural policy. Some Marxist writers, for example, have attacked the original introduction and continuing emphasis on organized cotton growing as a typical imperialist policy designed to procure cheap raw materials for foreign industry. The latest five-year plan evolved by Soviet advisers, however, continues the primary stress upon expansion of irrigated cotton production as the sector with the most dynamic potential for near-term growth.

Irrigation Development

Qash and Tawkar

The Qash and Tawkar desert deltas of eastern Sudan were the first areas in the country to be exploited for systematic growing of a commercial cotton crop (see fig. 14). The idea was introduced by a farsighted governor in 1867, during the period of Egyptian rule before the Mahdiyyah, using natural flood irrigation. Disrupted during the Mahdiyyah movement, irrigated cotton cultivation was resumed in Tawkar during British rule in 1896 but neglected in Qash until after World War I. The canals to control the flood of the Qash River were built between 1924 and 1926. The Baraka River at the Tawkar delta has never been harnessed by definite channels and regulators, as it is judged that the local duststorms would make maintenance too costly; natural flood irrigation continues to be used there. Qash and Tawkar consist of intermittently cultivated, flush-irrigated cropland, in contrast to the perennially cultivated, gravity-irrigated cropland of the Jazirah and associated schemes.

The Jazirah Scheme

The extensive tableland of Al Jazirah triangle, between the Blue Nile and the White Nile south of their confluence at Khartoum, slopes gently toward the north and west, permitting natural gravity irrigation from the dam at Sannar. The land is very flat, so that it is easily reached by the system of small canals and minor distributory channels; and it consists of cracking clays well suited for irrigation (see ch. 3).

The Jazirah Scheme was conceived as early as 1904. Work on the Sannar Dam was started in 1913, interrupted by World War I, and resumed in 1921. Water began to flow in the main canal at Jazirah in 1925, and by 1931 the Jazirah Scheme proper had reached its ultimate extent of 987,000 feddans. By 1941 the first small extension at Abd al Majid had been added.

One of the greatest agricultural undertakings in the world, Jazirah had been the inspiration, if not the model, for a number of projects in other developing areas as well as for subsequent schemes in Sudan itself. Few areas in the developing world, however, can match the natural advantages of the Jazirah area, which have permitted extension of the scheme on a scale hardly advisable for the average centrally managed crop project.

Long-staple cotton was produced in the Jazirah area from the first. In its first decade the Jazirah Scheme suffered from the effect of the worldwide depression of the 1930s on cotton prices, coinciding with a catastrophic decline in yield because of erratic rainfall, pests, and disease. Before long, however, the choice of long-staple cotton as the crop most likely to repay the cost of investment appeared justified. In 1965, for example, a working party reported that net revenue per irrigable feddan had been found to be at least twice as high for cotton as for nearly all the alternative crops or crop sequences. Moreover, there was greater price fluctuation on world markets among many crops other than cotton.

After World War II expansion of gravity-flow irrigation in Al Jazirah triangle lagged until the renegotiation of the Nile Waters Agreement in 1959 permitted work to begin on the vast Manaqil extension. In the interim, expansion of irrigated area along the Nile took the form primarily of the proliferation of private diesel pump schemes.

In 1970 the Jazirah Scheme and its Manaqil extension were still accounting for much of the aggregate output of the modern agricultural sector: 60 percent of the cotton and about 50 percent of the wheat. They even accounted for a sizable portion of more traditional crops: 12 percent of the year's output of durra and 30 percent of the lubia crop, for example. (Lubia is a forage bean.) For all its importance, however, Jazirah was but one of a growing number of government modernization or improvement projects for agriculture.

Private Pump Schemes and Alternative Livelihood Schemes

Private irrigation schemes using diesel pumps began to develop in Khartoum Province in the 1920s, raising crops to supply the Three Towns—Khartoum, Omdurman, and Khartoum North—

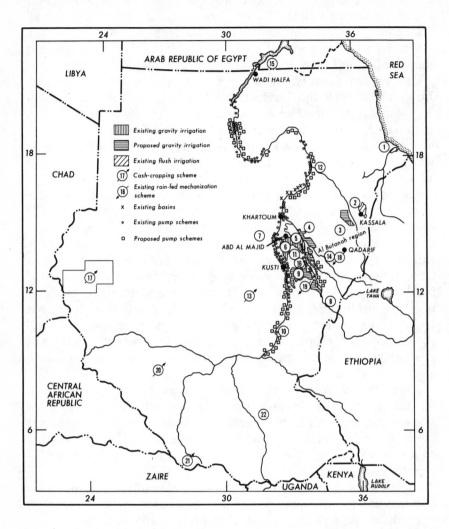

Source: Adapted from: D. J. Shaw (ed.), *Agricultural Development in the Sudan*, Khartoum, Philosophical Society of the Sudan, 1966.

Figure 14. *Location of Principal Improvement Schemes, Existing and Proposed, Sudan, 1971*

with dairy products, fruits, and vegetables. One of these was founded by the son of the Mahdi, who at about the same time established the large private Aba Island Pump Scheme near Kusti on the White Nile. In the 1930s other private entrepreneurs brought some 33,000 feddans under irrigation in the White Nile area. During the same period pump irrigation along the Nile in Northern Province was in its incipient stage.

More than a decade after completion of the Sannar Dam, a second dam was constructed at Jabal al Awliya on the White Nile in 1937 to impound the water annually from August until April, under an agreement to regulate water supplies flowing to Egypt. Although its primary benefit was to Egypt, it did permit acceleration of the development of local pump schemes; however, it also caused the annual flooding of a large area of tribal grazing and cultivation land, extending upstream for some 180 miles. The riverine tribes involved had to be compensated by the construction of seven pump schemes known as the alternative livelihood pump schemes, which were financed partly by a payment from the Egyptian government. Although the tribesmen had considerable difficulty in adapting themselves to this enforced change in their way of life, the schemes eventually came to produce large surpluses of cotton and durra. By World War II their financial success was so evident as to inspire eager emulation by a number of private entrepreneurs.

After 1950 the founding of private pump schemes, particularly along the White Nile, continued to grow in popularity, and from then until 1958 they accounted for most of the new additions to the country's irrigated cotton acreage. Such schemes were particularly stimulated by the high cotton profits during the worldwide boom at the beginning of the Korean conflict in 1950 and 1951, when a number of private cotton fortunes were made. In the five years from 1953 to 1958 the total area under cotton of private estates in Blue Nile and Upper Nile provinces increased from 91,000 feddans to 197,000 feddans, with a gross cultivable area of about 650,000 feddans. By 1958 almost half of the country's irrigated cotton was grown under pump irrigation, but ten years later this proportion had dropped to one-third.

After the sharp fall of cotton prices in 1959, a shortage of capital led to a decline in development of private estates. Subsequent short-term downward movements in the fluctuation of cotton prices from 1960 to 1963 and again from 1965 to 1967 not only discouraged investment but also led to the failure of many private pump schemes, mainly because of disputes between licensee-entrepreneurs and their tenants following low yields and poor crop returns. In 1967 failures occurred in as much as 45 percent of the area in working schemes on the White Nile and in Khartoum Province, 24 percent in Blue Nile Province, and 11 percent in Northern Province.

Because of the high rate of failures and for other policy reasons, the government in 1968 decided that it would gradually take over ownership and operation of the private pump-irrigated estates. A new body, the Agricultural Reform Corporation, was created for this purpose. The larger estates were taken over in 1968, and thereafter the private pump schemes along the White Nile were brought under the control of the corporation as their leases expired. In May 1970 the remaining leases were revoked, and the land involved was placed under the corporation. By the time the 1970/71 crop was planted, therefore, the government had assumed a monopolistic position in cotton growing.

The Junayd Scheme

Because the Blue Nile is more deeply incised in the plain than the White Nile, its waters required a greater and therefore more costly lift by diesel pumps during the low-water season, and the growth of pump schemes there before and after World War II was somewhat slower. The government's rather expensive Junayd pump scheme near Rufaah on the right bank of the Blue Nile went into operation in 1955 to provide alternative livelihood for the nomadic pastoralists of the Shukriyyah and Rufaah tribes, who had become progressively impoverished and were subject to occasional famine. For five years the Junayd Scheme produced mainly cotton, but in 1960 it was decided to introduce sugarcane, and a factory was built at Junayd to process the crop. Under the Five-Year Plan of Economic and Social Development, 1970/71–1974/75, a new extension was being planned at Junayd.

Irrigation Schemes in the 1960s

The Nile Waters Agreement of 1959, based on plans for Egypt's Aswan High Dam, paved the way for renewed expansion of gravity-flow irrigation in the 1960s. It entitled Sudan to draw the equivalent of about 20.5 billion cubic meters of water a year. By 1971 about half this entitlement was being drawn, and projects in the planning stage were expected to make it possible for Sudan to utilize all of its entitlement within about five years.

Heavy investment in irrigation engineering took place in the early 1960s and thus came formally under the financing of the Ten-Year Plan of Economic and Social Development, 1961/62–1970/71, although much it it had actually been planned or proposed before the drafting of that plan. The plan period also saw the completion of the large 290,000-feddan Manaqil extension, lying to the south and west of the Jazirah Scheme proper and utilizing waters from the Sannar Dam. Manaqil was put into operation in five stages, the first of which was completed by 1958 and the last, in the mid-1960s. With the completion of Manaqil, the total gross cultivable area of the Jazirah Scheme was 1.8 million feddans. Irrigation absorbed about 70 percent of total expenditure on agriculture under the ten-year plan and was one sphere in which the original objectives of the plan were actually met in practice.

The construction of the Aswan High Dam lent urgency to the irrigation investment of the early 1960s. The Sudanese government wished to proceed as rapidly as possible with construction of a new dam at Al Russayris, which had been selected in 1954 as the best spot at which to impound the additional entitlement of Nile waters for extended irrigation below Al Jazirah triangle.

First priority, however, had to be accorded to the Khashm al Qirbah Scheme in the Butanah plain, a project for resettlement of the Nubians displaced from Wadi Halfa by the creation of Lake Nasser. As completion of Aswan and the flooding of Wadi Halfa rapidly neared, the Khashm al Qirbah project had to be readied under tremendous time pressure, and it was not possible to prepare the scheme as well as had been hoped, particularly in its sociological aspects.

Khashm al Qirbah was partly financed by a payment from the Egyptian government. Resettlement of the Nubians was carried out during 1964 and 1965 (see ch. 4). The storage dam at Khashm al Qirbah, on the Atbarah River below Kassala, had been completed at the end of 1964, permitting the irrigation development of some 500,000 feddans. Not all of this has been developed. About 125,000 feddans were set aside for resettlement of the Nubians from Wadi Halfa and a further 25,000 feddans for the people of the locality. Medium-staple cotton, groundnuts, and wheat were originally the principal crops. Another 45,000 feddans have been planted to sugarcane, and a second sugar factory has been built to supplement the output of the Junayd Scheme.

The Rusayris Dam on the Blue Nile, begun before 1961 but delayed because of the urgency of Khashm al Qirbah, was finally completed in 1966, but utilization of water from its reservoir was still lagging at the end of 1971.

Irrigation Plans for the 1970s

The water from Rusayris was intended principally for use in the proposed massive Rahad River east bank gravity-irrigation project, tentatively slated to be planted about one-half to cotton and one-third to groundnuts with the remainder in fallow. This project had been under discussion for some ten years, but delays in financing and uncertainty as to the most economical irrigation method had intervened. Pumps had been under consideration as the quicker method, but after agreement in principle on financing had been obtained from the International Bank for Reconstruction and Development (IBRD), it was decided to use the gravity-irrigation method, and the first year's budget for the five-year plan allocated funds for digging the fifty-six-mile canal and general preparatory work on the project. The final loan agreement was not expected to be signed until spring 1972, but the press reported that the IBRD would cover the foreign exchange costs, expected to amount to about 60 percent of the project's estimated cost of £S35 million. The Rahad East Bank Scheme is designed to occupy about 410,000 feddans and could form the first part of an eventual million-feddan expansion of irrigated agriculture to the east of the Rahad River that would utilize the capacity of the first stage of the Rusayris Dam.

A small proportion of the water from Rusayris Dam will also serve the Jazirah Scheme extensions, supplementing that from the Sannar Dam. In the two years 1970 and 1971 about 20,000 feddans of new land were added to the Jazirah Scheme, and its cultivation was being intensified by reduction of the fallow periods. Some of the water from Rusayris Dam was also in use along the Blue Nile, where it had permitted some extension as well as intensification of irrigated cultivation. In the meantime, feasibility studies were progressing on other potential areas of utilization, including Dindar, Kinanah, the Rusayris area, and Suki.

The Suki Scheme between Sannar and Sinjah on the Blue Nile has a potential irrigation area of 85,000 feddans. In September 1970 a group of Japanese firms announced an agreement with the Sudanese government by which they would provide construction equipment and farm machinery for Suki, where it was intended

282

over the ensuing five years to introduced cultivation of cotton, sorghum, and oliseed.

Altogether, the ambitious target of the five-year plan is to bring some 700,000 feddans under irrigation, compared with 450,000 during the previous five years and a total of 750,000 feddans during the previous ten years. Besides the initial 300,000 feddans of the 410,000-feddan Rahad project and the 85,000-feddan Suki Scheme, the plan target estimate would include 150,000 feddans fed by the Sannar Dam and five small projects totaling 163,000 feddans.

Rain-fed Mechanization Schemes

Although the irrigation projects have priority, the five-year plan also calls for increasing the area of rain-fed cultivation by an unprecedented 2.8 million feddans, compared to an estimated increase of 500,000 feddans in the preceding five years and about 1.2 million in the preceding ten years as a whole. The proposed target would include about 900,000 feddans in the Qadarif area of Kassala Province, 550,000 feddans in Blue Nile Province, 450,000 in Upper Nile Province, 500,000 around the area of the Nuba Hills, and 400,000 in Darfur Province.

Government projects for mechanization of dry-land agriculture go back to about 1944, when the first pilot project was established at Wad al Huri, about nine miles southwest of Al Qadarif on the rail line to Sannar. The government took over an area of largely unoccupied grassland with black clay soil, an average annual rainfall of more than nineteen inches, and a short growing season suitable for durra sorghum. Because of the shortage of water for drinking and livestock, no tenure rights had been established to most of the land. By 1963 there were about 1.25 million feddans of cultivatable land in the scheme, not all of which were under crops.

The government-operated estates were at first not entirely successful, proving somewhat too costly for the returns involved. After independence in 1956 the new government encouraged Sudanese merchants and other entrepreneurs to take up private tenancies; these were later increased in size to 1,000 feddans so that the tenants could use their own machinery, and government rental of machines was abandoned. Plans to improve the drinking water supplies met with only limited success. The tenants and their workers occupied the land only seasonally, most of the tenants having other occupations in town.

Further areas were devoted to mechanized rain-land production east of the Blue Nile not far from the railway line from Qadarif in the area of the Rahad and Dindar rivers. By 1960 a total of about 800,000 feddans were planted to durra in the mechanized rain-fed belt as a whole, and large reserves of fallow were available. By the 1968/69 crop season about 1.3 million feddans were actually under crops in the mechanized rain-fed areas of Qadarif in Kassala Province and Dali and Mazmoun districts near the rail line in Blue Nile Province. The Dali and Mazmoun schemes were planted principally to durra, with a little sesame. The Qadarif Scheme was planted 70 percent to durra, 27 percent to sesame, and 3 percent to cotton.

Other Schemes

Among the other government schemes that figured prominently in plans for the 1970s were the Uwayl rice-growing scheme, the Jabal Marrah and Nuba Hills cash-cropping schemes, and the Malut Scheme. One of the most ambitious projects under consideration was that for the Jonglei Canal. It had long been under debate, but funds had been lacking. In December 1971 Sudan and Egypt agreed to begin digging the canal in the marshlands of Upper Nile Province. It was expected that the scheme would cost the equivalent of about US$122 million and that the first stage would be completed in 1977, the second in 1982, and the third in 1987. Each stage would provide 6,000 cubic meters of extra water a year, which would be shared equally between the two countries. A high-level Sudanese delegation was planning to visit the tropical lakes area of southern Sudan to study the feasibility of projects to utilize the waters.

The preparatory investigation for the proposed Jabal Marrah cash-cropping scheme was completed by the FAO in 1968. It recommended that the scheme be devoted to developing peasant agriculture among the Fur rather than to large-scale publicly managed enterprise on the Jazirah model. The project area includes the foothills of the Jabal Marrah range and the plain to the west, roughly coinciding with western Darfur district. The basin of the Wadi Azum provides some 150,000 feddans of good land, and the piedmont another 100,000 feddans. The area is more suitable than other parts of the country for growing crops such as navel oranges, cigarette tobacco, softwood, and probably deciduous fruits as well. Crops that could be produced at seasons when they are scarce elsewhere include citrus fruits, potatoes, tomatoes, and chilies.

Administration and Problems of Government Schemes

Of all the land under cultivation in the country in 1970, more than 27 percent was managed by government corporations that leased the land to tenants under some sort of crop-sharing arrangement. A semiautonomous managerial board, known as the Jazirah

284

Board, had charge of agricultural operations and maintenance at Jazirah, the Manaqil extension, and the Khashm al Qirbah Scheme in the 1960s. In 1967 it was reported that a special board was to be established for future management of Khashm al Qirbah. Private pump schemes, licensed by the Nile Pumps Control Board until the government took them over after 1968, have since been managed by the Agricultural Reform Corporation, reportedly with a view to eventually forming them into cooperatives. Other government-sponsored schemes have similar semiautonomous managing bodies, such as the Qash Board, the White Nile Alternative Livelihood Board, or the Equatoria Products Board.

Until the concession expired in 1950, Jazirah was managed by two private British firms. The Jazirah Board was established in 1950, and sudanization of its staff took place between 1954 and 1957. The government provides the land and maintains and operates the dams and the principal irrigation canals. The board maintains subsidiary canals, allocates tenancies, advances credit, and controls agricultural operations through a staff of resident Sudanese inspectors. The resident inspectors enjoy high status and remuneration but have no technical qualifications or previous experience in agriculture, confining their supervision to seeing that the prescribed operations are carried out. In 1970 there was one such inspector for every 250 tenants. A recent development as of 1971 was the inauguration of a comprehensive extension system for tenants. If qualified extension staff can gradually be trained, this may eventually permit improvement in the outlook and agricultural efficiency of the tenants, which in the mid-1960s was reportedly at a low level.

Despite its nationalization with the advent of independence, Jazirah in early 1972 had not changed significantly in its organization and operation since the 1920s. The scheme retained its initial pattern of government-owned land parceled out in revocable tenancies (only about 1 percent of which are actually revoked in any year). No clear policy option had been taken between the extremes of communal and independent peasant-style farming repeatedly urged by opposing critics.

In the 1950s and 1960s a fairly copious literature developed on the Jazirah Scheme in particular and the Sudanese example in general, as their problems and achievements might serve to illuminate the prospects of development efforts in other areas. Because of its large scale and relatively long history, the interest of foreign observers has tended to center on the Jazirah Scheme, which is sometimes said to be the social laboratory of the country. This is true in the sense that, as the first large-scale theater of economic change in the society, it affords a useful illustration of the probable interaction of traditional and modern forces in the gradual conversion from subsistence to cash farming. By the 1960s the same effects and trends observable in Al Jazirah were already apparent in a number of the other schemes adapted from the Jazirah model, with certain variations. With the exception of the Zande Scheme in the south in the 1950s, however, fewer published details were available in 1972 on the organizational and social problems of the other schemes.

Moreover, the usual time lag is observable between the publication of production data and that of sociological studies. Most analysis and criticism of the functioning of Jazirah or other schemes dates from the early or mid-1960s, when yields in commercial cotton growing had failed to show the expected improvement. A limited economic report published in early 1971, on the other hand, reported that cotton yields per feddan had been appreciably improved over the preceding five years by the use of fertilizers and insecticides, better management, and better cultivation practices. There were no data, however, on cotton productivity per man hour, which was the criterion most directly affected by the social problems described by the schemes' critics.

As an organizational model for development projects in Sudan or elsewhere, Jazirah is said by these critics to exhibit some of the defects of its virtues. Although it has been hailed in the international press for many years as an example of a successful modernization scheme, its success has been most evident in keeping down overhead costs of irrigation and marketing and in raising the income level of the original tenants. Through increasing employment of migrant labor, it has also had a favorable impact on the redistribution of income to other classes and regions. It has been less successful, however, in raising productivity per unit of scarce labor.

Uneconomic use of labor on the Jazirah and similar development schemes has had a favorable effect on the redistribution of income; but the opportunity cost of the labor—that is, the cost of sacrificing its potential employment elsewhere in the economy—may be high. In the Jazirah twice as many people were being used in 1953, at far more than twice the cost, as were required twenty years earlier to produce the same bale of cotton or ton of grain. In other areas, where labor might have been more productively used, it was in short supply. The sparsity of population and shortage of labor was one factor that retarded rainland production of food grains.

This declining labor productivity and uneconomic use of labor was attributed by more than one foreign observer in the mid-1960s to the social orientation of northern Sudanese, who constitute the bulk of the official tenants at Jazirah, Qash, Tawakar, and Qadarif and at least 30 percent of the labor force at Jazirah. The term *northern Sudanese* is commonly used to embrace all those ethnic groups—largely Muslim, arabized, and of pastoral tradition—other than Nilotic and other negroid peoples of the south, the Nuba, and the people of far western Darfur Province (see ch. 4).

The traditional social values connected with agricultural work among the northern Sudanese are such that many—and not only the most uneducated or tradition-bound—regard it as the modern equivalent of tasks that within living memory were "slave's work," and they will not perform it unless obliged to by force of circumstance (see ch. 5). The economic impact of this value heritage is less evident where food is in short supply or where cultivation is temporary or highly seasonal in nature but becomes obvious where planned agricultural development is in progress and is bringing structural or social changes.

In the early days of the Jazirah Scheme, and particularly during the worldwide depression of the 1930s, not enough Sudanese volunteered for tenancies, and many were therefore granted to so-called westerners. The term *westerners* is loosely applied to migrants of largely cultivating tradition from anywhere in Africa outside Sudan or even from western Darfur (see ch. 4). By 1946 there were just over 3,000 tenancies, or 12.6 percent, held by westerners on the Jazirah Scheme.

According to one British observer, the average westerner in Sudan, when contrasted with the average northern Sudanese, takes on the aspect of "economic man." Though often Muslim, he is usually from a predominantly agricultural rather than pastoral society, does not regard field labor as demeaning, and will readily undertake other essential tasks that the northern Sudanese will not perform, such as canal cleaning. He has greater stamina. He increases his income by moving between cash cropping and wage labor markets; he is the most efficient, reliable, and productive member of the country's working force.

When cotton prosperity mounted in the early 1950s and the advantages of Jazirah tenancy became evident, resentment against the more productive westerners in Jazirah grew to such an extent that they were officially excluded from further tenancy, and the proscription has since remained in force. A corresponding development took place on the Qash Scheme. This ban on western tenants has reduced the efficiency of the average holding but has augmented the landless labor force of the Jazirah area.

Rising income among Jazirah tenants in the early 1950s permitted them to realize deeply internalized traditional values by employing labor to the limit of their incomes and beyond; in less prosperous years tenants may go into debt to attract and hold workers. As some tenants grew more conspicuously prosperous, the striving to keep up with them in status and ostentation mounted. Concurrently, as more labor from traditionally low-status (non-northern) groups was employed, the tenant's social aversion to participating in field labor increased. Reduction in the size of holdings, designed to counteract the prevailing labor shortage by permitting cultivation by the tenant and his family during all but peak seasons, has not had the desired effect. The increased use of hired labor is not necessarily related in direct ratio to crop returns or income. As a result labor costs have mounted, yields per man-hour have declined, and productivity has suffered. Statistics for the 1957–65 period showed that annual variations in cotton income resulted more from variations in yield than from price fluctuations, severe though these had been.

The inflationary effect of declining productivity has reportedly been enhanced by the consumption habits of tenants of northern Sudanese tradition, which place a higher value on status and ostentation than on improved physical living standards. Relief from manual labor has first priority, and the number of laborers hired is a direct indication of status.

In 1962 about 40 percent of the Jazirah working force (that is, labor, excluding tenants) was resident on the scheme, securing year-round wage employment from tenants, with the Jazirah Board or other official agencies, or in town and village trade. The other 60 percent consisted of seasonal migrants, lending a serious element of uncertainty to labor supply. Of the migrants, about half were nomads from the adjoining semidesert or from the drier northern portion of the central clay plains. The other half included both westerners and Sudanese cultivators from the qoz regions and central clay plains districts. Most of the Sudanese cultivators and nomads visit Al Jazirah in search of wage work only when the yield of their own crops or herds has been unsatisfactory. Consequently the years of favorable climate and absence of locusts and other pests are those when labor is in shortest supply.

Another feature of the pastoral tradition is its stress on flocks and herds as the foundation of social position and the principal store of wealth (see ch. 5). As a result, tenants on improvement schemes tend to save surplus income in the form of gold jewelry and cattle, investing their cotton profits without regard to productivity or economic return. On Jazirah, for example, there has been a constant attempt to keep animals in totally unsuitable places. In the late 1960s, however, an effort was being made to provide for the integration of livestock husbandry into the scheme in more productive form. Fodder crops such as lubia, a soil-restoring legume, were being allotted a place in the prescribed crop rotation.

In the Qash and Tawkar delta schemes, there was never an intention of creating a class of peasant farmers. The original tenure claims to the land resided with the Hadendowa, a group of nomadic Beja pastoralists who traditionally disdained cultivation. The Hadendowa were granted tenancies for political reasons and as compensation for loss of their grazing. They hire laborers to do their work, often pilgrims on their way to Mecca or other westerners, whose share of official tenancies has been restricted to about 30 percent. A similar practice is followed by other northern Sudanese tenants, many of whom live and hold full-time occupations in Kassala.

Herd owners generally do not undertake wage labor. Cotton picking in the Qash and Tawkar deltas and wage labor in nearby Port Sudan are performed by those who have no animals at home; it has been suggested that they are predominantly the descendants of former serfs or slaves of the Beja and other pastoralists. The working force is augmented by seasonal migration of westerners who move on to Qash and Tawkar after the Jazirah crop is picked. Tawkar in particular is the last stop on the pilgrimage to Mecca and draws temporary labor from among the pilgrims. Because the labor supply is uncertain and contains a large element of target labor—persons aiming to earn money for a particular purpose rather than persons wholly dependent on their earnings—as much as one-third of the cotton crop is often wasted for lack of picking.

This pattern of economic relationships, reflecting the former slaveholding hierarchy, is found in western and west-central Sudan as well as across northern Sudan and the central clay plains. On the Nuba Hills cotton-growing scheme, the Nuba, who are of cultivating tradition, still work for the Baggara cattle nomads, taking part of their wages in cash and trade goods and part in grain and cattle. Southerners such as the Dinka and Shilluk also cultivate food crops for the pastoralists.

The Zande cotton-growing and resettlement scheme, which was established in Equatoria Province in the 1950s, affords a valuable illustration of a case, contrasting with Jazirah, in which rigid centralized supervision, inflexible allocation of plots, and a commercially oriented marketing board contributed to the failure of an originally well conceived plan devised by a prominent agronomist with some knowledge of the area. Whereas the highly centralized organization of Jazirah facilitated the adaptation of a largely pastoral people of uneconomic social tradition to a cultivating system, the Azande were cultivators by tradition and by many years of trial and error had evolved cultivation patterns that appeared disorderly to European eyes but were minutely adapted to local conditions. Though unaccustomed to production for cash, they proved to have a lively appreciation of the comparative value of monetary rewards as measured against local purchasing power or against the higher crop prices obtainable in the nearby Belgian Congo. They gave every evidence that they would have responded positively to reasonable price incentives and to greater independence and flexibility in the choice of location of residence, cultivation plots, and crop rotation patterns.

The Zande Scheme was not modelled primarily on the Jazirah experience. Instead it acquired its major features as piecemeal decisions by the local British administrator, who had valuable experience in effective administration through the local chiefs but an inflated estimate of the chiefs' status and popularity among their people, which had been seriously undermined by British rule. Other features evolved by majority decisions of a committee of British civil servants, who also lacked agricultural expertise as well as local knowledge and who arbitrarily rejected some features of the original plan intrinsically inseparable from some of the features retained. According to a field study by an American anthropologist from 1952 to 1955, the scheme was characterized throughout by a superficial understanding of Zande traditions, values, and economic attitudes. Its economic failure may have been attributable above all to the inadequate price incentives offered to the Zande growers, owing to the misguidedly low estimate of their potential economic sophistication entertained by the British and later the northern Sudanese administrations.

The Equatoria Products Board, intent on making its accounts balance, ran an unprofitable cotton fabrics mill at the expense of the cotton growers and transported the finished cotton fabric at great expense to Khartoum, where it was offered at a far lower price than on the local market. Yet the cloth failed to develop a market in Khartoum, while it was not available to meet the demand at home. The Zande Scheme came to an end when a riot by the cotton mill workers at Nzara in July 1955 touched off the south's smoldering resentment against northern Sudanese rule into active revolt (see ch. 2). Long before that, however, the scheme had been foundering. After an initial enthusiasm in the expectation of higher earnings and increased social recognition from the authorities, the Zande cultivators progressively lost interest in cotton growing as the anticipated economic and social rewards failed to materialize.

MINERALS

Small concessions for the mining of gold, manganese, mica, and salt were operating in the Red Sea Hills, but mineral extraction accounted for only about 0.4 percent of GDP in 1968. In the early 1970s intensive mineral surveys were being conducted, and a high-quality deposit of copper had been found at Hfrat al Nahas near Port Sudan. In January 1972 a British and an American firm had applied for concessions to exploit these copper deposits, which according to the Sudanese Ministry of Industry and Mining were worth at least £S150 million. Traces of a long list of other useful minerals had been identified at one time or another but not in commercially exploitable form (see ch. 3).

In the late 1960s two gold mines in Northern Province were producing about 530 pounds of gold a year. There were four mica mines producing the muscovite type of mica for export to Great Britain, the United States, and the Federal Republic of Germany (West Germany). Four manganese mines in eastern Sudan produce about 20,000 metric tons a year. Salt is obtained by evaporation at the Red Sea coast. Annual production was about 70,000 metric tons, of which 42,000 metric tons were exported, mostly to Japan. A Yugoslav company was working the iron ore deposits 163 miles north of Port Sudan. Only about 87,500 metric tons were produced in 1967, but there are thought to be plentiful reserves. Besides copper deposits in southern Darfur Province, prospecting had revealed deposits of magnesian talc at Qala al Nahl, of gypsum along the Red Sea, and of wollastonite to the west of Port Sudan.

MANUFACTURING

Modern manufacturing was still only very slightly developed in 1972. In 1968 it had been estimated that the modern manufacturing sector contributed approximately 4.8 percent of GDP out of the 7.9 percent contributed by the entire manufacturing and traditional handicraft sector. Employment in modern industry, in establishments of more than ten persons, amounted to only about 50,000 persons, or 1 percent of the active population.

Moreover, the growth of manufacturing during the 1960s had been halting, uneven, and beset with problems. At the end of the decade some unsound aspects of the structure remained. A number of the government-owned factories operated by the Industrial Development Corporation (IDC) were operating at a loss and well below full capacity. Some of the projects financed by East European countries, such as a Yugoslav cardboard factory and two Soviet-built canneries, had been criticized as failures.

The usual problems of a country in the initial stage of industrial development were being encountered. Lack of trained manpower and managerial talent, dearth of capital, and inadequate transportation were the most conspicuous. Two main types of manufacturing were being introduced: agricultural processing industries, which were suffering difficulties of raw material supply, and import-substitution industries, which were having problems in keeping costs low enough to compete with imports.

Until 1970 many of the manufacturing units were privately owned and operated. The IDC had been established in 1962; by 1971 it was operating nine plants, all of them processing agricultural products. There had thus long been a mixed economy, the government intervening both directly through the operations of the IDC and more indirectly through incentives to investment in priority lines. After the inauguration of the nationalization policy in May 1970, however, the government sought greater dominance in the industrial sector by confiscating sixteen large Sudanese firms and several foreign-owned companies, including a British cement factory and a Canadian shoe factory.

The problems that already beset the government, arising from the unprofitable administration of the nine IDC plants, were thus multiplied. In 1971 and 1972 there were some reports by foreign newsmen that the government had regrets about some aspects of its nationalization policy and might seek a return to a more mixed economy. It was not clear, however, whether these reports referred to industry or commerce.

In the ten years of the 1960s the private sector had invested £S36 million in industrial development, of which £S16 million were from domestic and £S20 million were from foreign private sources. The largest private investment had gone into textiles, soap, oil pressing, footwear, soft drinks, printing, packing, flour, and knitwear. The foreign capital came largely from unrepatriated profits made in the import-export business in Sudan.

At the end of the 1960s most industries were still operating at well below capacity. According to the five-year plan, some branches of industry in both the private and public sector were operating at only 15 to 30 percent of capacity in 1970, and rarely was a branch utilizing more than 50 percent of capacity. This was true in textiles and footwear as well as in food processing. The plan, drafted by Soviet advisers, blamed the lack of assured regular supply of domestic raw materials, unorganized imports of materials, and lack of adequate protection against competition from imported goods or, in the case of government-owned plants, from private firms. It advocated a greater degree of centralized control by government.

The expansion of output had been somewhat uneven (see table 12). There had been successful import substitution in petroleum refining, cement, and flour production. Two new flour mills and a new cement plant had been added during fiscal year 1969/70. The soap industry was also able to increase production significantly in 1969/70. On the other hand, the government's sugar program had suffered from a decline in sugar cane output on the schemes at

Junayd and Khashm al Qirbah, and an increase in excise taxes had slowed demand for beer and cigarettes.

The country's first important modern industry had been cotton ginning, which was established early in the twentieth century and was taken over by the Jazirah Board in 1950. It now operates the largest ginning enterprise under single management in the world. Other early industries were oil pressers, soap, and soft drinks. The most rapid increase in manufacturing—though from a very low base—took place in the 1960s. The first government industrial enterprise—apart from the Jazirah Board and the cotton mill established by the Equatoria Products Board at Nzara in 1959—was the Junayd sugar factory opened in November 1961. The IDC also opened a tannery in 1961, and the Khashm al Qirbah sugar factory was started in 1963. The IDC operates five other food-processing plants: one cannery and one date-processing plant in Kuraymah, a cannery in Waw; an onion dehydrating plant in Kassala, and a dairy plant in Babanusah. All have suffered problems of raw material supply.

Table 12. Output of Principal Manufactures, Sudan, 1965/66 to 1969/70*

Manufacture	Unit of Quantity	1965/66	1966/67	1967/68	1968/69	1969/70
Cement......thousand metric tons....		73.2	101.1	128.7	140.7	194.0
Flour...............do............		44.8	39.9	48.8	51.5	111.6
Sugar...............do............		11.3	85.9	93.2	90.8	86.2
Soap...............do............		18.8	18.8	18.4	19.3	23.6
Wine.......million quarts.........		1.1	1.5	1.4	1.3	1.8
Beer.............do.............		6.6	6.9	6.5	6.3	4.1
Cigarettes....metric tons...........		535.0	647.0	661.0	532.0	601.0
Matches.....billions...............		3.1	3.9	4.0	3.9	4.9
Shoes.......million pair...........		7.2	8.2	9.5	10.7	2.7

* Data are taken from excise tax collections, and thus reported by fiscal year.

Most private industry had been centered on Khartoum, and the opening of these factories by the government in the 1960s was designed in part to introduce more decentralized operations at the local level. Among the plants located in Khartoum at the end of the 1960s were a large brewery, a dairy, a large tannery, a shoe factory, and a spinning and weaving factory. Other plants included a cigarette factory in Wad Madani, a cement plant at Atbarah, and a petroleum refinery at Port Sudan.

SECTION IV. NATIONAL SECURITY

CHAPTER 14

NATIONAL SECURITY

In early 1972 the country had just concluded a major conflict that for seventeen years had pitted south against north, resulting in the deaths of an estimated 500,000 persons. Since independence the various military and civil governments had been confronted with the problem of holding together diverse ethnic groups and politicoreligious factions under a system of controls that was understood by few Sudanese outside the major towns. The structure of the national government and its approach to internal security were based upon principles derived from British, Egyptian, Indian, and Islamic law. Only a small percentage of the population was aware of the concept of a national state and was willing to accept and support it.

Most people were primarily loyal to family, ethnic group, or religious ties and looked to their elders or local leaders in matters of social control, security, and the trial and punishment of violators of their customary laws. In the six northern provinces the majority of people (including most government officials and other influential townsmen) were at least partially nomadic or proudly traced their familial and cultural inheritance to nomadic forebears, who had traditionally rejected any authority outside their own group (see ch. 5). Most adhered to the Islamic faith, but Muslims were divided into several groups that had often conflicted in religious, political, and even military matters.

Most people in the three southern provinces, which contain about one-fourth of the total population, were linked culturally and otherwise with peoples of black Africa. A very small minority had adopted the Christian religion (see ch. 6). The differences between north and south had led to the protracted rebellion that began in 1955.

As succeeding military and civilian governments attempted to suppress the growing demand for southern autonomy or secession, they increased the national military forces from a strength of about 5,000 men in 1956 to nearly 50,000 in early 1972. Extensive military aid from the Soviet Union facilitated the task of equipping the expanding forces. Nevertheless, the government was unable to gain a decisive victory over the southern rebel forces, which had come to be known as the Anya Nya. A settlement achieved through negotiation was signed on March 28, 1972. In addition to military units engaged in the south, a Sudanese force of brigade size had been stationed along the Suez Canal since the end of the brief Arab-Israeli War in June 1967.

Even without the southern problem, there were complex crosscurrents of dissidence, intrigue, and subversion. Throughout the years since independence, plotting against the government and coup attempts had been common among military and civilian groups who were out of power. Secular governments, for example—whether military or civilian—were openly or covertly opposed by the political arms of strong Islamic factions with traditional and mystical as well as political claims upon the loyalty of their followers (see ch. 9).

The communist movement also has been involved in matters affecting the country's internal security. Its activities were complex: it functioned for a time as an overt political party and later as a covert subversive organization with worldwide connections and external support. Despite several setbacks Communists continued to function on both levels for much of the 1956–71 period. After they shared in a briefly successful coup against him in July 1971, President Jaafar al Numayri followed up earlier and more cautious attempts to restrict the communist drive for power by initiating a thoroughgoing purge. A drive to remove all party members or supporters from influential positions continued into 1972.

The executions of top-level Communists in 1971 contrasted with the policies usually followed by police, secular courts, and prisons when dealing with ordinary lawbreakers. Police were usually well trained and functioned with restraint. Sentences in criminal courts were not usually severe, and probation and amnesty were common. Long-established rehabilitation programs for prisoners had a history of considerable success.

THE ARMED FORCES

Military Traditions

Much of the history of Sudan has provided a record of continuing warfare and struggles for supremacy among clans, tribal groups, or larger local kingdoms. Individual and tribal military prowess have always been highly valued, and the warrior enjoyed a special status. Nevertheless, after the first large-scale foreign invasion of the area in modern times, carried out in 1820, Sudan was annexed to the Ottoman Empire. The ease with which the invaders overran the northern area has been attributed to the unwillingness or inability of the various ethnic groups in the area to join forces against the invaders; these peoples were just as alien to one another as they were to the Ottomans, who subdued them group by group. From 1820 to 1880 the Sudanese, particularly the various ethnic groups in the south, were targets of the slave traders. Some slaves were sold; others were pressed into the Ottoman army.

In 1881 the religiously inspired wars of the Mahdiyyah provided an emotional starting point for a concept of Sudanese nationality (see ch. 2). The ideal of Sudanese unity was encouraged by British governors general serving the Anglo-Egyptian Condominium (1899–1952). The beginnings of national institutions—including the Sudanese army—thus were fostered by foreign administrators.

The armed forces of independent Sudan developed from these condominium forces, first organized in 1898 as part of the Egyptian army. For decades Sudanese troops were commanded almost entirely by British and Egyptian commissioned and noncommissioned officers serving in Sudan until a mutiny in 1924, after which Egyptian officers and units were returned home. In 1925 local forces were designated the Sudan Defense Force (SDF), and the Sudanese assumed an increasing share of responsibility for its operation.

The relatively calm period of the early 1930s was devoted to training. As World War II approached, 5,000 carefully selected, disciplined, and trained Sudanese officers and men were available. After neighboring Ethiopia was occupied by the Italians, Sudanese troops were sent to guard the long eastern and southern borders of the country. The SDF eventually had 4,500 men on border defense. Meanwhile 2,500 British troops provided security and support in Khartoum, Atbarah, and Port Sudan.

By using hit-and-run tactics, moving constantly, and appearing in unexpected places, the SDF caused the Italian command in Ethiopia to overestimate Sudanese strength and capabilities. Nevertheless the Italians, with vastly superior strength, attacked in several places along the east-central border during the summer of 1940. They advanced toward Kassala and by October had penetrated eighty miles into Sudan in the Blue Nile area but suffered heavy losses at the hands of the SDF defenders. They had also been delayed by heavy rains and flooded streams and were unable to hold some of the forward positions, as Sudanese military and police continued to harass them.

Before the end of 1940 large numbers of British colonial and commonwealth troops reinforced the SDF defenders. The Italian troops were demoralized and driven back to Ethiopia by May of 1941, except for some disorganized small units. Some SDF units later served with the British Eighth Army in North Africa but, for most of the SDF, security of the home area was the World War II mission.

As nationalist feeling increased after 1945, Sudanese officers continued to assume larger shares of control of the military forces, and British officers departed or retired. Meanwhile an attempt was being made to integrate the non-Muslim southern peoples into the independent Sudanese state envisioned by nationalistic leaders in Khartoum.

In the 1950–56 period, the last preindependence years, Sudanese leadership included a number of well-educated military officers. Many of them were, like other members of the educated elite, scions of influential families and graduates of Gordon Memorial College, later renamed the University of Khartoum. The armed forces had absorbed a useful nucleus of military traditions, derived from service in the SDF. Very few of its members had been demobilized after World War II, and the unit retained an effective structure.

During the last few years of the condominium, the British trained 400 additional Sudanese officers and supported the sudanization of the army in other ways. British officers sent to serve in Sudan were carefully picked. Sudanese officer candidates were selected on merit and carefully screened. With a central core of experienced military officers and noncommissioned officers, who were familiar with the organizational structure and tactics of a modern military force, the army could readily be expanded if necessary.

Meanwhile the northern government continued its efforts to integrate southern leaders into the political structure and southern men into the armed forces. The southerners were skeptical about the intentions of northern politicians during the preindependence electioneering and political maneuvering of the early 1950s. Among other evidences of unrest, a conspiracy to mutiny was discovered, allegedly involving a number of army personnel.

The enlisted men of the Equatoria Corps of the SDF were southerners, but most officers, especially in the higher ranks, were from the Muslim, arabized north. In 1955 resentment led to weeks of open rebellion, until the government sent in northern troops and imposed emergency laws (see ch. 9). The Equatoria Corps was disbanded officially after its members went into hiding. Troops from the northern provinces maintained order.

Despite these problems, the move toward independence and sudanization of the army continued. The longstanding warrior traditions of many of the ethnic groups in the SDF and the generally commendable performance of Sudanese fighting men before and during World War II became a part of the attraction of military service. After the country became independent in 1956, the national army drew many more volunteers than were needed.

Personnel Resources

Officers

Before World War II most Sudanese officers were from middle and upper class families, with inherited wealth and prestige. Between 1945 and 1972 greater numbers were drawn from the slowly growing class of merchants and civil servants. In preindependence days and during the early years of independence, educational and physical requirements for entrance were rigorous. As a result, the majority of those who qualified and entered officer-training programs were able to complete the course.

Cadets were selected on merit through competitive examinations. They came from all provinces, but entrants from the south were rare for many years. Most southerners were unable to compete for entry because they did not know the Arabic language (see ch. 8). Most applicants came from the Three Towns (Khartoum, Khartoum North, and Omdurman) or from other towns, where secondary schools were available.

On February 15, 1972, the graduation of the largest annual class of officer cadets ever trained by the Arab Military Academy—formerly the Military College—was ceremonially observed. General Numayri, in his multiple role as president, minister of defense, and commander in chief of the People's Armed Forces, congratulated the group.

The 512 graduates in 1972 contrasted with 400 in 1971 and an average of about sixty officers each year during the 1950s. The increases were necessitated by the rapid growth of the army, losses to southern rebels, defections of southerners, and purges or resignations following several coups or coup attempts.

Originally the Military College granted commissions to students upon completion of a two-year program. After 1960 the course was extended to three years, but it may have been shortened for the 1971 and 1972 classes. The previously high standards become variable after 1958, as many of the best trained and most competent officers were diverted into political positions in government, became preoccupied with political maneuvering, or were purged by political or military superiors. After independence officers were often engaged in police and security duties instead of maintaining combat skills.

In addition to the Arab Military Academy at Omdurman, Sudan operated technical schools for junior officers and noncommissioned officers in engineer, ordinance, service, and signals specialties. Refresher courses in tactics and general ground forces combat skills were given at the infantry school at Jubayt in the Red Sea Hills of Kassala Province.

For training beyond normal military college levels, some technically oriented officers and trainees for senior staff positions were sent to advanced military courses abroad. In 1970, for example, officers were in Great Britain for training in communications and in Pakistan for academic work. Many officers served for extended periods in the Egyptian armed forces. In earlier years, some officers had attended schools in other countries, including the United States; General Numayri, for example, was a graduate of the United States Army Command and General Staff School at Fort Leavenworth, Kansas.

Enlisted Men

Under the Anglo-Egyptian Condominium, many Sudanese gained a reputation as excellent fighting men. Beja tribesmen from the northern deserts, with their cultural inheritance of survival under rigorous conditions, were regarded by their English officers as especially good soldiers. Once they and men from other northern nomadic ethnic groups had developed trust and confidence in their leaders, they were reportedly fearless and extremely loyal to their commanders. Condominium officers also regarded the Nuba of central Sudan as excellent soldiers or policemen. Military life did not attract men from the sedentary groups along the Nile River, and few of them enlisted. Townsmen who joined the armed forces were more likely than nomads to be able to read and write and were often assigned to administrative duties.

Few non-Muslim southerners joined the army during the condominium period. Until 1955 those who joined usually served in the south, but recruitment in southern provinces was temporarily suspended after the 1955 mutiny in the Equatoria Corps (see ch. 2). When recruitment in the south began again in 1956, southerners were required to serve in the north under northern officers. Despite the typical southerner's hostility toward northerners, the southerners who served in the military after 1956 generally became good soldiers.

Recruiting has generally been a function of the major regional command. Before independence a particular corps might attract large numbers of men from one ethnic group, and the corps (later called a command) became known by their tribal name. Since independence this has been avoided, as the army and the central government have tried to attract the primary loyalty of the troops.

Conscription

Until the 1970s the prestige and material benefits of military service had attracted a surplus of volunteers. Usually there were ten applicants for every billet. An army career was attractive to men who had not had the opportunity to acquire advanced schooling or a technical skill that provided security, prestige, and family care. As the military service expanded, however, the surplus of well-qualified volunteers was reduced.

The ruling Revolutionary Command Council (RCC) established a system of conscription, effective July 1, 1971. It applied to all men eighteen to thirty years old and required young men to report to draft officials in the month of March after their eighteenth birthday. The decree provided many possibilities for deferment or exemption from service, including the types of educational and humanitarian exemptions familiar in Western nations. The standard term of service for draftees was two years, with shorter tours for university or higher secondary school graduates.

An estimated 3 million men were in the eighteen-to-thirty age group in 1972 and subject to the new draft laws. At least 175,000 men were reaching their eighteenth birthday each year during the early 1970s, and the pool of eligible draft material exceeded the needs of the military services and the capacity of the nation to support enlarged armed forces.

An unspecified number of these men were to be assigned to the newly developed National Guard. Government spokesmen announced the completion of basic instruction for a second increment of guard trainees in January 1972. The only duty publicly specified for these men at that time was the protection of government institutions.

Manpower and Defense Costs

Military budgets were limited during the early years of independence, then increased during the 1960s as the problem of the southern rebellion began to dominate other needs. The military budget for fiscal year 1957/58 was about £S4.8 million (one Sudanese pound equals US$2.87), the equivalent of US$13.8 million, or 11 percent of the total national budget. Since there had been few replacements or additions to the armed forces' equipment since 1952, this budget included expenditures for arms, vehicles, communications equipment, and aircraft.

The armed forces listed more than 18,000 men by 1966, ten years after independence. The defense allocation of £S14 million (the equivalent of US$40 million) was nearly 20 percent of the total budget. At various times during the early and mid-1960s the government was also receiving a modest level of military aid, in some cases in the form of training as well as equipment, from

Great Britain, the United States, Ethiopia, Pakistan, the Federal Republic of Germany (West Germany), and other nations.

After the 1967 Arab-Israeli War the Sudanese government drastically reduced or cancelled all overt aid from the United States and West Germany. During 1968 government leaders arranged for extensive aid from the Soviet Union. When Numayri and his supporters took over the government in May, they accepted the aid arranged by their predecessors. Reports indicated that weapons, vehicles, and aircraft worth more than US$50 million had been delivered to Sudan by the end of 1970 in accordance with the 1968 agreement with the Soviet Union, which also provided training missions and technical advisers.

The military expanded rapidly from 1968 to 1972, as the government continued its attempt to subdue the rebels in the south. Because of growing economic problems, the government depended more upon force or the threat of force to protect itself and to maintain control. By 1971 there were roughly 37,000 men in the armed forces, up from 18,000 in 1966. About 35,000 were army troops. By early 1972 army strength approximated 50,000 men. The small air force had increased to more than 1,500. The navy, with little part to play in internal security, increased only slightly to about 600 men.

The 1969/70 fiscal year budget originally projected expenditures of £S30.3 million (the equivalent of US$87.6 million), but actual costs were probably higher. The projected 1971/72 military budget was £S46.4 million (the equivalent of US$133.2 million). The armed forces were much larger and much better equipped than ever before.

Military Structure

The armed forces were organized under the Ministry of Defense, with major headquarters in Khartoum. There were six major regional command headquarters: the Khartoum Garrison; Central Command at Al Ubayyid; Eastern Command at Qadarif; Western Command at Al Fashir; Northern Command at Shandi; and Southern Command at Juba.

The army also had installations in or near the Three Towns for engineer, ordinance, service, signal, and medical corps. An artillery regiment was based at Atbarah, and an infantry school was at Jubayt in the Red Sea Hills.

The Army

The primary missions of the army were the defense of national borders and the preservation of internal security. The separation of military and civilian components of the national government was blurred by the 1958 military coup and the period of martial law that followed. Military men continued to be influential in government from 1958 to 1972, even when civilian leaders occupied the most important posts. In practice, much of the military mission during the 1960s and early 1970s consisted of the attempt to control southern rebels and the protection of the government, whether it was led by military officers or by civilians approved and supported by the armed forces.

The decree of October 26, 1971, formally placing the armed forces under the minister of defense specified several additional army missions. These included the "protection of the (national) revolution" and active participation in national construction and development; the latter made it a matter of legal record that the revolutionary government may use army personnel on development or reconstruction projects.

Army organization was based on military concepts adopted by Great Britain and other Western nations. The largest separate units in existence in 1972 were brigades divided into regiments, which were further divided into battalions.

Core units during most of the 1960s were six infantry brigades and a parachute regiment. Additional large units may have been formed during the continuing growth between 1969 and 1972, but information on such units was not available. Primary units could be supported by at least three artillery regiments, an engineer regiment, and an armored brigade. Besides normal light weapons, bazookas, and machineguns, the army was equipped with heavy and medium tanks, several types of armored personnel carriers, and scout cars. Artillery included 105-millimeter, 122-millimeter, and forty-millimeter guns and howitzers; a small number of Soviet-made eighty-five-millimeter antiaircraft guns; and other smaller artillery weapons.

An air defense brigade, with headquarters at Port Sudan, reportedly had the nucleus of a surface-to-air-missile (SAM) battalion in training. Two missiles had been exhibited in parades during the early 1970s.

The rank structure was patterned after that of the British army. The military commander in chief was a *ferik*, equivalent to a lieutenant general. Insignia for all officer ranks consisted of stars, eagles, or combinations of both. Junior officer insignia ranged from one star for a second lieutenant to three stars for a captain. Majors wore an eagle; lieutenant colonels, colonels, and brigadiers wore an eagle with one, two, and three stars, respectively. A major general wore a star, crossed swords, and baton; insignia of the *ferik* consisted of an eagle, crossed swords, and a baton. Noncommissioned officers wore chevrons or combinations of chevrons and a star or eagle on the upper sleeve.

The Air Force

The mission of Sudan's small air force included the security of Sudanese air space, support of ground forces, airlift, and aerial reconnaissance. In 1972 air units were still no more than a nucleus for an eventual full-fledged military air organization.

The air force, with headquarters at Khartoum, had about thirty combat aircraft in 1971, including jet interceptors from the Soviet Union. Other aircraft included light attack or ground support planes; Soviet-made helicopters; Soviet light and medium transports; and light transports obtained from Western nations.

Small numbers of pilots and other skilled specialists had received training in the United Kingdom, or in Sudan under British instructors, before 1967. In early 1972, however, there were probably no fully trained Sudanese jet pilots and few well-trained technicians. Technical personnel and a few pilots were reported in training in the Soviet Union since Sudan received Soviet helicopters and jet fighters in 1969 and 1971. The nation was completely dependent on foreign sources for all air equipment, fuel, training, and parts.

A few helicopters and jet fighters were active in 1971 in reconnaissance and tactical support of ground troops in the south. News reports indicated strikes by jet fighters and helicopters. All of these aircraft were believed to have been piloted by Soviet or Egyptian personnel.

The Navy

The Sudanese navy, the smallest component of the country's military establishment, was formed in 1962. Although it is directed by the government to share in the defense mission, the actual mission of the navy has been the control of smuggling along the Red Sea coast. The modest force was organized into a coastal patrol unit at the Port Sudan naval base and a Nile River patrol unit at Khartoum. In early 1972 naval operations were directed from a headquarters in the national capital.

The navy was formed originally around a nucleus of four armed coastal patrol boats provided by Yugoslavia. Since then two armed river patrol boats have been added to the original equipment inventory along with two landing craft, an oiler, a water carrier, and a survey vessel—all obtained from Yugoslavia. Training of naval personnel in the operation and maintenance of the vessels also has been provided by Yugoslavia.

INTERNAL SECURITY

The independent government established in 1956 was inexperienced and soon was troubled by major economic problems and social cleavages. Within two years the population, accustomed to strong family and governmental control, was uneasy and ready for change. There was little opposition among the general population when a military government took over in 1958 and imposed strict controls in matters of public order.

In 1972 many people in rural areas still were little aware of any national government and paid little attention to government-instituted changes. In most communities the central government was able to do little except provide some degree of police protection and collect taxes. Small-scale dissidence, feuds, or other disturbances were often handled by family, ethnic, or community elders or by local police. In the absence of any pervasive influence from the central government, customary laws and courts continued to function (see ch. 9).

Armed forces personnel had sometimes investigated subversive groups during the 1960s as military influence in government increased, but military intelligence had never had a large or fully trained staff. After 1969 a military intelligence branch received greater support. A few officers were sent to the United Kingdom for technical training in skills related to intelligence and counterintelligence activities. Until the attempted countercoup of July 1971 and the subsequent purge of Communists in government a few intelligence specialists were reportedly being trained by the Soviet Union.

A cabinet-level committee of senior officers was authorized in 1970 to provide policy and coordinate military and civilian security agencies, and a centralized security organization that would report directly to President Numayri's RCC was established. New security units were formed with broad powers to investigate and arrest suspects.

A decree issued on April 26, 1970, made acts related to subversion of the state punishable by death. Such acts included strikes damaging to the economy or obstructing the government in other ways. Revised sequestration laws increased the power of the Numayri government to confiscate the property of opponents.

A December 1971 decree established the Office of State Security within the Ministry of Interior. The new agency was charged with evaluating information gathered by various security organizations. Its goals included the preservation of order and security and the "protection of the socialist revolution"; control of the police; prevention and detection of crime; control and licensing of weapons; administration of passports, immigration, and related activities; administration of prisons; and liaison with police in other nations. The central files of security documents associated with these operations were to be maintained in the custody of the president rather than within the Office of State Security. In February 1972 an army major was appointed as the new chief of state security.

Criminal Law

The development of Sudan's Penal Code, like other facets of Sudanese law, was influenced by the criminal codes of Great Britain, Egypt, and India. This amalgam was further modified to accommodate customary laws and the dictums of the *sharia* (Islamic law). In the modern Sudanese secular courts, alleged violators were charged and prosecuted in accordance with the Code of Criminal Procedure (see ch. 9). Punishments authorized by the Penal Code included death or any specified lesser sentence. Defendants had the right of appeal to the chief justice, who reviewed all decisions.

Courts-martial and other military legal activities, including the people's courts set up by the military government to try alleged enemies of the state, were controlled by the military leaders through the Branch of Military Justice of the armed forces.

The people's courts were being reviewed in January 1972 with the announced purpose of removing court officers whose loyalty to the May revolution—that is, to the Numayri government—was open to question. Local courts in Blue Nile Province and the Jazirah were also being reviewed by committees of local and central government officials. Their findings were scheduled for review by province officials.

The Police

The Sudan Police Force had its beginning in 1898 when a British army captain was placed in the central administration for police duties, and thirty British army officers directly responsible to him were detailed to organize provincial police establishments. Complete decentralization of police control was introduced in 1901, and great differences arose in the performance of the police in the various provinces. In 1908 a modified form of administrative control by the central government was reinstituted.

In 1924, when the late Sir John Ewert of the Indian Police was invited to Sudan to make a survey and report, his recommendations resulted in the drafting of a new police ordinance and new regulations. A school was opened in Omdurman in 1925 for the training of police officers and senior noncommissioned officers from the ranks. The school offered courses in criminal law and police science with the object of training a force that could deal efficiently with professional criminals and with other problems inherent in the growth of urban and suburban areas.

In early 1972 the Sudan Police Force—a single national force under the supreme command of the president—was responsible to the minister of interior. Police headquarters in Khartoum was organized and functioned according to the guidelines initiated by the British during the earlier period of condominium rule. Headquarters divisions included those responsible for criminal investigation, administration, and training. Separate departments handled passports and immigration and the staffing of prisons. Police personnel responsible for security investigations were a separate organization that reported directly to the interior minister.

The Sudan Police Force was enlarged during the first years of national independence, from 169 officers and 7,300 policemen in 1956 to approximately 184 officers and 8,800 policemen in 1959. Strength was reported to be above 11,000 by 1970 and was probably increased, along with that of the army and other security forces, between 1970 and 1972. There was also a separate force of about 700 railway police, who guarded trains, railway installations, and river steamers.

The total police establishment was distributed throughout the nine provinces and along the Sudan Railways roughly in proportion to population density but was specially reinforced in areas where there was some likelihood of trouble. Within each province the police were under the control of a commandant of police who was directly responsible for administration, organization, training, and discipline. The provincial police had both mounted and foot branches; the mounted police, mainly motorized, were still furnished with camels, mules, and horses for special assignments. In addition to the regular police there were a number of police reserve companies that were completely motorized and staffed by specially selected men trained along semimilitary lines to deal with all types of emergencies.

All police officers were volunteers, and the large number of applicants for each vacancy made it possible for the service to be highly selective. Recruits were drawn from all groups in the country and particularly from the Nuba, to whom the idea of police work seemed especially attractive. Pay was comparable to that of the armed forces. The police wore khaki uniforms similar to those worn by the army.

Police recruits usually received two years of training at the modern Sudan Police College near Khartoum. Opened officially in 1959, the school was well equipped to provide theoretical and practical instruction; it also provided training for military personnel who required police skills in their assignments. In addition to recruit training the college offered instruction in aspects of criminal law, general police duties, fingerprinting, clerical work, photography, and the use of small arms. Since independence some police personnel have received additional training abroad. Although a number of Western nations had provided advanced training for Sudanese police officials, the emphasis shifted in the late 1960s to training in the German Democratic Republic (East Germany) and in the United Arab Republic (UAR).

Many police were well trained and had absorbed some of the British police tradition. Provincial police often had good relations with the community except in the south, where the police and the military had thoroughly frightened and alienated the population as they attempted to suppress the separatist movement Programs to improve the public image of the police system in the south during the late 1960s had not succeeded. In attempts to placate the southern peoples, however, the government had recruited 600 policemen from the southern area. By the end of 1969 about 300 southerners had been trained and were ready for duty. The government, however, continued to assign northerners as police commanders at the provincial level in the south.

The Prison System

The general supervision of the Sudan Prison Service was the responsibility of the minister of interior, acting through a commissioner of prisons. The central prisons at Khartoum North, Port Sudan, and Sawakin were directly administered by the commissioner, who was also responsible for the five reformatories, the Kober Institution for the Insane, Port Sudan Local Prison, and the Prison Service Training School at Khartoum North. All provincial detention camps and jails were under the control of provincial authorities. Provincial prisons were classified as local class I or local class II according to their size and importance. In the early 1960s, the latest period for which data were available in 1972, about sixty-eight local prisons and fifty detention camps were in use or available at provincial level if needed.

Prison guards were trained at the Prison Guard School in Khartoum. Their treatment of prisoners was generally reported to be humane. Prisoners—particularly in Khartoum and the larger cities—were quartered in large barracks or dormitory rooms, which were kept clean and well ventilated.

Education in prison was compulsory. The system was geared to a policy of rehabilitating inmates and equipping them for useful work and a complete return to society. First offenders and trusted prisoners were given a fifteen-day annual holiday with their families.

Prisoners could be put to work and were paid a small sum, which was held until the date of release; they could be employed outside the prisons on roads or other public works projects. "Hard labor" as a rule was barred. Within the prisons small industries had been developed; rug weaving, furniture making, and ornamental ironworking were taught, and the products were sold at low cost to the public.

After completing their sentences—which were often shortened by probation or amnesty—prisoners received discharges that rated them according to their behavior, attitude, and training. Employers, including the government, and society in general usually assumed that an offender had accepted his punishment and would henceforth be a good citizen; he was therefore employable. Recent statistics on recidivism were not available in 1972, but in earlier years probationary programs had shown a high rate of success. Less than one-fifth of all prisoners were returned to prison for second offenses, and only a small number were convicted and sentenced a third time.

An amnesty announced during March 1972 illustrated the government's tendency to be lenient with prisoners convicted of less serious offenses. The sentences of many lawbreakers, excluding murderers, often have been reduced by presidential edict. Prisoners whose sentences were to expire within three months were released immediately.

About 10,000 men were serving sentences in 1967, the date of the latest information on prison population available in 1972. Few Sudanese women commit serious crimes, so there were few female prisoners. Reform schools handled offenders under fifteen years of age, giving them regular schooling while detained.

The most common crime was theft, usually of animals. Sentences for such crimes ranged from a period of probation to ten years in prison. Killings in tribal fights were also common. The sentence was usually about seven years in prison for a murder in a tribal conflict, but it might be twice as long for a killing in some other situation.

Threats to Public Order and Security

The historical record of the period from 1956 to 1972 has shown that there was usually at least one group making tentative plans for an attempt to overthrow whatever government was in power. Several governments thus came to power through successful coups d'etat, including that of President Numayri. His security investigators claimed to have detected nine plots against him during a six-month period in 1970.

New security legislation and the expanded internal security and counterintelligence forces available in 1972 had reduced the danger of plots against Numayri, but the various conflicting factions within Sudan clearly held the potential for subversion or open conflict with the government. In early 1972 the Numayri regime had achieved at least a respite from the two most persistently troublesome problems: the Sudanese Communists and the southern rebels.

Sudanese Communism

During the postindependence years communism in Sudan had drawn support from urban workers and middle class citizens, without having reached the rural population. Devout Muslims regarded communism as inimical to their beliefs.

In most communities active Communists could be watched by local leaders or by provincial police. Despite opposition they advanced their cause through their ability to organize and direct dedicated followers. Communist doctrine and alleged solutions to social and economic problems were presented in simple terms. Most of the nation's ills were attributed to a single cause: "Western imperialism." Party members also professed to favor more democracy in government. After 1959 they presented the only effectively organized opposition to the military government of General Ibrahim Abboud, although some of their leaders were cabinet members.

During the troubled decade after independence—from 1956 to 1966—Sudanese Communists developed considerable influence among students at the University of Khartoum, in students' organizations in secondary schools, and in some of the urban professional associations. Their attempts to organize farmers appeared to have had only limited success, but they did succeed in winning some strength among tenants in the Jazirah agricultural region by taking up the cause of grievances concerning rentals paid on government-owned land.

Sudanese Communists sponsored or supported other political parties during the mid-1950s and proselytized diligently among the small but growing educated elite in an attempt to develop a political base for a coalition of parties or a national front.

Party membership was about 750 in 1958, when the first post-

310

independence military government assumed control; another 2,000 to 3,000 people were estimated to have supported the movement actively in front organizations or unions. All political parties and political however, were banned by the Abboud military regime, which also initiated other measures against the Communists. A number of party leaders were arrested; elections were suspended; the press was monitored; and communist political activities were restricted or suppressed in other ways.

The Communists were successful at forming effective covert opposition organizations that encompassed nonmembers and at forming coalitions with modernist elements in the other parties and in the army. This allowed them to play a major part in the successful coups of 1964 and 1969. Both times the coups were followed by periods during which individual Communists were able to exert considerable influence on the government. In 1964 and 1969, however, they came into conflict with the rest of the government. Numayri and the other leaders of the May 1969 revolution had depended heavily on the Communists and installed several in government posts. In that period Sudanese communist strength was estimated at 5,000 to 10,000 members. This was a small number in comparison to the size of the population, but it represented a significant portion of the educated elite on whom the military government had to depend.

Despite an apparently warm relationship in 1969, the Communists came into stronger conflict with the RCC during 1970. Their position in government had been considerably weakened by the RCC during late 1970 and early 1971.

On July 19, 1971, a section of the army, apparently guided or at least supported by members of the Sudan Communist Party, arrested Numayri and gained control of the government for three days. Numayri's resumption of power was supported by a show of force by Egypt and Libya. News observers indicated that the Egyptian show of force consisted of several companies of paratroops flown to Jabal al Awliya, a base near Khartoum. The failure of the coup attempt was brought about, however, by the Communists' lack of popularity among the soldiers and civilians. Major military and civilian forces rallied to Numayri while he was still a prisoner. After regaining power, Numayri indicated a firm belief that the Communists were responsible for the short-lived countercoup attempt, and he proceeded to purge them.

Party members or supporters were searched out and removed from government positions not only in the central government but also at provincial and lower levels. Six military courts held brief trials, which were closed to the public. The original list of suspects scheduled for trial contained 400 names; included were

100 military officers and 300 civilians who were alleged to be Communists or participants in the plot. Fourteen were executed after the first group of trials, including the military leader of the coup, Major Hashim al Atta; the Sudan Communist Party secretary general, Abdal Khalig Mahgoub; the secretary of the Sudanese Workers' Trade Union Federation, Shafi Ahmad al Sheikh; and Joseph Garang, minister of southern affairs. The few Sudan Communist Party officials who remained at large fled or remained abroad.

In December 1971 government spokesmen announced that, of the more than 3,000 people who had been detained, 1,300 had been released. Another 560 were released in increments during January and February 1972, and several small groups were freed during March.

At the same time, however, other alleged communist supporters were being searched out. Trade unions, in which the party had had considerable representation and power, were dismissing party members from their leadership committees, according to the government-controlled press. Reviewing the losses over the eight-month period since the abortive countercoup attempt, some Middle Eastern newspapers alleged that the Sudan Communist Party had collapsed.

Surviving party spokesmen, however, claimed that they had held a meeting in November 1971 and announced a hard-line attitude toward Numayri, threatening revenge and death. They reportedly elected a new secretary general, Muhammad Ibrahim Nogod, a surviving member of the old communist central committee, and acknowledged that the Sudan Communist Party had been involved in the attempted countercoup against the Namayri regime.

President Numayri continued to berate the Communists in early 1972. On one occasion he described a group of Communists meeting in Beirut, Lebanon, as "International agents who have sold their consciences and lost their will." In late March 1972 his government spokesmen announced that still another "fugitive" Communist had been captured and was to be questioned in Khartoum.

Religious Conservatism

Other potential threats to the Numayri government were posed by essentially conservative religious groups that had developed political structures; none of them, however, had a history of subversion similar to that of the Sudanese Communists. Included were the Ansars, or followers of Imam al Hadi al Mahdi; their numbers were estimated at about 3 million. In 1970 approximately one-half of the active military forces were believed to be members. As a conservative politicoreligious leader with inherited power and prestige, Imam al Mahdi had considerable influence but, when he attempted to exert political and military pressure on the government in early 1970, Numayri ordered a strong military response. His forces attacked the Ansar stronghold on Aba Island in the lower White Nile River and gained a decisive victory. Imam al Mahdi was killed at the border while apparently fleeing to Ethiopia (see ch. 9).

The Khatmiyyah, another conservative sect, reportedly had as many adherents as the Ansars, but they were quiescent from 1969 to mid-1972 and had no activist tradition. The traditionalist Muslim Brotherhood was also quiet, apparently deprived of its strength by the attractiveness to potential supporters of the RCC, particularly after the RCC broke with the Communists. As did other conservative political or religious organizations in Sudan, the brotherhood opposed the communist movement (see ch. 9).

The Southern Rebellion

The number of northern troops assigned to combat guerrilla activity in the south increased throughout the 1960s. Bloodshed and destruction were most widespread from 1964 through 1966 and continued at a reduced level thereafter.

Army troops and police struggled to maintain control of the larger towns and main roads. In the process, they further developed a reputation among the southerners for ruthlessness. Southern spokesmen and foreigners who were able to visit the southern provinces reported accounts of widespread killings in Juba, Waw, Yambio, Rumbek, and other towns. Southerners reported that groups of men, women, and children had been shot while attending church services and that the churches were burned. Hundreds of schools—some reports say all schools in the south—were closed, burned, or occupied by government forces.

As stories of being shot on sight spread among the southern townsmen and homesteaders, they either moved away from the roads and trails to hide in the forests or fled into neighboring countries. Small numbers of southerners joined the hard-core rebels or formed separate rebel bands to attack vehicles, troops, police outposts, bridges, and roads; sometimes they preyed on other southerners as well.

Large numbers of Sudanese refugees fled to Ethiopia, Uganda, Zaire—until late 1971 Congo (Kinshasa)—and the Central African Republic. Many southern political leaders were among those who fled to neighboring countries during the early years of the rebellion. Other educated southerners joined them. Together they formed a political group known as the Sudan African National Union (SANU), which sponsored guerrilla units that eventually developed contacts with other spontaneously formed groups of rebels. The uncoordinated, conflicting guerrilla units began to be known as Anya Nya, originally the name for a poison made from cobra or scorpion venoms (see ch. 9).

During the late 1960s the rebels developed better contact between widely separated bands and became more adept at obtaining arms. They bartered for weapons in the black markets of neighboring countries, solicited aid from foreign powers, and purchased guns and supplies with taxes and contributions collected from southern supporters. Government sources in Khartoum repeatedly charged that Israel was supporting the Anya Nya with weapons and training.

Northern forces in the south increased to about 12,000 in 1969. Central direction of these units was reported to be poor, lacking clear-cut lines of command. Various units were necessarily widely separated, and small units were under the leadership of noncommissioned officers, who received little guidance from their headquarters. There was little effective control or discipline from central headquarters in Khartoum. Although they received extra pay and other benefits, northern troops disliked service in the remote, humid southern provinces. The rebels had even greater problems; they were scattered over great distances, and guerrilla groups had very little contact with each other.

Government forces retained control of the main towns and roads, but the enlarged northern forces were somewhat short of weapons and equipment until 1969. In keeping with a military agreement between the Soviet Union and the Sudan government in power in 1968, military supplies began to arrive in 1969. Deliveries between 1969 and 1971 included infantry weapons, motor vehicles, and small numbers of helicopters and jet fighters. Both types of aircraft were used against the southerners. The jet fighters operated from Juba airfield in Equatoria Province, reportedly with Egyptian or Soviet pilots.

The deliveries alleviated most of the shortages of basic weapons and other matériel that had limited the scope of operations. Government forces in the south, better equipped than in earlier years, increased to 25,000 or 30,000 men by late 1971. Government action against the rebels declined for a brief time after the May 1969 coup that brought General Numayri to power. The new regime then resumed the use of military pressure, meanwhile urging negotiation leading to autonomy for the south.

Southerners who had moved away from the roads and towns into the forests remained hidden, unwilling to accept government promises of safety if they returned to their home areas. Refugees who had fled the country were equally dubious about the value of government promises; fearful of new violence by northern troops, they remained outside the borders of Sudan. Officials in Uganda charged that Sudanese government troops made forays into Uganda territory—shooting, looting, or kidnapping Sudanese refugees and sometimes Ugandan citizens as well.

Meanwhile rebels, including members of the Anya Nya, damaged or destroyed several bridges during 1970 and showed improved skills in their attacks on government posts and other targets. Although government troops and vehicles could not move effectively or safely except on a few main roads, the army was able to hold the major towns. The guerrillas continued to operate from remote camps, but their poorly organized units were too small and scattered to be highly effective in any single area. Between 1969 and early 1972 the maximum strength of the rebel forces approximated 5,000 to 10,000 members, of whom only a few thousand had modern rifles and machineguns. Many had only spears and bows and arrows.

Contacts between the opposing forces were sporadic and inconclusive between 1968 and 1972. Despite their successes in limited areas, the government forces were unable to enforce a military settlement. Although President Numayri had offered autonomy to the southern provinces and amnesty to the rebels soon after he took over the government in May 1969, the southern guerrillas did not have a unified organization or spokesman to represent all factions. Little progress toward a negotiated settlement was made before late 1971. Meanwhile, with more weapons, ground vehicles, and aircraft available, military pressure on the rebels continued. At the same time the Anya Nya forces increased their resistance. They were obtaining more weapons and training in guerrilla tactics, reportedly from Israel. From 1969 through 1971 they slowly developed an improved organization and command structure with key power in the hands of younger former Sudanese army officers, particularly, Major General Joseph Lagu.

By 1971 various observers were estimating that attacks by government troops, forced movement out of home areas, disease, and malnutrition had killed about 500,000 southerners. The extensive suffering and the large investments in manpower and matériel had brought the government no nearer to a settlement by force.

Having talked since 1969 in favor of granting autonomy to the south and amnesty to members of the southern resistance, President Numayri and his assistants moved from preliminary arrangements into advanced negotiations in late 1971. In February 1972 they arrived at tentative agreements with southern spokesmen.

As negotiations progressed, the government ordered a ceasefire for its military forces. On March 6, 1972, Major General Lagu, spokesman for the southern forces, issued similar directives to the Anya Nya rebels. In what appeared to be a gesture of good faith, President Numayri replaced the generals in command of the military forces in Upper Uile, Bahr al Ghazal, and Equatoria provinces. His comments as he announced the appointments indicated that he regarded the new commanders as men who understand the problems of the south.

Along with political and administrative arrangements, the military and security provisions of the north-south agreement provided amnesty for the Anya Nya and other resistance groups. Internal security in the south, including control of the police, was to be directed by the new Southern Region government. Control of the Sudanese armed forces in the south was to be retained by the central government.

About 12,000 Sudanese military personnel were to be stationed in the south—half of them to be northerners and half southerners. They were to be organized in separate units, at least until a referendum in the south could be held. Former Anya Nya who were not taken into the army were to be employed in construction units to repair war damage.

BIBLIOGRAPHY

SECTION I. SOCIAL

Albino, Oliver. *The Sudan: A Southern Viewpoint.* London: Oxford University Press, 1970.

Al-Rahim, Muddathirabd. *Imperialism and Nationalism in the Sudan, 1899–1956.* Oxford: Clarendon Press, 1969.

Arkell, A.J. *A History of the Sudan from the Earliest Times to 1821.* (2d ed., rev.) London: Athlone Press, 1961.

Asad, Talal. *The Kababish Arabs: Power, Authority and Consent in a Nomadic Tribe.* Praeger: New York, 1970.

Barbour, Kenneth Michael. *The Republic of the Sudan: A Regional Geography.* London: University of London Press, 1961.

Barclay, Harold B. "Muslim Prophets in the Modern Sudan," *Muslim World,* LIV, No. 4, October 1964, 250–255.

———. "The Nile Valley." in Louise E. Sweet (ed.), *The Central Middle East.* New Haven: Human Relations Area Files, 1968.

———. "Notes on a Village in the Jazirah Area of the Republic of Sudan," *Muslim World,* LV, No. 1, January 1965, 46–57.

Beaton, A.C. "Bari Songs, III Funeral Songs," *Sudan Notes and Records* [Khartoum], XIX, Part 2, 1936, 327–355.

———. "Some Bari Songs," *Sudan Notes and Records* [Khartoum], XVIII, Part I, 1935, 277–287.

Bedri, Ibrahim. "Dinka Beliefs in Their Chiefs and Rainmakers," *Sudan Notes and Records* [Khartoum], XXII, No. 1, 1939, 125–131.

Berry, L., and Whiteman, A.J. "The Nile in the Sudan," *Geographical Journal* [London], CXXLV, No. 1, March 1968, 1–37.

Beshir, Mohammed Omer. "Some Problems of University Education in the Sudan," *Comparative Education Review,* V, No. 1, June 1961, 50–53.

———. *The Southern Sudan: Background to Conflict.* London: C. Hurst, 1968.

———. *The Southern Sudan: Background to Conflict.* New York: Praeger, 1968.

———. "The Sudan: A Military Surrender," *Africa Report,* IX, No. 11, December 1964, 3–6.

Boccassino, Renato. "Il contributo delle antiche fonti sulla religione dei Latuca, Obbo, Bari, Beri, Denca, Nuer e altre popolazioni," *Annali del Laternanensi* [Rome], XV, 1951, 79-138.

———. "Le varie forme della sciavitù in uso tra le popolazioni nilotiche e nilo-camitiche del già Sudan Anglo-Egiziano e dell' Uganda," *Annali del Lateranensi* [Rome], XXIX, 1965, 325-395.

Branchesi, Oliver. "The Sudan: Conspiracy for Destruction," *World Missions*, XV, No. 4, Winter 1964-1965, 8-21.

Brown, Carl L. "The Sudanese Mahdiyyah." Pages 145-168 in R. Rotberg and Ali Mazuri (eds.), *Protest and Power in Black Africa*. New York: Oxford University Press, 1970.

Buchler, I.R. "Semantique descriptive de categories religieuses Nuer," *Homme* [Paris], XI, No. 4, October–December 1966, 35-38.

Burns, Donald. "Educational Development in the Sudan," *Leeds African Studies Bulletin* [Leeds, England], VI, March 1967, 11-12.

Butt, Audrey. *The Nilotes of the Sudan and Uganda*. London: International African Institute, 1964.

Buxton, S.C. *Chiefs and Strangers*. Oxford: Clarendon Press, 1963.

Caravita, Gianni. "L'arta dei Dinka," *Africa* [Rome], XXIII, No. 3, September 1968, 350-369.

"The Church in the Sudan Today," *DIA* [Kinshasa], May 8, 1968, 204.

Clark, W.T. "Manners, Customs, and Beliefs of the Northern Bega," *Sudan Notes and Records* [Khartoum], XXI, No. 1, 1938, 278-295.

Collins, Robert O. and Herzog, Richard. "Early British Administration in Southern Sudan," *Journal of African History* [London], II, No. 1, 1961, 119-135.

Comte, Pierre M. "Les Peintures Zandes: L'Art populaire africain," *Connaissançe du Monde* [Paris], X, June–July 1957, 21-26.

Cook, Christopher L. "The Church in the Southern Sudan," *East and West Review* [London], XIX, No. 4, October 1953, 110 ff.

Crapanzo, Vincent, and Kramer, Jane. "Life in a Small Arab Town—A World of Saints and She-Demons," *New York Times Magazine*. June 22, 1969, 14-38.

Cunnison, Ian. *Baggara Arabs, Power and the Lineage in a Suddanese Nomad Tribe*. Oxford: Clarendon Press, 1966.

Deng, William. *The Problem of Southern Sudan* (Institute of Race Relations.) London: Oxford University Press, 1963.

Dima, S.A. "Southern Sudan: A Southern Student's Experiences," *African Forum*, III, No. 2/3, Winter 1968, 58–74.

Drower, Margaret S. *Nubia, A Drowning Land*. Harlow: Longman House, Burnt Mill, 1970.

Etzkorn, K. Peter. "Goerge Stimmel and the Sociology of Music," *Social Forces*, XLIII, No. 1, 1964, 101–106.

Evans-Pritchard, Edward Evan. *The Azande*. Oxford: Clarendon Press, 1971.

————. *The Nuer*. Oxford: Clarendon Press, 1940.

————. "Some Zande Folk-Tale, No. 1," *Sudan Notes and Records* [Khartoum], XLIV, 1963, 43–68.

————. "Sources, with Patricular Reference to the Southern Sudan," *Cahiers d'Etudes Africaines* [Paris], XXI, No. 1, 1971, 129–179.

————. "Variations in a Zande-Tale," *Journal of African Languages* [London], III, No. 2, 1964, 103–135.

————. "Zande Trickster and Other Tales," *Journal of African Languages* [London], V, No. 2, 1966, 125–160.

First, Ruth. *The Barrel of a Gun: Political Power in Africa and the Coup d'Etat*. London: Penguin Press, 1971.

"A Functional Literacy Poject in Sudan," *UNESCO Chronicle* [Paris], XV, No. 2, February 1969, 70–71.

Gero, Fil. "Caccia e Magia, *Nigrizia* [Rome], LXXXVII, No. 3, March 1969, 30–33.

————. *Death Among the Azande of the Sudan* (Beliefs, Rites and Cult). Bologna: Editrice Nigrizia, 1968.

————. *La Superstizione Zande*. Bologna: Editrice Nigrizia, 1966.

Giorgetti, Filiberto. "Ritmo e musica dei balli Bor e Bviri," *Annali del Lateranensi* [Rome], XXIX, 1965, 233–242.

Graham, Anne. "Man-Water Relations in the Central Sudan," Pages 409–445 in M.F. Thomas and G.W. Whittington (eds.), *Environment and Land Use in Africa*. London: Methuen, 1969.

Gray, Richard. *A History of the Southern Sudan, 1839–1889*. London: Oxford University Press, 1961.

Greener, Leslie. *High Dam over Nubia*. New York: Viking Press, 1962.

Haaland, Gunnar. "Economic Determinants in Ethic Processes." Pages 58–73 in Harold B. Barth (ed.) *Ethnic Groups and Boundaries*. Boston: Little, Brown, 1969.

Hale, Gerry A. "Urbanization in the Northern Sudan: Trends and Problems." (Paper presented to Symposium on the Arid Lands, Chicago, December 26–27, 1970.) Los Angeles: University of California, Department of Geography, December 1970. (Unpublished manuscript.)

Hale, Sandra. "Arts in a Changing Society: Northern Sudan," *Ufamo* [Khartoum], I, No. 11, 1970, 64–79.

————. "Sudanese Cultural Renaissance: Social Themes Have Brought About a Flowering of the Written, Sung, and Spoken Word," *Africa Report*, XV, No. 9, December 1970, 29–31.

Hance, William. *The Geography of Modern Africa.* New York: Columbia University Press, 1964.

Hassan, Yusuf Fadl. "The Penetration of Islam in the Eastern Sudan," *Sudan Notes and Records* [Khartoum], XLIV, 1963, 9–20.

————. "The Sudanese Revolution of October 1964," *Journal of Modern African Studies* [London], V, No. 4, December 1967, 491–509.

Henderson, K.D.C. *Sudan Republic.* (Nations of the Modern World Series.) New York: Praeger, 1966.

Henin, Roushdi A. "Second Thoughts on Sudan's Population Census." Pages 142–151 in J.C. Caldwell and C. Okonjo (eds.), *The Population of Tropical Africa,* New York: Columbia University Press, 1968.

Herzog, Rolf. "Die Ergebnisse der ersten sudanischen Volkszählung in ethnologischer Sicht," *Zeitschrift für Ethnologie* [Braunschweig], LXXXIV, No. 2, 1959, 173–204.

Hill, Richard L. *A Biographical Dictionary of the Sudan.* (2d ed.) London: Frank Cass, 1967.

————. "Government and Christian Missions in the Anglo-Egyptian Sudan," *Middle Eastern Studies* [London], I, No. 2, 1965, 113–134.

Hitti, Philip K. *Islam, A Way of Life.* Minneapolis: University of Minnesota Prses, 1970.

Hodgkin, Robin. *Sudan Geography.* London: Longmans, Green, 1951.

Holt, Peter M. *A Modern History of the Sudan . . . to the Present Day.* New York: Grove Press, 1961.

————. "Two Traditional Sudanese Historical Works," *Research Bulletin of the Center of Arabic Documentation* [Ibadan], V, No. 12, December 1969, 1–20.

Hoogstraal, Harry H., and Heyneman, Donald. "Leishmaniasis in the Sudan Republic," *American Journal of Tropical Medicine and Hygiene,* XVIII, No. 6, November 1969, 1091–1210.

Huffman, Ray. *Nuer Customs and Folklore.* London: Frank Cass, 1970.

International Yearbook of Education, 1969, XXXI. Paris: United Nations Educational, Scientific and Cultural Organization, 1970.

"Islamic Pressure of Sudan Constitution," *DIA* [Kinshasa], February 27, 1968, 87.

Jungraithmayr, Herrmann. "Rock Paintings in the Sudan," *Current Anthropology*, II, No. 4, October 1961, 388–389.

Keating, Rex. *Nubian Twilight*. New York: Harcourt Brace, 1963.

Kirwan, L.P. "A Contemporary Account of the Conversion of the Sudan to Christianity," *Sudan Notes and Records* [Khartoum], XX, No. 2, 1937, 289–295.

Konrad, Walter. "Ueber Buduma-Lieder und den Bau einer funfsaitigen Buduma-Harfe," *Jahrbuch des Museums für Volkerkunde* [Leipzig], XXIII, 1966, 64–74.

Kronenberg, Andreas. "Jo Lou Tales," *Kush* [Khartoum], VIII, 1960, 237–251.

Kronenberg, Andreas, and Kronenberg, W. "Die Bevoelkerung im Stauseegebiet Sudanisch-Nubiens," *Paideuma* [Wiesbaden], II, 1965, 119–124.

———. "Der gegenwaertige Stand der Literatur ueber ethnische Gruppen in Suedsudan," *Bulletin, International Committee on Urgent Anthropological, Ethnological Research*, VII, 1965, 107–123.

———"Wooden Carvings in the South Western Sudan," *Kush* [Khartoum], VIII, 1960, 274–281.

Krotki, K.J. *The Population in Sudan*. (Report on the sixth Annual Conference.) Khartoum: Philosophical Society of Sudan, 1958.

Lebon, J.H.G. *Land Use in Sudan*. (Regional Monograph No. 4 in the World Land Use Survey, edited by Sir Dudley Stamp.) Bude, Cornwall, England: Geographical Publications, 1965.

Lee, David R. *Land Utilization Along the Nile from the Sixth Cataract to Abu Hamed, Sudan*. Davis: University of California, Department of Geography.

———. *Village Morphology and Growth in Northern Sudan* (Paper presented to the Annual Meeting of the Association of American Geographers, Ann Arbor, Michigan.) Davis: University of California, Department of Geography, 1969.

Legum, Colin. "Sudan's New Split Adds to Chronic Strife," *Africa Report*, XV, No. 6, June 1970, 14–15.

———. "Sudan's Three Day Revolution," *Africa Report*, XVI, No. 7, October 1971, 12–15.

Lienhardt, Godfrey. *Divinity and Experience, the Religion of the Dinka*. London: Oxford University Press, 1961.

Maan, W.J. "Church and State in the Sudan," *Frontier* [London], VII, No. 1, 1964, 36–40.

MacGaffey, W. "History of Negro Migrations in the Northern Sudan," *Southwestern Journal of Anthropology*, VIII, No. 4, 1961, 178–197.

McLoughlin, Peter F.M. "Economic Development and the Heritage of Slavery in the Sudan Republic," *Africa* [Rome], XXXIII, No. 4, October 1962, 355–391.

Mair, Lucy. *Primitive Government*. Harmondsworth, England: Penguin Books, 1962.

Middleton, John. *Black Africa*. London: Macmillan, 1970.

Nadel, Siegfried F. "A Shaman Cult in the Nuba Mountains," *Sudan Notes and Records* [Khartoum], XXIV, 1941, 85–112.

————. "Two Nuba Religions: An Essay in Comparison," *American Anthropologist*, LVII, No. 4, August 1955, 661–679.

————. "Witchcraft in Four African Societies: An Essay in Comparison," *American Anthropologist*, LIV, No. 1, 1952, 17–31.

Nebel, Arturo. *I Dinca sono cosi. Ricordi di une vita fra i dinca del Bahr el-Ghazal Sudan*. Bologna: Editrice Nigrizia, 1968.

Nordenstam, Tore. *Sudanese Ethnics*. Upsala, Sweden: Scandinavian Institute of African Studies, 1968.

"Nubia: Excavation and Preservation of Nubia's Sites and Monuments." Pages 690–691 in *Encyclopaedia Britannica*, XVI. Chicago: Encyclopaedia Britannica, 1969.

Olderogge, Dmitry, and Forman, Werner. *The Art of Africa: Negro Art from the Institute of Ethnography, Leningrad*. New York: Paul Hamlyn, 1969.

Oliver, J. "Problems of the Arid Lands: The Example of the Sudan." Pages 219–239 in *Land Use and Resources: Studies in Applied Geography*. London: Alden and Mowbray, 1968.

Paulme, Denise. "Carved Figures from the White Nile in the Musée de l'Homme," *Man* [London], LIII, No. 172, August 1953, 113–114.

Prothero, R. Mansell. *Migrants and Malaria in Africa*. Pittsburgh: University of Pittsburgh Press, 1965.

Rahim, M.A. "Early Sudanese Nationalism, 1900–1928," *Sudan Notes and Records* [Khartoum], No. 47, 1966, 39–64.

"Recolonization of Southern Sudan," *Neue Zuercher Zeitung*, Zurich, 1971. [Translated by U.S. Department of Commerce, Office of Technical Services, Joint Publications Research Service (Washington). JPRS: 53,087, *Translations on Africa*, 1971.]

Reining, Conrad. *The Zande Scheme: An Anthropological Case Study of Eocnomic Development in Africa*. Evanston: Northwestern University Press, 1966.

"Religious Instruction in Government Schools," *Fides* [Rome], No. 2,144, November 16, 1968, 588.

Roden, David. "Lowland Farms for a Mountain People," *Geographical Magazine* [London], XLII, No. 3, December 1959, 201–206.

Said, Beshir Mohammed. *The Sudan, Crossroads of Africa*. Chester Springs, Pennsylvania: Dufour Editions, 1966.

Sanderson, Illian. "A Survey of Material Available for the Study of Educational Development in the Modern Sudan, 1900–1968," *Sudan Notes and Records* [Khartoum], XLIV, 1963, 68–81.

Santandrea, Stefano. "Aggiornamenti sul gruppo Ndogo del Bahr al Ghazal (Sudan) : Tribu Ndogo, Sere, Bai, Bviri e Golo," *Annali del Lateranensi* [Rome], XXIX, 1965, 42–231.

————. *The Luo of the Bahr el Ghazal: Historical Notes*. Bologna: Editrice Nigrizia, 1968.

————. "Morte violenta per i re divini Schilluke Dinka," *Africa* [Rome], XX, No. 1, March 1965, 15–32.

————. *A Tribal History of the Western Bahr al-Ghazal*. Bologna: Editrice Nigrizia, 1964.

Sasnett, Martena, and Sepmeyer, Inez. *Educational Systems of Africa*. Berkeley: University of California Press, 1966.

"Seven Sudanese Deacons to be Ordained Priests," *Fides* [Rome], No. 2,150, December 11, 1968, 634.

Sharma, B.S. "Elections in the Sudan During the Military Regime," *Parliamentary Affairs* [London], No. 4, Summer 1967, 274–280.

————. "Failure of Local Government/Democracy in the Sudan," *Political Studies* [London], XV, No. 2, February 1967, 62-71.

Shaw, D.J. (ed.) *Agricultural Development in the Sudan*. Khartoum: Philosophical Society of the Sudan and Sudan Agricultural Society, 1966.

Shepherd, G. "The National University in Multi-National Societies: The Case of the Sudan," *Africa Today*, XIV, No. 2, 1967, 9–11.

Shoush, Muhammad Ibrahim al. "Some Background Notes on Modern Sudanese Poetry," *Sudan Notes and Records* [Khartoum], XLIV, 1963, 21–41.

Sokiri, Yugusuk Mori. "The Folk-Tales from the Southern Sudan," *Folklore* [London], LXXVI, Autumn 1965, 196-201.

Stamp, Dudley L. *Africa: A Study in Tropical Development*. New York: John Wiley and Sons, 1953.

Stevenson, R.C. "Some Aspects of the Spread of Islam in the Nuba Mountains," *Sudan Notes and Records* [Khartoum], XLIV, 1963, 1–8.

Sudan. Ministry of Planning. Research and Statistics Section. *Economic Survey, 1969*. Khartoum: Government Printing Press, December 1970.

————. *The Five Year Plan of Economic and Social Development of the Democratic Republic of the Sudan for the Period 1970/71–1974/75*, I: Major Trends of Development. Khartoum: 1970.

Sudan. Ministry of Social Affairs. *First Population Census of the Sudan, 1955–56.* Khartoum: Government Printing Press, 1958.

Sudan Almanac, 1968: An Official Handbook. Khartoum: Government Printing Press, 1967.

"Sudan Democratic Republic." Pages B44–B58 in Colin Legum (ed.), *Africa Contemporary Record: Annual Survey and Documents, 1970–1971.* London: Rex Collings, 1971.

"Sudan Democratic Republic." Pages B47–B68 in Colin Legum and John Drysdale (eds.), *Africa Contemporary Record: Annual Survey and Documents, 1969–1970.* Exeter: Africa Research, 1970.

Sudan Today. Tavistock: University Press of Africa, for the Sudan Ministry of Information and Culture, 1971.

Sweet, Louis E. (ed.) *The Central Middle East: A Handbook of Anthropology*, I. New Haven: Human Relations Area Files, 1968.

Tayib, Griselda al. "Women's Education in Sudan," *Kano Studies* [Kano, Nigeria], I, September 1965, 43–46.

Tothill, J.D. (ed.) *Agriculture in the Sudan.* London: Oxford University Press, 1948.

"The Tragedy of Southern Sudan," *Reporter* [Nairobi], December 13, 1968, 14.

Trigger, B.G. "Languages of the Northern Sudan: A Historical Perspective," *Journal of African History* [London], VII, No. 1, 1966, 19–25.

Trimingham, John Spencer. *The Christian Church in Post-War Sudan*, World Dominion Press [London], 1949, 1–44 (pamphlet).

————. *The Influence of Islam upon Africa.* New York: Praeger, 1968.

————. *Islam in Sudan.* London: Oxford University Press, 1949.

"Two Tanzanian Priests Go to Southern Sudan," *Fides* [Rome], No. 2,119, July 3, 1968, 683.

United Nations. Department of Economic and Social Affairs. *Population and Vital Statistics Report, Statistical Papers.* (Series A.) XXIII, No. 4, October 1971, 10–11.

United Nations. Department of Economic and Social Affairs, jointly with Department of Statistics, Council of Ministers, Republic of Sudan. *Population Growth and Manpower in the Sudan.* (Population Study No. 37.) New York: UN, 1964.

United Nations Educational, Scientific and Cultural Organization. *Repertoire d'ecoles normales superieurs*, Geneva: UN, 1969.

U.S. Agency for International Development. *Economic Data Book, Africa*. Washington: 1971.

U.S. Department of State. Bureau of Intelligence and Research. *International Boundary Studies, Central African Republic-Sudan*. (Series No. 16.) Washington: 1962.

——. *International Boundary Studies, Chad-Sudan*, (Series No. 15.) Washington: 1962.

——. *International Boundary Studies, Congo-Sudan*. (Series No. 106.) Washington: 1970.

——. *International Boundary Studies, Libya-Sudan*. (Series No. 10.) Washington: 1961.

——. *International Boundary Studies, Sudan-Uganda*. (Series No. 104.) Washington: 1970.

——. *International Boundary Studies, UAR-Sudan*. (Series No. 18.) Washington: 1962.

Wenzel, Marian. "A Note on the Cat-lore of Nubia," *Folklore* [London], LXXV, Summer 1964, 121.

Willis, C. Armine. "The Cult of Denge," *Sudan Notes and Records* [Khartoum], XI, 1928.

——. "Religious Confraternities of the Sudan," *Sudan Notes and Records* [Khartoum], IV, No. 4, 1921, 175.

World Christian Handbook, 1968. (Eds., H. Wakelin Coxill and Kenneth G. Grubb.) London: Butterworth Press, 1967.

The World of Learning 1970–1971. (21st ed.) London: Europa Publications, 1971.

Yassein, Osman. "Social, Economic and Political Role of Urban Agglomerations in the Developing States: The Sudan's Experience," *African Administrative Studies* [Tangier], December 1967, 1–11.

(Various issues of the following periodicals were also used in the preparation of this section: *Kush* [Khartoum], X, 1962, through XIV, 1966. *Sudan Notes and Records* [Khartoum], XLIII, 1962, through XLVII, 1966.

SECTION II. POLITICAL

Abd al Rahim, M. "Arabism, Africanism and Self-Identification in the Sudan," *Journal of Modern African Studies* [London], VIII, No. 2, July 1970, 233–249.

Africa South of the Sahara. London: Europa Publications, 1971.

Albino, Oliver. *The Sudan: A Southern Viewpoint.* London: Oxford University Press, 1970.

Ammar, B. "Regional Autonomy Brings Peace to Southern Sudan," *New Middle East* [London], Nos. 42 and 43, March/April 1972, 12–13.

Beshir, Mohammed Omer. *The Southern Sudan: Background to Conflict.* New York: Praeger, 1968.

Bettinghaus, Erwin P. *Persausive Communications.* New York: Holt, Rinehart and Winston, 1968.

"Economic Notes," *New Africa* [London], XIII, Nos. 9–10, 1972, 12.

Europa Yearbook, 1971. London: Europa Publications, 1971.

"Eye Witness in the Southern Sudan," *New Middle East* [London], No. 31, April 1971, 32–33.

Fellows, Lawrence. "The Unknown War in the Sudan," *New York Times Magazine,* September 22, 1968, 25–27, 122–130.

Gandy, Christopher. "Sudan 1972: Pragmatism Replaces Ideology," *New Middle East* [London], Nos. 42 and 43, March/April 1972, 14–16.

Hare, A.P., et al (eds.). *Small Groups: Studies in Social Interaction.* New York: Knopf, 1965.

Horton, Alan W. *The Splendid Isolation of the Sudan: An Arab-Speaking Country Holds Itself Aloof—Even from the Arab World.* (American Universities Field Staff Reports Service, *Northeast Africa Series,* XI.) New York: AUFS, June 1964, 39–48.

Howell, J., and Hamid, M.B. "Sudan and the Outside World, 1964–1968," *African Affairs* [London], LXVIII, No. 273, October 1969, 299–318.

Hyman, Herby H., and Singer, Eleanor (eds.). *Readings in Reference Group Theory and Research.* New York: Macmillian, 1968.

Ismael, Tareq. "The People's Republic of China and Africa," *Journal of Modern African Studies* [London], IX, No. 4, December 1971, 507–510.

———. *The UAR in Africa: Egypt's Policy Under Nasser.* Evanston: Northwestern University Press, 1971.

———. "United Arab Republic and the Sudan," *"Middle East Journal,* XXIII, No. 1, Winter 1969, 14–28.

Kelman, Herbert C. (ed.) *International Behavior: A Socio-Psychological Analysis.* New York: Holt, Rinehart and Winston, 1965.

Kilner, Peter. "Better Outlook for Sudan," *World Today* London, XXVIII, No. 4, April 1972, 181–188.

Klinghoffer, Arthur Jay. "Israel in Africa: The Strategy of Aid," *Africa Report,* XVII, No. 4, April 1972, 12–14.

Legum, Colin. "Sudan," *Africa Report,* XVII, No. 4, April 1972, 4.

————. "Sudan's New Split Adds to Chronic Strife," *Africa Report*, XV, No. 6, June 1970, 14–15.

————. "Sudan's Three Day Revolution," *Africa Report*, XVI, No. 7, October 1971, 12–15.

Mahgoub, Mohammad Salih. "The Sudanese Press," *Sudan Notes and Records* [Khartoum], XLVI, 1965, 1–7.

The Middle East and North Africa, 1971–1972. London: Europa Publications, 1971.

Mustafa, Zaki. *The Common Law in the Sudan.* London: Oxford University Press, 1972.

"Radio Broadcasting in Africa," (Michael Diroks, ed.) *Afrika Heute*, Bonn, October 1, 1971. [Translated by U.S. Department of Commerce, Office of Technical Services, Joint Publications Research Service (Washington). JPRS: 54,749, *Translations on Africa*, No. 1,094, 1971.]

Reed, Allan. "The Anyanya: Ten Months' Travel with Its Forces Inside the Southern Sudan," *Munger Africana Library Notes*, No. 11, February 1972.

Rondot, Pierre. "L'Experience Politique du Sudan," *Revue Defense National* [Paris], XXV, July 1969, 1190–1212.

"Slaughter in Africa: Arab Against Black," *Atlas*, XIV, No. 10, October 1967, 14–19.

Statistical Yearbook, 1969. Paris, United Nations Educational, Scientific and Cultural Organization: 1970.

Statistical Yearbook, 1970. New York: United Nations, 1971.

Sudan. *Internal Statistics, 1969.* Khartoum: Ministry of Planning, Department of Statistics, 1969.

Sudan. Ministry of Planning. Research and Statistics Section. *The Five Year Plan of Economic and Social Development of the Democratic Republic of the Sudan for the Period of 1970/ 1971–1974/1975,* I: Major Trends of Development. Khartoum: 1970.

Sudan Almanac, 1968: An Official Handbook. Khartoum: Government Printing Press, 1967.

"Sudan Democratic Republic." Pages B44–B58 in Colin Legum (ed.), *African Contemporary Record: Annual Survey and Documents, 1970–1971.* London: Rex Collings, 1971.

"Sudan Democratic Republic." Pages B47–B68 in Colin Legum and John Drysdale (eds.), *Africa Contemporary Record: Annual Survey and Documents, 1969–1970.* Exeter: Africa Research, 1970.

"Sudan Moderates Policies at Home and Abroad," *Washington Post*, December 16, 1971, G-8.

"The Sudan." Pages 128–152 in Arnold Rivkin (ed.), *Nations by Design: Institution Building in Africa*. Garden City: Anchor Books, 1968.

"Sudan's Trade Unions: Communist Stronghold," *Africa Report*, IV, No. 1, January 1959, 12.

Sudan Today. Tavistock: University Press of Africa, for the Sudan Ministry of Information and Culture, 1971.

Sylvester, Anthony. "Muhammad Versus Lenin in Revolutionary Sudan." *New Middle East* [London], No. 34, July 1971, 26–26.

Thompson, Cliff F. "The Sources of Law in the New Nations of Africa: A Case Study from Sudan." Pages 133–176 in Thomas Hutchison (ed.), *Africa and Law*. Madison: University of Wisconsin Press, 1968.

United Nations Educational, Scientific and Cultural Organization. *World Communications: Press, Radio, Television, Film*. Paris: UNESCO, 1964.

United Nations. *Report of the United Nations High Commissioner for Refugees*. (General Assembly Official Records, 26th Session Supplement No. 12.) New York: UN, 1971.

————. *United Nations High Commissioner for Refugees Report: The Promise of M'Boki*. Geneva: United Nations High Commissioner for Refugees, 1969.

United Nations. General Assembly Official Records. *Addendum to the Report of the United Nations High Commissioner for Refugees*. (General Assembly Official Records, 26th Session Supplement No. 12–A.) New York: United Nations, 1971.

————. *United Nations High Commissioner for Refugees Report: Refugees in Africa*. Geneva: UNHCR, 1966.

U.S. Department of Commerce. Office of Technical Services. Joint Publications Research Service—JPRS (Washington). The following items are from the JPRS series *Translations on the Near East*.

"President Decrees New Organization of Government," *Al-Ayyam*, [Khartoum], October 14, 1971. (JPRS: 54,847, Series No. 694, January 4, 1972, 103–118.)

"The Struggle in the Sudanese Communist Party," *Al-Nahar*, [Beirut], March 26–31 and April 1–3, 1971. (JPRS: 53,946, Series No. 647, August 31, 1971, all pages in issue).

U.S. United States Information Agency. Office of Policy and Research. *Communications Data Book for Africa*. Washington: August 1966.

World Radio-TV Handbook, 1972. (Ed., J.M. Frost.) Hvidovre, Denmark: World Radio-TV Handbook, 1972.

Yearbook of International Organizations, 1968–69. Brussels: Union of International Associations, 1969.

Zanotelli, Alex. "Muslim Sudanese Students: Marx or the Koran," *Insight and Opinion* [Accra, Ghana], III, No. 2, 1968, 107–114.

(Various issues of the following periodicals were also used in the preparation of this section: *Africa Research Bulletin* [London], January 1971–April 1972; *Middle East Economic Digest* [London], January 1971–April 1972; *New York Times*, January 1971–April 1972; and *Washington Post*, January 1971–April 1972.)

SECTION III. ECONOMIC

Barbour, Kenneth Michael. *The Republic of the Sudan: A Regional Geography*. London: University of London Press, 1961.

Barclay's Bank, D.C.O. *The Sudan: An Economic Survey*. Khartoum: Local Head Office, September 1967.

Bowring, Philip. "Potential of War-Torn South," *Financial Times* [London], November 23, 1971, 30.

———. "Transport System Inadequate," *Financial Times* [London], November 23, 1971, 28.

Chambers, Robert. *Settlement Schemes in Tropical Africa*. New York: Praeger, 1969.

L'Economie des Pay Arabs [Beirut], XIV, No. 36/162, July 1971.

"L'Economie du Soudan," No. 3,536 in the series *Notes et Etudes Documentaires*. Paris: Secretariat General du Government, La Documentation Française, November 16, 1968.

Food and Agriculture Organization. *Monthly Bulletin* [Rome], XXI, No. 1, January 1972.

Garner, John. "Difficult Year for Cotton," *Financial Times* [London], November 23, 1971, 28.

Germany, Federal Republic of. Statistisches Bundesamt. "Landerkurzberichte: Sudan." (In a series *Allgemeine Statistik des Auslandes*.) Wiesbaden: Statistisches Bundesamt, 1970.

Gerster, Georg. "Weisses Gold vom Blauen Nil," *Neue Zurcher Zeitung* [Zurich], Overseas Weekend Issue No. 27, No. 177, July 1, 1962, 6A–6D.

Graham, Anne. "Man-Water Relations in the East Central Sudan." Pages 409–445 in M.F. Thomas and G.W. Whittington (eds.), *Environment and Land Use in Africa*. London: Methuen, 1969.

Gretton, George. "Sudan Takes Stock After the Coup," *African Development* [London], August 1969, 9–12.

Güsten, Rolf. *Problems of Economic Growth and Planning: The Sudan Example: Some Aspects and Implications of the Current Ten-Year Plan.* (No. 9 in the series Afrika-Sudien of the IFO-Institut für Wirtschaftsforschung.) West Berlin: Springer-Verlag, 1966.

Hodgkin, Robin A. *Sudan Geography.* Khartoum: Sudan Department of Education, 1946.

Hodgkin, Robin A., and Lock, K.C. *How People Live in the Sudan.* London: Education Supply Association, 1963.

Honsch, Ingrid. "Die Republik Sudan: Ein ökonomisch-geographischer Uberblick unter besonderer berücksichtigung agrargeographische probleme," *Geographische Berichte* [Gotha, East Germany], XI–XII, No. 1, 1966, 1–11.

International Monetary Fund. *International Financial Statistics.* Washington: IMF, December 1971.

International Monetary Fund. *International Financial Statistics.* Washington: IMF, March 1972.

Jeune Afrique. *Afrique, 1970.* (Annual Reference Volume). Paris: Société Presse Africaine Associée, 1971.

Johns, Richard. "Economy in Trouble," *Financial Times* [London], November 23, 1971, 26.

———. "In Search of Real Stability," *Financial Times* [London], November 23, 1971, 25.

———. "More Planning Finance Needed," *Financial Times* [London], November 23, 1971, 26.

Lavrencic, Karl. "Attempts to Broaden the Trading Base," *Financial Times* [London], November 23, 1971, 29.

———. "Water Is the Key to Prosperity," *Financial Times* [London], November 23, 1971, 30.

Lebon, J.H.G. *Land Use in Sudan.* (Regional Monograph No. 4 in the World Land Use Survey, edited by Sir Dudley Stamp.) Bude, Cornwall, England: Geographical Publications, 1965.

———. "On the Human Geography of the Nile Basin," *Geography* [Sheffield], XLV, 1960, 16–26.

McLoughlin, Peter F.M. "Economic Development and the Heritage of Slavery in the Sudan Republic," *Africa* [London], XXXIII, 1962, 355–390.

———. "Population Growth Projections 1906–2006, for Economic Development in the Sudan, *American Journal of Economics and Sociology,* XXIV, No. 2, April 1965, 135–156.

Mahgoub, Sayed Mirghani. "Land Policy and Settlement in Sudan." Pages 175–188 in El Ghonemy and Mohammad Riad (eds.), *Land Policy in the Near East.* Rome: United Nations Food and Agriculture Organization, 1967.

May, Jacques M., and McLellan, Donna. *The Ecology of Malnutrition in Eastern Africa and Four Countries of Western Afica.* New York: Hafner, 1970.

Oden, Bertil. *Sudans Ekonomi.* Uppsala, Sweden: Nordiska Afrikainstitutet, April 1969.

Oliver, J. "Problems of the Arid Lands: The Example of the Sudan." Pages 219–239 in *Land Use and Resources: Studies in Applied Geography.* London: Alden and Mowbray, 1968.

Production Yearbook, 1969. Rome: United Nations Food and Agriculture Organization, 1971.

Production Yearbook, 1970. Rome: United Nations Food and Agriculture Organization, 1971.

Reining, Conrad. *The Zande Scheme: An Anthropological Case Study of Economic Development in Africa.* Evanston: Northwestern University Press, 1966.

Roden, David. "Lowland Farms for a Mountain People," *Geographical Magazine* [London], December 1969, 201–206.

Said, Beshir Mohammed. *The Sudan: Crossroads of Africa.* Chester Springs, Pennsylvania: Dufour Editions, 1966.

Shaw, D.J. (ed.) *Agricultural Development in the Sudan.* Khartoum: Philosophical Society of the Sudan, in conjunction with the Sudan Agricultural Society, 1966.

——. "Resettlement from the Nile in Sudan," *Middle East Journal,* XXI, No. 4, Autumn 1967, 463–487.

Simpson, I.G. "New Approaches to Irrigated Farming in the Sudan: Organization and Management," *Land Economics,* XLVI, No. 3, August 1970, 287–296.

Stucken, Rudolf (ed.). *Entwicklungsbedingungen und Entwicklungschancen der Republik Sudan.* West Berlin: Duncker and Humblot, 1963.

Sudan. Economic Planning Secretariat. *The Ten Year Plan of Economic and Social Development, 1961/62–1970/71.* Khartoum: Government Printing Press, 1962.

Sudan. Ministry of Planning. Research and Statistics Section. *Economic Survey, 1969.* Khartoum: Government Printing Press, December 1970.

——. *The Five Year Plan of Economic and Social Development of the Democratic Republic of the Sudan for the Period 1970/71–1974/75,* I: Major Trends of Development. Khartoum: 1970.

"Sudan Fights for Freedom from Thirst," *New Africa* [London], XIII, Nos. 1 and 2, 1971, 7.

"Sudan: Joining Federation?" *Africa: An International Business, Economic, and Political Monthly* [London], May 1971, 52.

Thornton, D.S. "Human and Social Aspects of Irrigation Development." Pages 50–63 in *Economics of Irrigation Development: A Symposium.* (Development Study No. 6.) University of Reading, England, Department of Agricultural Economics, May 1969.

Tothill, J.D. *Agriculture in the Sudan.* London: Oxford University Press, 1948.

United Nations. United Nations Development Program and Food and Agriculture Organization. *Land and Water Resources Survey in the Jebel Marrah Area, the Sudan.* (FAO/SF:48/SUD–17.) Rome: UNDP/FAO, 1968.

Verrier, Anthony. "Sudan: A Rethink over Economic Policy," *Middle East International* [London], No. 4, July 1971, 37–38.

Wynn, R.F. "Sudan's Ten Year Plan of Economic Development, 1961/62–1970/71: An Analysis of Achievement to 1967/68," *Journal of Developing Areas,* No. 5, 1970, 55–76.

SECTION IV. NATIONAL SECURITY

"Agreement to End 15-Year War in the South," *Middle East Economic Digest* [London], XVI, No. 9, March 3, 1972, 247–248.

Albino, Oliver. *The Sudan: A Southern Viewpoint.* London: Oxford University Press, 1970.

Bechtold, Peter. "The Military in Sudanese Politics," *Africa Today,* XV, No. 2, April–May 1968, 23–25.

Beeri, Eliezer. *Army Officers in Arab Politics and Society.* New York: Praeger, 1970.

"Church Helps End Sudan Split." *Washington Post,* March 11, 1972, C–21.

Dupuy, T.N. (ed.) *Almanac of World Military Power.* Dunn Loring, Virginia. T.N. Depuy Associates, 1970.

"Eye Witness in the Southern Sudan," *New Middle East* [London], No. 31, April 1971, 32–33.

Fellows, Lawrence. "The Unknown War in the Sudan," *New York Times Magazine,* September 22, 1968, 25–27, 122–130.

First, Ruth. *The Barrel of a Gun: Political Power in Africa and the Coup d'Etat.* London: Penguin Press, 1971.

———. "Sudan: Behind the Coups," *Africa: An International Business, Economic, and Political Monthly* [London], No. 3, August 1971, 60–61.

Klinghoffer, Arthur Jay. "Israel in Africa: The Strategy of Aid," *Africa Report,* XVII, No. 4, April 1972, 12–14.

Lee, J.M. *African Armies and Civil Order*. New York: Praeger, 1969.

The Military Balance, 1969-70. London: Institute for Strategic Studies, 1969.

The Military Balance, 1970-71. London: Institute for Strategic Studies, 1970.

The Military Balance, 1971-72. London: Institute for Strategic Studies, 1971.

"Military Forces in Sudan," *Air Force Magazine*, LIV, No. 12, December 1971, 78-81.

"Playing War," *Atlas*, XX, No. 2, February 1971, 34-35.

Reed, Allan. "The Anya Nya: Ten Months' Travel with Its Forces Inside the Southern Sudan," *Munger Africana Library Notes*, No. 11, February 1972.

Rouleau, Eric. "Sudan's Communists: Routed by Arabism," *Le Monde* [Paris], (Weekly English edition) No. 123, August 28, 1971, 11-13.

"Second Biafra," *Atlas*, XX, No. 2, February 1971, 33, 34.

"Slaughter in Africa: Arab Against Black," *Atlas*, XIV, No. 10, October 1967, 14-19.

Sudan. *Central Budget of the Democratic Republic of the Sudan: Estimates of Revenues and Expenditures*. Khartoum: Government Printing Press, 1968.

"Sudan: A Victory for Humanity," *Time*, XCIX, No. 11, March 13, 1972, 39-40.

"Sudan Democratic Republic." Pages B47-B68 in Colin Legum and John Drysdale (eds.), *Africa Contemporary Record: Annual Survey and Documents, 1969-1970*. Exeter: Africa Research, 1970.

"Sudan—Joining Federation?" *Africa: An International Business, Economic and Political Monthly*, [London] No. 5, 1971, 52.

"Sudan Salute Your Rebel General," *Economist* [London], CCXLII, No. 6,707, March 11, 1972, 44-45.

United Nations. Department of Economic and Social Affairs, jointly with Department of Statistics, Council of Ministers, Republic of Sudan. *Population Growth and Manpower in the Sudan*. (Population Study No. 37.) New York: UN, 1964.

Wood, David. *The Armed Forces of African States*. (Adelphi Papers No. 27.) London: Institute for Strategic Studies, 1966.

Yangu, Alexis Mbali. *The Nile Turns Red*. New York: Pageant Press, 1966.

"A Year of the Revolution," *Atlas*, XX, No. 10, October 1970, 375-376.

GLOSSARY

awqaf (sing., *waqf, q.v.*)—Muslim religious endowments.

cadi (Arabic, *qadi*)—A Muslim judge who interprets and administers the religious law of Islam.

Coptic Orthodox Church—The ancient Christian church of Egypt, surviving in modern times mainly among the peasants or laborers, particularly agricultural laborers, in Arabic-speaking countries.

extended family—A husband, his wife (or wives), his children, and his married sons and their wives and children.

feddan (pl., feddan or feddans)—Sudanese unit of area equal to 1.038 acres.

fiqi (pl., *fuqaha*)—Arabic term for traditional Koranic teacher in small *khalwa* (*q.v.*), usually in rural areas.

hadith—A narrative record of the deeds, sayings, and customs of the Prophet Muhammad and his companions, as reported by witnesses and handed down by tradition. One of the sources of the *sharia* (*q.v.*).

Haj—One who has made the pilgrimage to Mecca; it is often used as a title of respect.

haji—The pilgrimage to Mecca required of all Muslims able to go.

imam—The prayer leader of a mosque. Also, any Muslim who is followed as an authority in Islamic theology and law or an authoritative Muslim who has founded a school of religious interpretation.

jihad—A religious duty imposed on Muslims by the *sharia (q.v.)* for the spread of Islam. Popularly known as "holy war," it is waged against unbelievers and enemies of the faith. Followers may fulfill their *jihad* duty in four different ways: by the heart, the tongue, the hand, and the sword.

khalwa—Small Islamic schools, usually in rural settlements, that stress rote memorization of the Koran. In Sudan *khalwa* are classified as village schools as contrasted to public institutions.

lineage—A group of people who can trace descent from a known common ancestor. Most ethnic groups in Sudan are patrilineal in that they trace descent through the male line. A large lineage tracing descent from a relatively remote ancestor may include smaller lineages, each of which traces descent from a less remote ancestor.

335

Nilotic—Refers to semisedentary pastoralists living in the flood plains of the Blue Nile and White Nile rivers and also to the related languages they speak.

nuclear family—A man, his wife, and their unmarried children.

Ramadan—In the Muslim year, the ninth month, when strict fasting is observed from dawn to sunset, commemorating the revelation of the Koran.

salat—A ritual prayer made by Muslims five times daily, in a standing position alternating with inclinations and prostrations, while the worshiper faces toward Mecca.

sawm—Arabic term for abstinence; applied particularly to the fasting practices during the month of Ramadan (*q.v.*).

shahadah—Arabic term denoting: to give testimony, to declare acknowledgment, or to witness. It is commonly applicable to the act of professing the Islamic faith by declaring: "There is no God but Allah, and Muhammad is his prophet."

sharia—The body of formally established, sacred Islamic law. It is based primarily on Allah's commandments found in the Koran. In theory it governs religious matters and also regulates political, economic, civil, criminal, ethical, social, and domestic affairs in Muslim countries. In practice it is commonly supplemented by the customary law of a region and by government legislation and administrative practice. Courts applying this law are called *shariat* courts.

sheikh (Arabic, *shaykh, shaikh,* or *sheykh*)—Head of an Arab family, clan, tribe, or village. Also used as a title for a religious scholar or as a form of respectful address. Literally, it means "old man."

Sudanese pound (£S)—The Sudanese basic monetary unit composed of 100 piasters; 1 Sudanese pound equals US$2.87.

suq (also, *souk, souq, suk,* or *sukh*)—A marketplace in the Muslim world. In English-speaking areas it is frequently called a bazaar.

tariqa (pl., *turuq*)—Arabic term literally meaning "path" or "way." It is used in Sudan to denote the various Islamic religious orders.

Three Towns—Sudanese reference to the cities of Khartoum, Khartoum North, and Omdurman. Located in close proximity to the juncture of the White Nile and Blue Nile rivers, they form a single metropolitan area.

ulema (also, *ulama*)—Muslim theologians and scholars who are concerned and occupied with the interpretation of the Muslim legal system as derived from a study of its sources in the Koran and *hadith* (*q.v.*). *Ulema* are usually gathered in groups in various urban centers, where they function individually as teachers, as consultants in religious law, and as theologians. They are the highest religious authorities in Islam.

wadi—The channel or bed of a watercourse that is dry except in the rainy season; also, a ravine through which a stream flows.

waqf (pl., *awqaf, q.v.*)—In Islamic law, an endowment of property to be held in trust for a charitable or religious cause.

Zaire—Short-form designation for the Republic of Zaire, the new name of the former Democratic Republic of the Congo (Kinshasa), which was officially changed on October 27, 1971.

zakat—An annual alms tax or offering to the poor, expected to be paid by each Muslim as a religious duty. It is used for charitable or religious purposes.

INDEX

Arabs (*see also* northern area of Sudan): 15, 17, 32, 71, 72-77; self-image, 107; social system, 94-95, 104
archeology: 10, 159-160, 161
architecture: 157, 159-160
area: vii, 1, 49; arable land, 258
armed forces (*see also* coups d'etat): x, 38, 41, 179, 295, 296-304; in southern region, 190; military expenditures, 222-223, 246, 301
army: x, 302-304
artistic expression: 151-161
Ashigga party: 172
Aswan High Dam (*see also* Lake Nasser): 22, 79, 159, 198, 230, 255, 281
Atbarah: 2, 66, 103, 138, 229; River, xiv, 53, 56
Atta, Hashim al: 180, 312
Atuot: 72, 85
Avungara clan: 98
Awadallah, Babikir: 46, 47, 180
awqaf: 140
Ayam Printing Company: 214, 215
Az Zaydab Scheme: 265, 278
Azande peoples (*see also* Zande language): 29, 72, 74, 87, 118, 233; agriculture, 274, 289; civil war and, 107; customs, 124, 156, 157; health, 131, 133; social organization, 98, 105
Azania Liberation Front: 187
Azhari, Ismail al: 30, 34, 35, 43, 44, 45, 46, 172, 173

Ba'ath movement: 184
Badawiye language: 80
Baggara nomads: 76, 91, 126, 129, 174, 267; customs, 156, 289
Bahr al Arab: xiv, 53, 56
Bahr al Ghazal: ix, xiv, 53
Bahr al Ghazal province: xiv, 49, 52, 134, 135, 262; industry, 233, 235; language, 75, 84; population, 64, 72, 74, 88
Bahr al Jabal. *See* White Nile River
Baka peoples: 72, 74, 75, 88, 96
Baker, Samuel: 20
Bakr, Ahmed: 16
Bakr peoples: 174
balance of payments: 233, 237, 238
Banda peoples: 88

banking system: 249-250; commercial banks, 7, 222, 249
Barakah River: 56, 259, 276
Barclays Bank: 249
Bari peoples: 72, 74, 86, 88, 96, 97, 107, 118, 122; customs, 156, 157; language, 75
Beir peoples: 72, 87
Beja Congress: 43, 178
Beja peoples: 80-81, 126, 131, 158, 184; language, 75; population, 72, 73, 74, 77; religion, 73, 111; social system, 91, 289
Belanda peoples: 72, 88
Belgium: 25
Berber historic province: 24
Berber peoples: 73
Berkid peoples: 72
Berta peoples: 72, 83
Berti peoples: 72, 82
bilharziasis: viii, 133, 134
Biri peoples: 88
birth rates: 66, 87
Bisharin peoples: 80
Bishop Gwynne College: 149
Blemmyes: 14
Blue Nile province: xiv, 52, 150, 306; agriculture, 271, 280, 283; health, 133, 134; peoples, 64, 72, 74, 75, 76, 82
Blue Nile River: vii, 53, 56, 245
Bonaparte, Napoleon: 18
Bongo peoples: 72, 74, 75, 87, 88, 96, 157; religion, 123
boundaries: xiv, 1, 25, 50-52; border problems, 196, 199, 297, 302
British colonial rule (*see also* Anglo-Egyptian Condominium of Sudan): viii, 4, 119, 168, 202; administration, 97, 98
broadcasting (*see also* radio; television): 151, 153, 155
budgets (*see also* tax collection): 245-249, 293; military, 301, 302
Bulgaria: 205, 245

cabinet: 43, 47, 165, 166, 180
Cairo, University of: 149, 150
camels (*see also* nomads): 91, 266
caravans: 13, 16, 230
cassava: 271, 275
cattle ownership (*see also* livestock): 93, 105, 268

cattle people (see also nomads): 76, 84, 99, 230–231, 265, 268
cement production: 229, 292, 293
censorship. See freedom of the press
census: 64, 66, 71, 82; cattle, 93
Central African Republic: 51, 199, 313
Chad: 51, 199, 200, 231
children (see also education): 66, 309
China, People's Republic of: 195, 206, 207; trade, 242, 243
Christianity (see also missionaries): 15, 110–112, 118–120
civil war (see also Addis Ababa agreement; north-south separation: refugees): v, viii, 3, 194, 295, 310, 313–316; effects, 71, 143, 163; toll, 107, 126, 164, 315
climate: vii, 56–58, 69
clothing: 130–131
coeducation: 145
Commercial Code: 167
communication: 209–220
communists (see also Sudan Communist Party): 182, 184, 189, 193, 211; internal security and, 296, 310–312; purges of, 170, 296, 305, 311, 312; relations with communist countries, 204–207
condominium rule. See Anglo-Egyptian Condominium of Sudan
conscription: 300–301
constitution: viii, 5, 31, 41; draft, 36, 37, 46, 47, 166
consumer goods: 46, 125, 230, 293
copper: 7, 255, 291
Coptic church: 111
Coptic language: 15, 79
cost of living: 226
cotton (see also agricultural schemes; cotton exports): 139; crop, 6, 19, 27, 229, 234, 256, 257, 260, 263–265, 273, 279, 283, 284; crops lost, 289; ginning, 229, 293; manufacturing, 265, 293; new variety, 243
cotton exports: viii, ix, 6, 222, 239, 240, 241, 242; marketing, 36, 37, 205, 237, 275–276
coups d'etat: 5, 12, 13, 38, 46, 183–184, 305
cowhouse: 130
crime (see also penal codes; prisons): 97, 309; punishment, 305, 306; rehabilitation, 296

crops (see also cotton; food grains): 235–236, 260, 262–265, 271, 274; irrigated farming, 277, 281, 283, 284
cults: 98, 110, 122, 123
cultural organizations: 161–162
currency: ix, 19, 250
Cush: 13, 14
customary law: viii, 167, 168
Czechoslovakia: 218, 269

Daju peoples: 72, 82, 122
Dali Scheme: 278, 284
dams (see also Aswan High Dam): 59
Danagla peoples: 79
Darfung peoples: 74, 82
Darfur province: xiv, 9, 16, 25, 52, 95, 111; agriculture, 266, 283; health, 134, 135; language, 75; people, 64, 72, 74, 76, 79, 81, 94, 230
death rate: 66, 132
decree laws: 166, 167
Democratic Unionist Party: 45, 46, 175
Deng, William: 45, 187
Denmark: 269
desert areas: 49, 53, 58, 60, 258; oases, 230; spread southward, 231
development plans. See Five-Year Plan of Economic and Social Development; Ten-Year Plan of Economic and Social Development
Didinga Hills: 55
Didinga peoples: 72, 74, 87, 122
diet and nutrition (see also milk): 3, 6, 126, 131–132, 231, 262, 268
Dindar game reserve: 65
Dindar River: 53, 56, 282
Dinka peoples: 72, 74, 76, 84–85, 96, 107, 118, 129, 133; agriculture, 274, 289; customs, 105, 138, 156; language, 75; religion, 121, 123; social organization, 100, 101, 102
Diori, Hamani: 200
diseases: viii, 3, 132–136, 138
doctors: 136
Dongolawin peoples: 79
Dongotona mountains: 53, 54, 55
dukhn millet: 257, 258, 259, 262, 263, 271, 272, 273
Dunqulah: 24, 64, 94, 174
durra sorghum: 257, 258, 259, 262, 263, 270, 271, 272, 273, 274, 275, 277, 283, 284

economy: viii, 6, 221–225; economic regions, 226–236, 270

educated elite. *See* elite class

education (*see also* schools; vocational and technical training): vii, 2, 141, 142–151, 218; history of, 27, 29, 114, 120; prisoners, 309

educational broadcasting: 157

Egypt (*see also* Arab Republic of Egypt; Nile Waters Agreement; United Arab Republic): 172, 174, 265; aid from, 245, 269; diplomatic relations with, 196, 197, 204, 311; historic country, 3, 10, 11, 12, 13, 17–20, 159; trade, 237, 242

elected assembly: 31, 35, 165, 166, 190

elections: 35–36, 40, 190; national, 42, 43, 44

electric power: 7, 229

elite class: 4, 11, 32, 34, 89, 128; communism and, 310; educated, 42, 44, 109, 176; in armed forces, 298, 299

English language: 32, 71, 118, 142, 148, 150, 190, 202; public information, 211, 213, 214, 217

Equatoria Corps: 298

Equatoria province: xiv, 20, 49, 52, 123, 143; agriculture, 262, 266; health, 134, 135; industry, 233, 234, 235; language, 75, 84; population, 64, 72, 74, 86

Ethiopia: 15, 302, 311, 313; border, 25, 52, 297; diplomatic relations, 195, 200–201; Sudan peace treaty, 164, 190–191, 201

ethnic groups: 71–78

European Economic Community: 242

evil eye: 124

Ewert, John: 306

Export-Import Bank: 204

exports (*see also* cotton exports): ix, 158, 205, 241, 251; agriculture, 225, 256, 271, 273

Fajelu peoples: 86

family. *See* kinship groups

famine and hunger: 125, 131, 280

Fashoda historical province: 24

Feroge peoples: 72, 88

Fertit peoples: 88

films: 218–219

fiscal year: 245

fish and fishing: 62, 131, 132; industry, 162, 207

Five-Year Plan of Economic and Social Development: 7, 137, 147, 222, 223, 240, 303; agriculture, 274, 280; budget, 245, 246, 247, 292; communication facilities, 216–217, 219, 220; for southern area, 234–236; irrigation, 256, 268, 282

Flinders Petri Library: 161

Food and Agriculture Organization: 161, 231, 235, 258

food grains (*see also* dukhn millet; durra sorghum; wheat): 228, 258; silos, 260

foreign affairs (*see also* foreign aid; foreign trade): 5–6, 7–8, 36, 37, 40, 44, 193–208

foreign aid: x, 180, 223, 235, 243; from United States, 36, 37, 204; military aid, 205, 301–302

foreign residents: 66, 67, 73, 83, 149

foreign trade (*see also* exports; trade agreements): 236–245; government role, 222; monetary area, 250; wild animal products, 87; with communist countries, 236, 242, 245, 264

France: 23, 24, 149

Free Officer Movement: 179

Freedom from Thirst campaign: 268, 269

freedom of religion: 45, 110, 120, 166

freedom of the press: 211, 212, 213, 214

Fung kingdoms: 10, 17

Fung peoples: 18, 75, 82, 110

Fur peoples (*see also* Darfur province): 16–17, 111, 178; agriculture, 232, 273, 284; language, 75; population, 72, 74, 81; social system, 69, 94

Gaaliin Arabs: 76

gabily: 91

game reserves: 62

Garang, Joseph: 184, 189, 312

Gaylani, Abd al Qadral al: 117

generation gap: 102

geography: vii, 1, 49–61; arable land, 258

Gerkid peoples: 79

Germany: East, 308; West, 180, 195, 198, 242, 302

goats: 266

gold: 13, 62, 230, 290

Golo peoples: 88
Gordon, Charles George: 20, 22
Gordon Memorial College: 27, 29, 149, 298
government, national (*see also* local government): 5, 45, 94, 95, 100, 163–170, 295; finance, 245–249, 257; role in communications, 211, 212, 216; role in economic activity, 222
government workers: 139, 179, 224, 249
Graduates' General Conference: 171, 183
Great Britain (*see also* British colonial rule): 198, 202, 204; aid from, 243, 245, 269, 302; military structure from, 300, 303, 305; trade, 241, 242, 244
gross domestic product: 222, 224, 255, 266, 290, 291
groundnuts: ix, 229, 241, 257, 263, 273, 275, 282
Guhani, Abdalla al: 76
Guhayna Arabs: 76
Gule peoples: 72, 83
gum arabic: ix, 228, 229, 232, 240, 241, 256, 273

Habbaniya Arabs: 74
Hadendowa peoples: 80, 174, 289
hair styles: 130
Hamadallah, Faruk Uthman: 180, 183
Hamza, Mirghani: 36
handicrafts: 86, 153, 157, 158, 212
hariq cultivation: 271–272
Hassib, Muhammad: 180
Hawazma Arabs: 76
health (*see also* diet and nutrition; diseases; medical care; public health): viii, 3, 132
Hicks, William: 22
higher education: 142, 149–150
Hill Nubians: 72, 79
history (*see also* Anglo-Egyptian Condominium of Sudan): 9–47, 163–165, 168, 172
holidays and festivals: 114, 119, 120, 158
Homr Arabs: 76, 91, 105, 129
hookworm: 133, 134
hospitals: 136
housing: 127–130

Idris, Ahmad ibn: 117
Idrisiyyah: 117
imam: 113, 114

Immatong mountains: 53, 54, 55
import substitution: 292
imports: ix, 37, 205, 237, 240, 241, 244, 251; food, 236, 240, 241, 260
independence: v, vii, 11, 12, 26, 30–31, 35, 142, 185, 212, 222
India: 195, 241, 242, 264
indigenous religion: (*see also* ancestors; cults; rainmaking; witchcraft and sorcery): 82, 109, 120–124
Industrial Bank: 249–250
Industrial Development Corporation: 222, 291
industry: viii, 218, 222, 236, 255, 290–293, 309
inflation: 223, 246, 288
Ingassana peoples: 72, 83, 84, 122
interest rates: 249, 250
internal security (*see also* communists; police): 295–296, 305–316
International Bank for Reconstruction and Development. *See* World Bank
International Development Association: 245
International Finance Corporation: 245
International Monetary Fund: 237, 238
international organizations (*see also* United Nations): x, 162, 244–245; memberships, 207–208
iron ore: 62, 291
Ironstone Plateau: 53, 55, 61, 227, 233; agriculture, 270, 274
irrigation (*see also* agricultural schemes): 6, 14, 27, 49, 54, 56, 221, 230, 255, 256, 259, 269, 272; pump projects, 270, 277, 278, 279, 280
Islam (*see also* Khatmiyyah brotherhood; Mahdiyyah revolt): 2, 112–118, 142, 147, 310; mosques and shrines, 110, 114, 115–116; spread, 16, 73, 80, 111, 176
Islamic law (*see also* sharia): viii, 19, 112, 117, 167
Islamic University: 149
Ismail, Khedive: 19
Ismailiyyah: 117
Israel (*see also* Arab-Israeli War): 180, 195, 196, 314, 315
Italy: 242, 269, 297

Jabal al Awliya: 278, 279
Jabal Barkal: 13, 159

Mahdi, Abd al Rahman al: 29, 39, 118, 171
Mahdi, Imam al Hadi al: 44, 46, 177, 178, 179, 181, 312, 313
Mahdi, Sadik al: 39, 44, 45, 46, 177, 181, 186
Mahdiyyah revolt (see also Ansar sect): 20–24, 117, 297
Mahgoub, Abdal Khalig: 45, 182, 184, 206, 312
Mahgoub, Muhammad Ahmad: 43, 44, 45, 187
malaria: viii, 133, 134, 136
Malut Scheme: 265, 278
Manaqil extension: 231, 277, 278, 281, 285
Mandala peoples: 88
Mandari peoples: 72, 86
manufacturing (see also handicrafts): 224, 230, 291–293
marriage: 68, 99, 101, 103–105; payments, 104, 268
mass communication: 209–220
Massalit peoples: 178, 200
matrilineal descent groups: 73, 95
Mayen, Gordon: 188
Mazmoun Scheme: 278, 284
medical care: 3, 66; modern, 136–137, 207; traditional, 137–138
Meroe kingdom: 14
Messiriyyah Arabs: 76
mica mines: 291
Midob peoples: 72, 79
midwives: 137
migrant labor: 225, 286–288, 289
migration (see also migrant labor; nomads): 67–69, 83, 92, 114; seasonal, 73–74, 126, 221, 231, 256, 266–267
milk: 131, 139, 266, 268
millet (see also dukhn millet): 126, 131, 272
minerals: 7, 62, 222, 255, 290–291
ministries: 166–167
Ministry of Agriculture: 161, 260
Ministry of Animal Production: 139
Ministry of Communications: 212, 216, 219
Ministry of Defense: 302
Ministry of Economy and Trade: 194
Ministry of Education: 145, 146, 148, 159, 218

Ministry of Finance and Economics: 246
Ministry of Health: 137, 139, 161
Ministry of Higher Education and Scientific Research: 149
Ministry of Housing: 127
Ministry of Industry and Mining: 291
Ministry of Information and Culture: 153, 212, 214, 216, 218
Ministry of Information and Labor: 211
Ministry of Information and Social Affairs: 212
Ministry of Interior: 305
Ministry of Local Government: 137, 235
Ministry of Planning: 234, 246, 252
Ministry of Religious Affairs and Religious Trusts: 115, 120, 147
Ministry of State for Presidential Affairs: 194
Ministry of State for Southern Affairs: 167, 215
Ministry of Transport: 251
Mirghani, Ali al: 34, 35, 38, 117, 171
Mirghani, Muhammad Uthman al: 117
Mirghani family: 29, 34, 117
missiles: 303
mission schools: 2, 32, 85, 118, 119, 120, 142–143
missionaries (see also mission schools; Roman Catholicism): 32, 111, 118, 119, 120, 140; expelled, 39, 109, 143, 186; Islamic, 111
Mondire, Ezbon: 189
Moru peoples: 74, 87, 88, 96, 118, 275; language, 75
motor vehicles: ix, 125, 252, 307
mountains: 50, 53, 54–55
Muhammad, Abdullahi ibn: 21, 22, 23
Muhammad, Prophet: 112
Mundi peoples: 88
Muqurra kingdom: 15
Murle peoples: 72, 87
museums: 160–161, 216
music and dance: 152, 153, 155–156
Muslim Brotherhood: 173, 175, 178, 179, 313
Muslim Islamic Charter Front: 43, 175

Naguib, Muhammad: 30, 172
Napata: 14, 159

Tombalbaye, Francois: 200
Toposa peoples: 72, 74, 75, 86, 123
trade agreements: 198, 204, 206–207, 218
trade union movement: 176, 182, 183, 226, 312
transportation system (see also roads; water transport): 6–7, 62–64, 241, 250–253, 262, 291
treaties and agreements. See Addis Ababa agreement; foreign aid; Nile Waters Agreement; trade agreements
tribal feuds: 5, 97, 100, 101, 105, 118, 309
tsetse flies: 86, 131, 234, 258
tuberculosis: viii, 133, 135
Tungur peoples: 111
Turkish rule: 17–20

Udak peoples: 72, 83
Uganda: 51, 199, 313; relations with, 194–195, 197, 315
Ummah party: 29, 35, 36, 37, 38, 42, 43, 44, 45, 172, 173–174, 177, 211
unemployment: 225
United Arab Emirates of the Persian Gulf: 195, 196
United Arab Republic (see also Nile Waters Agreement): 35–36, 37, 51, 193; relations with, 40, 193, 308
United Kingdom. See Great Britain
United Kingdom Export Credits Guarantee Department: 202
United National Front: 41
United Nations (see also Food and Agriculture Organization; World Health Organization): x, 145, 151, 160, 161, 195, 207, 220; Economic Commission for Africa, 207; High Commissioner for Refugees, 199, 203, 208, 235; UNICEF, 151, 203, 208
United States: v, 180, 184, 193, 195, 198; aid from, 36, 202–204, 236, 244, 253, 302; trade, 242
University College of Khartoum: 149, 310
University of Khartoum: 2, 137, 149, 160, 161, 177
Upper Nile province: xiv, 49, 52, 235, 284; agriculture, 266, 271, 283; lan-

guage, 75, 84; population, 64, 72, 74, 86
Upper Nile River: 53
urban society: 125, 127, 128; areas, 65, 69, 90; social organization, 35, 102, 225
Uwayl Scheme: 278, 284

Vegetation: 52, 59, 60, 231, 259
veterinary science: 139, 150, 207, 266
Vietnam, North: 195
visual arts: 151–153, 157
vocational and technical training: 148, 149, 225, 257; military, 299, 307, 308

Wad al Huri Scheme: 278, 283
Wad Madani: 66, 103, 138, 250, 293
Wadi al Ku: 56
Wadi Azum: 56, 284
Wadi Halfa: xiv, 54, 58, 198, 320
Wadi Howar: 53, 56
Wahab, Ahmad Abd al: 38
Wanji, Barri: 188
water supply (see also Nile River; wells): 55–56; 59, 232, 255, 256; for drinking, 259, 267, 268–269, 283; population, 138, 139 water transport: ix, 64, 219, 240, 251, 252
watermelon: 273
Waw: 252, 275
wealth: 93, 100, 104, 288
welfare programs: 139–140
wells: 235, 266, 268
West Africans: 72, 74, 75, 287; pilgrims, 83 114
wheat: 263, 273, 277; imports, 236
White Nile River: vii, xiv, ix, 53, 55, 280; agricultural scheme, 265
wildlife: 62
witchcraft and sorcery: 4, 98, 115, 124, 138
women: 42, 82, 128, 129, 130; crime, 309; cults and, 96, 116, 123; dancing, 152, 156; education, 145, 146, 147, 150; employment, 226; position, 103, 107, 118, 130
work force. See labor supply
World Bank: 236, 243, 245, 282
World Council of Churches: 189
World Health Organization: 133, 135, 161, 208
Yugoslavia: 195, 206, 243, 291; ships from, x, 304

PUBLISHED AREA HANDBOOKS

550-65	Afghanistan	550-41	Korea, Republic of
550-98	Albania	550-58	Laos
550-44	Algeria	550-24	Lebanon
550-59	Angola	550-38	Liberia
550-73	Argentina	550-85	Libya
550-20	Brazil	550-45	Malaysia
550-61	Burma	550-161	Mauritania
550-83	Burundi	550-76	Mongolia
550-50	Cambodia (Khmer Rep.)	550-49	Morocco
550-96	Ceylon	550-64	Mozambique
550-159	Chad	550-35	Nepal, Sikkim and Bhutan
550-60	China, People's Republic of	550-88	Nicaragua
550-63	China, Republic of	550-157	Nigeria
550-26	Colombia	550-94	Oceania
550-91	Congo (Brazzaville)	550-48	Pakistan
550-67	Congo (Kinshasa) (Zaire)	550-46	Panama
550-90	Costa Rica	550-156	Paraguay
550-152	Cuba	550-92	Peripheral States of the Arabian Peninsula
550-22	Cyprus	550-42	Peru
550-158	Czechoslovakia		
550-54	Dominican Republic	550-72	Philippines, Republic of the
550-155	East Germany	550-160	Romania
550-52	Ecuador	550-84	Rwanda
550-150	El Salvador	550-51	Saudi Arabia
550-28	Ethiopia	550-70	Senegal
550-29	Germany	550-86	Somalia
550-153	Ghana	550-93	South Africa, Republic of
550-87	Greece	550-95	Soviet Union
550-78	Guatemala	550-27	Sudan
550-82	Guyana	550-47	Syria
550-151	Honduras	550-62	Tanzania
550-21	India	550-53	Thailand
550-154	Indian Ocean Territories	550-89	Tunisia
550-39	Indonesia	550-80	Turkey
550-68	Iran	550-74	Uganda
550-31	Iraq	550-43	United Arab Republic
550-25	Israel	550-97	Uruguay
550-30	Japan	550-71	Venezuela
550-34	Jordan	550-57	Vietnam, North
550-56	Kenya	550-55	Vietnam, South
550-81	Korea, North	550-75	Zambia